EDUCATION IN INDUSTRIAL WALES
1700 - 1900

PLATE 1 DOWLAIS SCHOOLS WITH EXTENSIONS.
Reproduced by kind permission of the Guest, Keen Iron and Steel Co. Ltd., Cardiff.

EDUCATION IN INDUSTRIAL WALES

1700 - 1900

A study of the Works Schools System in Wales during the Industrial Revolution

by

LESLIE WYNNE EVANS

First Published by
Avalon Books in 1971.
Printed by Heanton Press, Cardiff.
© Leslie Wynne Evans, 1971.

TO MY PARENTS IN DEEP
GRATITUDE WHOSE MEMORY
I DEARLY CHERISH
ELIZABETH JANE EVANS
JOHN MADDOCK EVANS
LLANELLI

Preface

THIS BOOK does not pretend to cover the whole story of elementary education in Wales from 1700 to 1900. Rather, it is an attempt to deal with a particular phase of elementary education in the Principality, that of the efforts made by employers of labour to provide a modicum of basic education for 'the hewers of wood and the drawers of water' in rapidly developing industrial areas. It is an aspect of education which has hitherto been neglected by Welsh educational historians of the nineteenth century, namely, the Works Schools System. In the initial stages of this inquiry my intention was merely to explore what I conceived to be a fascinating cul-de-sac in Welsh educational historiography. This conception proved to be quite erroneous. As the investigation proceeded it became increasingly evident that I was dealing with a topic which had far-reaching implications springing from a deep-rooted and fundamental theme in the history of education in the industrial areas of western Europe and Britain of which this Welsh contribution is an integral part.

It deals simply with the problem of educating 'the greatest number' of working-class children in the industrial areas of Wales before the advent of a State system and attempts to assess the efforts of employers of labour—often in partnership with the Voluntary Societies—to combat 'educational destitution' in rapidly expanding industrial communities. The viability, effectiveness and beneficial results of such efforts, together with the limitations, were dictated by industrial demands and social attitudes prevailing at the time. But, numerically, in terms of schools, the educational opportunities afforded were so substantial as to constitute a school system comparable in stature with that of the two Voluntary Societies.

If this work has any value at all it lies in the wealth of detail presented regarding individual schools, (an inevitable result of the treatment adopted, namely, that of relating the provision of education for the working classes to the various phases of industrial development in Wales) and the gap which they filled in the voluntary school pattern before 1870. No apology is made for the inclusion of generous helpings of Welsh economic history or for emphasizing the geographical setting, for the whole theme of this book revolves around the works which in turn produced the industrial community with its particular sociological background, its workmen and children, its religious and educational problems, and its typical works school.

This aspect of Welsh educational history has for the first time brought many new names into prominence. In addition to familiar ones such as Thomas Gouge, Sir John Philipps, Griffith Jones, Thomas Charles and Sir Hugh Owen, there are the less familiar like Sir Humphrey Mackworth, Joseph Tregellis Price, Sir Josiah John Guest and Lady Charlotte Guest, the Vivian and Nevill families of Swansea and Llanelli respectively, George Thomas Clark, Sir Thomas Phillips, William Williams M.P., the Revs. John Phillips, William Roberts (Nefydd), and David Rees (Capel Als, Llanelli); celebrated officials and inspectors of schools such as Hugh Seymour Tremenheere, Joseph Bowstead, William Edwards, and the Rev. H. Longueville Jones (the last three all H.M.I.s) which have not appeared before in their proper contexts in Welsh education in the nineteenth century.

The reasons why this subject has escaped the attention of Welsh educational historians and has not been included in any treatment of elementary education in Wales are not far to seek. In the first place the theme is complex and often intricately interwoven with questions of religion, economics, industry, politics, and sociology. Secondly, during the initial phases of their establishment, works schools were independent of government subvention, were not inspected by the Committee of Council's inspectors and were often excluded from the official *Annual Minutes* of that Committee. Thirdly, the Committee of Privy Council made no comprehensive survey of these schools. Again, source material on this subject is widely diffused though not by any means wanting and full use has been made of masses of official government publications relating to the mining and factory districts and other special reports, more especially the nineteenth century Blue Books which are so much more exciting than is commonly supposed by those who have never made them the basis of investigation.

Choice of dates for the delimitation of certain historical studies is not always easy. The theme of this study has its roots in the seventeenth century and extends almost to the Education Act of 1902. The educational background of Wales was intimately bound up with the religious awakening of the eighteenth century and gave rise to the predominance of Nonconformity and Sunday Schools in the nineteenth century which coincided with the rapid expansion of industry and growth of population in the Principality. Hence the dates 1700-1900 were chosen for the scope of this work.

For a book of this kind my debt to others has been heavy and is gladly acknowledged. Professor Emeritus William Rees, formerly of University College, Cardiff, has been both adviser and friend and at all stages of my researches his criticism and wide scholarship in Welsh history have been invaluable. I am also grateful to the late Professor Emeritus R. T. Jenkins, Bangor, Professor Emeritus E. G. Bowen, Aberystwyth, and the late Dr. Thomas Jones, C.H., for many kindnesses and references. The librarians and staffs of the British Museum, Public Record Office, the National Library of Wales, the libraries at University College, Cardiff and Bangor, the Glamorgan County Record Office, the Central libraries at Cardiff, Swansea, Llanelli and numerous other town libraries in Wales, have all been ready in their help and guidance. I have also, unashamedly pestered scores of individuals who had their mite to contribute on points of detail, and it is a pleasure to record the courtesy and information which I received from directors of education and other county officials throughout the Principality.

My thanks are due to the Librarian of the National Library of Wales for permission to reproduce material from my articles in the *Journal* of that Library and for making available certain of the photographs. The skill and care with which the maps were re-drawn and prepared for publication by Mr. Morlais Hughes of the Department of Geography and Anthropology at the University College of Wales, Aberystwyth deserves the highest praise. I am also grateful to Professor and Mrs. Brian Simon of the School of Education, University of Leicester, for many useful criticisms and suggestions. Dr. R. Brinley Jones, of the University of Wales Registry, read the whole of the work in manuscript. For this and many other kindnesses great and small I am deeply in his debt. My warm thanks are accorded to Mr. Stephen Murgatroyd, one of my Honours class, for compiling the Index. I record my gratitude to the directors of Avalon Books for their kindness in inviting me to contribute the second in their series of educational works, and to the printers for their workmanship in the production of this volume. Finally, I wish to thank my wife, whose patience and understanding during the preparation of this book will scarcely be rewarded by its appearance.

LESLIE WYNNE EVANS.

Department of Education,
University College, Cardiff,
January, 1971

CONTENTS

PREFACE

INTRODUCTION

CHAPTER I	Background and Early Schools	1
CHAPTER II	Educational Destitution and the Establishment of Works Schools	15
CHAPTER III	Ironworks Schools	37
CHAPTER IV	Sir John Guest's Education Scheme	95
CHAPTER V	Works Schools of the Non-Ferrous Metal Industries	121
CHAPTER VI	Tinplate Works Schools	157
CHAPTER VII	Colliery Schools	169
CHAPTER VIII	Slate Quarry Schools and the Voluntary Societies in North Wales	203
CHAPTER IX	Nonconformity and Sunday Schools in the Industrial Areas	231
CHAPTER X	School Attendance and Further Education	261
CHAPTER XI	Characteristic Features of Works Schools	287
CHAPTER XII	Works Schools in relation to the Voluntary Societies and School Boards	305

EPILOGUE   333

APPENDICES   (at the end of each chapter)

BIBLIOGRAPHY   339

INDEX   351

Maps and Plates

MAP 1   Wales: Distribution of Works Schools

MAP 2   South Wales: Ironworks Schools

MAP 3   South Wales: Colliery, Tinworks and Non-Ferrous Metal Works Schools

MAP 4   North Wales: Slate Quarry Schools

PLATE I   Dowlais Schools with Extensions, 1890 (frontispiece)

PLATE II   Sir Josiah John Guest, M.P. (1785-1852)

PLATE III Lady Charlotte Guest (later Schreiber) (1812-1895)

PLATE IV   Sir Thomas Phillips (1801-1867)

PLATE V   Rev. David Rees, Capel Als, Llanelli (1801-1869)

PLATE VI   Pupil Teacher's Indenture (facsimile)

Introduction

IT HAS been asserted by one writer that 'the history of education is not just a tale about schools and thinkers, but an aspect of social history'.[1] This pronouncement has a peculiar significance when an attempt is made to interpret the story of elementary education in the regions of heavy industries, coal mining and slate quarrying in Wales, for it involves a deep consideration of the whole elaborate drama of a changing society in an economic and industrial revolution. In short, it is necessary to pursue the study of the history of education in the eighteenth and nineteenth centuries in its appropriate and relevant context, so long neglected, that of social and economic history. In this connection several recent writers have paid particular attention to the struggle for education by the middle and working classes in England in the nineteenth century and this background should prove fruitful for those readers who wish to delve deeper into the social context. The story has been told so well by Simon—along with Pollard, Silver and Thompson—that it is unnecessary to repeat it here.[2]

Wales, in common with England, experienced the full onslaught of economic and industrial changes which produced fundamental and far-reaching modifications in the structure of Welsh society and mode of life. On the educational side the provision of schools for the new and rapidly expanding industrial communities was one of the major social problems. In the absence of a State system of education this problem was tackled in the industrial areas in part by the Voluntary Societies but mainly by 'enlightened employers of labour' who voluntarily established works schools for the children of their employees. But although

---

1 Sir Fred Clarke, The Widening Scope of the Study of Education, Section L, Education *The Advancement of Science, Vol. VI, No.* 23, British Association for the Advancement of Science, London.
2 Brian Simon, *Studies in the History of Education*, 1780-1870, London, 1960 (reprinted 1964).
Sidney Pollard, *The Genesis of Modern Management* (A study of the Industrial Revolution in Great Britain), London, 1965.
Harold Silver, *The Concept of Popular Education* (A study of ideas and social movements in the early nineteenth century), London, 1965.
E. P. Thompson, *The Making of the English Working Class*, London, 1963.
ibid, Time, Work-Discipline and Industrial Capitalism, *Past and Present*, No. 38, December, 1967, pp. 56-97.
Brian Harrison, Religion and Recreation in Nineteenth-Century England, *Past and Present*, ibid, pp. 98-125.

works day-schools became an important and common feature of the Welsh industrial communities, Wales already possessed her own successful system of part-time education, the Sunday schools, which enjoyed the loyalty not only of the Welsh rural peasantry but also that of the working-class populations in the industrial regions. It should be remembered that the works proprietors or Companies also vigorously promoted and encouraged denominational Sunday schools in their works communities in addition to day-schools.

The provision of education by industrialists was a common activity in most of the industrial areas of England and Wales but so far as schools were concerned there were important differences between the textile manufacturing areas and the regions of coal-mining and heavy metallurgical industries. Sanderson, in his study of education in industrial Lancashire between 1780 and 1840[1] has shown that one of the social consequences of industrial change in England during that period was the 'increased importance of part-time as opposed to full-time education' and cites the demand for child labour in the cotton factories 'which reduced the possibility of the lower-class child being able to attend a day-school, together with the great rise in population which demanded other educational institutions such as Sunday schools, night schools, Mechanics Institutes and infant schools to meet the educational problems of the Industrial Revolution'. In addition there was 'the further device of the *factory school* whereby in a strange compromise the economic institution that had done much to change the pattern of eighteenth century education sought to provide a solution, as it were, by associating to itself schools for its child workers'.[2] Between 1802 and 1833 the various Factory Acts, which only applied to cotton and wool mills, placed the responsibility for education on the factory owner, but after 1833 the factory owner was not obliged to provide education but children between certain ages were required to attend external day schools.

In Wales, however, we are dealing with the device of the *works school* in the regions of heavy industries, coal-mining and slate quarrying which were so characteristic of the Industrial Revolution in that country. Similar industrial regions in England also had their works schools some of which are noted later. One of the social consequences of industrial change in England and Wales in such regions during the late eighteenth and the whole of the nineteenth centuries was the increased importance of both *full-time* and *part-time* education. The main aim of works schools was to provide—not during working hours—orthodox *full-time day-schooling* by the direct participation of the works proprietor in education

1 Michael Sanderson, Education and the Factory in Industrial Lancashire, 1780-1840, *Economic History Review*, 2nd Series, Vol. XX, 1967, pp. 266, ff.
2 ibid

both before and after the introduction of Factory legislation which applied to the coal and metallurgical industries after 1844 as we shall see later on. Moreover, the works schools in England and Wales in such industries, unlike factory schools[1] were separate external institutions built expressly by benevolent, philanthropic or paternalistic proprietors for the education of the children of their employees. Such schools established voluntarily were independent of any State intervention in the form of factory legislation. Indeed, this kind of legislation never demanded that proprietors in the heavy industries should provide, or be responsible for education, or to build schools.

For the period with which we are dealing, many factors have to be considered when discussing education in the Welsh industrial areas. Among the most important of these are questions of religion and moral standards, the Welsh language, the attitude of parents towards secular education, and the genuine concern of the employers of labour for the welfare of their workers. These were some of the main elements in the social structure of the Welsh working-class community. With regard to religion the social historian has to acknowledge the pre-eminent position which Nonconformity occupied in the life of Wales during its industrial evolution. Religion probably exercised a greater influence on the lives of the Welsh people during the last century than was the case in England or in any other Protestant country. Socially and culturally, and often politically, their lives were centred on the chapel, and class differences in outlook coincided with religious differences, and this cleavage was intensified by a language barrier.[2] In the industrial areas the workers were mainly Welsh in speech and strongly Nonconformist in religion, while the works proprietors and officials were predominantly English-speaking and members of the Established Church.[3] There were other problems in relation to religion and education in the industrial regions which will be dealt with fully in the chapter on Nonconformity and Sunday schools.

The attitude of parents towards secular education before 1870 raised special problems of irregular attendance and early withdrawal from schools which caused concern to inspectors of schools and works proprietors alike. Again, there is abundant evidence to show that the humane employers, anxious for the welfare of their employees, spared no efforts to promote a healthy socio-economic industrial community, for besides establishing schools, they built churches and provided reading

1 Sanderson, op. cit. p. 269. Some cotton factories did provide a separate external school.
2 C. R. Williams, The Welsh Religious Revival, 1904-5, *British Journal of Sociology*, Vol. III, No. 3, p. 242.
3 One of the reasons for the phenomenal success of Sunday schools was the use of the Welsh language, especially in the industrial areas.

rooms and libraries. The Commissioner stated the case quite clearly in his evidence to the Mines Commission in 1846: 'Whatever may be the theory, as to the duties of employers towards their work-people—and I am happy to say I have met with very few who say pay fair wages only, nothing else is required of us—the fact, according to my observation, is nearly universal, viz. that where other responsibilities are neglected, the result is moral injury to the people and pecuniary loss to their employers ... the wise employer raises his views also to a higher point. He conceives that, in the present low average state of education among so many of the working classes, to leave them without other spiritual guides than those whom they may themselves select, often from among themselves, is to shut them out from an important and valuable source of enlightened advice and instruction: and that to take no steps to encourage them to attend to the education of their children, is in most cases, virtually to allow the latter to grow up with the smallest possible amount of elementary instruction, or without any at all'.[1]

The genesis of the works school in Wales was related to the exploitation of its natural resources which was, in the main, the province of foreign and English immigrant industrialists. The foreign element was a feature of the industrial awakening of the country in the sixteenth and seventeenth centuries associated with the Chartered Companies of the Mines Royal and of the Mineral and Battery Works.[2] Before this time Wales was a poor and backward country with regard to mineral exploitation and the industrial skill of its people. It was not until 1536 that Wales, incorporated within the English legal system by the Act of Union, offered scope for industrial enterprise and, after 1568, when the above Companies were granted their Charters, the first industrial ventures were inaugurated.[3]

Many of the skilled workers engaged in these early activities came from industrial communities in western Europe where the works school was an old and familiar institution. Such schools were quite common in Sweden, Germany, and some parts of Holland.[4] The Swedish works schools had a long history, especially those found in the central part of that

1 *Reports of the Commissioner ... under the provisions of the Mines Act, 5 and 6 Vict.c.99, to inquire into the working of that Act and into the State of the Population in The Mining Districts,* 1844-59: 1846, p. 426.
2 William Rees, *Industry before the Industrial Revolution,* 2 volumes, Cardiff, 1968, Vol. II, pp. 384, ff.
3 ibid, Vol. I, p. 21.
4 *Svenska folkskolans* (*History of the Elementary School in Sweden*): under redaktion av Viktor Fredriksson. Albert Bonniers forlag, Stockholm, 1940, Tome 1: *Den svenska folkundervisniggen fran reformationen till* 1809. (*Swedish popular Education from the Reformation to* 1809). Albin Warne. Tome 2: *Det svenska folkundervisningsvasendet,* 1809-1860. (*The Swedish Popular Educational System*), Klas Aquilonius, 1942. In Sweden, foreign workers, e.g. Walloons and Dutchmen were often called in for the new industries and they established schools for their children: Tome 1, supra, pp. 167, ff.

country. At the beginning of the seventeenth century copper was one of Sweden's important industries, and a copperworks school existed at Avesta in southern Dalarna as early as 1642.¹ In the Uppsala region, north of Stockholm, 'works schools were in existence at every works'.² Numerous free schools for poor people were also established by industrialists on the pattern of Francke's *Armenschulen*.³ A brass-works school was in operation at Skultuna in the mining district north of Lake Malaren intended for the workers' children, but a few peasant children were allowed to use it.⁴ The ironworks district in the diocese of Karlstad, north of Lake Vener, abounded in works schools.⁵ The scope of teaching included reading, writing, and arithmetic (quattuor species), and the Bible, hymn-book, and Luther's catechism were studied. Very poor children received free books from the works proprietors.⁶

In common with Wales, the industrial areas of England had works schools in the nineteenth century, e.g. Cumberland, Durham, Warwickshire, Staffordshire, and Cornwall.⁷ In the county of Durham there were colliery schools at Black Boy Colliery (Darlington), Seaton, Thornley, and Wearmouth; the large schools of the Consett Iron and Coal Company, ironworks schools at Escomb and Witton Park, and the Washington chemical works school. Others in the north of England were those in east and west Allendale and Weardale connected with the mining establishments of Wentworth Blackett Beaumont, Esq., M.P., and the London Lead Mining Company's schools under the agency of R. W. Bainbridge, Esq., in Teesdale and Alston Moor which were in operation in 1818.⁸

It is quite evident that the early works schools in England and Wales were related to a similar tradition of schools in western Europe which in addition to having a long history were an integral part of the elementary school structure of industrial regions. They could not be designated Charity schools in the eighteenth century usage of the term in Britain although the earliest works schools of Sir Humphrey Mackworth were of that type. Again, as in Sweden, some industrialists, e.g. Nevill at Llanelli,

1 *Avesta skola*, 1642-1872, P. Norberg, Stockholm, 1924, published by Sveriges allmanna folkskollararforenings litteratursallskap, Stockholm.
2 *Svenska folkskolans*, Tome 2, pp. 40, ff., especially pp. 42, ff.
3 ibid, Tome 1, pp. 432-444.
4 ibid, Tome 2, pp. 66-68.
5 ibid, pp. 85-89.
6 ibid, pp. 66-68.
7 Report of Commissioners appointed to Inquire into the State of Education in England and Wales, 1861 (The Newcastle Commission Report), pp. 245-367. *Minutes of Committee of Council*, 1865-66.
8 ibid, vol. 2, Report of A. F. Foster, Esq., Assistant Commissioner, on the mining districts of Durham and Auckland, Weardale, Penrith and Wigton in the counties of Durham and Cumberland.

v

Carmarthenshire, established 'free schools' in connection with his copperworks and collieries. But there is no reason to doubt that the provision of education for the working classes had a close relationship with the Humanitarian movement. The *'tabula rasa'* doctrine propounded by John Locke in his philosophical *Essay Concerning Human Understanding* published in 1690 fostered humanitarian feeling. This in turn 'engendered philanthropy which in the eighteenth century became almost a catchword and its practice influenced both private persons and statesmen and extended to education'.[1] Robert Owen, one of the first employers of labour to build a school for the children of his employees at New Lanark accepted Locke's doctrine and proceeded to frame a New Order of Society.[2] Another of Locke's works *Some Thoughts Concerning Education* and his two *Treatises on Government* discussed the principle of utility as the criterion in morals—the greatest happiness principle. In the nineteenth century the principle formed the basis of the philosophy which saw the standard of moral value in 'the greatest happiness of the greatest number'. This was voiced by Bentham and the Philosophical Radicals, was essentially a middle-class creed and numbered amongst its adherents those who agitated for a State system of education.[3]

The method of establishing works schools where a payment was exacted from the workmen's earnings for their maintenance has some connection with Adam Smith's *Wealth of Nations* 1776. In this work he outlines a scheme of education where 'for a very small expense the community can facilitate, encourage, and even compel the general mastery of the three R's. In every parish there should be a little school whose master should be paid in part by voluntary contributions, in part by the pupil's fees, these being such as to be within the means of a common labourer. The contributions from public funds to the upkeep of the school and the payment of the teacher must only make good any deficiency in these other sources'.[4]

A scheme of this kind was operated in the industrial areas by the employers of labour in the nineteenth century but the phrase compulsory contributions has to be substituted for voluntary. The massing of people around a new colliery or works in effect created a new parish, and where proprietors of works built a school for that population it was the parochial school endowed by the proprietors but maintained by a small levy well within the means of the 'common labourer'. This nineteenth century expression of Adam Smith's idea was aptly described by one of the

1 J. W. Adamson, *English Education* 1789-1902, Cambridge, 1930, p. 2.
2 ibid. Robert Owen, *New View of Society or Essays on the Principles of the Formation of Human Character and the Applications of the Principles of Practice*, 1813.
3 Frank Smith, *A History of English Elementary Education*, 1760-1902, London, 1931, p. 104.
4 J. W. Adamson, op. cit.

Commissioners in 1847: 'by the denomination "workmen's schools" I intend to designate schools directly connected with particular works and maintained wholly or in part by a stoppage from the people's wages employed in those works, the proprietors usually providing the site and the schoolroom . . . I found twenty-four such schools. The stoppages upon the people's wages vary considerably in amount, as ½d., 1d., or 2d. per week; 2d., 4d., or 6d. per month; ½d., 1d., or 4d. in the pound (in the latter instance the sick fund is maintained from the same source)'.[1] He went on to describe the 'gigantic character of the works as a feature not to be passed over which had rendered the ancient divisions of the country a dead letter. The basis of the old parochial terrier was the manor whilst the basis of the new one was the works'. He therefore regarded a workmen's school in no other light than 'as a parochial school and a works to which no school was attached in the same light as a parish containing no school. Nor could it be justly deemed an exaggeration to speak of the works as parishes, e.g. four proprietors employed all the labouring population of Merthyr and Dowlais representing some 40,000 souls. So that, just as when parishes were first instituted, it was every man's interest to think what parish he belonged to, because his rights of relief, employment and redress were all parochial or manorial, so now did the same interest make him think of these or those works, and not at all—or very remotely—of the parish. In the works was his sick fund, his benefit society, his hope of employment and, by a tolerated system of fining, his ordinary court of justice'.[2] The Commissioner dwelt upon these circumstances because as long as there was such contradiction between the parochial and the veritable distribution of the population it was impossible to deal with its educational necessities through any adaptation of the existing parochial machinery. But 'not only the physical distribution, still more, the moral and social relations of these mining and manufacturing communities required new and special provision. They contained no middle-class such as those who commonly constituted a vestry. For although the absence of the truck-system in this district allowed the growth of shopkeepers, yet those were only an offshoot. The works themselves contained no middle-class. There were the proprietors and their agents of administration on the one hand and the mass of operatives on the other. The elimination of a middle class was rendered still more complete when, to the economic causes tending to produce it was super-added the separation of language'.[3]

Inspectors of schools reporting on the state of popular education in the industrial areas were very partial to the phrase 'enlightened employers

1 *Reports of the Commissioners of Inquiry into the State of Education in Wales*, Three Parts, London, 1847, Part 1, pp. 12, ff.
2 ibid
3 ibid

of labour'. It is true that some proprietors in Wales up to 1847 promoted schools as a form of enlightened benevolence, but after 1850 most of them sought government grants through the Voluntary Societies for the upkeep of the schools in addition to poundage on wages and school-pence. In these circumstances the benevolent motive needs qualification and must be viewed more dispassionately. Employers of labour voluntarily shouldered their responsibilities up to a point, but thereafter their employees were called upon to bear a generous load of financial support whether they liked it or not. Rather, it was a case of enlightened benevolence coupled with compulsory contributions. In the matter of schools, the workman was at least an equal partner with the proprietor.

The story of the establishment of works schools in Wales, their numbers, their relationships with other educational bodies, their achievements, and the difficulties they had to contend with are described in the following pages. They were established in connection with all the major metallurgical industries, with collieries, and in quarrying districts. By 1870 the Works Schools System was a major partner in the voluntary elementary schools structure of the nineteenth century and the works schools were invariably described in successive Inspectors' Reports as the best in their inspectorial districts. Even in 1850, one Inspector stated that 'the only day-schools of any value in the mining and manufacturing districts are the works schools of the large employers'.[1] In consequence, it is singularly unfortunate that certain writers have failed to assign any significance to these schools, and to have assumed that they were few in number and of no import.[2]

The modern State system of elementary education owes the Works Schools System a very special debt. Before the Education Act of 1870 and well on to the end of the century it took over a vast burden of educational provision from the Voluntary Societies. Works schools had also shown how small, evenly distributed payments could meet educational expenditure and prepared the way for an education rate. It has already been noted that they were among the best in the industrial areas in the middle of the nineteenth century. When they were finally absorbed by the School Boards at the end of the century they were still acknowledged to be the most efficient schools within their respective areas.

1 *Minutes of Committee of Council*, 1850, General Report by J. Fletcher, H.M.I.
2 A. H. John, *The Industrial Development of South Wales*, Cardiff, 1950, p. 72. Idwal Jones, The Voluntary System at Work, *Trans. Cymm. Society*, 1931-32, p. 87. Sidney Pollard, op. cit., pp. 179 and 202.

Note: In this book, the word British denotes a school associated with the British and Foreign School Society, e.g. British School, British system. National schools and National system refer to the National Society of the Established Church.

CHAPTER I

Background and Early Schools

ALTHOUGH the Works Schools System was one of the important practical by-products of industrial society in the nineteenth century, the origin of such schools can be traced back to the early industrial communities of the seventeenth and eighteenth centuries. As a preliminary to discussing the main system, it is worth including here and examining briefly the background and establishment of the earlier schools.

1. BACKGROUND

For Wales, the year 1701 was of major importance in the story of elementary education for it initiated a century in which was launched a comprehensive movement for the provision of the rudiments of learning for the children of the poor. Many years before the beginning of large scale industrialism, before the Circulating Schools of Griffith Jones and his successors, and before the Sunday Schools of Thomas Charles, the Charity School Movement co-ordinated by the formation of the Society for Promoting Christian Knowledge in 1699 had, as its object, the further extension and promotion of charity schools throughout the country. In effect, it was a Voluntary Society of the Established Church which carried on the work of the Gouge Trust, and between 1700-1735 distributed large numbers of Welsh books and set up parochial libraries. Sir Humphrey Mackworth (1657-1727), M.P. for Cardiganshire in 1701, and from 1702 to 1705, one of the five philanthropic enthusiasts who founded the S.P.C.K., was a leading entrepreneur of the day and deputy-Governor of the Mine Adventurers 'who combined his interest in education for children with Company promotion of a questionable character'.[1] When the Society started its work in earnest in Wales around 1699-1700 it received excellent support in money and influence from the clergy, the Welsh landowners and squires, especially John Vaughan of Derllys and

---

1 M. G. Jones, *The Charity School Movement in the Eighteenth Century*, Cambridge, 1938, p. 39. Thomas Gouge (1605?-81). Educated at Eton and King's College, Cambridge. Ordained in 1634 and became Vicar of St. Sepulchre, London, in 1638. He was ejected from his living for disagreeing with the Act of Uniformity. He came to Wales and in 1674 formed the 'Welsh Trust' which established 300 schools in the Principality to teach poor Welsh children to read.

Sir John Philipps of Picton Castle, Pembrokeshire. Mackworth was determined, in his charitable projects, that industry should follow the lead of the land and that the charity schools he envisaged in connection with his Company were to provide education for the children of the miners and workmen belonging to it.

The work of the S.P.C.K. expanded rapidly particularly in south-west Wales through the guidance and enthusiasm of Sir John Philipps who established many schools in that area. When he died in 1737 'his mantle fell upon the shoulders of Griffith Jones, the most distinguished figure in the history of education in Wales, who put into practice the idea of circulating or itinerant schools or, more correctly, "school sessions".'[1] These schools spread rapidly because Welsh was used as the medium of instruction and by 1761 when Griffith Jones died, no less than 3,495 schools had been set up. His work was continued by Madam Bevan, but at her death in 1779 the system came to an abrupt end. They were simply catechetical schools, taught reading, but no writing or arithmetic.[2] Further efforts were made to resuscitate the Circulating Welsh Charity Schools and Thomas Charles succeeded to a limited extent. However, his greatest work was the organization of the Welsh Sunday schools during the last two decades of the eighteenth century (the early phase of the Industrial Revolution) which became so popular during the nineteenth century especially in the new industrial areas.

After 1800 the educational background was inevitably bound up with the many fundamental changes in the social, economic and political life of the country. Perhaps the most striking feature of the nineteenth century was the dilatory attitude and consequent procrastination on the part of the government of the day to legislate on a comprehensive scale for the education of the working classes which by the middle of the century comprised the greater part of the population. There was, however, during the early years of that century a growing interest in popular education. Some continental countries were ahead of Britain and had organized education on a national basis for, after 1789, free, compulsory, state-controlled education had become one of the leading conceptions of continental liberalism.[3] But liberalism of the English kind, while favourable to a general extension of education, distrusted State control as being a political danger to civil liberty. So did those who regarded education as essentially a sphere of religious training and believed in ecclesiastical

1 M. G. Jones, op.cit., p. 298.
2 ibid
3 J. W. Adamson, op. cit., p. 9, ff. H. C. Barnard, *Short History of English Education, 1760-1944*, London, 1947, pp. 49-51.

control. Others still clung to the view so characteristic of the eighteenth century that education was a charity to the poor and not a right to which everyone in the realm was entitled. The interaction of these and other opinions delayed for many years the planning of a State system.

The establishment of the two Voluntary Societies, the British and Foreign School Society and the National Society in the early years of the nineteenth century carried the main burden of providing education for the common people and they received the support of all sections of the community. There was little enthusiasm for State intervention in the first half of the century and when the issue was brought to a head between the voluntary principle, backed by the religious bodies, and State intervention supported by Dr. James Phillips Kay in 1833, the result was a compromise and not a solution.[1]

Parliament had more than once attempted to devise some scheme to which all religious denominations could agree. In 1807 Whitbread had tried to introduce education through the Poor Law, but failed. In spite of protests, agitation continued for popular education especially by Sir Thomas Bernard in the *Reports of the Society for the Betterment of the Poor*, 1798-1808, by David Stow's *Accounts of Infant Schools* and Robert Owen's *Essays on the Formation of Human Character*.[2] Owen, a strong supporter of a State system of education like the Philosophical Radicals 'was chiefly concerned to find the solution to the problem of pauperism. But his approach was... not merely rational within the limits of the iron laws of political economy, but broadly humanist. It was his argument that industry could be rendered efficient and profitable by humane treatment of the workers and by an education designed to develop potentialities of all kinds.'[3] His famous day-school, the Institution for the Formation of Character at New Lanark was planned as an ideal centre for the education of his workmen's children as well as the workmen themselves. Monitorial learning by rote was unknown here and the curriculum far from being cramped, comprised the basic skills, geography, history, natural science, music, dancing and elementary musket drill. Owen's example was followed by more than one leader of industry in the mining and metallurgical industrial areas of south Wales. The nearest approach to New Lanark were Guest's schools at Dowlais, Vivian's Hafod schools at Swansea, and Nevill's schools at Llanelli.

1 M. G. Jones, op.cit., p. 329.
2 Owen's educational theory is discussed in the third essay *A New View of Society*, 1816.
3 Brian Simon, op. cit. pp. 194, ff.

But to return to Parliamentary efforts. Even the eloquence of Brougham availed nothing in 1816 and the Education Bill which he introduced in 1820 foundered on religious jealousy and dislike of change. It was in 1833 that Parliament compromised and voted its first annual grant of £20,000 to be divided equally between the two Voluntary Societies and in 1839 established the Committee of Privy Council on Education and an Education Department in 1856. Thus the State acquired a modicum of control over education at a time when a general education Bill had no chance of passing the Upper House and yet it was becoming more involved in education by the circuitous route of factory legislation.[1]

To a certain extent the Factory Acts did help to further the cause of the working classes and to check the oppression of children by the demands of industry for their labour, for every Factory Act included educational clauses and were in effect a series of unpretentious education Acts which heralded the first Education Act of 1870. The provisions of these Acts in relation to education in the industrial areas are treated in some detail later on. Other factors of importance were the varying attitudes of employers of labour to the educational clauses of the Factory Acts and the extent to which they cooperated or otherwise with voluntary bodies to provide educational facilities in their areas.

In the meantime the dominant problem in the industrial regions was educational destitution. The Works Schools System of the nineteenth century emerged to face this challenge.

2. EARLY SCHOOLS

One of the most obvious and important features of industrial civilization, a large concentration of urban living around a particular works or industry has become familiarly known as the industrial community. In many industrial areas this kind of community depended almost entirely upon the proprietor of the works or Company for most of its wants, physical, moral and educational. Although the provision of educational facilities in the form of works schools and other kinds of social welfare in industrial communities was pre-eminently a feature of the Industrial Revolution which made rapid headway from the latter half of the eighteenth century onwards, the earliest examples of these institutions and the first industrial communities can be traced back to the 'First Industrial Revolution' of the Age of Elizabeth the First (and her immediate successors) which were associated with the activities of the large mineral exploiting and smelting Companies.[2]

1 Frank Smith, op. cit., p. 117, ff.
2 William Rees, op. cit., Vol. 1, Foreword.

BACKGROUND AND EARLY SCHOOLS

In 1568 the Crown granted rights to two joint-stock Companies, the Society of the Mines Royal and the Society of the Mineral and Battery Works, to exploit the mineral resources of certain areas in English and Welsh counties. Rees has described in considerable detail the former Society's first activities at Keswick, Cumberland, where the skilled immigrant German smelters and their families called for a close community life and the 'circumstances which brought together a foreign community into this remote region gave the organization a special character which was to influence future industrial practice in this country'.[1] This is our example of the earliest industrial community and the forerunner of scores of others in Wales in which 'the total environment was under the control of a single employer'[2] or Company which made itself responsible for the living conditions of its key-workers and, indeed, for the general welfare of the entire colony.

The Society of Mineral and Battery Works on the other hand provides us with the earliest example of a works school. One of the main activities of this Society was the manufacture of iron wire and after various searches in south Wales for sites with adequate water-power the wire works were finally established on the banks of the Angevy, a tributary stream of the river Wye at Tintern. It was probably during the 1630s that the Iron Wire-works school was started at Tintern and it was recorded that 'while the Corporation did not find it necessary to establish at Tintern a hostel for its foreign workers and an elaborate system of supply, such as had been instituted by Mines Royal at Keswick, it was not unmindful of the welfare of its employees at Tintern when the works were under its direct control'.[3] Indeed, attached to the works and on the pay-roll of the Company was 'a preacher in receipt of a salary of £8 a year. The workers' children too, were taught at the works school by the works' schoolmaster passing rich on a salary of 40/- a year'.[4] This pattern of church and school—religion and education—in the welfare context of these early industrial communities emerges again in the Works Charity Schools of the early eighteenth century associated with the industrial ventures of

1 William Rees, op. cit., Vol. I, p. 406.
2 Sidney Pollard, op. cit., p. 197.
3 William Rees, op. cit., Vol. 2, p. 614.
4 ibid. Vol. 2, p. 645. Wire-making as a young industry had to combat competition from the long-established Continental product, and Thomas Foley at the Tintern and Whitebrook works promised to carry on its manufacture if Parliament prohibited the importation of foreign wire. The Act of 1678 was passed to this end, and Foley demanded certain adjustments in the terms of the new lease in his favour 'the Corporation agreeing to put the Whitebrook works (some four miles away from Tintern) in repair and to take over the pensions of the schoolmaster and minister'.

5

BACKGROUND AND EARLY SCHOOLS

Sir Humphrey Mackworth and the Company of the Mine Adventurers of England, in Cardiganshire and at Neath, Glamorgan. William Waller, Steward of the Mines in Cardiganshire, described Mackworth who was a keen Churchman 'as taking delight in bringing advantage to others, especially to his miners and labourers' and with 'giving encouragement to his workmen to be careful and industrious in their own interest as well as in that of their masters', and as a subscribing founder member of the Society for the Propagation of Christian Knowledge in Foreign Parts.[1] Before dealing with his schools it should be noted that under the constitution of the Company provision was made for the maintenance of 'aged and impotent miners and labourers out of the profits of the mine'. In addition, the workers had to observe strictly the rules of the works in such matters as personal conduct and swearing, quarrelling and drunkenness, and attendance at Divine Service on Sundays was expected.[2] Mackworth's first venture in the industrial development of south Wales was his exploitation of collieries in the Neath district which he had acquired by marriage. By 1698 he had extended his industrial interests to non-ferrous metal mining in Cardiganshire when his Company bought the shares of Sir Carbery Pryse at Esgair Hir.[3]

In 1700 the Company published *A Familiar Discourse concerning the Mine Adventure* which described the objects and constitution of the concern.[4] One of its clauses referred to the use of part of its profits, of which one-twelfth was to be appropriated to charitable uses under Mackworth's direction, which included among other things the relief of 'poor Miners and Labourers at the works, their wives and children, and the provision of schooling for the latter'.[5] The two schools promoted by the Company at Neath and Esgair Hir were, next to Tintern, the earliest of the works schools established in Wales. They were, in name at least, charity schools and were maintained for a few years at the expense of the Company. But by 1709 the miners themselves were required to

---

1 Note by E. D. Jones in *Mackworth and the S.P.C.K.* N.L.W. MSS., V. iii., p. 232.
2 William Rees, op. cit. Vol. 2, pp. 544-5. Note that these rules of conduct and attendance at church on Sundays were features of many of the works schools of the nineteenth century.
3 D. J. Davies, *Economic History of South Wales prior to* 1800, University of Wales Press, Cardiff, 1933, p. 126. William Rees, op. cit. gives the full account in Vol. 2, pp. 521-572.
4 *A Familiar Discourse, etc.*, 1700, issued under the name of William Sheere, the Secretary of the Mines Royal. This was later reported to have been written by Waller himself.
5 *The Mine Adventure or an expedient for composing all Differences between the partners of the Mines late of Sir Carbery Pryse*, 1698, 'for the augmentation of poore Vicaridges in Wales . . . the relief of poore miners and labourers at the works, their wives and children*', etc. B.M.552.M 12/6.

BACKGROUND AND EARLY SCHOOLS

contribute the sum of half a crown per quarter towards the education of their children.[1] This deduction from wages was similar to the 'poundage' system which was to be adopted as a general practice by the works schools of the nineteenth century.

The first works charity school was established in 1700 by Mackworth at the Esgair Hir Mines in north Cardiganshire[2] and in the following years various sums were allocated by the Company of the Mine Adventure towards its maintenance.[3] An annual grant of £20 was made to the school in 1705 and 1706 and an additional £30 per annum 'for a chaplain to the miners in the County of Cardiganshire to read prayers, preach, and catechise the workmen and their children'.[4] The Company also provided houses for the isolated mining communities together with some kind of truck shop, for in 1699 the Steward was ordered to encourage 'some convenient person or persons to settle on the mountain who would bake . . . and provide cheap butter, tobacco and other necessaries for the workmen at reasonable prices, of which you are to be the judge that the workmen are not cheated by them'.[5]

Waller had made the most extravagant claims for the Esgair Hir mine with the result that the Company eventually opened twenty-eight mines and levels in the area. In 1708 matters deteriorated, the mines proved disappointing, the partners quarrelled, and Mackworth and Waller began to blame one another. One of the feuds arose in connection with the schoolmaster's salary at Esgair Hir. A certain Mr. Hawkins, assistant Steward to Waller, was inveigled into giving evidence against his former manager. Hawkins maintained that Waller had paid the schoolmaster only £5 instead of the stipulated £15 per annum. Waller, in addition to his work as Chief Steward, seems to have maintained a boarding establishment, for Mr. Watson the schoolmaster and Mr. Evans the parson lived at his house. Waller deducted £10 per annum from Watson's salary in lieu of board-residence. In *The Answer of Mr. Waller to Mr. Hawkins's Report*[6] Waller asserted that he charged 'Mr. Evens the Parson £13 per

1 *A General Account of the Mine Adventure*, Folio 2, 1709, B.M. 522.M. 12/15.
2 ibid.
3 T. Shankland, Pennod Anghofiedig yn Hanes Addysg Elfennol Cymru'r ddeunawfed ganrif, *Seren Gomer, Mai*, 1903, *Rhif.* 3. *Cyf. XXIV*, App. 1, pp. 152-160.
4 T. Shankland, Sir John Philipps and the Charity School Movement in Wales, *Trans. Cymm. Soc.* 1904-5, p. 74.
5 D. J. Davies, op. cit., p. 82.
6 W. Waller, *The Answer of Mr. Waller to Mr. Hawkins's Report, Given in at the General Court of the Governor and Co., of the Mine Adventure of England, December 15, 1709.* Published by John Baker, London, 1710, p. 16. Waller explained that he charged Watson £10 per annum for his board and lodging and gave him £5 in addition.

7

annum for his keep, but in view of the fact that Watson teaches my two sons, I only charge the schoolmaster £10'.[1] Moreover, Watson in his *Deposition* said: 'James Watson, late of Graystock in the County of Cumberland, Gent, maketh Oath, That he hath been ever since November, 1706, keeping a Schoole at the Chapel near the Silver Mills in Cardiganshire, and did Dyet at Mr. Waller's house near the said Chapel, ever since he came into the County; and was informed by Mr. Waller That the Company of Mine Adventurers did allow him 15 pounds per annum towards his keeping the said Schoole; whereof this Deponent did allow the said Mr. Waller ten pounds per annum towards his Dyet, and has, and is to receive from the said Mr. Waller the sum of five pounds per annum more; and that the said Mr. Waller gives this Deponent Liberty to Dyet himself where he thinks fit'.[2] The deficit in Watson's salary was overcome by levying an education rate on the workmen in the sum of 'thirty pence per quarter from their wages, since the miners were eager to have their children educated'.[3] The school at Esgair Hir was shortlived, for by 1721 there was not a single charity school left in Cardiganshire.[4]

Mackworth established another charity works school at Neath, recorded in the *Minutes of the S.P.C.K.* for 26 July 1705 when 'Mr. Edward reported that the Governour and Company of the Mine Adventure have allowed £40 per annum for the education of 40 children of the miners and workmen belonging to the said Company whereof one moyety is allowed for a Charity School in the County of Glamorgan (Neath), and the other for another in the County of Cardigan . . .'.[5] The Neath charity school also received its £20 annual grant from the Company and Mr. Williams the schoolmaster there was more fortunate than Watson at Esgair Hir for he was paid an annual salary of £30 for the 'education of the children of the poor workmen'.[6]

Mackworth was the pioneer of charity works schools and no others of this kind were established in Wales in the eighteenth century. His two schools were small, the curriculum unpretentious and rudimentary, mainly concerned with religious instruction and the teaching of reading. In 1709 the children attending the schools were described as being 'illiterate' and were taught through the medium of English.[7] Labour for

1 W. Waller, op. cit. p. 15.
2 ibid, p. 16.
3 *A General Account of the Mine Adventure*, 1709.
4 R. T. Jenkins, *Hanes Cymru yn y Ddeunawfed Ganrif*, Caerdydd, 1931, p.34.
5 T. Shankland, *Seren Gomer*, op. cit., p. 145.
6 D. R. Phillips, *History of the Vale of Neath*, Swansea, 1925, p. 169.
7 *A General Account of the Mine Adventure*, 1709.

BACKGROUND AND EARLY SCHOOLS

the mines was recruited from the local freeholders along with some immigrants and very often women and children were employed in the less arduous duties of mining.[1] The school at Neath was in existence in 1718 but nothing was heard of it after that date.[2]

There is an interesting postscript to Mackworth's work. In a *S.P.C.K. Abstract of Correspondence* was a letter, dated 17 September 1719 from a Mr. O'Connor at Neath, Glamorgan: 'that he is desired by Sir Humphrey Mackworth to acquaint the Society that there has been several overtures for a schoolmaster at Neath, but that they seem not altogether qualify'd especially to sett up the first school. He therefore submits to the Society's consideration whether it may not be proper to pitch upon one of the best schoolmasters in London to begin the setting up of schools in Wales, *who may be a sort of Itinerant Master*, when he has sett up one, *and brought up an usher*, then to sett up another.' Is not this letter and the ideas conveyed in it rather significant? Mackworth after all might have been the originator of both the monitorial system of the nineteenth century associated with the names of Lancaster and Bell, and the Circulating Welsh Charity Schools later promoted by Griffith Jones after Mackworth's death in 1727.

The initial phase in the industrialization of south Wales between 1750 and 1800 produced the first ironworks school. It was a small venture at Capel Waun y Pound, midway between Beaufort and Sirhowy in Monmouthshire and promoted by two ironsmelting concerns, Kendall of Beaufort and Messrs. Atkinson and Barrow the proprietors of the Sirhowy furnace. The schoolmaster was a curate who conducted services on Sundays and was appointed directly by the three ironmasters and not by the diocesan Bishop. About twenty-five to thirty children attended out of a total population of 250 employed mainly in the ironworks. The works proprietors also built the church and appointed the clergy.[3]

This small works school, opened in 1784, unlike the schools of Sir Humphrey Mackworth, was not conceived in the tradition of the charity school background though it might have been inspired by its example. Rather, Capel Waun y Pound was the forerunner and the prototype of scores of other works schools which abounded in the Welsh industrial areas after 1800. Indeed, the rapid development and multiplicity of such

---

1 W. Davies, *Agriculture and Domestic Economy of South Wales*, 1815, Vol. 1, p. 92.
2 T. Shankland, *Trans. Cymm. Soc.* op. cit., p. 93. In 1718 Mackworth was in London 'intends to wait on the Society . . . to recommend to him a Master for school at Neath'.
3 A. Gray Jones, The industrial development of Ebbw Vale, unpublished M.A. dissertation, University of Wales, 1929, p. 34.

BACKGROUND AND EARLY SCHOOLS

schools was, in reality a new and unique system of works elementary schools which were identified with the new industries and essentially a nineteenth century phenomenon. This system sought to combat educational destitution among the rapidly expanding industrial communities centred around works and collieries right up to the genesis of a State elementary school system in 1870. Additionally, this system of works schools represented a striking continuity of tradition from the eighteenth century. Mackworth had envisaged the setting up of 'Free' works charity schools and promoted his early schools under the aegis of the S.P.C.K., i.e. combined philanthropy and benevolence administered through a seventeenth century voluntary society. The industrialists of the nineteenth century did likewise but with one vital difference. Having established works schools, the promoters of the majority of them sought the support of the National or the British and Foreign School Society for the purpose of inspection and securing monetary grants and also ensured that their employees helped to maintain the schools by imposing a poundage on wages. In that sense the nineteenth century works schools were not charitable institutions but 'pay' schools within the voluntary system before State intervention.

There is one example of a works charity school which was established in the early years of the nineteenth century. Exactly a hundred years after Mackworth's efforts at Neath and Esgair Hir a 'Free' school was opened at Llanelli, Carmarthenshire. This school, again associated with the non-ferrous metallurgical industry was promoted by R. J. Nevill and Co., who had built the Llanelli copperworks in 1804. The Company also owned numerous collieries in the district and the *Returns of the Free School* for March and April 1818 show that children attended whose parents worked at the copperworks and the Caemaen and Box collieries. It was a school of fifty-nine pupils with an average attendance of twenty-eight.[1] In 1823, £31 was subscribed by the local industrialists and gentry to the school which later became the Llanelli copperworks schools, opened in 1847, and ranked as one of the outstanding schools of their type in the nineteenth century.[2]

---

1 *Returns of the Llanelli Free School* for March and April 1818, rendered for R. J. Nevill, Esq., of Field House and the Copperworks, Llanelli, by W. Williams. Appendices 2a and 2b to this chapter.
2 Names of subscribers to the Llanelli Charity School, 1823. Appendix 3.

BACKGROUND AND EARLY SCHOOLS

APPENDIX 1

About 1705, Sir Humphrey Mackworth of Neath, M.P. for Cardiganshire, and Deputy Governor of the Mine Adventurers of England persuaded his Company to allow £40 per annum for the education of 40 children of the miners and workmen belonging to the said Company: whereof one moiety is allowed for a Charity School in the County of Glamorgan (Neath) and the other for another in the County of Cardiganshire (Esgair Hir).[1]

'Mr. Edward reported that the Governor and Company of the Mine Adventure have allowed £40 per annum for the education of 40 children of the miners and workmen belonging to the said Company . . . and also £30 per annum for a Chaplain to the miners in the County of Cardiganshire to read prayers, preach, and catechise the workmen and their Children.'[2]

'It may be observed that Sir Humphrey Mackworth and tenants do pay near two-thirds of the rates of the whole parish (Neath) and therefore having a due regard to his own interest and to the interest of the Parish, did provide in the original establishment of the Mine Adventure a considerable share of the profits of the said Mine to be applied to the maintenance and support of poor decayed workmen and their families: and the Company does now allow thirty pound per annum to Mr. Williams, a schoolmaster at Neath, for the education of the children of the poor workmen.'[3]

In 1706, the Governour and Company of the Mine Adventurers allowed £20 per annum for a Charity School for the children of the Miners and workmen belonging to the Company. In addition an annual grant of £30 was made to a Minister for reading Prayers, preaching, and catechising the children.[4]

In 1706, Neath, Glamorganshire, 1 school. The Company of Mine Adventurers pay £20 annually for a Charity school for the children of the Miners and Workmen of the Said Company.[5]

1709. Waller attempted to fleece the employees of some of their wages in order to swell his personal income, as in the case when Mr. Murgatroyd had paid £15 to Waller in wages for the schoolmaster at the Charity school, and of the £15 the Schoolmaster had received £5 and 2/6 per quarter from each miner whose children were intended to be taught at the Company's expense. The poorly paid Masters gave a very inadequate tuition to the already very illiterate children.[6]

1 *Trans. Cymm. Soc.* 1904-5, op. cit., p. 74.
2 Phillips, D. R. op. cit., p. 170.
3 ibid, p. 169,
4 ibid.
5 *Trans. Cymm. Soc.* ibid supra.
6 *A General Account*, 1709, op. cit.

BACKGROUND AND EARLY SCHOOLS

APPENDIX 2(a)

TABLE OF RETURNS FOR R. J. NEVILL, ESQ., COPPERWORKS, LLANELLI.
RETURN OF THE LLANELLI FREE SCHOOL, MARCH, 1818, RENDERED BY W. WILLIAMS.[1]

Attendance	Strength of the School			Present			Absent			Total
	Copper Works	Cae Maen	Box	Copper Works	Cae Maen	Box	Copper Works	Cae Maen	Box	
Monday 23rd	24	28	4	–	–	–	–	–	–	Easter
Tuesday 24th	24	28	4	10	15	3	14	13	1	56
Wednesday 25th	24	28	4	12	18	3	12	10	1	56
Thursday 26th	24	28	4	11	18	3	13	10	1	56
Friday 27th	24	28	4	13	14	3	11	14	1	56
Saturday 28th	24	28	4	8	14	2	16	14	2	56

W. WILLIAMS.

1 Miscellaneous Papers, Llanelli Public Library.

BACKGROUND AND EARLY SCHOOLS

APPENDIX 2(b)

TABLE OF RETURNS FOR R. J. NEVILL, ESQ., of FIELD HOUSE, LLANELLI.
RETURN OF THE LLANELLI FREE SCHOOL, APRIL, 1818, RENDERED BY W. WILLIAMS.[1]

Attendance	Strength of the School			Present			Absent			Total
	Copper Works	Cae Maen	Box	Copper Works	Cae Maen	Box	Copper Works	Cae Maen	Box	
Monday 27th	24	31	4	12	17	1	12	14	3	59
Tuesday 28th	24	31	4	13	19	2	11	12	2	59
Wednesday 29th	24	31	4	12	19	2	12	12	2	59
Thursday 30th	24	31	4	–	–	–	–	–	–	Fair Day
Friday May 1st	24	31	4	10	16	1	14	15	3	59
Saturday May 2nd	24	31	4	8	10	1	16	21	3	59

W. WILLIAMS.

APPENDIX 3.

LLANELLI CHARITY SCHOOL
NAMES OF SUBSCRIBERS TO LLANELLI CHARITY SCHOOL, 1823.[2]

Amount of Subscriptions per annum		Due June 25, 1823	Due Christmas 1823
£ s. d.		£ s. d.	£ s. d.
5 5 0	Ralph Stephen Pemberton, Industrialist	2 12 6	
5 5 0	Richard Janion Nevill, Industrialist	2 10 0	
5 5 0	Rees Goring Thomas	2 12 6	
5 5 0	Most Noble Marquis of Cholmondeley	2 10 0	2 10 0
1 1 0	Arthur Raby, Industrialist	10 6	10 6
2 2 0	Haynes Day and Co.	1 1 0	1 1 0
2 2 0	Rev. Ebenezer Morris (Vicar of Llanelli)	1 1 0	1 1 0

Total Subscription for 1823—£31 0s. 0d.

1 Miscellaneous Papers, Llanelli Public Library.
2 ibid

CHAPTER II

Educational Destitution and the Establishment of Works Schools

THE MOST significant feature of industrialization in Wales during the nineteenth century was the remarkable growth and concentration of population in the metallurgical and coalmining areas. This phenomenon not only produced new problems of various kinds involving the health and working conditions of the labouring population, but it also raised more sharply than before the question of education. It is no exaggeration to state that the provision of elementary education for the working classes attracted most public attention in the Principality during the greater part of the nineteenth century.

The absence of a State system of education, and the reluctance of successive governments during the nineteenth century to participate directly, was chiefly due to the question of religion. In Wales before 1840 education was provided mainly, apart from a small number of National and British schools, by the large numbers of private adventure schools which gave some kind of instruction for a penny or two per week for those who could afford it, and by the Sunday schools which were universally popular and attended in large numbers by all age groups. Before 1840 the activities of the two Voluntary Societies were limited in extent although by that year the National Society was bestirring itself and according to several Reports issued by the diocesan Education Boards was striving to appropriate as much money as possible due to them under certain conditions from the Committee of Privy Council on Education. But, viewed as a whole, and from a proliferation of evidence from the monumental Blue Books of 1847, although there were hundreds of schools of a sort in Wales, most of them were in a languishing and unsatisfactory state both in terms of buildings and quality of teaching.[1]

The many government and official reports of the first half of the nineteenth century employed the term 'educational destitution' to denote the poor provision for education in south Wales. This is precisely what the employers of labour had to face together with problems of housing,

---

1 *Reports of the Commissioners of Inquiry into the State of Education in Wales* 1847.

sanitation, and moral welfare. This was the first ever population explosion with all its inherent problems in an age bereft of any precedent to act as guide for seemingly insoluble situations. So far as education was concerned the masters of industry had to provide on the spot facilities for their workers and their progeny, and the works schools appeared, spasmodically at first up to 1840, but by 1870 were characteristic landmarks in every industrial community or parish in the iron, copper-smelting, tinplate, colliery, and slate quarry districts of Wales. Indeed, every new works created a new township and the more humane employers of labour assumed their civic responsibilities.

After 1800 the growth of population in the two counties of Monmouthshire and Glamorgan was phenomenal. Between 1801 and 1851 the increase for Glamorgan was 223 per cent, and for Monmouthshire 244 per cent, whereas the national average, i.e. Britain, was $93\frac{1}{2}$ per cent. For the inter-censal period 1841-1851 the population of Glamorgan had increased by more than 35 per cent.[1] Waves of immigrants invaded the new industrial regions from the rural parts of Wales, the contiguous counties of England, especially south-western England, and from Ireland.[2] From a social standpoint some parts of the industrial areas fared worse than others. In the Monmouthshire valleys, in Merthyr Tydfil and Dowlais, and a few other places 'whatever is unsettled or lawless or roving or characterless among working men has felt an attraction for these districts. It was from these areas that most of the followers of John Frost in his march on Newport in 1839 were drawn . . . living conditions were often deplorable and in those places where works proprietors built houses for their work-people they did so without the slightest attention to comfort, health, or decency, whilst the work-people, although never deficient in natural ability, were grossly ignorant.'[3] But these places were the worst and could not be taken as indicative of conditions generally in the industrial districts. Many proprietors paid special attention to housing conditions and the social welfare of their work-people. Even at Dowlais, for example, conditions were much better than at Merthyr Tydfil nearby.[4]

In the industrial area around Cwmavon in west Glamorgan, conditions were much improved. There, the Company considered the welfare

1 *Minutes of the Committee of Privy Council on Education*, 1854-55, p. 635.
2 A. E. Trueman, Population changes in the eastern part of the S. Wales Coalfield, *Geographical Journal*, 1919, p. 415.
3 1847 *Reports*, Part 2, pp. 290-93. *Report to the General Board of Health on a preliminary enquiry into the sewerage . . . and the sanitary condition of the inhabitants of the town of Merthyr Tydfil*, London, 1850.
4 Due mainly to the work of Sir John and Lady Charlotte Guest. The social and educational conditions at Dowlais are dealt with in detail in Chapter IV.

ESTABLISHMENT OF WORKS SCHOOLS

and interests of the working classes. Employers showed more discrimination about the type of workman employed, and always insisted on enquiring about the character of a new employee. These precautions contrasted with the reckless manner in which workmen were absorbed in the works around Merthyr Tydfil and the valleys of Monmouthshire. Also, at Cwmavon the workmen's houses were well arranged 'in an orderly manner in rows of moderate size in different parts of the valley'.[1] On the whole, the new populations of the mining and smelting districts were generally poor and unskilled, whilst the use of the vernacular and the variety of religious denominations made educational provision difficult. The major problem in these areas was the serious deficiency of schools which caused no little anxiety for those who cared. The question of educational destitution in the growing industrial areas was frequently voiced in the House of Commons not only in conjunction with Factory legislation but also by those who advocated elementary schools for the labouring population.

The *Annual Reports of the National Society* up to 1831 were gravely concerned with the state of the working classes and yet in the twenty years of its existence, that Society had done very little, if anything, to provide National schools in such areas. The Society seemed to take the view that it was the duty of the proprietors to supply the deficiency. In its *Annual Report* for 1831 this attitude was made quite clear: 'In colliery and mining and manufacturing districts large masses of population have often been rapidly collected without any of that mixture of rank and intercourse between the rich and poor which is so beneficially exercised in most parts of the kingdom. Children in industrial areas are suffered to grow up in utter ignorance of all their duties and privileges as Christians. Why has this state of things been permitted to exist? Have not the proprietors of such estates and manufactories relieved those grievous wants? . . . The answer to such questions is direct and plain. In some places the owners of such works have, greatly to their credit, provided at their own expense schools on an adequate scale for the education of the poor, but instances of this kind are not common.'[2]

The activities of the British and Foreign School Society for the same period were no more impressive and if anything in a more moribund state than that of the National Society, for in 1833 there were less than a dozen schools established throughout Wales. There was little improvement by 1845 for in that year the Rev. John Phillips, the Society's Agent,

1 1847 *Reports*, Part 1, p. 29.
2 *National Society*, 20*th Annual Report*, 1831, p. 16.

said that he 'never thought that Wales was so destitute of the means of instruction for the children of the working classes until his late journeyings to and fro through the country'.[1] Compared with the National Society, the work of the British and Foreign School Society was considerably hampered by lack of organization and administration. Whilst the former had all the machinery of the Established Church with its diocesan education Boards and inspectors behind its activities, the latter had only one Agent for the whole of Wales and moreover had to deal with Nonconformity in all its denominational array.

The *Education Inquiry of* 1833 and the *Reports of the Select Committee on Education* in succeeding years emphasized the need for more schools particularly in the industrial regions.[2] Although the State had applied grants for elementary education to be disbursed through the Voluntary Societies from 1833 the money available was totally inadequate to meet the need and in 1839, through the publication of the first *Minutes of the Committee of Privy Council on Education* the country became aware of the continued state of educational destitution in the South Wales Districts by the 'gloomy' Report drawn up for the Mining Districts by Hugh Seymour Tremenheere.[3] The whole of this Report is a heart-rending human document incorporating stirring pleas and arguments for educational facilities, and in the following excerpt he describes conditions in the ironworks around north Monmouthshire: 'It is not likely to be forgotten that this part of the country was the seat of the Chartist outbreak in 1839. The ironworks are on high moorlands from 800 to 1,000 feet above sea-level, with their populations of 5,000 and 10,000 clustered around them, the growth of comparatively recent years and now again rapidly on the increase . . . this district had very little educational facilities except Sunday schools. Vast populations were left without any adequate means of moral and religious superintendence and control and without opportunities of any effectual education for their children. Little had been done at that time either by the proprietors of works or by the landowners deriving large revenues from their mineral property, to supply

---

1   *British and Foreign School Society, Annual Report,* 1833, p. 18. Also, ibid. *Report for* 1845, p. 58.
2   i. *Education Inquiry, Abstracts of Answers and Returns made pursuant to an Address of the House of Commons,* 24*th May,* 1833, printed 1835: Vol. 2, Monmouth. Vol. 3, Surrey-Radnor (containing Glamorgan).
ii. *Report from the Select Committee on the education of the poorer classes in England and Wales,* 1834, IX; 1835, VII; 1837-38, VI, *p.* 163.
iii. *Abstract of Answers and Returns relative to the State of Education in England and Wales,* 1836, XLI, XLII, XLIII.
3   H. S. Tremenheere, 1804-93, first an Inspector of Schools then an Assistant Poor Law Commissioner; served on a number of Government Inquiries.

ESTABLISHMENT OF WORKS SCHOOLS

the manifest deficiencies.'[1] In September, 1841, Rhys William Jones, who compiled a report on the Ebbw Vale District for the Commissioners of 1842 stated that 'the extensive and populous neighbourhood of Ebbw Vale remains destitute of almost every educational resource, excepting that of inferior Sunday Schools at the sectarian chapels where large numbers attended but few teachers were forthcoming'.[2] 1846 was a significant year for education in Wales. William Williams, M.P. for Coventry and a native of Llanpumsaint, Carmarthenshire, proposed in the House of Commons that an Inquiry be made into the state of education in the Principality.[3] The detailed *Report* which appeared in 1847 involved three large volumes which gave for the first time a comprehensive picture of education in every parish in Wales, caused a furore among the Welsh people, and was the major national controversy of the first half of the nineteenth century.[4] Briefly, the *Report* re-affirmed the findings of previous government inquiries that in the industrial regions apart from a few works schools, educational facilities were meagre. The lengthy paragraphs of written evidence submitted by hundreds of individual witnesses throughout the Principality are exciting sources of study for the sociologist in addition to the masses of detailed tables, statistics and lists of schools, including Sunday schools.[5] Two years later, Sir Thomas Phillips in his book on *Wales* with particular reference to the work of the National Society, refers in some detail to the lack of schools in the populous parishes of his native Monmouthshire.[6] Even the denominational bodies raised an outcry against the deficiency of schools,

1 *Minutes of Committee of Council*, 1839-40. *Report on the Mining Districts of South Wales by H. S. Tremenheere*, p. 415.
2 *First Report of Commissioners for Inquiring into the Employment of Children in mines and manufactories*, (Mines), 1842, XV, p. 343. Also: *Reports and Evidence of Sub-Commissioners for same*, 1842, XVII, p. 186.
3 Daniel Evans, *The Life and Work of William Williams*, Gomerian Press, Llandysul, 1940, p. 82.
  William Williams, 1788-1865, born at Tredarren, Llanpumpsaint, Carmarthenshire; wealthy London cloth and cotton merchant; M.P. for Coventry 1835-1847, M.P. for Lambeth, 1850-1865. On December 1st, 1863, at a memorable meeting held at the Freemasons Tavern, London, at which he was chairman, was proud to initiate steps to promote University education in Wales, and gave £1,000 and a substantial sum in his will for the venture.
4 The Blue Books of 1847 became known in Wales as 'Brâd y Llyfrau Gleision' (The Treachery of the Blue Books). The three Commissioners who conducted the Inquiry (Englishmen) were accused of bias against the Welsh language. They also accused the Welsh people of immorality and ignorance.
5 ibid, Reports of Hundreds, Parishes, and Schools. Part 1, Glamorgan and Carmarthenshire; Part 2, Monmouthshire; Part 3, North Wales.
6 Sir Thomas Phillips, *Wales: The language, social conditions, moral character, and religious opinions of the people considered in their relation to education, etc.* 1849, pp. 401, ff.

especially from 1843 onwards, and many attempts were made to build unsectarian schools independent of State aid, but these efforts were spasmodic, uncoordinated, and delayed rather than encouraged the establishment of schools by the British and Foreign School Society.[1]

The Factory Acts in their relation to works schools and nineteenth century education merit some consideration. Factory legislation from 1802 onwards had attempted to provide some kind of education for children and young persons employed in industry. These attempts were in the educational clauses embodied in the Acts, but were always abused and often ignored. In Wales however, during the initial phases of the industrial revolution when iron-smelting was dominant, child labour was much less in demand as compared with the cotton and woollen factories of England. Towards the end of the eighteenth century coppersmelting had assumed importance in south Wales and both iron and copper industries demanded a more mature and experienced type of workman, although many children were employed in the unskilled processes and general labouring. Factory legislation up to 1844 (the Acts of 1802, 1819, and 1833) were wholly inapplicable to Wales[2] with the exception of a few rural woollen factories, and for that reason do not concern the Welsh industrial areas. This inapplicability of the early Factory Acts to the metallurgical industries of Wales was one of the main reasons for educational destitution, for the proprietors of works were under no obligation to provide schools. One attempt on the part of the government to establish factory schools was put forward in a special report drawn up by R. J. Saunders, a Factory Inspector in 1842[3] when he pleaded for the immediate establishment of a few experimental 'Government Factory Schools' financed wholly by the State. Saunders had already seen some schools opened by what he termed 'enlightened employers of labour' who had either covered the costs of the buildings themselves, or who had opened subscription lists in their localities to defray the costs with help from the Voluntary Societies.[4] But this scheme 'was not successful in the south Wales areas where works schools were so badly needed because few people were wealthy enough to support schools'.[5] As a result, where

1 *Y Diwygiwr*, 1863, p. 247; 1864, p. 218.
2 1802 *Act:* 42. Geo. III. *c.* 73.
  1819 *Act:* 59. Geo. III. *c.* 66.
  1833 *Act:* 3 and 4, Will. IV. *c.* 103.
3 *Parliamentary Paper* XXVII, 1843. Report of R. J. Saunders upon the establishment of schools in Factory Districts, p. 385.
4 *Transactions of the National Association for the Promotion of Social Science*, 1859, p. 377.
5 Sir Thomas Phillips, op. cit. pp. 401, ff.

works schools were built in south Wales, they were built by the employers, maintained by the employees and the majority were affiliated to the Voluntary Societies.[1]

However, the sponsoring of factory schools by the State was looked upon with some favour by the House, and on this basis in 1843, Sir James Graham presented his controversial *Education of Factory Children's Bill* to Parliament which included a definite proposal for the building of schools in the industrial areas—but on the National system. A bitter quarrel ensued between the Established Church and the Dissenters which ended in the complete withdrawal of the Bill.[2] Had the Bill been passed 'it might well have led in time to a general provision of schools in all industrial districts'.[3] Graham introduced a further Bill, which became the Factory Act of 1844 but no further attempt was made to aid the provision of schools.[4] It reinforced the Act of 1833 by insisting, *inter alia*, on the production of written proof of attendance at school of those children employed in factories, and they were also required to attend school for three hours daily.[5]

With the rapid expansion of the smelting and coalmining industries after 1840 subsequent factory legislation was extended to cover children and young persons employed in those industries and it is in this connection that the operation of works schools comes into the picture especially with reference to the twin evils of irregular attendance and early withdrawal which will be dealt with later. Here the battle starts between the working-class parents and the State on the one hand and the proprietors who had provided works schools on the other. It was a paradoxical and to some extent ludicrous situation. Both employers of labour and the State (by means of grants to the Voluntary Societies) were tackling the problem of educational destitution, and, where no schools existed, the work-people complained. Yet, when employers of labour provided schools, the work-people and their children proved extremely uncooperative. The works and collieries attracted young people and the parents encouraged them to start work at an early age. This attitude persisted relentlessly after the Factory Act of 1860 which stated that children between ten and twelve years of age could be employed if certificates were produced

1 See Chapter XII.
2 *Bill for regulating the employment of children and young persons in factories and for the better education of children in factory areas.* Parl. Paper II, 1843, p. 495.
3 A. H. Robson, *The Education of Children Engaged in Industry in England*, 1833-1876. 1931, p. 78.
4 *Bill for Regulating the employment of children ... in factories*, Parl. Paper II, 1844, p. 149.
5 7. Vict. c. 15.

showing proficiency in reading and writing.¹ The government continued to promote more effective education in the industrial areas. In 1862, the *Third Report of the Commissioners*² dealt with the employment of children in blast furnaces, rolling-mills and forges. It recommended the abolition of night work for young children, a half-time system of hours of work and education for all children under thirteen, together with a more rigorous supervision of works and factories by Inspectors. In 1867 the Factory Acts Extension Act³ applied the provisions of the previous Factory Acts to ironworks, blast furnaces, mills, foundries and forges. Its educational clause required the half-time attendance at school of all children between the ages of eight and thirteen. Three years later the Education Act of 1870 placed education on a national footing and subsequently gave authority to the local School Boards to make by-laws to compel children to attend school.⁴ The decade 1870-1880 produced a coalition between Factory and educational legislation and thereafter education became a national responsibility.

Although the Factory Acts had made it possible for some kind of education to be given to working-class children, they achieved very little in the way of establishing schools.⁵ The Select Committee of 1841 contained the views of two witnesses who were proprietors of factories: 'Schooling either belongs to the parents or it belongs to the State: it does not belong to the employer, in my opinion: it is either a parental or a national duty.'⁶ The second witness stated that 'there are situations in which it would be very onerous and expensive for the mill-owner to provide schooling to the extent which the population or those employed in the manufactory might require. The owner had better pay higher wages to older hands than incur the expense of having to employ children if he must undertake to educate them.'⁷ The Committee however, did no more than remark that they could devise no precise remedy and that 'it would be dangerous in many respects to hold the government responsible for providing schools in such cases; and the Committee can only express their sincere and cordial hope that the rapid progress of the prevailing feeling in favour of a moral and religious education of the operative

1 23/24. Vict. c. 151.
2 *Parliamentary Paper*, XXIX, 1864, *Third Report of the Commissioners* (*Children's Employment Commission*,) 1862, p. 547.
3 30/31. Vict. c. 103.
4 Universal compulsory education came in 1880.
5 *Parliamentary Paper*, IX, 1841. *Report from the Select Committee on the Act for the Regulation of Mills and Factories*, p. 575.
6 ibid
7 ibid

classes will speedily come in aid of the difficulty.'[1] The practical effects of the Factory Acts was to throw on the proprietors the obligation, in the last resort, of providing education for the children of those whom they employed. Unless a school already existed near a works or factory, the owners usually provided it.

The deficiency of day-schools in the industrial areas was counteracted to a very great extent by the popularity, universality, and conspicuous success of the Sunday schools.[2] Everywhere, these schools were particularly attractive to the working-classes, and in the industrial areas were more popular than the day-schools even where the latter schools existed. The reason for this enthusiasm for the Sunday schools was a simple one—they were carried on in the Welsh language, taught Bible reading, and were freely available to all age groups. Many works proprietors who had not built day-schools maintained with some measure of justification that Sunday schools already supplied whatever deficiencies existed in educational provision, and, indeed, many Sunday schools had both secular and religious curricula and also employed paid teachers. Moreover, the workmen themselves subscribed to the same view, for attendance at school on Sundays meant no loss of work or wages for young boys, and consequently no loss of income for the family.

It is worth probing a little deeper into this attitude of the working-classes of that period. Tremenheere in the same Report of 1839-1840 describes the appalling conditions under which people in the south Wales mining districts lived, and also the lack of educational provision. One of the blackest areas was the Merthyr-Bedwellty region which he analyses in some detail. He calculated that of the whole number of the working classes in that district for whom daily instruction should have been provided, more than two-thirds or 70.8 per cent did not attend any day school.[3] The plain fact was that the ordinary working man did not consider schooling essential for the type of work he was doing—which did not require high intellectual proficiency. In addition, adults and children alike, readily obtained employment and the economic or class

1 *Report from the Select Committee*, 1841, op. cit., p. 577.
2 See Chapter IX.
3 *Minutes of Committee of Council*, 1839-40, p. 178: 'In a district the population of which is, to a considerable extent, composed of immigrants, and subject to fluctuations to fix upon satisfactory data for arriving at an approximation to the number of children between the ages of 3 and 12, the period there usually devoted to education, would have been difficult without an accurate census of a definite portion of that district, affording a fair average of the whole. With this I have been furnished by the kindness of one of the proprietors of the Varteg Ironworks in the Parish of Trevethin, who caused it to be taken for the purposes of the present inquiry. In a

value of a good education did not appeal to them.[1] The workmen were far more concerned with the evils of the truck and shop systems than with the education of their children. In his evidence before the Commission of 1861, the manager of the Dowlais ironworks stated 'that there is no very active demand for education is evident from the fact that the absence of schools has seldom, if ever, formed a topic of complaint against the proprietors. The men, and those who employ themselves in setting forth their grievances, are in some slight degree awake to other abuses, but in those works, now indeed happily but few, in which no schools are provided, this is not urged against the masters, and I have only known one case in which the men expressed an opinion in their favour. Still, where the means are at hand, the people are very far indeed from being indifferent to education. They willingly pay the weekly penny .... and take great interest in the progress of their children. But this is not so everywhere, but is certainly the case here with us in Dowlais where we have excellent schools. Schools of this kind generally do not originate with the workmen—the stimulus comes from the proprietors. Workmen do not, as a rule, establish efficient day schools for themselves,

population of 8,598 attached to his own and two neighbouring works, the number of children between 3 and 12 years of age was found to be 1,717, or one-fifth (19.96 per cent) of the population. Taking this as a basis of calculation applicable to the whole district, the result, as respects the proportion of those who attend day-schools to those who do not will be as follows:—

One-fifth of 85,000	17,000
Deduct children of superior workmen and agents sent elsewhere for education, or frequenting a few schools of superior description; also children of the working classes sick, or prevented by casualties from attending school; one-third of 17,000 ..	5,666
Total children of working classes for whom education should be provided at day schools	11,334
Deduct children going to day schools	3,308
Total children uneducated at day schools	8,026

It thus appears that upwards of two-thirds (70.8 per cent)* of the whole number of the working classes in this district, for whom daily instruction should be provided do not attend any day school.'
Note* this is mis-printed 7.08 per cent on page 178 of the *Minutes*.
[1] ibid: 'Their occupations are such that in general the absence of any previous mental culture is no obstacle to their obtaining good employment. Success in their calling being the result of mechanical skill, rather than, as in some of the mining operations, of careful judgement and previous calculation, the higher qualities of the mind are called for in a comparatively small degree . . . their employments have but a slight tendency to impress upon them the value of intellectual proficiency. The great majority, therefore, are content to remain without any instruction.'

ESTABLISHMENT OF WORKS SCHOOLS

or support them voluntarily, but they submit in some of the works to a small deduction from their wages.'[1]

Apart from the examples already given of educational destitution in certain areas of south Wales it would be superfluous to describe them all at this juncture since they will be referred to in greater detail in subsequent chapters dealing with each particular industry which established works schools. Statistically the numbers of schools established by each industry are impressive: Ironworks, 45; Non-ferrous metal industries, 15; Tinplate works, 12; Collieries, 47; Slate-quarries, 12; Textile industries, 2; Stone-quarries, 1. Total number of works schools: 134.

During the early period of the Industrial Revolution, Capel Waun y Pound school (1784), already described, was the sole representative. The opening years of the nineteenth century saw the establishment of several schools in the coppersmelting district around Swansea, at Melingriffith tinworks near Cardiff, and at the lead mines at Gloddaith, Llandudno, all opened by 1810. From 1810 to 1839 more works schools appeared, promoted mainly by individual proprietors, many of whom were Quakers. In the iron smelting areas schools were opened at Blaenavon, Varteg Hill (Trevethin), Machen, and Nantyglo in Monmouthshire; at Neath Abbey, Hirwaun, Dowlais, Venallt, and Pentyrch in Glamorgan, and at Yniscedwyn in Breconshire. In the coppersmelting district, schools were established at Llanelli, and Margam (which also had a tinworks school). There were a few small colliery schools at Hirwaun and Dinas in central Glamorgan and also the Aberdare 'Free Schools' supported mainly by the Marquis of Bute; at Cilybebyll (Crynant), and the schools promoted by the Llewellyn family of Penllergaer near Swansea, at Llangyfelach, Gorseinon, and Penllergaer.

On his first visit to south Wales in 1839 Tremenheere was worried that few owners had bothered to provide schools, hence his 'gloomy' Report. After 1840 the memory of the Chartist disturbances of 1839, and the period of general depression in the iron trade with unemployment and low wages between 1839 and 1845 (which however tended to produce better relationships between employers and employed),[2] brought the question of the education of the working classses into the limelight by long discussions in Parliament together with the efforts of individual Welshmen. Graham's Factory Bill of 1843 had long sessions in the House and the

1 *Newcastle Commission Report*, 1861, *Reports of the Assistant Commissioners*, Vol. II, pp. 572-634: Evidence of G. T. Clark, Manager, Dowlais Ironworks.
2 *Reports from Commissioners, Mines*, 1846, op. cit., p. 414.

south Wales M.P.s, many of them leading industrialists, had taken part in the debates on the proposed Factory schools mentioned earlier. Secondly, Hugh Owen's *Letter to the Welsh people* urging the provision of elementary schools on the British system throughout Wales was published in 1843 and was enthusiastically received everywhere, especially in north Wales.[1] Thirdly, the motion of William Williams, M.P. and the publication of the Blue Books of 1847 no doubt served to bestir those employers who had taken no action to date. These events occurred, or rather, coincided with the rapid establishment of works schools between 1840 and 1850 in the iron and coppersmelting areas, and after 1850 in the tinplate and colliery regions.

Tremenheere is our authoritative recorder of the various stages of the establishment of works schools—a record which was methodical and in considerable detail. On his second visit to the industrial areas of Monmouthshire and Glamorgan in 1845 (when he had to report on the working of the Mines Act), he was very impressed by the efforts made by employers to establish schools.[2] During this visit he only reported on the iron-smelting and colliery districts, and mentions no schools in other industries. His Report of 1846 however, is important not only for his account of the state of the population in the industrial districts of Monmouthshire, Breconshire, and Glamorgan (Carmarthenshire was omitted) but it was also the first comprehensive survey of works schools in south Wales. He described the schools established at Blaenavon, Rhymney, Courtybella, Tredegar, Sirhowy, Nantyglo, Pontypool, Abersychan, and Pontnewynydd in Monmouthshire; the Cwmavon, Llynfi, Maesteg, Ystalyfera, Neath Abbey, Bryndu, and the Dowlais schools in Glamorgan, and the Yniscedwyn school in Breconshire.[3] By 1850 he was able to report 'a continued improvement in school provision for the south Wales industrial areas' and gives details of further developments: 'As regards school buildings, it may now be said that, considering those already erected, and those about immediately to be built, then out of the sixteen principal masses of populations collected around the great coal and ironworks from Pontypool to Aberdare, are, or will shortly be furnished with excellent ones, conducted by properly qualified masters and mistresses, namely, the Pontypool Valley, Blaenavon, Nantyglo, Blaina, Ebbw Vale and Victoria, Sirhowy, Blackwood, Gelligaer, Rhymney, Merthyr, Dowlais, and Aberdare. In proportion to its need, Merthyr,

1 Daniel Evans, op. cit. p. 276 ff.
2 *Reports from Commissioners, Mines*, 1846, op. cit.
3 ibid for 1847.

ESTABLISHMENT OF WORKS SCHOOLS

containing the large population employed at the Cyfarthfa, Penydarren, and Plymouth Works, is the least adequately provided. There are schools at Clydach (Breconshire) and very large ones at Tredegar and Dowlais, but not yet provided with appropriate buildings. The spots presenting the most marked deficiency are Brynmawr and Beaufort.'[1]

Between 1852 and 1855 new school buildings had been erected by many proprietors—who had by this time become affiliated to the Voluntary Societies thus qualifying for building grants, teachers' salaries, and equipment—at Abersychan, Sirhowy, Tredegar, Blaenavon, and other places. In his 1850 Report, Tremenheere mentions for the first time the 'important' schools connected with the copperworks of Vivian and Grenfell in the Swansea district and the Nevill copperworks schools at Llanelli.[2] His most encouraging and cheerful Report appeared in 1856 when he stated that practically all the new works schools had been erected and educational provision in the densely populated south Wales districts had improved 'beyond his wildest dreams', and he went on to say that 'the spirit actuating the very great majority of the employers of labour in the great mining district of Monmouthshire and Glamorgan in reference to their responsibilities to the labouring populations is unquestionably now of a very much higher kind than was visible when I was first called upon to report on the condition of these districts. After the Chartist outbreak of 1839, Company after Company, and employer after employer has in successive years taken steps towards providing for their people better means of moral and religious and general instruction, and towards facilitating the physical comforts and decencies of life among those large and rapidly collected populations.'[3]

Tinworks and colliery schools appeared after 1850, for it was after that date that the mid-Glamorgan coalfield was exploited when scores of new collieries and new mining communities occupied the Rhondda and neighbouring valleys. In marked contrast to the slow establishment of works schools in the metallurgical areas of south Wales up to 1850, the colliery schools were built in rapid succession, some between 1850 and 1860, the majority between 1860 and 1870 and a few more in the period 1870-1885.[4]

There were several reasons for this extraordinary school-building activity in the colliery districts. One was the tremendous enthusiasm

1 *Reports from Commissioners, Mines, for* 1850, p. 334.
2 ibid, Vol. XXIII, p. 542.
3 *Reports from Commissioners, Mines, for* 1856, *Parl. Paper* XVIII, p. 293.
4 See Appendices to this Chapter.

27

shown by the colliers who were fortunate in having first-rate leaders[1] and sympathetic and cooperative coalowners. Another important factor was the close relationship between school establishment and voluntary effort. For many years, and long after the passing of the Education Act of 1870 (which authorised the setting up of local School Boards), education in the mining valleys went hand in hand with self-help within the community. This entailed local subscriptions, a poundage levy on the miners' wages, with the colliery owners providing the buildings. For example, 'up to 1878, in the parish of Ystradyfodwg (the Rhondda valleys), the whole responsibility of supplying school education had been thrown on voluntary agency, and it must be admitted that, while trade was flourishing, the joint sacrifices of coalowners and colliers had sufficed to bear the burden.'[2] Again, the British and Foreign School Society had started its activities in earnest in south Wales in 1853 with the appointment of its first south Wales Agent, the Rev. William Roberts (Nefydd) of Blaina, Monmouthshire. According to the reports of the National Society similar rejuvenation infected the scholastic work of the Established Church in the colliery areas. Where local voluntary effort failed to carry on a school, the local committee usually sought the aid of one of the Voluntary Societies in order to benefit from State grants. The time arrived when the majority of works schools became integrated with the two Voluntary Societies and this sometimes produced the inevitable religious problems. The triumph of the British and Foreign School Society over the National Society in the industrial areas was primarily due to its undenominational character which appealed to the working classes, the majority of whom were Nonconformists. It should be remembered that whilst all education in England and Wales up to 1870 was voluntary, and promoted by the State through the two Voluntary Societies, the working-class population who had schools provided for them by employers were compelled to submit to a contribution from their wages towards the upkeep of such schools. Very often the schools would be organized on the National system, and the workmen would be very largely Nonconformist. This arrangement, which was unacceptable to the workmen, often caused friction between employers and employed. But where such schools were organized on the British system the men gladly paid their poundage and supported the schools.[3]

1 Rev. William Morris, Treorchy; William Abraham (Mabon); William Jenkins, Ystradfechan, Treorchy, Managing Director, Ocean Collieries.
2 *Minutes of Committee of Council*, 1881, p. 305. Report of Wm. Edwards, H.M.I.
3 See Chapter XII.

ESTABLISHMENT OF WORKS SCHOOLS

This dichotomy in Welsh society in the industrial areas—the proprietors of works and officials predominantly English-speaking and members of the Anglican communion, and the working-classes, Welsh in speech and background, and strongly Nonconformist in religion, was an important and often unpleasant aspect of the educational, political, and religious life of nineteenth century Wales. Nowhere was this more evident than in the story of the establishment of works schools for the labouring classes.

The north Wales coalfield was singularly deficient in works schools, with the exception of the insignificant Cotton Company's school at Mold, Flintshire. The mountainous region of the west had a few slate-quarry schools, and one school promoted by a granite quarry company. The paucity of works schools in north Wales was no doubt related to the much earlier activities of the Voluntary Societies there as compared with south Wales,[1] and to the fact that the Welsh Calvinistic Methodists raised no objection to being led into the fold of the British and Foreign School Society.[2]

---

1 *Report of the British and Foreign School Society*, 1845, pp. 58-9.
2 ibid, *Report for* 1849, p. 4.

APPENDIX 1

WORKS SCHOOLS BEFORE 1750

Works School	County	Date of Establishment
Neath	Glamorgan	1706
Esgair Hir	Cardiganshire	1700

WORKS SCHOOLS ESTABLISHED 1784-1810

Works School	County	Date of Establishment
Capel Waun y Pound	Monmouth	1784
Kilvey Juvenile Copperworks, Swansea	Glamorgan	1806
Melingriffith Tinworks, near Cardiff	Glamorgan	1808
Gloddaith Lead Mines, Llandudno	Caernarvonshire	1810

APPENDIX 2

IRONWORKS SCHOOLS, 1810-1839

Ironworks School	County	Date of Establishment
Blaenavon	Monmouth	1816
Neath Abbey	Glamorgan	1816
Hirwaun	Glamorgan	1820
Varteg Hill	Monmouth	1823
Dowlais	Glamorgan	1828
Trevethin	Monmouth	1832
Venallt	Glamorgan	1834
Pentyrch	Glamorgan	1834
Machen	Monmouth	1837
Nantyglo	Monmouth	1837
Yniscedwyn	Brecon	1839

ESTABLISHMENT OF WORKS SCHOOLS

APPENDIX 3

COPPERWORKS, TINWORKS, AND COLLIERY SCHOOLS, 1810-1839

Works School	County	Date of Establishment
Llanelli Free School (Nevill's Copperworks and Collieries)	Carmarthen	1818
Hirwaun Colliers	Glamorgan	1820
Llangyfelach National Colliery	Glamorgan	1822
Margam Tinworks	Glamorgan	1829
Dinas Colliery	Glamorgan	1830
Margam Copperworks	Glamorgan	1830
Penllergaer Colliery Swansea	Glamorgan	1834
Cilybebyll Colliery	Glamorgan	1839
Kilvey Copperworks, Swansea	Glamorgan	1839

APPENDIX 4

MONMOUTHSHIRE IRONWORKS SCHOOLS, 1840-1850

School	Proprietors	Date of Establishment
Tredegar	S. Homfray	1841
Cwmbran	Ebbw Vale Co.	1842
Pontnewynydd	W. Williams	1842
Pontypool	C. Hanbury Leigh	1842
Rhymney (National)	Rhymney Iron Co.	1843
Rhymney (British)	Rhymney Iron Co.	1849
Abersychan	British Iron Co.	1845
Blaina and Cwmcelyn	Blaina Iron Co.	1845
Ebbw Vale	Ebbw Vale Co.	1844 (Girls) 1845 (Boys)
Victoria (Ebbw Vale)	Ebbw Vale Co.	1845
Sirhowy	Darby and Co.	1845
Dos Nailworks School, Newport, Mon.	J. J. Cordes	1848

EDUCATIONAL DESTITUTION AND THE

APPENDIX 5

GLAMORGAN IRONWORKS SCHOOLS, 1840-1850

School	Proprietors	Date of Establishment
Maesteg	Maesteg Iron Co.	1841
Taff Vale	Taff Vale Iron Co.	1842
Ystalyfera (Wern) Girls	Palmer Budd	1842
Cwmavon	English Copper Co.	1844
Llynfi	Llynfi Iron Co.	1845
Bryndu	H. Ford	1846
Bryn (Cwmavon)	English Copper Co.	1845
Oakwood (Cwmavon)	English Copper Co.	1846
Tonmawr	Tonmawr Iron & Coal Co.	1846
Cyfarthfa (Merthyr Tydfil)	R. Crawshay	1848
Georgetown (National) Merthyr Tydfil	R. Crawshay (by support only)	1850
Plymouth, Merthyr Tydfil	Plymouth Iron Co.	1850
Aberaman	Crawshay Bailey	1850
Tondu	Llynfi Iron Co.	1850
Aberavon	Messrs. Llewellyn	1850
Penydarren, Merthyr Tydfil	Penydarren Iron Co.	1852

APPENDIX 6

CARMARTHENSHIRE AND BRECONSHIRE, IRONWORKS SCHOOLS
1840-1860

School	Proprietors	Date of Establlshment
Trimsaran, Carmarthenshire	Messrs. Norton, Upperton & Stone	1843
Amman, Carmarthenshire	Amman Iron Co.	1856
Gwendraeth, Carmarthenshire	T. Watney & Co.	1860
Yniscedwyn, Breconshire	George Crane	1839
Clydach, Breconshire	Messrs. Powell	1842

ESTABLISHMENT OF WORKS SCHOOLS

APPENDIX 7

COLLIERY, COPPERWORKS, AND TINWORKS SCHOOLS
1840-1860

1 *Colliery Schools*

School	County	Date of Establishment
Llansamlet National	Glamorgan	1841
Courtybella, National	Monmouth	1842
Rhigos Colliery	Glamorgan	1856
Bryndu (Pyle)	Glamorgan	1846
Llanfabon	Glamorgan	1846
Cwmllynfell	Glamorgan	1850s
Cymmer, Porth	Glamorgan	1850s
Gors Eynon (Gorseinon)	Glamorgan	1846

2 *Copperworks and non-ferrous metal works schools*

School	County	Date of Establishment
Hafod Copperworks, Swansea	Glamorgan	1847
Copperworks, Llanelli	Carmarthen	1847
Pembrey Copper Works	Carmarthen	1855
Crown Copper Works, Neath	Glamorgan	1841
Spelter Works, Maesteg	Glamorgan	1854?
Pontamman Chemical Works	Carmarthen	1850s
Ysbyty Ystwyth Lead Mines	Cardiganshire	1842
Goginan Lead and Silver Mines	Cardiganshire	1843

3 *Tinworks Schools*

School	County	Date of Establishment
Aberdulais	Glamorgan	1842
Carmarthen	Carmarthen	1844
Pontardawe	Glamorgan	1846
Ystalyfera	Glamorgan	1850?
Dafen (Llanelli)	Carmarthen	1850

APPENDIX 8
Tinworks Schools Established After 1860

School	County	Date of Establishment (where known)
Brynamman	Carmarthen	1872
Ynyspenllwch (Swansea Valley)	Glamorgan	?
Melincrythan	Glamorgan	?
Hendy Higher Grade, Pontarddulais	Glamorgan	1885
Tydee, Rogerstone	Monmouth	?

APPENDIX 9
Colliery Schools Established After 1860

(*Note:* With the exception of the Duffryn Schools, the following schools were opened after 1860. The dates for most of the schools are uncertain, and are therefore queried.)

School	County	Date of Establishment
Treherbert (British)	Glamorgan	1860
Bodringallt (Ystrad)	Glamorgan	1861
Llwynypia	Glamorgan	1865
United Collieries, Treorchy	Glamorgan	1866
Dunraven	Glamorgan	1863
Blaenycwm	Glamorgan	1863
Pentre	Glamorgan	1875
Ton, Ystrad	Glamorgan	1869
Penygraig	Glamorgan	1869
Ferndale	Glamorgan	1869
Cwmparc	Glamorgan	1871
Clydach Vale	Glamorgan	1872
Blaengarw	Glamorgan	1883
Ynysybwl	Glamorgan	1886
Duffryn	Glamorgan	1857
Cwmpennar (Mountain Ash)	Glamorgan	1860s
Miskin Infants (Mountain Ash)	Glamorgan	?
Newtown Infants (Mountain Ash)	Glamorgan	?
Cwmamman	Glamorgan	?
Garth Colliery, Maesteg	Glamorgan	?
Coegnant Colliery, Maesteg	Glamorgan	1870
Merthyr Colliery, Maesteg	Glamorgan	1870
Varteg Hill Colliery	Monmouth	?
Gilfach Goch	Glamorgan	?
Clydach Vale	Glamorgan	?
Tynewydd (Wyndham Colliery)	Glamorgan	?
Nantymoel	Glamorgan	?
Resolven	Glamorgan	?
Court Herbert Colliery, Skewen	Glamorgan	?
Dyhewid (Llantwit Fardre)	Glamorgan	?
Pentrebach (Merthyr Vale)	Glamorgan	?
Kenfig Hill	Glamorgan	?
Pits (Ebbw Vale)	Monmouth	?
Yard School (Chas. Pit Colliery, Llansamlet)	Glamorgan	?

ESTABLISHMENT OF WORKS SCHOOLS

APPENDIX 10

NORTH WALES WORKS SCHOOLS

Oakeley Slate Quarry Schools:
Ffestiniog National School, 1829: Established by W. G. Oakeley.
Llwynygell, Blaenau Ffestiniog, 1836: Established by Mrs. W. G. Oakeley.
Maentwrog Church School, 1835: Established by W. G. Oakeley.
Gellilydan (Tynant) School. Mr. and Mrs. W. G. Oakeley.
Penrhyndeudraeth National School, 1859: Established by Mrs. L. J. Oakeley.

Tanygrisiau School, established by Samuel Holland.
Penrhyndeudraeth British School, 1835, established by Samuel Holland.
Tremadoc British School, 1810: opened by W. A. Madocks.
Gerlan National School, 1872: Lord Penrhyn.
Llandegai National Schools: Boys (1844); Girls (1810): Lord and Lady Penrhyn.
Llanllechid National Schools: Lord Penrhyn.
Bron y Foel School: Cilgwyn Company (1820s).

Welsh Granite Company's School, Trevor, Llanaelhaiarn, Caernarvonshire.

Gloddaith Lead Mines or Great Orme Copper Mines school, 1810-11.

Mold Cotton Company's School, Mold. 1834.

Shrewsbury: Flax Mill Company's School.

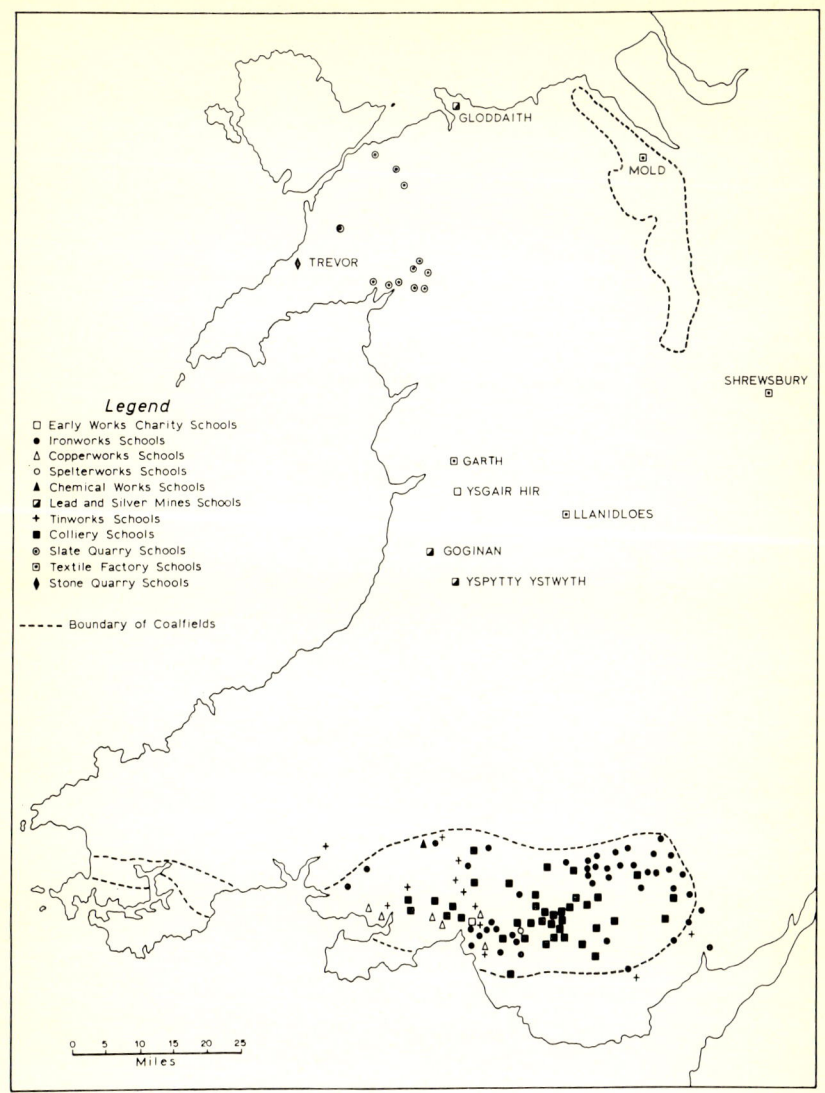

MAP 1 WALES: DISTRIBUTION OF WORKS SCHOOLS.

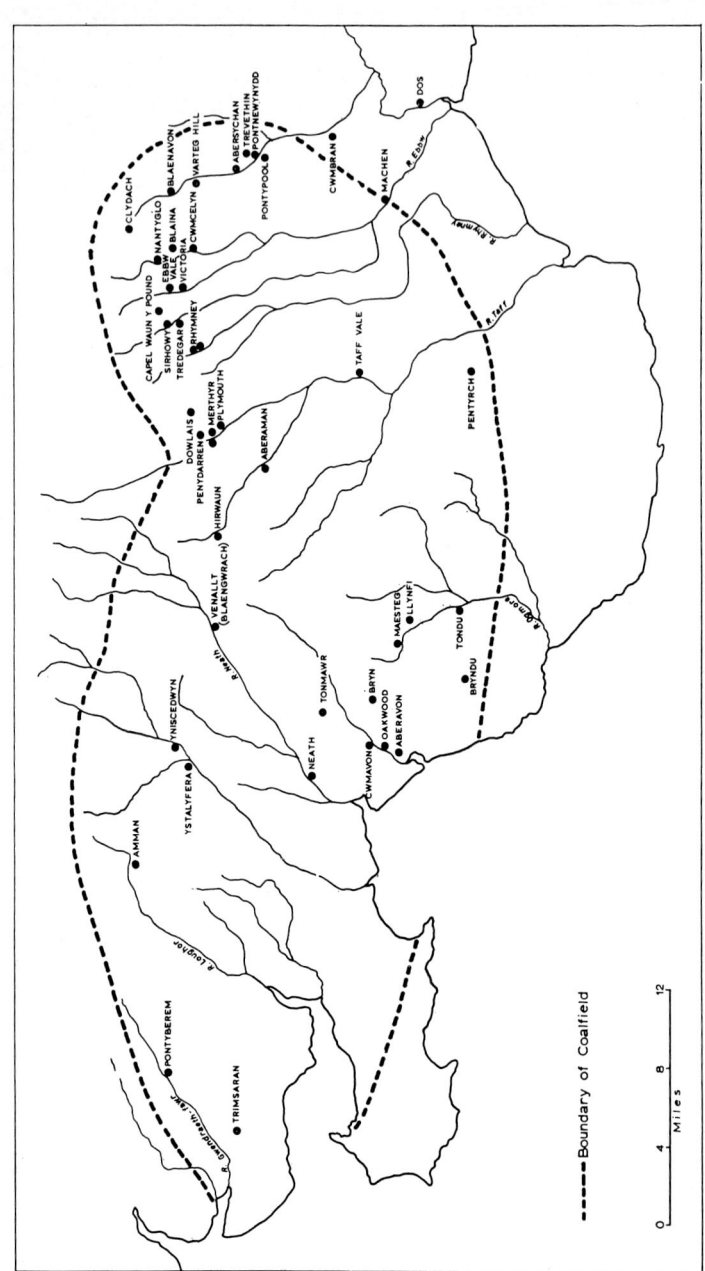

MAP 2 SOUTH WALES: DISTRIBUTION OF IRONWORKS SCHOOLS.

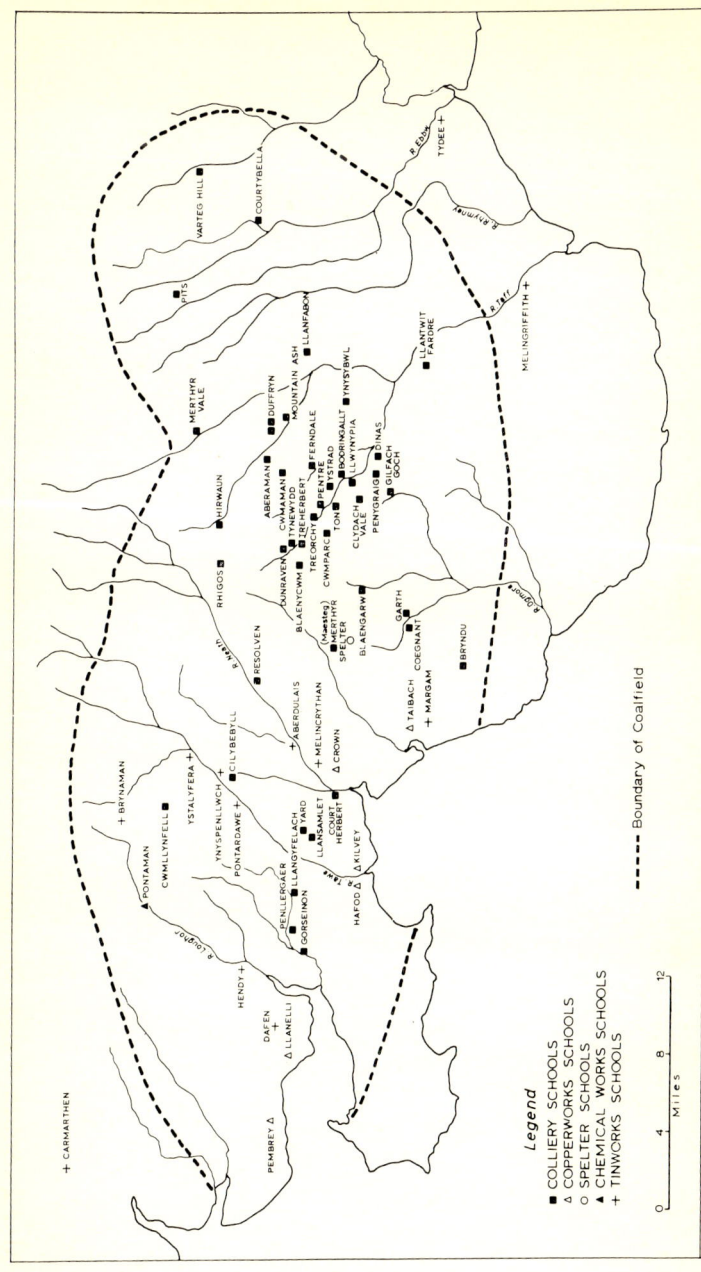

Map 3 South Wales: Distribution of Colliery, Tinworks and Non-Ferrous Metal Works Schools.

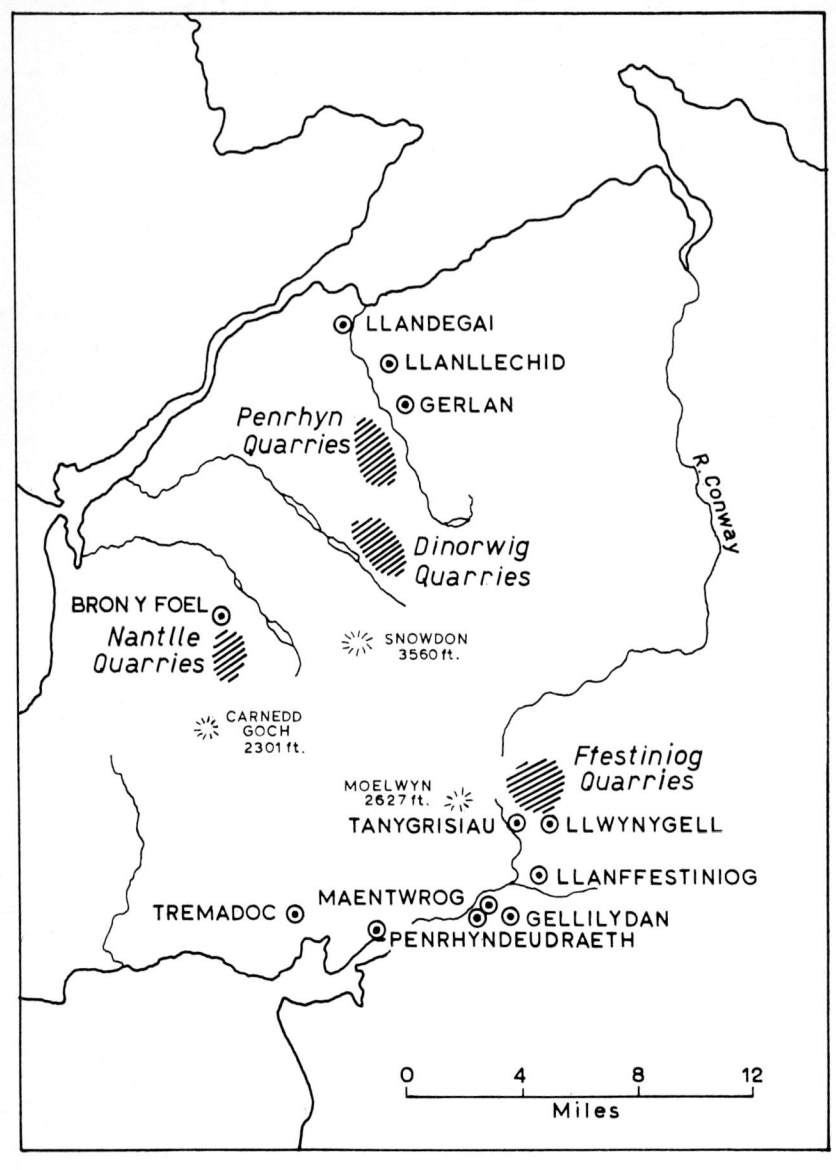

MAP 4   NORTH WALES: DISTRIBUTION OF SLATE QUARRY SCHOOLS.

CHAPTER III

Ironworks Schools

THE INITIAL phase of industrialism in south Wales was concerned with iron and coppersmelting.[1] The iron industry of the north-eastern outcrop of the south Wales coalfield, involving south Breconshire, north Glamorgan and north Monmouthshire, developed during the latter half of the eighteenth century where the essential raw materials such as iron ore, limestone, and small timber for charcoal were at hand. The second stage in the evolution of the iron industry, which continued throughout the first half of the nineteenth century, was identified with the use of coal for smelting. In addition to the large ironworks of this second phase which were established on the north-eastern outcrop from Hirwaun and Merthyr Tydfil across to Blaenavon and Pontypool on the east, other centres developed on the coalfield. These were located mainly in the Maesteg and Aberavon districts, the Swansea, Gwendraeth, Amman and Aberdare valleys, at various scattered subsidiary centres at Yniscedwyn (Breconshire), Clydach (Breconshire), Newport (Monmouthshire), Pentyrch, Taff Vale, Tondu (Bridgend), and other centres.[2]

The ironsmelting industry in the south and north Wales coalfields was developed mainly by immigrant English industrialists who also brought with them the necessary capital resources. They arrived during the latter half of the eighteenth century from the Midlands, the north of England and London.[3] The majority of the ironworks schools of the first half of the nineteenth century were promoted by these ironmasters, e.g. Guest of Dowlais, Homfray of Tredegar, Darby of Sirhowy and Ebbw Vale, Hill and Hopkins of Blaenavon, and Harford and Bailey of Nantyglo. Forty-five ironworks schools were established in south Wales but the north Wales coalfield had none.

There were three phases in the establishment of ironworks schools on the south Wales coalfield:

(a) An insignificant pre-1800 phase with only one school at Capel Waun y Pound in 1784.

1 Coppersmelting is discussed in Chapter V.
2 See map of ironworks schools.
3 A. H. John, op. cit., Chapter II.

(b) The period 1800-1840, when several schools were established by individual proprietors of works.

(c) The hey-day period of ironworks schools, between 1840 and 1860 when over thirty schools appeared, promoted by individual proprietors and by large companies.

By the middle of the nineteenth century, especially after 1860, many ironworks were also manufacturing tinplate and thus some ironworks schools later became known as tinworks schools, e.g. the Amman Ironworks in Carmarthenshire.[1]

IRONWORKS SCHOOLS 1800-1840

School	Proprietor	Date of Establishment	County
Blaenavon	T. Hill and S. Hopkins	1816[2]	Monmouth
Neath Abbey	J. Tregellis Price	1816[3]	Glamorgan
Hirwaun	F. Crawshay	1820[4]	Glamorgan
Varteg Hill	Varteg Hill Iron Co.	1823[5]	Monmouth
Dowlais	Sir J. J. Guest	1828[6]	Glamorgan
Trevethin	C. Hanbury Leigh	1832[7]	Monmouth
Venallt	Messrs. Jevons & Wood	1834[8]	Glamorgan
Pentyrch	T. W. Booker	1834[9]	Glamorgan
Machen	Machen Iron Co.	1837[10]	Monmouth
Nantyglo	Harford and Bailey	1837[11]	Monmouth
Yniscedwyn	George Crane	1839[12]	Brecon

The first ironworks school of the nineteenth century was established in 1816 at Blacnavon, Monmouthshire. Thomas Hill and Samuel Hopkins of Staffordshire had started the Blaenavon ironworks in 1789[13] and as the

1 See Chapter VI.
2 *Reports from Commissioners, Mines*, 1846, p. 414. Date of foundation is given as 1815, but the *Blaenavon Church Schools MSS* denote 1816.
3 1847 *Reports*, Part 1, p. 62, also pp. 333-4.
  D. R. Phillips, op. cit., p. 173
4 1847 *Reports*, Part 1, p. 54
5 *Education Inquiry: Abstract of Answers and Returns . . . to An Address of the House of Commons*, 24th May, 1833, Vol. 2, Monmouth, p. 602.
6 *Minutes of Committee of Council*, 1844. Report on 138 schools in the Western District, p. 226
7 1847 *Reports*, Part 2, p. 234.
8 ibid, Part 1, p. 64
9 ibid, pp. 58-61
10 ibid, Part 2, p. 316
11 ibid, p. 301
12 *Reports from the Commissioners, Mines*, 1846, p. 430.
13 C. Wilkins, *History of the Iron, Steel, Tinplate and other Trades of Wales*, 1903, pp. 209-10.

township developed, the two ironmasters built the parish church in 1805. The ironworks schools were founded and endowed by Miss Sarah Hopkins of Rugeley, Staffordshire in memory of her brother.[1] Later, the original girls' school was re-designed for a mixed school of boys and girls, and by 1846 the buildings were considerably enlarged to house infants, girls and boys, but 'although the schools are very promising ones, yet due to the extreme youth of the children their attainments were not very satisfactory in the boys' school, but were superior in the girls' school, and both master and mistress would repay a year's training in a good Normal school.'[2] By 1860 three separate schools had been built and for the first half of the nineteenth century these schools were the only means of education available for the children of Blaenavon.[3] The Hill family were staunch Anglicans and conducted the schools on the National system with the clergyman as visitor. Although the schools were called 'Blaenavon Endowed schools' and sometimes 'Free Schools'[4] a nominal charge for upkeep was deducted from the workmen's wages in 1856 which caused considerable friction between the proprietors and the employees, since the majority of the latter were Dissenters. The Rev. William Roberts (Nefydd), the Agent of the British and Foreign School Society, maintained that nine-tenths of the population were Dissenters and persuaded them to open a British school in 1857.[5]

A Quaker ironmaster, Joseph Tregellis Price, promoted the Neath Abbey ironworks schools. The Neath Abbey works together with the houses around them formed a suburb of Neath and when the school was opened in 1816 it was held in premises attached to the works. Later, in 1825, additional accommodation was provided 'for boys, girls, and infants, in separate buildings, surrounded by a wall'. Price was responsible for the cost and the Lords of the Abbey furnished the land and materials.[6] In 1858 the schools were re-built and some years later became solely

1 *Blaenavon Church School Deeds and MSS*. The translation of the Latin words on the wall of the girls' school reads : 'That she may elicit the perpetual praises of God from the mouths of children and that she might in some measure—even when he is dead, carry into effect the benevolent intentions of her deeply lamented and most deserving brother towards his Glenavonians. Sarah Hopkins at her own expense caused this school to be erected and founded in the year 1816'.
2 1847 *Reports*. In the Tabular Reports of Schools, Part 2, p. 319, it states that the master had been at Chichester Training School for 10 months in 1843.
3 *Blaenavon Church Deeds*, ibid.
4 1847 *Reports*, Part 2, p. 287
5 40*th Annual Report of the National Society*, 1851, p. 16. *Parl. Paper* XIV, *Reports from Commissioners*, 1868-69 (*Inspectors of Factories*), *Sub-Inspector's Report*, p. 239. *Nefydd MSS*, 7106 E. N.L.W., Rev. William Roberts's *Journal for* 1855; ibid, *Journal for* 1856-57.
6 1847 *Reports*, Part 1, p. 338. *Education Inquiry*, 1833, Vol. 3, 1835, p. 1279.

an infants' school.[1] Reporting on the schools in 1846, the Assistant Commissioner gave some interesting details: 'There had been three masters at the boys' school. When it was being opened for the first time, a lad of 16 who had up to that age been in the National school at Neath occasionally assisting the master, applied to Mr. Price for work. Mr. Price thought him likely to make a good master, and bound him apprentice to himself to learn the art of a schoolmaster. In fulfilment of this agreement, he first sent him to the British school in Goat Street, Swansea, which was a Model School. On his return, the Neath Abbey school rapidly filled under his hands. During the vacations, Mr. Price sent him to London, Bristol, and elsewhere to see the best schools that he could hear of. The master, by taking advantage of these opportunities, had risen, at the time of my visit, to be head of Coalston School at Bristol. His successor at the Abbey school was less efficient. Under his hands the school declined and he had recently been induced to resign. The present master was just entering on his duties and seemed likely to discharge them well.'[2]

Price was one of the first ironmasters to introduce the practice of weekly stoppages for the support of a school and he had also extended benefits in the form of medical aid. He also considered that the ironmasters of south Wales 'had the power by these means to provide effectually for the education and welfare of their people without further assistance. It was also understood that should the surplus arising from the stoppages in good times fail to meet the expenses of the schools in bad times, that the Company would still keep the schools open. Thus the payment not only provided, but insured (on the honour of the employers), the means of education. The Kilvey schools (Llansamlet) nearby, were kept open by the Companies during a strike of the men.'[3]

The Abbey Boys' School was organized in three classes but there was little difference in age between the classes. But one result was evident, that the boys 'highest in position were also longest in attendance at school'. It appeared that parents generally withdrew their children from school about the same age, usually the tenth year when a boy's labour began to be valuable and he could earn ten-pence per day. Some parents sent their children to school at a much earlier age and it seemed that parental co-operation in extending the period of instruction at school only existed during the earlier years of childhood.[4]

1 D. R. Phillips, op. cit., p. 173.
2 1847 *Reports*, pp. 338-9; See note below.
3 ibid
4 *Minutes of Committee of Council*, 1847, p. 217, ff.
1847 *Reports*, p. 340

The importance of having Infants' Schools in manufacturing areas, stressed so much by the Inspectors, was given due attention by Price. He took great care in selecting good teachers, and it is important to note that he also got them to give a thorough practical training to the brighter boys that they might become engineers and key men 'in the Bristol Company's steamers'.[1] In his appraisal of the state of education in the Neath region, Price observed that 'apart from the schools supported by the proprietors and workmen in this area, there is still great room for additional schools among us; where there is a will, there is a way; the price, 1d. per week per man, and $\frac{1}{2}$d. per week per boy—enough to sustain three schools, one for boys, 80 to 100; one for girls, 60 to 80; one for infants, 100 to 120. So that education is obtained for a whole family for a trifle, and they are independent.'[2]

At Hirwaun, one of the bleakest parts of the Aberdare district, two schools existed in connection with the ironworks although only one is mentioned by name, the Firemen's or Furnace School established in 1820.[3] The furnace was owned by F. Crawshay, of Treforest, Pontypridd, and the school was conducted by a stoppage of a $\frac{1}{2}$d. in the pound from the workmen's wages, whilst the proprietor supplied the master with 'a house and garden rent free, and other emoluments'.[4] William Morris, the Assistant Commissioner, visited the schools in March, 1846 but had very little to say about them and must have been glad to get away from the 'bleak, desolate-looking spot on the table-land'. The population of some 2,000 were directly connected with the works, and the proprietor left the entire management of both schools to the workmen 'who administered the funds neither very amicably nor very efficiently'.[5] The schools were not in a very flourishing state, the parents had no confidence in them, and the children hated attending. Yet there were some salutary features, for example, Welsh was universally spoken in and out of school, the workmen were interested in reading and 'grasping after knowledge', and

1 1847 *Reports* Part I, p. 487.
   Price, no doubt, was in close touch with the merchant-men of Bristol for the export of his iron products. The "lad of sixteen" had the Headship at the (later) well-known Colston School, Bristol. Edward Colston was a Bristol merchant and a member of the Merchant Venturers. Originally Colston's Hospital, the school was opened 'to educate in the principles of the Church of England and to maintain and clothe a hundred poor boys and to place them out to apprentice'. Established in 1710, it catered for boys who were sons of Freemen or who were born within the city of Bristol. The school moved to its present site at Stapleton in 1858. (Arrowsmith's *Dictionary of Bristol*, and H. J. Wilkins, *Edward Colston*.)
2 1847 *Reports*, Part 1, p. 487, evidence of J. T. Price, Neath Abbey.
3 ibid, Part 1, p. 54
4 ibid, p. 57
5 ibid, pp. 333-4

the older boys and workmen requested winter lectures and were anxious to get a master to do this work.¹ But here again the strong Nonconformist elements resented the teaching of the catechism, and in 1849 an unsuccessful attempt was made to open a British school. The Rev. William Roberts made several efforts to preserve it, but by 1856 came to the conclusion that 'the miserable schools connected with the works causes the British school to languish, and the population of Hirwaun is almost entirely under the influence of the manager of the works. One of the works schools is superintended by a drunken man, who is in the habit of cursing the children and swearing.'²

In the parish of Trevethin to the north of Pontypool two schools were established in 1823 in connection with the ironworks of the Varteg Hill Iron Company. In 1833 there were '14 day schools in this parish, two whereof are called the Varteg Hill Iron Company's schools. In one are 70 males and in the other 60 females. These schools are partly supported by the house-holders at the above works, and partly by the proprietors, and have lending libraries attached to them.'³ It was one of the proprietors of the Varteg Hill ironworks who furnished Tremenheere with the statistics on which he based his estimate of 70.8 per cent of the children in that district who did not attend school.⁴

The most important of all the works schools established within any industry during the nineteenth century were those promoted by the Guest family at Dowlais, near Merthyr Tydfil. The first school was opened in 1828 with 110 pupils and by 1892 had over 2,000 pupils. These schools were so exclusive and such a feature of nineteenth century elementary education, not only in Wales but in the whole of Britain, and the Educational Scheme evolved by Sir J. J. Guest and his wife, Lady Charlotte so remarkable, that special attention is devoted to them in Chapter IV.

Small schools were found at the Trevethin, Venallt, Pentyrch, and Machen ironworks. In 1832, C. Hanbury Leigh, of Pontypool started an infants' school at the Trevethin Forge for 'the children of the workmen employed at his forges'.⁵ Messrs. Jevons and Wood established a school in connection with their Venallt Coal and Iron works at Blaengwrach in the parish of Glyncorrwg in the Neath Valley. The fluctuating character

1 C. Wilkins, *History of Merthyr Tydfil*, new ed., 1908, p. 267
2 *Nefydd MSS, Journal for* 1856
3 *Education Inquiry*, 1833, Vol. 2, Monmouth, p. 602
4 *Minutes of Committee of Council*, 1839-40, p. 178
5 *Education Inquiry*, 1833: 'Trevethan Parish: one infant school, recently commenced, contains about 45 children of each sex, and is supported at the sole expense of Capel Hanbury Leigh, Esq. It is conducted by a master and mistress.'

of the population made schooling almost impossible, and the parents took little interest in the school: 'a large proportion of our workmen are wanderers, who frequently change their place of abode and never remain more than a few months with any employer . . . the children were allowed to absent themselves from school for slight causes, or taken away to work before they had learnt anything well. There were 72 boys and girls on the school books but the attendances were too uncertain to be ascertained.'[1] The works had both day and Sunday schools and the parish was devoid of any other educational provision. The day school was not conducted very effectively and the discipline was most defective 'the boys sitting, in many instances, with their caps on, and the children generally seemed to quit their seats and stand around the fire as they pleased . . . and the room wore an untidy and slovenly air. The mode of teaching English in this school was very good, and was introduced by the patron. There was no one to teach the girls sewing, The master commenced teaching at the age of 16, was later a student at the Presbyterian College, Carmarthen, and became a Unitarian minister. His salary was £60 per annum for schoolmastering and £5 per annum as minister.'[2]

There were two small schools at Pentyrch, near Cardiff, and Machen in Monmouthshire, the former was a National school mainly supported by S. W. Booker, one of the proprietors of the ironworks,[3] and the latter was an 'appendage to some ironworks', merely a crèche for young children whose mothers were employed at the works.[4] The schools in connection with the Nantyglo ironworks which were started in 1790 by John Harford in partnership with the Hills of Blaenavon, originated in a schoolroom attached to the works as early as 1812. The Company made certain 'that the workmen and children should receive the rudiments of reading and writing'.[5] The first school was built in 1836, enlarged in 1837 and was also used for Sunday services. Later, Joseph Bailey acquired the ironworks, continued the educational work, and erected new school-rooms, one for boys and one for girls, 'the Company maintaining the schools which were conducted on the National system'.[6]

At the head of the Swansea Valley, within the border of Breconshire, Ystradgynlais had its ironworks at Yniscedwyn. George Crane, the local

1 1847 *Reports*, Part 1, p. 479.
2 ibid, p. 65.
3 ibid, p. 336.
4 ibid Part 2, p. 228: 'it is only an infants' school . . . and its principal object is that of affording an asylum during working hours for the young children of those who are employed during the day'.
5 D. Williams, *Monmouthshire*, 1796, p. 17; A. Gray Jones, op. cit., p. 35.
6 1847 *Reports*, Part 2, p. 278 and p. 285

ironmaster, one of the first to use anthracite coal successfully in the smelting of iron, started a school on his own account in 1839, and in 1842 applied for a government grant through the British and Foreign School Society and built a large school to accommodate boys, girls, and infants which was opened in 1843.[1] He appointed a trained master to teach the boys and girls, a female to teach sewing, and secured from the Training College of the Home and Colonial Infant School Society an infants' teacher well-versed in the Pestalozzian principles. Crane also 'contemplated establishing schools for the distant portions of his district for which a desire is already shown by the people. The new schools are supported by a small sum stopped from each person's wages, the rest of the cost being undertaken by the proprietor.'[2]

In addition to the British ironworks school there was also a National school in the parish which in later years caused a depletion in numbers at the works school. A further government grant of £375 was made to the works school in 1864 'for substantial improvements to the school'. This is rather difficult to explain in view of the evidence given by the Rev. G. Harries of Brecon before the *Select Committee on Education* in 1866. He said that in 1861 the British school at Ystradgynlais under the patronage of the Yniscedwyn Iron Company was hardly able to function because few children were in attendance and this situation was not due to lack of funds, yet the National school nearby was flourishing.[3] As a rule, in other areas with a similar duality of schools, the British school usually ousted the National one, and, in fact, not far from Ystradgynlais, at Ystalyfera and Abercrave, the workmen had built their own undenominational schools rather than send their children to the National works schools.[4] Nevertheless, the position continued to deteriorate at Yniscedwyn and the works school had to close in 1867. Since the buildings were in such good condition, they were re-opened with the formation of the Ystradgynlais School Board in March, 1871,[5] and in 1880 received a further grant of £370 for extensions to the buildings.[6] The school was

1 *Minutes of Committee of Council*, 1854, Schools Aided by Parliamentary grant, p. 250: 'Yniscedwyn Ironworks, £250, building grant, 15th Jan. 1842'.
2 *Reports from the Commissioners, Mines*, 1846, p. 430.
3 *Report from the Select Committee on Education, together with the proceedings of the Committee, Minutes of Evidence, Appendix, and Index*, 1866 (*the Pakington Committee*), p. 263, Minute 5369.
4 *Minutes of Committee of Council*, 1868-69: Mr. Bowstead's General Report for 1868, pp. 281-2.
5 *Parliamentary Paper, Accounts and Papers*, Vol. LII, 1873, *School Boards, Returns from all School Boards to September 30th*, 1872, p. 206.
  ibid: 1877-78, p. 237.
6 *Minutes of Committee of Council*, 1880-81, p. 732.

finally closed in 1889.[1] Roberts, the British Agent, provides some details of the school between 1854 and 1861 in his Diary, and when the attendance figures are compared for these two years they seem to bear out what the Rev. Harries had stated. In 1854, 200 children attended as compared with 75 in 1861.[2] *The Newcastle Commission Report* gave statistics for both schools:

PUBLIC SCHOOLS: OCCUPATION, ETC. OF PARENTS.

School	Total number of children in schools	Children of Farmers	Children of Traders	Children of Mechanics	Children of Labourers
Yniscedwyn Ironworks	75	–	–	2	73
Ystradgynlais National	81	3	–	18	60

IRONWORKS SCHOOLS 1840-1850
During this decade, the period *par excellence* of the establishment of ironworks schools, over thirty schools were promoted, in the main, by large Iron Companies. On account of their number and compact distribution pattern they will be considered geographically on a regional basis.

Monmouthshire Ironworks Schools

School	Proprietors	Date of Establishment
Tredegar	S. Homfray	1841[3]
Cwmbran	Ebbw Vale Co.	1842[4]
Pontnewynydd	W. Williams	1842[5]

1 *Minutes of Committee of Council*, 1889-90, p. 684.
2 *Nefydd MSS*, Diary for August, 1854, Entry for August 15th, 1854: 'Yniscedwyn: this was the first place where I met Mr. J. Bowstead, M.A., H.M.I. This school was established and supported in connection with the works in this place. The Upper School under the tuition of Mr. Williams was in an efficient state, but the Lower School Mr. Bowstead found very backward. The attendance in the Upper School was 60; in the Lower School, 140.'
Education Commission 1861, *Reports of Assistant Commissioners*, Vol. II, Appendix E, p. 636.
3 1847 *Reports*, Part 2, p. 312
4 *Nefydd MSS, Journal for* 1854
5 1847 *Reports*, Part 2, p. 203

IRONWORKS SCHOOLS

School	Proprietors	Date of Establishment
Pontypool	C. Hanbury Leigh	1842[1]
Rhymney (National)	Rhymney Iron Co.	1843[2]
Rhymney (British)	Rhymney Iron Co.	1849[3]
Abersychan	British Iron Co. (later Ebbw Vale Co.)	1845[4]
Blaina & Cwmcelyn	Blaina Iron Co.	1845[5]
Ebbw Vale	Ebbw Vale Co.	1845 (Boys)[6] 1844 (Girls)
Victoria (Ebbw Vale)	Ebbw Vale Co.	1845[7]
Sirhowy	Messrs. Darby & Co.	1845[8]
Dos School, Newport	J. J. Cordes	1848[9]

The Monmouthshire ironworks schools fall naturally into five main regions:[10]
1. Rhymney Valley containing the Rhymney ironworks schools.
2. Sirhowy Valley containing the Tredegar and Sirhowy schools.
3. Ebbw Valley, with ironworks schools at Ebbw Vale, Victoria (Ebbw Vale) and Machen.
4. Lwyd Valley with the Pontypool, Blaenavon, Trevethin, Pontnewynydd, Abersychan, Varteg Hill, and Cwmbran ironworks schools.
5. The Blaina area, on the borders of Monmouthshire and Breconshire with the Nantyglo and Blaina ironworks schools.

The Machen, Trevethin, Blaenavon, Varteg Hill, and Nantyglo schools have already been discussed. The five regions of Monmouthshire will be treated separately in order to relate the establishment of the schools to the social background. These five regional divisions are west of the River Lwyd or Pontypool valley and comprise the industrial core of Monmouthshire. This western part of the county contained roughly eighteen parishes 'some parts of which the inhabitants were engaged in mineral occupations either in mines or ironworks. Although these parishes

1   1847 *Reports*, Part 2, p. 324
2   ibid, Part 2, Appendix, p. 34
3   ibid
4   ibid, Part 2, p. 324
5   ibid, p. 312
6   ibid
7   ibid, p. 316
8   ibid, p. 312
9   John Warner, *Local Government in Newport*, 1835-1935, Newport, 1935, p. 63
10 See map of Ironworks schools.

IRONWORKS SCHOOLS

involve an area of 98,520 acres out of the area of the whole county which contains 324,310 acres, yet the population of this region amounted to no less than 86,079 in 1841, out of a total population in the county of 134,355. Thus in the agricultural part of the county there are 4.67 acres to each person; in the mining districts there are only 1.14 acres to each person.'[1] This account was written in the 1840s when Monmouthshire showed a population increase not exceeded in any other county in Britain. In the first census of 1801, the population was 45,852; in 1811, 62,127; in 1821, 71,833; in 1831, 98,130; in 1841, 134,355.[2] Almost every witness examined by the Commissioner in 1846 stressed the rapid growth of population in their parishes and the insufficient schools at their disposal to educate the labouring classes. The census of 1851 showed that the population of the county had further expanded to 177,130, with only 12,632 children attending school.[3] The situation was, that although the population of Monmouthshire had increased by 244 per cent. during the first half of the nineteenth century, the proportion of children at school to the whole population was only 9 per cent.[4]

In the old parish of Bedwellty (which included the small villages of Rhymney and Tredegar) the population had risen from 619 in 1801 to 22,413 by 1841, with only 1,236 children attending school.[5] The first *Reports of the Minutes of Committee of Council* showed that only 825 children attended day and Dame schools.[6] At Rhymney, several Nonconformist ministers had started elementary classes in their chapels for the workmen and their children.[7] The school established by the Rhymney Iron Company in 1843 was part of a general scheme of development which the Company envisaged for the growing town. The Company had already opened a Company shop and had also built a church and rows of houses for their workmen.[8] The school was built in Middle Rhymney near the ironworks, but soon after its erection was damaged by fire and 'it should be appreciated that the master and mistress have laboured under great disadvantage for the past few months and the dwelling house at present used as a schoolroom being too small to accommodate the scholars makes education difficult. It will be expected that the schoolroom

1 1847 *Reports*, Part 2, p. 271
2 *Census Returns, Monmouthshire*, 1801-1841
3 *Education Census*, 1851, H.M.S.O., 1854, detailed tables, p. 6
4 *Minutes of Committee of Council*, 1855, p. 636
5 *Census Returns*, 1801, p. 342, and 1841, p. 550
6 *Minutes of Committee of Council*, 1839-40, p. 157, Appendix 2
7 Thomas Jones, *Rhymney Memories*, Welsh Outlook Press, Newtown, 1938, p. 22. Reprinted, Gwasg Gomer, 1970.
8 ibid, pp. 11-24.

will be ready in a few weeks. The master and mistress seem to devote themselves entirely to their duties and to give great satisfaction. The master however did not always express himself grammatically, he said 'they goes and comes'.[1] In 1846 the school was known as the Rhymney Ironworks National school and no mention is made of stoppages from the men's wages for its maintenance. The 120 boys and girls who attended, moreover, paid 2d. per week. The salaries of both master and mistress were paid by the Company who also provided a house and garden rent-free, together with free coal.[2]

The British ironworks schools in Upper and Lower Rhymney were affiliated to the British and Foreign School Society, but were inferior to the National schools. In 1850 as a result of agitation on the part of a large number of Dissenting workmen, and later, after Roberts had been to see Mr. G. P. Hubbuck, the Works Manager, a new British school was established in 1854.[3] It was mentioned for the first time in the *Minutes* of 1858:[4]

School	Building grants £ s. d.	Books, etc. £ s. d.	Grants to Certificated Teachers £ s. d.	Grants to Pupil Teachers £ s. d.
Rhymney Ironworks British school	235 15 10	10 15 0¼	93 3 4	33 0 0
Rhymney Ironworks National school	—	—	46 10 0	152 0 0

In 1858 a new National school was built at a cost of over £3,000. It was on one floor, measured 100 by 50 feet, and was 'much superior to the rival British school'. Part of this new school was earmarked as a reading room to accommodate the library and Scientific Institution established in 1850.[5] The library, which had 80 subscribers, was managed by the officials of the Company and the local ministers of religion. Among the subscribers were 'the manager, three professional gentlemen, eight agents, twelve tradesmen, eleven accountants, fifteen shopmen, and thirty workmen'.[6] The Company's secretary informed the Inspector of Mines

1 1847 *Reports*, Part 1, p. 303
2 ibid, Appendix to this Chapter for details
3 *Nefydd MSS, Journal for April*, 1854, entry for 10th April.
4 *Minutes of Committee of Council*, 1858. Report by J. Bowstead on British schools: Monmouthshire, Tabulated Reports, p. 361
5 Thomas Jones, op. cit., pp. 24-27
6 *Reports from the Commissioners*, 1868-69. *Parliamentary Paper* XIV. *Reports of Sub-Inspectors for* 1868 *on the working of the Factory Acts Extension Act of* 1867, pp. 271, ff.

'that they expected many more workmen to join as soon as it was more known: the subscription was low at 1/6d. per quarter, and they already had about 200 volumes including history, biographies, science, and poetry. It was hoped that these libraries which were being established at most of the works would create a taste for reading among the workmen generally.'[1] In 1868 the British ironworks school was renovated and enlarged for a town of over 10,000 people by 'the liberality of the Rhymney Company which is again conspicuous in the provision they are now making for the education and improvement of the large population gathered around their works. Schoolbuildings are about to be erected which are to cost (inclusive of a parliamentary grant) upwards of £2,200. The classrooms will also be used as libraries and reading rooms; one for the adults, clerks, etc., and one for the workmen. The large schoolrooms will be capable of being thrown open into one, for the purpose of lectures or music, the latter being much cultivated by the workpeople.'[2] Both schools had evening classes which attracted the special class of skilled artisans—young men in the fitting and engine-making departments at the works. These classes at the National school had an attendance of 55 in 1865 and 168 in 1870.[3]

In the Sirhowy Valley, Samuel Homfray started his schools in the Town Hall at Tredegar in 1838, and in 1841 his works school was built under the guidance of the National Society. Homfray took a personal interest in the school and insisted that the clergy of the parish visited them regularly.[4] The school had four departments, girls, boys, infants and vestry school, the latter being opened in 1844.[5] The school was self-supporting, the catechism was taught to 'all and sundry irrespective of their religious creed and much dissatisfaction was expressed at the children being compelled to attend the Church Sunday schools, though many of the parents were Dissenters. Some of the workmen are therefore compelled to pay for schooling which they cannot conscientiously avail themselves of for their children'.[6]

But withal, according to the testimony of those who had inspected the schools, the Tredegar ironworks school was one of the best in the industrial districts of Monmouthshire. The new schools were well equipped,

1 *Reports from the Commissioners*, 1868-69, pp. 271, ff.
2 ibid, p. 287
3 *Minutes of Committee of Council*, 1865, General Report by the Rev. B. J. Binns, p. 213. ibid 1869, p. 621.
4 D. and E. Powell, *History of Tredegar*, Newport, 1902, p. 54
5 1847 *Reports*, Part 2, p. 312
6 ibid, p. 286

organized in three departments of boys, girls, and infants. The schoolmaster was a Mr. Coles, though one source mentions Mr. Frederick Sergeant who was an 'indefatigable teacher'. The new buildings 'were a real boon to the town by its being the chief academy for the workmen's children, staffed by a master and one monitor, and the workmen contributed 3d. in the pound upon all their earnings toward their children's education, the doctor's fund and other necessary things, the money being deducted from their accounts in the office of the works'.[1]

Not far from Tredegar was the growing industrial centre of Sirhowy, where, in 1778 Messrs. Atkinson and Barrow (who had joined with Kendall to establish the school at Capel Waun y Pound in 1784) had built a furnace. Later, Messrs. Darby and Co. took over the ironworks, and the Sirhowy ironworks school, consisting of 'one long narrow room' was opened in 1845 with 128 children attending.[2] Until 1850 however, the school was in a very poor state and almost languished, but the Company took down the 'long room', built new schools at a cost of £2,000, improved the staffing, and initiated a good system of evening schools. By 1868 they were recognized as among the best schools in the county, being 'large and well-organized, and if a general system of compulsory education were introduced forthwith, these works schools would be prepared to meet any demand'.[3]

Messrs. Darby and Co. had taken over the ironworks at Ebbw Vale from the Quaker ironmaster John Harford in 1842[4] and soon afterwards the ironworks became part of the Ebbw Vale Company which established several schools in connection with its ironworks at different places. Apart from Sunday schools which abounded in this area especially in connection with the Ebbw Vale and Victoria ironworks, there were no day schools.

1 D. and E. Powell, op. cit. pp. 60, ff.
2 *Results of the Returns to the General Inquiry made by the National Society into the the State and Progress of schools*, 1846-47. Published 1849, Monmouthshire, p. 3. 1847 *Reports*, Part 2, p. 286: 'This school belongs to the Company. The children were all very young and they sat in classes four-square, and were all reading, apparently without method or superintendence. The master complained that he had no assistant. It was impracticable to question much he said, and all that the children appeared to be learning was the mechanical art of reading and writing . . . they spelled tolerably well. In all points of geographical knowledge they were quite ignorant. Two thought the people in Scotland black, and two white. England was part of Wales, and Ireland was a town. The writing was indifferent . . . The school was badly housed, the furniture and apparatus poor. 128 children were on the school books, and average attendance was 72 boys and 43 girls. 86 stayed at school for less than one year; the master was aged 23 and had been a bricklayer. His salary was £60 per annum.'
3 *Minutes of Committee of Council*, 1868-69, p. 281
4 C. Wilkins, op. cit., pp. 172-3

In 1844 and 1845 the Company started the girls' and boys' schools which cost over £3,000 'to afford means of instruction and intellectual gratification to the large mass of people assembled around their great Ebbw Vale and Victoria Works. The large lecture room is 62 feet by $21\frac{1}{2}$ feet, and 26 feet high. It is well warmed and lighted with a large central chandelier: the windows are ornamented with coloured glass: the arrangement for lectures and for its use as an ordinary reading room is complete.'[1] After 1850 the Ebbw Vale Company (then called Messrs. Darby and Brown) extended their schoolbuilding programme with two new schools near their works at Cwmbran and Abersychan, again vigorously promoting evening schools and lectures, and one lecture 'which had reference to the mechanical operations and the geology of the district attracted over 600 workmen'.[2]

To the north-west of Pontypool, near Pontnewynydd were the ironworks and collieries of the British Iron Company at Abersychan. This school was listed among the most efficient in Monmouthshire, was well managed, and had an elaborate list of regulations drawn up by the committee of management. It was described as the only day-school with an efficient master and mistress within the district and could accommodate 300 children.[3] Opened in 1845 it was situated on the premises of the Company with boys' and girls' departments. The Committee of Management consisted of the proprietors, agents, and workmen's representatives, the first meeting being held at the office of the New British Iron Company on the 20 May 1845.[4] The school had as its object 'the imparting to the children of its workmen of a sound religious, moral, and suitable education'.[5] The following were eligible, and were admitted in the following precedence:

(a) Children of parents working in the works.

(b) Children having lost their parents who died in the Company's employ, and who were supported by brothers or other relatives employed in the works.

(c) Children of parents who died in the Company's employ but who had no relatives employed in the works.[6]

It was also stipulated in the regulations that the 'ladies of Abersychan be invited to pay periodic visits to the girls' school . . . to superintend

1 *Reports of the Commissioners in the Mining Districts: Mines Inspectors Reports for* 1856, XVIII, p. 311
2 ibid
3 1847 *Reports*, Part 2, p. 296
4 ibid, p. 375
5 ibid
6 ibid

the needlework and help the pupils with sewing or other work belonging to their department'.[1] By December, 1852 the Ebbw Vale Company had acquired the Abersychan works and soon afterwards embarked on a substantial expansion of school building which eventually cost over £3,500, and comprised lecture rooms, reading rooms, and a Mechanics Institute, 'all of which were of good design and artistic beauty'.[2] In that year however, the Company had sought the aid of the Committee of Privy Council which subsequently provided a grant of £2,000, an unusually large sum of money in those days, and the Company provided the remaining sum of £1,500. When H. S. Tremenheere visited Abersychan in 1853 someone had told him that the Company had, in some way, reserved this sum from the men's wages. He 'was assured by the resident manager, Mr. Beaumont, that this was not the case; that the Company had not any sum whatever so accumulated; that the payments to the sick fund were distributed under the supervision of the agents, and that the whole of the £1,500 was given by the Company. The opinion to the contrary—very common in this district in similar cases, is, I fear, a proof of the rare occurrences of such instances of liberality in times past, and the consequent difficulty the men have in believing that anything can be proposed for their benefit by the masters without some selfish object in view, or without the design of making the men pay for it in the end.'[3]

The new Abersychan school was organized in three departments of boys, girls, and infants, evening schools were opened, and lending libraries started.[4] All in all, the school provision in the whole of the Pontypool valley in 1854 gave great satisfaction to the Mines Inspector: 'As regards school buildings in the Pontypool valley in eastern Monmouthshire, it can be said that in a few years it will be most completely provided in this respect. This has been brought about almost entirely through the efforts of employers of labour and their own works schools. In addition to the schools already built in connection with the works of, or liberally assisted by Mr. C. Hanbury Leigh, the Lord Lieutenant of the county, and by Mr. Williams of Pontnewynydd and Varteg works, the British Iron Company at Abersychan and Blaenavon there will then be in that valley containing a population of about 20,000, accommodation in day schools for 2,500 children.'[5]

1 1847 *Reports*, Part 2, p. 375.
2 *Reports of the Commissioners*, (*Inspector of Factories*), 1854: *Sub-Inspector's Reports on the South Wales District*, pp. 273-4
3 *Reports of the Commissioners: Inspector of Mines Report* for 1854, Vol. XXIII, *State of the Population in the Mining Districts*, p. 267
4 ibid
5 ibid p. 312

Pontnewynydd, in the parish of Trevethin (Pontypool) owed its importance to the large ironworks owned by W. Williams, of Snatchwood House.[1] It had two schools, British and National, the latter being the works school, promoted by the proprietor. The population of the parish included people from the neighbouring counties of Brecon and Hereford, Gloucester and Somerset. High wages were the attraction, which varied between £3 and £25 per month.[2] Before 1843, when the two schools were opened, Pontnewynydd, apart from Sunday schools, had no day schools. It was said in 1847 that there had been a marked improvement in the morals, conduct, and knowledge of the population, for before the schools were opened there 'was great ignorance amongst a large portion of the poor, especially those who had come from Gloucester and Somerset'.[3] Little is known of the works National school which for a few years assembled in the 'second storey of a warehouse' with 130 children on the books, until a new school was built in 1846, towards which Williams gave £100 and the site. It was described as a 'commodious building, and the master and mistress fully competent'.[4]

Midway between Pontypool and Newport were the nut, bolt, and nail works of the Ebbw Vale Company at Cwmbran which are not mentioned in the 1847 Blue Books, although they were established in 1842, conducted on the British system, with 100 pupils on the registers. The chief feature of this school was the special attention paid to evening classes which were organized by an energetic and enthusiastic works manager, Mr. Robins-Davis.[5]

In the old parish of Aberystruth on the borders of Monmouthshire and Breconshire were the large ironsmelting centres of Blaina and Nantyglo. The latter had a population of 8,000 in 1839, two day schools for the working classes, several Dame schools for young children aged three to five, and over a dozen Sunday schools.[6] By 1846, the parish population had increased to 12,000, with ten day schools and eighteen Sunday schools, but the largest schools were those of Nantyglo and Blaina Ironworks.[7] Blaina, where the champion of unsectarian or undenominational schools, and the first Agent of the British and Foreign School Society in south Wales, lived and worked for many years—the

1   1847 *Reports*, Part 2, p. 297
2   ibid
3   1847 *Reports*, Part 2, p. 297
4   *Minutes of Committee of Council*, 1845, p. 225
    1847 *Reports*, Part 2, p. 298
5   *Reports of Commissioners, Inspectors of Mines*, 1850, p. 248
6   *Minutes of Committee of Council*, 1839-40, Appendix 2, p. 157
7   1847 *Reports*, Part 2, p. 273

Rev. William Roberts (Nefydd)—had two schools established in connection with the Blaina ironworks, viz. the Blaina and Cwmcelyn British Schools. The Blaina school became one of the best of its type and ranked in importance, though not in numbers, with such schools as Cwmavon (Port Talbot or Aberavon), Hafod (Swansea), and Llanelli copperworks. It was opened in 1845, and became well known in Monmouthshire as the school which gave excellent training to pupil-teachers.[1] Similarly, the Blaina and Cwmcelyn Company's school was looked upon as a training-ground of older boys for the better and higher occupations in the works.[2] Another special feature of the Blaina school was the Instruction Society which was formed in 1852 'in order to attract young persons who had left school at an early age—to get them to use the schools during the evenings'.[3] Both schools were enlarged and re-organized between 1853 and 1858 with liberal grants from the Committee of Privy Council totalling £1,500.[4]

At Newport, Monmouthshire, the Dos nail-works school was established in 1848 by the proprietor, J. J. Cordes.[5] The Dos works were in production in 1835, and by 1867 employed 320 boys. The school was opened 'to attract boys of ability to come to the works, and also as a place of educational pioneering'.[6] Cordes kept meticulous records of those boys who received three-year diplomas, and their names were inscribed on the Honours Board in the school hall. All boys received their education free of charge.[7] Evening classes were, if anything, more important than the day school. There were three types of pupil: half-day pupils (half-timers of the Factory Acts)—part of each day spent at school; night pupils—those who worked during the day; private pupils taken by the schoolmaster. Boys who were preparing to enter the works had to pay 3d. per week, but boys in employment had free education. There are no records of fees paid by private pupils. But it must have been a long and tiring day for the Dos working boy—he was required to work a ten-hour day and then attend school in the evening. The curriculum was meagre, professing no more than reading, writing and arithmetic, and strange to relate, no technical instruction of any kind was given. Cordes was assisted by annual grants from the Committee of Council, but by

1 *Minutes of Committee of Council*, 1852, p. 376
2 *Reports of Commissioners, Mines*, 1856, op. cit. p. 274
3 ibid, 1868-1869, *Parliamentary Paper* XIV, p. 232
4 *Minutes of Committee of Council*, 1858, *Report on British Schools by J. Bowstead, H.M.I.*, p. 216
5 Date on the school tablet is 1851, but the works' Records give 1848
6 J. Warner, op. cit., p. 64
7 ibid.

1878 there were only 98 boys attending. The school continued until the end of the nineteenth century and 'many of Newport's leading men were educated there'.[1]

Glamorgan Ironworks Schools

School	Proprietors	Date of Establishment
Maesteg	Maesteg Iron Co.	1841[2]
Taff Vale	Taff Vale Iron Co.	1842[3]
Ystalyfera (Wern Girls' School)	Palmer Budd	1842[4]
Cwmavon	English Copper Co.	1844[5]
Llynfi	Llynfi Iron Co. Maesteg	1845[6]
Bryndu	H. Ford	1846[7]
Bryn (Cwmavon)	English Copper Co.	1845[8]
Oakwood (Cwmavon)	English Copper Co.	1844[9]
Tonmawr	Tonmawr Iron & Coal Co.	1846[10]
Cyfarthfa (Merthyr)	R. Crawshay	1848[11]
Georgetown (Merthyr National School)	R. Crawshay (by support only)	1850[12]
Plymouth (Merthyr)	Plymouth Iron Co.	1850[13]
Aberaman (Aberdare)	Crawshay Bailey	1850[14]
Tondu (Bridgend)	Llynfi Iron Co.	1850[15]
Aberavon	Messrs. Llewellyn	1850[16]
Penydarren (Merthyr)	Penydarren Iron Co.	1852[17]

1 J. Warner, op. cit., p. 64. *Minutes of Committee of Council*, 1879, p. 409
2 1847 *Reports*, Part 1, p. 66
3 ibid, p. 298
4 ibid, pp. 328-9
5 ibid, pp. 62, 70 and 353
6 ibid, p. 66
7 ibid, pp. 70 and 352-4
8 *Cwmavon Ironworks School, MSS and Papers*, Public Library, Port Talbot
9 1847 *Reports*, p. 353, and *School MSS Cwmavon*
10 1847 *Reports*, Part 1, p. 64; Part 2, p. 142. *Nefydd MSS, Journal for August*, 1854
11 *Reports from Commissioners, Mines*, 1850, p. 307
12 *Report of Pakington Select Committee*, Minutes 3794-7. *Reports from Commissioners, Children's Employment*, 1862, p. 395. C. Wilkins, *History of Merthyr Tydfil*, p. 511
13 Date of establishment uncertain, between 1850-52.
14 *Reports from Commissioners, Mines*, 1850, p. 307
15 Information given by W. Bowen, Esq. Blaengwynfi, Port Talbot.
16 *Nefydd MSS, Journal for July*, 1854, entry for 11th July
17 *Reports from Commissioners, Children's Employment*, 1862, p. 395

As in Monmouthshire, five main regional divisions, with a few subsidiary centres, contained the important ironworks of the county of Glamorgan:
1. The north-eastern Area, with ironworks schools at Hirwaun[1], Dowlais[2], Merthyr Tydfil, including the Cyfarthfa, Plymouth, Penydarren, and Georgetown schools, and Aberaman (Aberdare).
2. The Neath Area, containing the Neath Abbey and Venallt (Glyncorrwg), ironworks schools.[3]
3. The Swansea Valley, with the Pontardawe, Cwmllynfell, and Ystalyfera ironworks. Ystalyfera alone had an ironworks school.
4. The Maesteg Area, with the Maesteg and Llynfi ironworks and schools.
5. The Aberavon-Port Talbot Area with the Aberavon, Cwmavon, Bryndu ironworks and their schools; Margam ironworks with no school.
6. Subsidiary centres at Taff Vale, and Tondu, with ironworks and schools, also Pentyrch.[4]

The North-Eastern Area.

The best description of educational conditions at Merthyr Tydfil, Glamorgan, in the forties of the nineteenth century is that given in the Blue Books of 1847 already referred to. Among other masses of detailed information the Reports contain lengthy on the spot evidence of witnesses about conditions in all the industrial parishes, many of the informants being proprietors of works and mines. Summarizing the various pieces of evidence regarding educational facilities in Merthyr Tydfil (as distinct from Dowlais nearby) no provision had been made 'for the children of the men employed at the Cyfarthfa, Plymouth, and Penydarren ironworks except some trifling subscriptions by the proprietors to the National schools but new National schools and a British school were contemplated.' The proprietor of the large Cyfarthfa ironworks, Robert Crawshay, told the Assistant Commissioner that it was proposed to erect a school-house and establish a school, by the usual plan of stoppages for its support, in connection with the Cyfarthfa Works, in the course of the year. The same investigator was unable to ascertain whether similar measure was likely to be adopted at the Penydarren and Plymouth ironworks.[5] Another Report for the year 1849 again deplored the lack of educational facilities

1 Already discussed earlier
2 See Chapter IV
3 Discussed earlier in this Chapter
4 ibid
5 1847 *Reports*, Part 1, p. 305

IRONWORKS SCHOOLS

in the area, and emphasized the need for more schools in Merthyr Tydfil, for the large population employed at the Cyfarthfa, Plymouth, and Penydarren ironworks.[1]

Until 1846, apart from an abundance of Dame and private adventure schools, the town only boasted two schools, the Georgetown and High Street National schools, opened in 1843 and 1845 respectively.[2] These day schools were financially supported by most of the local ironmasters including Crawshay who was a staunch Churchman and one of the first to start Sunday schools in the town.[3] Cyfarthfa and Dowlais ironworks were the largest in Britain at this time but there could be no greater contrast between the two ironmasters—Crawshay and Guest, in so far as their efforts for the provision of education among their workpeople was concerned. Crawshay, although benevolent and generous in his support of Merthyr's National schools, and equally magnanimous in providing his own works school, never attained the stature and reputation which his neighbour John Guest achieved through his unique and remarkable Educational Scheme at Dowlais, which was acclaimed universally, not only in Britain, but in Europe, as the most comprehensive school system of the nineteenth century.[4]

It was in 1848 that Crawshay built the Cyfarthfa works school conducted on the National system 'for his own people at Cyfarthfa, the large suburb of Merthyr Tydfil'.[5] Charles Freeman the schoolmaster, 'who was well-versed in the practical bearings of the educational system' also successfully encouraged the organization of evening classes. He enlisted the support of the clergy to educate the adult population who might wish to make up for deficiencies in education incurred while young, and who might have no other method of informing and improving themselves.[6] The services of teachers were obtained by rotation, each set of teachers taking on duties a week or month at a time and were recruited from the clergy, the gentry and the tradespeople. The men and boys, girls and young women dressed themselves for the evening schools in their best clothes, came with clean hands and faces, as if to a feast, and when

1 *Reports from the Commissioners, Mines*, 1850, p. 300. Also, *Six Reports of the Commissioner on the operation of the Mines Act, on the State of the Mining Populations in England, Scotland, and Wales*, 1844-1849.
2 C. Wilkins, op. cit. p. 511.
3 ibid, p. 267
4 *Memorandum issued by the Trustee* on 1st March, 1892, relative to the Dowlais Iron Company's Schools.
5 *Minutes of Committee of Council*, 1850: Rev. H. Longueville Jones's Report on National Schools, Wales, p. 203.
6 ibid, 1856, p. 414; ibid, Vol. 2, 1850, p. 287.

within the school walls worked with a steadiness and diligence that soon produced its own reward.[1] Similar evening activities were a feature of the National school at Georgetown which had been considerably enlarged and re-equipped in 1850, and was rated one of the best schools under the inspection of the National Society.[2]

These developments in day schools and evening classes in Merthyr had no doubt been influenced by the extensive school arrangements which were carried on by Lady Charlotte and Sir John Guest at Dowlais nearby. Lady Charlotte Guest had, on several occasions, visited the Merthyr ironmasters to discuss welfare and educational matters with them, and in 1849 she was busy organizing schools at Merthyr like those at Dowlais.[3] It is difficult to decide whether this statement referred specifically to evening schools in Merthyr, but it is recorded that 'she was shocked at the large number of young people unprovided with school accommodation at Merthyr and was busily engaged in interesting other ironmasters like e.g. Hill of the Plymouth works, in her desire to establish evening schools there on the same lines as those that were proving so successful and beneficial at Dowlais'.[4] It is also mentioned in her *Journal* that she not only interested herself in the Merthyr evening schools for young people, but that she also had founded six schools (before her husband died in 1852) of which three were in Merthyr, for which she raised the necessary funds by her own gifts and subscriptions.[5] Whether these schools were private, or other day schools is not known, for no mention is made of them in contemporary sources or the official school returns of the *Committee of Privy Council*.

Very little is known of the other two ironworks schools in Merthyr— the Plymouth and Penydarren schools. In all probability the Plymouth school was opened in 1850, for on her visit to Dowlais on 13 April 1849, Lady Charlotte heard that following her example, Mr. Hill, the neighbouring ironmaster at the Plymouth works, contemplated establishing

1 *Minutes of Committee of Council*, 1850, p. 304
2 *Report of Pakington Committee*, Minutes 3794-7.
 Children's Employment Commission, 1862, p. 395.
 Reports from Commissioners, Mines, 1850, p. 507.
 Georgetown was the housing nucleus of poor industrial cottages to the west of Jackson's Bridge, and Cae-pant-tywyll and Williamstown to the east, near Cyfarthfa ironworks: see Harold Carter, *The Towns of Wales*, University of Wales Press, 1965, Plate XI and Note.
3 Earl of Bessborough: *The Diaries of Lady Charlotte Guest, Extracts from her Journal*, 1833-1852, Murray, 1950, p. 223.
4 ibid, p. 224.
5 ibid, pp. 9 and 223

day and evening schools at the end of the year.¹ The Penydarren school was opened in 1852, with two departments of boys and girls, with an average attendance of 200.² Both schools were conducted on 'neutral' principles. Sometime after 1860 a British School was built in Merthyr to which Crawshay, although a Churchman, was a liberal and frequent contributor. In 1867, he gave £300 to the Merthyr British schools, and 'was a warm supporter of Mr. Bruce and the Nonconformists'.³

In the Aberdare valley, which was singularly deficient of works schools, Crawshay Bailey had started ironsmelting at Aberaman around 1847 and had also intended to build a school there in 1850.⁴ There is no evidence to show whether or not this project materialised.

The Swansea Valley

Of the ironworks in the Swansea Valley, only Ystalyfera had a school. In 1838, Messrs. Treacher and James had erected ironsmelting furnaces which were sold later to James Palmer Budd who added tinplate mills, and in 1868 the Ystalyfera Iron and Tinplate Company was formed.⁵ Two schools were promoted by the Budd family, the Ystalyfera Wern Girls' school (principally supported by Mrs. Palmer Budd),⁶ and the Ystalyfera Tinworks schools established around 1852.⁷ The Wern school was opened in 1842, conducted on the principles of the National Society, had thirty girls in attendance and each was 'clothed in a clean white pinafore, provided by the patrons as a school dress. Sewing, reading, and writing were taught . . . and so much arithmetic as could be learnt from the cards on the walls, of which there seemed a pretty good supply.

1 Earl of Bessborough, op. cit., entry for April 13th, 1849.
2 *Reports from Commissioners, Children's Employment*, 1862. This school is not mentioned in the Minutes of Committee of Council before 1854. *Minutes of Committee of Council*, 1877, p. 411.
3 *Llanelli Guardian*, November 14th, 1867.
4 1847 *Reports*, Part 1, p. 332: 'This is a place that has risen entirely within the last eighteen months. Its present population is about 1200, from the turnpike to Crawshay Bailey's new furnaces. But Aberaman is not to be judged according to what it is now, but what it will be twelve months hence, when the furnaces are at work. My information is from Mr. Bailey's agents as delivered to me today. There will be here then four furnaces with about 300 men to each one . . . and is distant from the parish school at different points, a mile and a half, a mile, and three quarters of a mile. It is a long hamlet, and could be conveniently accommodated with a school situated somewhere in its centre. At present I have no authority to say we shall have any here; all will depend on Mr. Crawshay Bailey.' *Reports from Commissioners, Mines*, ibid, 1850, p. 262: 'the Vicar had been informed by Crawshay Bailey that he intended to build a school there in 1850'.
5 E. H. Brooke, *Monograph on Tinplate Works in Great Britain*, 1932, p. 104.
6 1847 *Reports*, Part 1, p. 329.
7 ibid, p. 54. See Chapter VI

This was a school doing real good in a quiet, unpretending way.'[1]

The Maesteg Area

The Llynfi valley, a tributary of the Ogmore, contained three ironworks schools. Two of these, the Llynfi and Maesteg ironworks, were at the head of the valley; the third, Tondu, was at the lower extremity. Describing the social conditions of the area in 1846, the Mines Commissioner emphasized the remoteness of the ironworks with the large and fast increasing populations gathered around them. Although the Maesteg district had not developed the moral evils to such a degree as in Merthyr Tydfil, there were examples where the men employed in the coal and iron works did not respond to the wishes of their employers. This was due mainly to the lack of interest displayed by their former masters, i.e. the old Cambrian Company. But on succeeding to these works in 1844, both the Maesteg and Llynfi Iron Companies appeared 'to have resolved to do what they could to correct the results of previous neglect, and introduced measures tending to raise the character of the population'.[2] In due course the Llynfi Iron Company, of which Dr. Bowring, M.P. was one of the principal proprietors, developed a well-ordered plan of real welfare for the neglected populations in three directions: building decent houses for the workmen and their families, which consisted of five rooms, gardens, and other conveniences attached; building places of worship for both Anglicans and Nonconformists for their spiritual welfare; building and partly maintaining proper schools for the children of their employees. Their schools were opened in 1845, were well-equipped and well staffed, and by 1850 flourishing evening classes were well attended.[3] Both day schools and Sunday schools had well-stocked libraries, and although the schools were under the superintendence of the clergyman, the catechism was not taught to those children whose parents objected.[4] In his General Report for 1853, Matthew Arnold, H.M.I. explained how the schools were maintained: 'The Llynfi works schools established for the children of the workpeople employed by an Iron Company in a very remote part of the country, are not maintained by the Company nor by the payments of the children who frequent them, but by a weekly deduction made from the wages of every person employed in the works, whether married or single, to form a fund to defray the expenses of the school, of a library, and medical attention. Those who have families pay no more than those who have none, and any number of children may be sent to the school

1 1847 *Reports*, Part 1, pp. 339-40; also Appendix 22 to this Chapter for details.
2 *Reports from the Commissioners, Mines*, 1846, Vol. XXIV, p. 429.
3 ibid, for 1850, p. 361; *Reports of the Committee of Council*, 1853, p. 294.
4 *Report of Pakington Committee*, Minutes 3034-3039

by the head of the family without his having to pay any additional subscription. The school is regarded as existing for the common benefit of all, directly or indirectly, now or at a future time. The deduction, I was assured, was submitted to without reluctance.'[1] Arnold was so impressed with the work being done at the schools that he discussed with the master, the possibilities of expanding the accommodation and also recommended the employment and training of a larger number of pupil-teachers. By 1860 the schools were considerably enlarged, with accommodation for three departments, and thenceforward the schools figured as among the best of their kind coming under annual inspection in all Inspectors' Reports from 1860 to 1870.[2] The school log-books showed that efficiency prevailed, a wide variety of subjects were taught, and special attention was given to the training of pupil-teachers.[3]

The Tondu ironworks school was also established by the Llynfi Iron Company and the same educational facilities were available there. Established about 1850, it became one of the most efficient British schools in the region, with flourishing day and evening classes, and the number of pupils rising from 112 in 1858 to over 500 in 1875.[4] This was due mainly to the opening of new collieries in the Ogmore Valley after 1870 which 'led to an influx of people into the area . . . and will cause a demand for additional schools, for the school at Tondu, which is supplied to a large extent from Aberkenfig, has outgrown all reasonable dimensions'.[5] The Tondu school was entirely rebuilt and enlarged in 1875.[6] The Maesteg ironworks school, built in 1844 by the Maesteg Iron Company to serve another neglected population, was under the supervision of the Rev. Hughes Jones, Curate.[7] It consisted of two schoolrooms which were to hold 250 to 300 children each, to replace the school kept by a female, set on foot by the Cambrian Company about eight months before they gave up the works.[8]

1 *Minutes of Committee of Council*, 1853, General Report by Matthew Arnold, H.M.I. Matthew Arnold: *Reports on Elementary Schools*, 1852-1882, H.M.S.O., 1910, pp. 9-10.
2 *Minutes of Committee of Council*, 1855-1870.
3 Tondu British Ironworks School, *Log-books, Vols. 1 and 2.*
4 *Minutes of Committee of Council*, 1859, p. 337. ibid, 1876, p. 21.
5 ibid, 1874, p. 75.
6 ibid, 1878, p. 408.
7 Year of foundation uncertain. The 1847 *Reports* mention 1841 (Part I, p. 66) but the 1846 *Mines Commission Report* states 1844.
8 *Reports from the Commissioners, Mines*, 1846, p. 428

The Aberavon and Port Talbot Area

Cwmavon, situated a mile or so away from Aberavon, was one of the most important industrial centres of west Glamorgan during the nineteenth century. As early as 1810 a Mr. S. F. Lettsom had erected blast furnaces there, but these were acquired by Messrs. Vigurs and Smith in 1820.[1] At that time 'there was no road for carriages, or any dwelling in the valley, with the exception of two or three cottages situated here and there'.[2] In 1841 the works were taken over by the English Copper Company which in 1846 consisted of 'the Cwmavon Iron, Coal, Copper, Tin, and Chemical works, four miles from Neath, Glamorgan, employing 4,500 men, women, and children, and the sum paid in wages per month was above £10,000'.[3] The Mines Commissioner had every praise for the proprietors of these works and issued the following 'satisfying report' of their activities: 'The Company ruled almost everything ... it could be said that nowhere in south Wales was an enterprise so well organized for the production of goods, and for the welfare of the working man. Nowhere at this time were there works organized so perfectly in internal and external affairs. The proprietors drew up rules and regulations, not merely for the conduct of the works and the welfare of the working-men, but also as to the type of workman that they wished to engage. With the view of getting a good-type population, the Company instituted strict inquiry into the character and life of the person they employed. The agent of each department in the works when selecting their labour force made each prospective employee complete a special form from the works office. Similar action was taken when an employee transferred from one department to another, or left the works.'[4] The Company also paid particular attention to the housing of their workmen, and, in addition, built the parish church, and evolved a complete system of schools.

It was in connection with education that the Cwmavon works excelled. There were at least four schools directly connected with the English Copper Company—schools which always came up for special mention in the annual reports of the Voluntary Societies and of the Committee of Council—and schools were often mentioned, e.g. those at Penycae and Pontrhydyfen, to which the Company gave generous donations annually.[5]

1   E. H. Brooke, op. cit., p. 58.
2   *Reports from the Commissioners, Mines,* 1846, p. 423
3   ibid
4   See Appendix 30 at end of this Chapter for specimen form.
5   *Cwmavon Works MSS,* Receipts and Payment Slips.
    Transactions of Aberafan and Margam District Historical Society 1931-32, p. 93.

IRONWORKS SCHOOLS

The four important schools were Cwmavon Works, Oakwood Works (across the river), Bryn, and Tymaen (Infants).[1] Two dates have been given for the establishment of the Cwmavon school. The 1847 *Reports* refer to the 'Cwmavon Schools promoted by the Governor and Company of Copper Miners in England: Resident Director, T. R. Guppy, Esq., Taibach, Glam. Stoppage of a 1d. in the pound upon the work-people's wages; schools established in 1845'.[2] An earlier *Report* refers to two day and Sunday National schools, commenced in 1830, containing 102 males and 73 females, supported principally by the English Copper Company, with the addition of 1½d. weekly from the head of each family of the workmen in the works: the salary of the master and mistress being £52 per annum, with house and coals.[3] Of all the industrial communities in south Wales in 1846, Cwmavon seemed to be the only example where schools were sufficient for the population: 'there are four boys' and four girls' schools in different parts of the valley placed conveniently for the large population, and one infant school at Cwmavon. That these are sufficient to meet the wants of the people is shown by the fact that there is only one small day school of the old kind in the valley.'[4]

So much detailed information is available concerning these schools that it is a difficult task to be selective and at the same time to be comprehensive. Only a brief survey of their development is possible here. In 1849, the schools were very much over-crowded and unwieldy, and the lack of an Infants' school 'overloaded the existing ones with babies'.[5] The Oakwood school, established in 1844, and the Cwmavon one, sent no boy to the works unless he could read and write, the girls were given a thorough training in house-craft, needle-work, and sewing, but were very irregular in attendance. For upwards of twenty years, from 1845 to 1865, the schools were entirely independent, managed their own affairs and did not seek government aid. For this reason, the story of the development of the schools does not feature in the annual reports of the Committee of Council before 1865. Neither did the National Society have any claim or basis for interference although they were National schools, but the Company invited the Inspector of National schools to visit them periodically, as a matter of courtesy and also in an unofficial advisory capacity. W. Gilbertson, the Cwmavon Works Manager, told

---

1 *The Cambrian*, January 4th, 1849: Cwmavon Schools, 250 boys, 200 girls. Oakwood Schools, 100 boys, 80 girls. Bryn School, 40 boys, 60 girls. Tymaen Infants, 120. Total of 850 in four schools.
2 1847 *Reports*, Part 1, p. 62.
3 *Education Inquiry: Abstract of Answers and Returns*, Vol. III, 1833, p. 1285
4 *Reports from the Commissioners, Mines*, 1846, p. 425.
5 1847 *Reports*, pp. 343-4.

the Newcastle Commissioners in 1861 that 'the day schools connected with the works did not receive government grants, nor were they under government inspection. They did not wish to be interfered with in the arrangement made for these schools, and there were some points which, if they accepted aid, would be insisted upon, that would be unnecessary there. The schools were visited, at their request, by the diocesan inspector, and were noticed in his Report.'[1]

In 1849, just as the schools were beginning to develop along successful lines, the English Copper Company were in a state of financial embarrassment and the Bank of England had to manage its affairs.[2] Before this crisis, in 1848, evening schools had been inaugurated on a sound footing which were well attended by the young men, most of whom could read and write. A circulating library was about to be commenced, lectures were given in the evenings, and a band of twenty instruments had been formed, as well as a good cricket club.[3] Again the indications were quite clear, several years before the crisis, of the excellent work done by the schools and the vigilance and guidance so obviously evident on the part of the management, that the Commissioner felt bound to make the following observations on the substantial educational work promoted by the Company: 'If the bringing together of a large mass of people earning high wages, has not been accompanied in this case by their demoralization, the cause is clear: many wise precautions have been taken that it should not. These are, to a certain extent, costly to the Company, but they have this advantage over the contrary plan of laying out nothing upon moral safeguards, and trusting to chance for the results, that the cost is known. I know of no extensive works which betoken a providing spirit of justice and liberality in their management, more evidently than these of the English Copper Company at Cwmavon, or in which the wise moral government of a large assemblage of workpeople engages so much careful consideration.'[4] From a sociological standpoint this reflection on the part of the Commissioner demands further comment, for his argument was an important ingredient in the relationship between employers of labour and their workpeople, and so germane to the whole question of works schools in the densely populated industrial areas. In truth, it epitomized the whole *raison d'être* of the need and purpose of such schools

1 *Newcastle Commission Report* 1861. Vol. II, Appendix B, p. 611.
2 *Reports from the Commissioners, Mines*, 1846, p. 426.
3 ibid. Also, Aeron Afan, *Cyfansoddiadau Buddugol Eisteddfod Iforiaid Aberafan*, Mehefin 23 ain, 1853: Traethawd ar ddechreuad a chynnydd Gweithiau Cwmafan, gan Afanydd (Parch. John Rowlands, Gweinidog y Bedyddwyr, Cwmafan), p. 88-146.
4 *Reports from the Commissioners, Mines*, 1846, p. 426.

in the nineteenth century, before the genesis of a State system in 1870 and in those places where the Voluntary Societies were lethargic in their school activities.

As early as 1831, Matthew Arnold, in company with many others condemned the condition of the manufacturing towns where the Factory Acts had failed to improve educational facilities and described them as 'places where men have assembled together, not for the purposes of social life, but to make calicoes or broadcloth. A man set up a factory and wants hands: I beseech you, Sir, to observe the very expressions that are used, for they are all significant. What he wants of his fellow creatures is the loan of their hands: of their heads and hearts he thinks nothing.'[1] This might be true of some manufacturing districts in England, but in south Wales where 'good employers of labour did not neglect their responsibilities toward their workpeople' and were not merely motivated by a mixture of benevolence and self-interest to promote miniscule welfare communities around their works—but substantial educational establishments of a permanent nature—such industrialists had the 'improvement of the working classes as an object of paramount importance'.[2]

And now to return to Cwmavon in 1852. After three years of control by the Bank of England, the English Copper Company, took over again. In the interim period the Company's educational programme was continued and developed under the guidance of Mr. Biddulph, when the schools were enlarged and a new school was opened at Bryn including an infants' school. Tremenheere reported in detail on the new developments in 1850 and said that 'although in 1849 changes took place in the management of the company, it was carried on, on behalf of the Bank of England, under the management of Mr. J. Biddulph and the same conscientious regard for what was due to the workpeople continues to be conspicuous ... important additions have been made to their schools ... reading rooms have been formed, accessible to all their workmen. The principal one is near their offices, and the others held in the schoolrooms at the remoter parts of the valleys. To this is also attached a Mechanics Institute and both are to be opened shortly under the same roof. Good and well-organized evening schools are also available for men and women.'[3] Similarly, the Rev. H. Longueville Jones, Inspector of National schools, visited Cwmavon in 1849 and the following years and reported that 'one

1 W. H. G. Armytage, *Four Hundred Years of English Education*, Cambridge, 1964, pp. 101 and 110: Arnold's letter to the *Sheffield Courant* in 1831.
2 *Reports from the Commissioners, Mines*, 1846, p. 426.
3 *Reports from the Commissioners, Mines*, 1850, Vol. XXIII, p. 369

of the most pleasing features connected with my inspection of the Glamorganshire schools . . . has been my visit to Cwmavon. I cannot omit stating that these schools are of the highest order and importance to the peculiar and hard-working populations for whom they are intended: that they are supported in an easy and judicious manner . . . and that they are, on the whole, in very excellent condition. They are superintended with great perseverance and activity, and the aggregate number of children attending them were more than 800.'[1]

The resumption of control by the Company in 1852 was an event which was celebrated by the whole population of 8,000 'with every demonstration of respect and satisfaction'.[2] Moreover, by this time the religious problem had been settled mutually—between the Anglican proprietors who had hitherto conducted their schools strictly on the National system, even compelling the children to march to the Church Sunday schools and to learn the catechism—and the workmen who were mainly Nonconformists. The children of Nonconformist workmen were no longer required to conform to this regulation and even in the day schools were not compelled to learn the catechism.[3] Also, special attention was given to the problem of early school-leaving and methods were devised to keep the brighter children at school, including the provision of good technical instruction. When the schools were placed under the surveillance of the *Committee of Privy Council* in 1864, the Company's educational complex comprised six schools attended by 919 children 'whose appearance and demeanour spoke most favourably for the care and influence exercised over them'.[4] After 1870 the Cwmavon schools, housed in new buildings, including Oakwood (Pontrhydyfen), Bryn, Tymaen Infants, and Penycae continued to grow numerically, and the total school population in 1873 was over 1,200.

Unfortunately, for the second time, the Company had to cease operations for financial reasons in 1877 when the inspector of schools voiced his apprehension in his annual report: 'There is one portion of this Union (Neath) about which I feel considerable worry, namely, Cwmavon. For fourteen years past I have been in the habit of inspecting the large and important schools in connection with the works of the English Copper Company there, and have watched with great interest their gradual progress and improvement. Adverse affairs however have

1 *Minutes of Committee of Council*, 1851-52, Rev. H. Longueville Jones's Report on elementary schools (National), p. 247.
2 *Reports from Commissioners, Mines and Collieries*, 1854, p. 404.
3 *Nefydd MSS, Journal for July*, 1854, entry for 11th July.
4 *Minutes of Committee of Council*, 1865, p. 57.

led to the extinction of that Company and the whole of their buildings and property have this year, 1877, passed to other hands. How the schools with their six departments and attendance of nearly 1,400 children are to be supported in the future, I am unable to predict: I can only express my earnest wish that the new proprietors may extend to them the same liberality as their predecessors, and that there may be no occasion to call into action the means for providing for the education of this populous district.'[1] Fortunately, his fears were allayed, the new owners continued the tradition, and in 1880 over 1,500 children attended the schools.[2]

The remaining ironworks schools in Glamorgan were at Aberavon, Bryndu (Pyle), Tonmawr, and Glyn Tâf. The Aberavon schools are only mentioned once, viz. in Nefydd's *Journal* for July, 1854: 'there are two very good schools in this populous place, established in connection with the Messrs. Llewellyn's works. Both boys' and girls' day schools are good and efficient and carried on—on the British system. About 240 children are contained in them, and the population of this place is around 5,000.'[3]

Bryndu, near Pyle (Bridgend), had a colliery and ironworks school. The sole reference to the ironworks school is by the Commissioner who reported in 1847: 'I arrived too late to find this school in operation. It is in contemplation to supersede it by a larger and more efficient establishment to be jointly supported by stoppages from the wages of the people employed in the Bryndu (H. Ford's works), and Messrs. Malin and Robinson's works. The schools were established in 1846 in very indifferent buildings and there were 143 children on the school books, 100 of whom remained at school for less than one year . . . the schools were maintained by a stoppage of a 1d. in the £ upon the workmen's wages in the Bryndu works.'[4] Messrs. Malin and Robinson also owned works and collieries at Garth (Maesteg) 'where it was intended to convert the building in which the Company's shop was kept, since abandoned, into a day school'.[5]

The Tonmawr Iron and Coal Company established a school in 1846, maintained by a stoppage of 6d. per month on the men's wages, and 3d. per month on the wages of the boys. The master 'aged 18 was also librarian

1 *Minutes of Committee of Council*, 1878, General Report by the Rev. B. J. Binns, p. 89.
2 ibid, for 1881, pp. 664-732.
3 *Nefydd MSS*, entry for 11th July, 1854.
4 1847 *Reports*, p. 354 and pp. 70-3. *Reports from Commissioners, Mines*, 1846, p. 430.
5 1847 *Reports*, pp. 70 ff.

at the Neath Mechanics Institute, and there were 52 children on the school books'.[1]

The Taff Vale Iron Company merely provided a building for the 'holding of a school for the children of the workmen employed at the chain and plate works, and although the men are somewhat a picked class in these works . . . yet they will set their children, when scarcely older than infants, to work'.[2]

The Ironworks schools of Carmarthenshire and Breconshire

With the exception of the Clydach Ironworks in south Breconshire, ironsmelting in both counties during the nineteenth century centred around the use of anthracite coal. This coal did not play an important part in the earlier phases of the industrial revolution because of its slow combustion which did not suit the early furnaces and forges of the eighteenth century. Anthracite ironworks were not established until the third decade of the nineteenth century, more particularly after 1838 when George Crane of Yniscedwyn successfully smelted iron-ore by means of anthracite.[3] Anthracite ironworks appeared between 1838-1850 and it is interesting to note that each had a school; most of these schools were small, and bore no comparison with the large schools of Glamorgan and Monmouthshire.

Carmarthenshire: Anthracite Ironworks schools.

The Gwendraeth Valley.
   (*a*) Trimsaran—established in 1843[4]
   (*b*) Gwendraeth—established in 1860 at Pontyberem[5]
The Amman Valley.
   Amman Ironworks school (later tinworks)—established in 1856[6]

Breconshire:
   Yniscedwyn—established in 1839[7]
   Clydach—established in 1842[8]

Few details are available for the two works schools in the Gwendraeth, Valley, Carmarthenshire, 'Trim Saron school in the parish of Pembrey',

1 1847 *Reports*, Part 1, pp. 62-5.
2 ibid, pp. 9-10 and p. 298.
3 C. Wilkins, op. cit., *The History of the Iron, etc.* p. 228. E. H. Brooke, op. cit., p. 104.
4 1847 *Reports*, Part 1, pp. 6-9, and p. 216.
5 *Minutes of Committee of Council*, 1861-1865: Tabulated Reports of schools aided by Parliamentary Grants.
6 *Amman Ironworks British School Logbook*, p. 2.
7 1847 *Reports*, Part 2, p. 142. *Nefydd MSS*, Journal for August 1854.
8 1847 *Reports*, Part 2, pp. 214-217, and p. 133.

which was National, and the Pontyberem school which was British, both being no more than village schools. The ironmasters, Messrs. Norton, Upperton, and Stone supported the original school at Trimsaran, and in 1846 subscribed £100 to erect a new one for about forty pupils. The Company paid 4/- per week to a mistress 'for teaching their workmen's children', and the pupils paid 1d. per week, and farmers' children 2d. per week.[1] There was also another 'furnace school' in the same parish, but it is uncertain whether it was attached to another small ironworks.[2] In 1848, T. Watney and Co. had three furnaces in the Gwendraeth Valley and promoted a school after 1850.[3] The Amman Ironworks British school at Brynamman had two periods of life, first as the Ironworks school in the old premises, from 1848 to 1868, and secondly as the Brynamman Tinworks school, 1868-1898, when the works went over to tinplate manufacture, and new school buildings were erected.[4] Before 1848, a charcoal forge had been in operation, which was taken over by Mr. Llewellyn Llewellyn and he erected anthracite blast furnaces.[5] In 1859 the forge and furnaces became the property of Messrs. Strick, Francis and Thomas, and in 1865 a puddling forge was added. In 1872, a three-mill tinplate works was built. The ironworks closed down in 1891, the tinplate works ceased to operate in 1897, and the works were dismantled.[6]

The first school at Amman ironworks was started in 1856 in a building near old Gibea chapel, which was in use until the tinplate company built a new school in 1868, and an infants' department in 1874.[7] The complete story of the new buildings is set forth in the school logbook which was

1 1847 *Reports*, Part 1, p. 216.
2 ibid, p. 216: the entry is brief, 'the master is a clergyman's son, and has received a good education. The scholars were farmers' and labourers' children but few were present owing to the snow. The copybooks were kept very clean and were well-written". At the Trimsaran school the pupils stayed at school over the age of ten years, e.g., in 1846, there were 8 girls and 20 boys over the age of ten at school, out of an average attendance in the last year of 18 girls and 24 boys.
3 *Reports from Commissioners, Mines,* 1849, *Vol. XXII,* Appendix to H. S. Tremenheere's Report, pp. 419-420.
R. Meade, *The Coal and Iron Industries of the United Kingdom,* 1882, Appendix 2, Table IV, p. 833.
4 See Chapter VI.
5 E. H. Brooke, op. cit., p. 112, R. Meade, op. cit.
6 E. H. Brooke, op. cit., loc. cit.
7 *Amman Ironworks British School Logbook,* entries for 1st April, 1868; 11th August, 1868, and 30th January, 1874.

kept from August, 1863, and the new school became the Brynamman Tinworks school.[1]

At Clydach, near Llanelly, Breconshire, ironsmelting started about 1705 by Hanbury the grandson of Capel Hanbury of Pontypool.[2] In 1805 'there were two furnaces for smelting the ore, and two forges for converting the pig-iron into bars: from 40 to 100 tons of the latter ore are made weekly . . . 400 hands are usually employed, some of whom get near £100 and none of them less than £40 per annum'.[3] Messrs. Frere, Cook, and Powell owned the works later and the wages bill of the company averaged £4,000 per month. The works were dismantled in 1858.[4] The Company built a school in 1842 which was entirely maintained by the Clydach ironworks through the contributions of the proprietors and the poundage on the workmen's wages. It was conducted on the National system 'but was unconnected with either of the Voluntary Societies', and the master and mistress were trained at the diocesan school at Bristol.[5]

1 *Amman Ironworks School, Logbook*, 1864-68: 'the attendance in 1863 was 115, but in August, 1864 the numbers were increasing so steadily that the Inspector stated in his Report: "The school is in satisfactory order, and has passed an excellent examination under the Revised Code. I am directed to state that the size of your principal schoolroom does not satisfy the conditions of the Revised Code for the present average attendance (see Article 5a). My Lords have allowed the grant as they understand that the managers intend to begin new buildings. Their Lordships trust that they will be ready for the children's use by the next inspection." But matters were not any better a year later, owing to a difficulty about the site, the proposed new building has not yet been commenced. But a site having now been obtained, the works are to be started without delay. However, this was not done, for the proprietors of the ironworks (in order to conform with the regulations for accommodation pending the building of a new school) dismissed all the children whose parents were not employed at the ironworks because "only 100 children are to be taught in the present schoolroom." On August 11th 1868, the new building was ready, and 133 scholars were assembled.'
2 C. Wilkins, op. cit., p. 218.
3 Theophilus Jones, *History of the County of Brecknock*. 2 Volumes, 1898, Vol. I, p. 73.
4 C. Wilkins, op. cit., p. 218. *Reports from Commissioners, Mines*, 1849, Appendix to H. S. Tremenheere's Report, pp. 419-20.
5 1847 *Reports*, Part 2, p. 98. 'Attendances were extremely irregular, the girls' school was better than the boys' school, both schools having an average attendance of 180 in 1844. The master and mistress were aged 28 and 27 respectively and were trained for four months in 1842. Their combined salaries were £82 with house and garden rent free. They were two of the few teachers in the whole district who received more than £40 per year, who are on a footing, in point of money, or money's worth, with a gentleman's groom.'

IRONWORKS SCHOOLS

APPENDIX 1

BLAENAVON IRONWORKS SCHOOL

ATTENDANCES 1846-1872 BOYS AND GIRLS

Year	Attendance
1846	125
1849	166
1852	224[1]
1858	214[2]
1865	189[3]
1870	153[4]
1872	137[5]

1 *Minutes of Committee of Council,* 1852, p. 270.
2 ibid 1858, p. 318.
3 ibid 1865, p. 209.
4 ibid 1870, p. 621.
5 ibid 1872, p. 188, Appendix B to Mr. Waddington's Report.

APPENDIX 2

NEATH ABBEY IRONWORKS SCHOOLS

Proprietor	School	Accommodation	Attendances 1846
Joseph Tregellis Price, Esq. Neath Abbey	Boys'	Room 40 x 23 feet x 15 feet high. Fitted with raised gallery and a desk for the master; parallel desks and fixed slates for the scholars	No Registers kept[1]
	Girls'	Room 23 x 20 feet x 15 feet high	60[2]
	Infants'	One schoolroom	103[3]

1 1847 *Reports,* p. 62. Appendix, Parochial Tables of schools.
2 ibid. Also: p. 341.
3 ibid, p. 340.

APPENDIX 3

Neath Abbey Ironworks Schools[1]

The three schools: boys', girls', and infants' established in 1816 and 1825. Promoter, J. T. Price, Esq., Neath Abbey Works, Neath.

Boys' School:
Tenancy at will. Good building, sufficient outbuildings in good repair. 15 feet high 40 x 23 feet.
Sufficient furniture and apparatus in good repair.
76 on books. Average attendance in 1846, 50.
Monitorial: 8 monitors. Religious instruction by teacher.
Visitation by promoter. English books only. English grammar.
Master's Age: 22. Borough Road for 3 months in 1842. Started at 22, clerk before.
1d. per week from Neath Abbey workmen.

Girls' School:
Details as for boys' school. 60 on books. Average attendance in 1846, 45.
Monitorial, 6 monitors.
Subjects taught: Holy Scriptures; reading; writing on slates and paper; mental arithmetic; geography; vocal music.
Visitation by promoter. English books only.
Age of mistress: 28. Started teaching at 26. Bonnet maker before. Salary, £26 per annum.
1d. per week from Neath Abbey workmen.

Infants' School:
Details as for boys and girls school. 103 on books.
Average attendance in 1846, 70 girls and 25 boys.
Monitorial, 10 monitors.
Age of mistress: 30, started teaching at 16.
Age of Assistant Mistress: 44. Started teaching at 22. Salary: £20-16-0.
1d. per week from Neath Abbey workmen.

1   1847 *Reports*, Part 1, pp. 62 and 340.

APPENDIX 4

Hirwaun Ironworks (Firemen's) School[2]

Established 1820. Promoter: F. Crawshay, Esq., Treforest, Pontypridd.
Tenancy at will. Good building. No outbuilding. Building 9 feet high; area 18 x 13.
Insufficient furniture; apparatus in good repair.
40 children on books.
5 children attended less than 1 year.
6 children attended 1 to 2 years.
4 children attended 2 to 3 years.
15 children attended 3 to 4 years.
10 children attended 4 to 5 years.
Children under 5 years of age not admitted.
5 to 10 years: 10 boys; 14 girls.
10 and over: 6 boys; 10 girls.
Average attendance in last year: 25 girls; 30 boys.
Method: Teacher instructor. No monitors.
Curriculum: Religious Instruction; reading; writing; Learning first rules: 2. Writing on paper: 7. Rule of three: 1.
Visitation made by Trustees, Committee, Governors or Guardians.
English books only. Welsh spoken to explain English books.

2   1847 *Reports*, Part 1, pp. 54-57.

IRONWORKS SCHOOLS

APPENDIX 5

Venallt Ironworks School, Blaengwrach (Glyncorrwg)[1]

Established 1834. Messrs. Jevons and Wood, Venallt Coal and Iron works, near Neath.
Tenancy at will. Good building. No outbuildings. 18 x 30 feet, 19 feet high.
Sufficient furniture and apparatus in good repair.
72 children on books. Attendance too fluctuating to be ascertained.
Ages: under 5 years: no girls, 2 boys.
     5 to 10 years: 19 girls, 33 boys.
     Over ten years: 6 girls, 12 boys.
12 living over $1\frac{1}{2}$ miles from school.
Monitorial with 4 monitors.
Subjects: reading: 35; writing on paper: 25; First rules, 16.
Visited by promoter.
English books only. Welsh spoken to explain. Grammar of both languages.
Master's age: 38, started at 16. Previous occupation: student at Presbyterian College, Carmarthen.
Other emoluments—Unitarian Minister, £5; Salary, £60. School pence, £4.
1d. per week from each man in the Venallt Coal and Iron works.

1 1847 *Reports*, Part 1, p. 62.

APPENDIX 6

Machen (Infants), Ironworks School[2]

Established 1837. Tenancy at will.
Good building, with no outbuilding. Size: 20 x 14 feet.
Accommodation at 6 square feet: 47.
Insufficient furniture and apparatus in good repair.
64 on books   22 less than 1 year.
                     23 more than 1 year less than 2 years.
                     11 more than 2 years less than 3 years.
                     8 more than 3 years less than 4 years.
Attending under 5: 18 boys and 16 girls.
Attending 5-10: 15 boys and 15 girls.
Attending over 10: No boys and no girls.
Average attendance: 20 boys and 26 girls.
Monitorial, 4 monitors.
Age of mistress: 23. At Newport National school for 18 months in 1841 and 1842.
Dressmaker before. Salary: £16; from school pence: £12.
Annual income of school from subscriptions: £16.
Annual income of school from school pence: £12.

2 1847 *Reports*, Part 2, p. 288 and p. 302.

IRONWORKS SCHOOLS

APPENDIX 7

Nantyglo Ironworks School[1]

Original schoolroom, 1812.

Boys' School:
Established 1837. Tenancy at will. Good building, no outbuildings. Dimensions 60 x 20. Accommodation at 6 square feet: 200. Sufficient furniture and apparatus in good repair. Number of children on books: 90 (39 less than 1 year), 2 boys under 5; 62 between 5 and 10; 26 above 10; Average attendance: 85.
Monitorial method, 10 monitors. Some simultaneous teaching. Scripture taught and catechism. Religious instruction given by master and minister. Visitations by minister. Instruction given in English language. Master's age: 35. Did not attend Normal or Model school. Commenced vocation at 16. No other occupation. Salary £70. Annual income by subscriptions of boys and girls schools: £120. From school pence: £40.

Girls' School:
Established 1837. Details as for boys' school. Number on books: 120 (77 for less than one year).
Under 5 years: 12; between 5 and 10: 65; Above 10: 43. Average attendance in last year: 105.
Monitorial, 8 monitors.
Age of mistress: 27. Not at Normal school, but 2 months at Bridgend National School. Commenced vocation at 25. No previous occupation. Salary £50.

1   1847 *Reports*, Part 2, p. 278, 285, and 296.

APPENDIX 8

Rhymney Ironworks National School[2]

Rhymney Iron Company, Church school, established 1843.
Good building, no outbuildings. 2 rooms, 33 x 17 each, 9 feet high. Insufficient apparatus, in bad repair.
120 children on books. Under 5 years of age: 3 girls, 0 boys. 5-10: 47 girls, 48 boys. Over 10: 10 boys, 12 girls. Average attendance in last year: 65 girls, 65 boys. 1 living over 1½ miles from school. Monitorial, 17.

Reading letters and monosyllables:	33.
Reading simple narratives:	14.
Reading with ease:	12.
Writing on slates:	3.
Writing on paper:	33.
Learning first rules:	9.
Rule of three:	2.
Vocal music:	86.

Religious instruction by teacher, minister, and visitors. Visitations made by committee and minister.
English books only. Master aged 56, mistress aged 46.
Trained at Bristol Modern school 2 weeks in 1846. Master's previous occupation: sub-agent and machine weigher.
Master's salary: £52 per annum. Secretary to Benefit Society brings him £1-15-0 p.a. Income from school pence £31-4-0. House and garden rent free. Coals given.

2   1847 *Reports*, Part 1, p. 34.

IRONWORKS SCHOOLS

APPENDIX 9

RHYMNEY IRONWORKS SCHOOLS, DAY AND EVENING ATTENDANCES, 1865-1873

		Day	Evening
1865:	Rhymney National School	369	55
	Rhymney British School	224	—[1]
1870:	Rhymney National School	488	168
	Rhymney British School	199	60[2]
1873:	Rhymney National School	527	?
	Rhymney British School	264	?[3]

1 *Minutes of Committee of Council*, 1865, p. 213.
2 ibid 1870, p. 621.
3 ibid 1827, p. 188.

APPENDIX 10(a)

TREDEGAR IRONWORKS SCHOOL[4]

Boys' School:

Established 1841. Tenancy at will. Good building, and out-buildings, sufficient.

Dimensions: 60 x 30 feet. 300 at six square feet. Sufficient furniture and apparatus in good repair. No. of children on books: 158. 79 at school less than 1 year; 5 to 10 years: 125; Above 10: 33. Average attendance in last year: 130. Monitorial and simultaneous. One monitor.

73 doing letters and monosyllables; 158 writing on slates; 60 writing on paper; 46 learning first rules in arithmetic; 13 deduction and compound rules; 37 rule of three; 20 mental arithmetic; 58 geography; 35 history of England; 158 vocal music.

Religious instruction by master and minister.

Visitation by minister, Language of instruction—English.

Master's age: 43, at Model school, Bristol Diocesan school 2 years, and at Wells Central school.

Commenced vocation at 21. Merchant's clerk before this.

Salary £80 p.a. with house and garden rent free.

The four Tredegar Works Schools comprising Girls, Boys, Infants, and Vestry schools receive £500 in subscriptions annually.

4 1847 *Reports*, Part 2, Monmouthshire

APPENDIX 10(b)

Tredegar Ironworks School[1]

Girls' School:
Established 1841. Dimensions, 30 x 80 feet. 150 at six square feet. As per boys' school in other details. 114 on books. 26 less than 1 year. Under 5 years of age—0. 5-10 years: 64. Over 10 years: 50. Average attendance in last year: 96.

Method: Individual and monitorial. 12 monitors.

Simultaneous instruction, Scripture and catechism. Religious instruction by mistress and minister.

Age of mistress: 31. At Westminster Training school for 2¼ years. Commenced teaching at 19. Salary £40, house and garden rent free.

Infants School:
Established 1843. 149 on books. 33 less than one year. Under five years of age: 70 boys, 71 girls. Average attendance: 65 boys, and 68 girls.

Method: individual and monitorial, 4 monitors.

Mistress aged 22. Trained at Bristol Infant school in 1843. Commenced vocation at 16 Salary, £35 p.a.

Vestry School:
Established in 1844. 58 in school.

1   1847 *Reports*, Part 2, p. 312. D. and E. Powell, op. cit., p. 54.

APPENDIX 10(c)

Expenses of Tredegar Ironworks Schools[2]

At Tredegar, Mr. Homfray writes me thus:

'I send you the account of the expenses as requested. The 1d. in the £ alluded to by the master of the school is for the schools and any other purposes connected with the schools that can tend to the mental and moral welfare of the workmen. This income varies according to the rates of wages paid, and amounts at present to about £500 per annum. The overplus, after paying the expenses, is kept as a fund for the purposes alluded to above. The schoolrooms are at present in the Town Hall, no buildings having yet been provided.'

I remain, etc.,

Samuel Homfray.

Expenses of the maintenance of the Tredegar schools.	£.	s.	d.
Salaries to the master and two mistresses	155	0	0
Rent and lodgings allowed to above	30	8	0
Books and other expenses	50	10	0
Monitors' clothing, etc.	44	6	0
Total	£280	4	0

2   1847 *Reports*, Part 2, Report on Monmouthshire by Jelinger C. Symons.

APPENDIX 11
Sirhowy Ironworks School[1]

Established 1845. Dimensions, 45 x 14 feet. 105 at six square feet. Insufficient furniture in bad repair.
128 on books. 86 less than 1 year in school. Average attendance: 72 boys, 43 girls.
Monitorial and simultaneous. 7 monitors.
Scripture and catechism.
Visitation by Committee and patron.
Instruction in the English language.
Age of master, 23. Bricklayer before this.
Salary £60 per annum, with house and garden rent free.
£18 from school pence and £60 from subscriptions.

1   1847 *Reports*, Part 2, p. 319.

APPENDIX 12
Ebbw Vale Ironworks School[2]

Boys' School:
Established 1845. Dimensions 60 x 24 feet. 240 at six square feet. 174 children on books.
135 for less than 1 year. Under 5 years of age: 32. Between 5 and 10 years: 130. Above 10: 12. Average attendance in last year: 145.
Monitorial and simultaneous instruction. 9 monitors.
Scriptures and the catechism.
Master's age about 35. At Weymouth National Model school for 6 years. Commenced vocation at 22; student before this.
Salary £70 per annum, with house and garden rent free.

Girls' School:
Established 1844. 157 on books. 90 for less than 1 year. 58 girls under 5 years of age. 29 above 10 years of age. Average attendance: 130.
Monitorial, 8 monitors.
Age of mistress: 23. Commenced vocation at 18.
Salary £60 p.a. with house and garden rent free.

Victoria Ironworks School[3]

Very inadequately described in the sources available. But this school had an unusual number of Sunday schools associated with it. In 1870, the day-school had an average attendance of 202. It also had thriving evening classes. In 1873, there were two departments, boys and girls, with an average attendance of 197.

2   1847 *Reports*, Part 2, pp. 312, ff.
3   *Minutes of Committee of Council*, 1870. Tabulated Reports of schools, p. 621.
     ibid for 1873, Appendix B, to Mr. Waddington's Report for 1872, pp. 196-7.

IRONWORKS SCHOOLS

APPENDIX 13

ABERSYCHAN IRONWORKS SCHOOL[1]

Boys' School:
Established 1845. By lease for a term.
Good buildings, with sufficient outbuildings. Dimensions: 30 x 20 feet; 100 at six square feet. Sufficient furniture and apparatus in good repair.
140 on books. 80 attend for less than one year. Average attendance: 115.
Monitorial, 10 monitors. Visitation by Committee.
Age of master: 32. Salary, £70 with house and garden rent free.
£70 from subscriptions.

Girls' School:
Established 1845. Rest of details as per boys' school.
108 on books. Average attendance 80.
Mistress aged 21. Previous occupation: Milliner.
Salary, £50 per annum.

1   1847 *Reports*, Part 2, p. 296.

APPENDIX 14

MINUTES OF THE COMMITTEE OF MANAGEMENT, ABERSYCHAN IRON COMPANY'S SCHOOL[2]

Abersychan British Iron Company: Government and Regulations of the school:

1. The children eligible to be admitted are the following: They take precedence in the order they are arranged:—
   (a) Children of parents working in the works.
   (b) Children having lost their parents, who died in the Company's service, and who are supported by brothers or other relatives employed in the works.
   (c) Children of parents who died in the Company's employ, but who have no relatives employed in the works.
2. That the school shall be opened and closed, morning and evening, with prayer and hymn, and the Bible shall be the only textbook for religious instruction.
3. That the children shall attend at 9 o'clock in the morning and go to dinner at 12. Return at 2 o'clock and break up for the day at 5 from the 1st March to 1st October and at 4 o'clock from the 1st October to the 1st March.
4. That every child must attend school with hands and face clean, and hair combed; in case this rule is not attended to, the master and mistress are required to send them home.
5. That children, having been admitted, must attend regularly, but in case they do not, a report to that effect must be made by the master and mistress, and delivered into the Company's Office every Saturday morning. That the parent or parents of the children absenting themselves must be visited by two or more Committee members and admonished. If the irregularity persists, the children may be suspended or dismissed the school at the discretion of the Committee, and not to be admitted without an order from them.

IRONWORKS SCHOOLS

6. Parents are not to interfere with the schoolmaster or mistress in consequence of any correction, which they may in discharge of their duty, inflict upon the children. If they consider unnecessary severity has been used, they must complain to the Committee, who will make inquiry into it, and adopt such measures as the case may require. Any interference contrary to this rule will occasion the immediate expulsion of the child or children.
7. That the schoolmaster and mistress keep a list of all the children, with the names of their parents and their occupation, and a daily account of their attendance in a book to be provided for that purpose.
8. That the children be dismissed from school in classes, with a short interval between each; and each class to be attended by the monitor beyond the limits of the school.
9. That a monthly report be rendered by the master and mistress of the general conduct of the children and of any irregularity not comprised in these regulations. That the said report be sent in to the New British Iron Company's Office on the last Saturday in each calendar month and that a meeting of the Committee be held on the first Monday of the following month at 12 o'clock, at the aforesaid New British Iron Company's Office.
10. That the holidays for the year shall be five weeks, and take place as follows: Two weeks at Christmas; Three days at Easter; Three days at Whitsuntide; Two weeks at Midsummer.
11. That two children out of each school shall be appointed by the master and mistress weekly, to sweep the rooms daily. That the said rooms shall be washed every fortnight, and the windows cleaned, and that £3 per annum be allowed for doing same, including brushes, flannels, soap, etc.
12. That neither the master nor mistress shall, on any consideration whatever, employ the children without their parents' consent, to carry coal into their houses nor manure into their garden, nor any other description of work not comprised in these regulations, nor with the parents' consent during school hours.
13. That no children in whose family there exists any infectious disease shall be permitted to attend the school till it shall be pronounced safe for them to do so by the Medical Officer of the works.
14. That any child absent after the time for opening the school shall be kept in by the master or mistress to learn some lesson for the same length of time after school hours.
15. That it is also desirable that the ladies of Abersychan district and neighbourhood be invited to pay periodical visits to the girls' school for the purpose of superintending the needle and other work belonging to their departments.
16. That the girls be taught some work of industry, such as knitting, straw plaiting, and plain needlework; or any other branch of industrial labour the ladies may suggest, and other work belonging to their departments, subject to the approval of the Committee.
17. That for the purpose of carrying out these regulations, any four members of the Committee shall form a quorum, and their decision shall be final. The meetings to take place in the Office of the New British Iron Company.

WILLIAM WOOD,
Chairman of Committee.

2   1847 *Reports*, Part 2, p. 284.

IRONWORKS SCHOOLS

APPENDIX 15

PONTNEWYNYDD IRONWORKS SCHOOL[1]

Established 1843. Tenancy in trust for ever. Good building, with sufficient outbuildings.
Dimensions: Boys' School: 60 x 25 feet. Girls' School: 24 x 19 feet. 362 at six square feet. Sufficient furniture and apparatus in good repair.
245 on books, 148 for less than one year. Average attendance: 90 boys; 70 girls.
Monitorial and simultaneous instruction. 8 monitors.
Religious instruction: 40 Holy Scriptures; 40 catechism. Religious instruction by master and minister.
Visitation made by minister and patron (W. Williams, Esq., of Snatchwood House).
Instruction in English.
Age of master: 27. Mistress: 20. Both commenced vocation at 20. Previous occupation: tailor; other, job-clerk and organist (£2 p.a.).
Salary: both £65 p.a. house and garden rent free.
Income from school pence: £31-3-4.
Annual income of schools: from subscriptions: £65.

1   1847 *Reports*, Part 2, pp. 320-3.

APPENDIX 16

BLAINA IRONWORKS BRITISH SCHOOL (BOYS')[2]

Established 1846. Tenancy in trust for ever.
Good buildings, with no outbuildings. Dimensions: 40 x 25 ft. Accommodation at six square feet: 167.
Number of children on books: 92. 92 at school less than one year.
Individual method and monitorial. 10 monitors. Also simultaneous instruction.
Scripture and catechism. Religious instruction by master. Visitation by Committee·
English grammar taught, and instruction in English only.
Master's age: 24. 7 months in Borough Road in 1846. Commenced vocation at 23. Previous occupation—private assistant. Follows no other occupation.
Salary: £40 p.a. Income from school pence: £20-16-0.

BLAINA AND CWMCELYN MIXED BRITISH SCHOOL

Established 1846. Tenancy by lease for a term.
Good building, no outbuilding. Dimensions: 30 x 25 feet. 125 at six square feet.
Number on books: 106. 106 at school for less than 1 year.
Monitorial, 8 monitors.
Scripture, but no catechism.
Simultaneous instruction.

2   1847 *Reports*, Part 2, p. 273.

IRONWORKS SCHOOLS

APPENDIX 17

Dos Nailworks School, Newport, Mon.

Messrs. J. J. Cordes and Co., Dos Works, Newport.

Mr. *Thomas Charles's evidence:*[1]

'Our works consist of a rolling and slitting mill and a patent process for the manufacture of nails. The latter part of the works and the process is peculiar to ourselves in this county.

Several boys are employed on this work. There are about 350 boys employed in the works. There are no girls employed here. The boys begin at 10-11 years of age; few would be under 11. All the boys who work in the nail manufacture are required to attend school 2 hours on four days in each week. These hours are from 4 to 6, or 6 to 8. All the boys work by day and night shifts. The day shift go to school from 6 to 8 and the night shift from 4 to 6.

The boys on the night turn get six days' wages, but they only work five nights. We allow our schoolmaster to take private pupils (day-scholars) before 4 o'clock. We have examinations of the working boys, and prizes are given. In the nail department the boys have regular meal times—½-hour for breakfast at 8.30; 1 hour at one o'clock for dinner. The boys in the mills get their meals during the same intervals.

We do not impose any qualification on the boys we employ, as to reading, or other education, but we always give a preference to the boys who have been in our master's day school. The boys generally leave our nailworks at about 16 years. They ought to attend school up to the time they leave their work. The boys are all paid by the firm on the piece-work system.'

1 *Report from the Commissioners, Children's Employment*, 1864. 3rd Report. p. 398

APPENDIX 18

Summary of Sirhowy Valley Ironworks Schools

School	Proprietors	Date Established	Number Attending
Capel Waun y Pound	Messrs. Kendall, Atkinson & Barrow	1784	30
Tredegar Ironworks	Samuel Homfray	1841	1840 — 157[1] 1847 — 421[2]
Sirhowy Ironworks	Messrs. Darby & Co.	1845	1847 — 128[3] 1856 — 250[4]

1 *Minutes of Committee of Council*, 1840-41. p. 225.
2 1847 *Reports*, Part 2, pp. 314-317.
3 ibid, p. 319.
4 *Reports from the Commissioners, Mines*, 1856, Parl. Pap. XVIII, p. 614.

APPENDIX 19

Summary of Ebbw Valley Ironworks Schools

School	Proprietors	Date Established	Number Attending
Ebbw Vale Ironworks	Ebbw Vale Co.	Girls' School, 1844 Boys' School, 1845	1844 — 157[1] 1845 — 174[1] 1868 — 423[2] 1873 — 382[3]
Victoria Ironworks, Ebbw Vale	Ebbw Vale Co.	1845	1870 — 202[4] 1873 — 197[5]
Machen Ironworks (Infants)	Machen Iron Co.	1837	1847 — 64[6]

1 1847 *Reports*, Part 2, p. 312.
2 *Minutes of Committee of Council*, 1868-69. Tabulated Reports, p. 621.
3 ibid, General Report for 1873, p. 188.
4 ibid for 1870, p. 261.
5 ibid Report for 1873, Appendix A, pp. 196-7.
6 1847 *Reports*, Part 2, pp 316-319.

IRONWORKS SCHOOLS

APPENDIX 20

SUMMARY OF IRONWORKS SCHOOLS IN PONTYPOOL VALLEY

School	Proprietor	Date Established	Attendances
Blaenavon Ironworks	Thomas Hill Samuel Hopkins	1816	1846 — 125[1] 1852 — 224[2] 1858 — 214[3]
Pontnewynydd Ironworks	W. Williams	1842	1846 — 245[4] 1870 — 218[5]
Abersychan Ironworks	British Iron Co.	1845	1845 — 248[6] 1865 — 218[7] 1870 — 299[8]
Trevethin Forge Infants	C. Hanbury Leigh	1832	1833 — 84[9]
Pontypool Ironworks	C. Hanbury Leigh	1842	1854 — 300[10]
Varteg Hill Ironworks	Varteg Hill Co.	1823	1833 — 130[11]
Cwmbran Ironworks	Ebbw Vale Co.	1842	1869 — 56[12] 1877 — 70[13]

1 1847 *Reports*, Part 2, pp. 316-319.
2 *Minutes of Committee of Council*, 1852, Tabulated Reports, p. 270.
3 ibid 1858, p. 318.
4 1847 *Reports*, Part 2, pp. 320-3.
5 *Minutes of Committee of Council*, 1871, p. 409.
6 1847 *Reports*, Part 2, pp. 324-7.
7 *Minutes of Committee of Council*, 1865-66, p. 324.
8 ibid for 1871, p. 621.
9 *Education Inquiry*, 1833, p. 602.
10 *Nefydd MSS, Journal for* 1854, entry February 6th.
11 *Education Inquiry*, 1833, p. 602.
12 *Minutes of Committee of Council*, 1869, p. 126.
13 ibid for 1877, p. 451.

IRONWORKS SCHOOLS

APPENDIX 21

SUMMARY OF BLAINA, NANTYGLO AND DOS IRONWORKS SCHOOLS

School	Proprietor	Date Established	Attendances
Nantyglo Ironworks	Harford & Bailey	Original school 1812 1836-37	1846 — 210[1]
Blaina Ironworks	Blaina Iron Co.	1845	1846 — 198[2] 1849 — 180[3] 1851 — 250[4] 1855 — 360[5]
Dos Nailworks, Newport	J. J. Cordes & Co.	1848	1878 — 98[6]

1 1847 *Reports*, Part 2, p. 278.
2 ibid, Appendix B, pp. 312-15.
3 *Minutes of Committee of Council*, 1850, Appendix 7.
4 ibid 1851, p. 402
5 *Reports from the Commissioners, Mines*, 1856, p. 274.
6 *Minutes of Committee of Council*, 1879, p. 409.

APPENDIX 22

YSTALYFERA IRONWORKS SCHOOL (GIRLS)[7]

Established 1842. Promoter: Mrs. Palmer Budd, Ystalyfera Ironworks, near Swansea. Tenancy at will.
Good building. Sufficient outbuildings, in good condition. 8 feet high, 15 x 12 feet.
Insufficient furniture and apparatus in good repair.
30 on books. Average attendance last year: 30. Religious instruction by teacher. Visited by minister and promoter.
English books only. Mistress's age: 48. Previous occupation: dressmaker. Commenced teaching at 45.
Salary: £13 p.a. School pence, £6.
House and garden rent free; also free coals.

7 1847 *Reports*, Part 1, pp. 329, 54, and 339-40.

APPENDIX 23

LLYNFI IRONWORKS SCHOOL[1]

Established 1845. Promoters: Llynfi Iron Company.
Resident Director: C. Bowring, Esq., Bowrington, Near. Bridgend. Tenancy at will.
Good building, sufficient and good outbuildings.
Dimensions: 46 x 20 feet, 12 feet high. Two rooms. Sufficient furniture and apparatus in good repair.
153 on books. Average attendance in last year: 83.
Teacher and monitorial: 9 monitors.
Religious instruction by teacher and visitor.
Master's age: 60. Started at 30, articled clerk to attorney.
Salary: £50 p.a. house and garden rent free, and free coals.
Mistress's age: 27. Started teaching at 16.
Salary £30 p.a.
Stoppage of 2d. per month on the wages of the Bowrington Company's workmen.

1   1847 *Reports*, Part 1, pp, 66-69.

APPENDIX 24

LLYNFI IRONWORKS SCHOOL LOG BOOK[2]

The log book of this school which dates from 1863, gives a description of school life in the mid-nineteenth century. It shows how much influence the works proprietors wielded over their workpeople, and their numerous visits to the schools are described. They came to listen to the children reading, reciting, and singing, and the children were given an annual tea-party.

The playground of the school was paved with stones. The school had three departments: 400 boys; 300 girls, and 100 infants:
'I remember a long, wide room, sloping down gradually to the dais at the bottom, where the head-teacher ruled. Discipline was unduly harsh. The children were very mixed—Welsh, English, and Irish. Several children were barefooted and pale. The curriculum was rather stereotyped and scanty. Reading, writing, and arithmetic mostly. Very little history, and geography consisted of map-drawing and remembering names.'[3]

The following entries from the log book describe some occurrences:
1863: Entry by head-teacher: "Fair school for Friday. I cannot possibly get a good school together on a Friday afternoon.'
'Sent after absent boys. Some of the parents burn the papers sent, and expressed a wish that I would not trouble them so much about the boys being away.'
'A boy named Fudge, nine years old, left school today to work in the tin-works.'
1864: 'A Government Inspector visited the school today to examine the children and to see whether they were vaccinated. Only three were not.'
'The boys appeared dull today—the copper smoke being very thick in the room.'

The reasons given for poor attendances on some days were: Llangyfelach Fair; Swansea Wool Fair; Animal shows.

2   *Llynfi Ironworks School Logbook*, 1863.
3   Williams, W. J: Llynfi school: *Cymru'n Galw*, 1938. Mr. W. J. Williams, M.A., H.M.I. who wrote this article attended the school in the 70's of the last century.

IRONWORKS SCHOOLS

APPENDIX 25

Maesteg Ironworks Schools[1]

Established 1841. Promoters: Maesteg Iron Company.
Resident Director: C. J. Hampton, Esq., Maesteg, Near Bridgend.
Tenancy at will. Good building, sufficient and good outbuildings. Area 30 x 36 feet.
Sufficient furniture and apparatus in good repair.
184 on books. Average attendance in last year: 70 girls, 50 boys.
Method: Monitorial with 10 monitors.
Visitation by minister and patron, English books; grammar of Welsh.
Age of master: 32. Started teaching at 22. Salary £60 p.a.
Age of mistress: 25. Salary £30 p.a.
Stoppage of 2d. per month on the wages of the Company's workmen.

1   1847 *Reports*, Part 1, p. 352.

APPENDIX 26

Inspector's Report on the Maesteg Ironworks School, 1851[2]

Boys' School:

100 present at examination; 82 left in last year. 80 admitted in last 12 months; 98 in ordinary attendance.

Desks and furniture moderate; fair books and apparatus; Organisation Monitorial, with sections for collective instruction. Fair. Fairish discipline.

Methods—want more finished application throughout. Master just gained his certificate, but has yet to make a commensurate progress in practical school management.

The faults of this school are as before—the want of a distinct and realised purpose to educate the whole of the children, which is at present, subordinate to that merely of instructing some of them, with a lower tone and discipline than ought to be witnessed, after making all allowances.

Girls' School:

120 present at examination; 74 left in last year; 86 admitted in last 12 months; 152 in ordinary attendance.

Moderate desks and furniture; fair books, and apparatus. Organisation Monitorial with enlarged classes, and sections for collective instruction. Good. Good discipline.

Methods very fair. Mistress—zealous and improving.

This school has made a good year's progress since November, 1850, and is essentially a good one in tone and discipline as well as in the work of an admirable set of reading classes, and a training to excellent needlework, with exemplary neatness. Its collective teaching to the little ones too, is steadily improving, while more effort is yet wanting with the writing and arithmetic. The general progress however, is exceedingly creditable to both teacher and managers, when the locality and the old habits of the population are considered.

2   *Minutes of Committee of Council*, 1852: General Report on schools in the Western District.

APPENDIX 27

Llynfi Schools (Report of Assistant Commissioner, 1847)

I visited these schools, for boys and girls separately, on the 9th March, 1847.

The schools are held in an upper and lower room of a building close to the works. The rooms are spacious, and that for the boys is well furnished with apparatus. In these schools books are found by the proprietors, and not out of the school fund. In the girls school I heard 23 read from the 12th Chapter of St. Luke. Only a third of the number read with ease. They answered extremely ill. Indeed I could obtain hardly any answers from them. The girls' room is not so completely furnished as that of the boys. I was told that they did not often go to receive instruction from the master in the other school. They are taught needlework.

The boys' schoolroom contains maps of Europe, Asia, Africa, America, and the World. Also of England, Jerusalem, and Palestine. I heard the First Class (seven) read from 20 St. John. The monitor of the class, the master's son, was a very sharp and well-informed lad. The other boys were the most ignorant that I have ever examined. I could get hardly a single answer from them, either upon what they had been reading, or upon the commonest facts of Christian knowledge. Apart from their ignorance of Scripture, their general information may be estimated from the fact that, after pressing them for some time to answer 'What countryman was Napoleon Bonaparte', one at length said 'a Russian'. On my requesting the master to give them a lesson in arithmetic, in his usual manner, upon the blackboard, he gave them one in compound addition only: none of those present, except the monitor, had advanced beyond the compound rules.

With good rooms and sufficient apparatus in one of them, the intelligence and proficiency of these schools was among the lowest which I have encountered. The proprietors are most willing to do everything in their power to render the schools efficient. It did not appear to me that they were well-conducted.

APPENDIX 28

Cwmavon Ironworks Schools[1]

Established 1845. Promoters: Governor and Company of Copper Miners in England.

Resident Director: T. R. Guppy, Esq., Taibach, Glam. Tenancy at will.

Good building, sufficient outbuildings in good repair. 30 x 20 x 9. Insufficient furniture and apparatus in good repair.

283 on books. Average attendance last year: 145.

By teacher only. Monitorial, 32 monitors.

Subjects: Holy Scriptures, reading, writing on slates and paper, geography, history, English grammar, Vocal music. 1 doing land surveying; 1 doing linear drawing.

Religious instruction by teacher. Visitation by patron. English books only.

Age of master: 40. Started at 23, copying clerk.

Age of mistress: 41: started teaching at 24. Milliner before.

Salary: £120 with house and coals.

Stoppage of 1d. in the £ upon the workmen's wages.

1   1847 *Reports*, Part 1, p. 62.

APPENDIX 29

OAKWOOD (CWMAVON), IRONWORKS SCHOOLS[1]

Established 1844. Promoters: Governor and Company of Copper Miners in England.
T. R. Guppy, Esq., Director.
Tenancy at will. Good building, no outbuildings. Both boys' and girls' schools 50 x 24 feet. Both furniture and apparatus insufficient but in good repair.
67 boys, 63 girls: 40 attend for less than one year.
Monitorial, with 7 monitors.
Religious instruction by teacher. Visitation by patron.
Subjects as per Cwmavon schools.
Master's age: 30. Started teaching at 27. Accountant before.
Mistress's age: 26. Started teaching at 18, dressmaker before.
Joint Salary: £109 p.a.
Maintained by the same Company as the schools at Cwm Afon, parish of Michaelston, Hundred of Neath, out of the same stoppages.

1   1847 *Reports*, Part 1, p. 62.

APPENDIX 30

CWMAVON WORKS SCHOOLS: AGENTS' EMPLOYMENT FORMS[2]

Every man employed at the Cwmavon Works had to complete the following form:

From the Manager:

To the..Agent.   184-.

You will engage one...

                              Signed..Manager

When a suitable person was found, the agent addressed the following:

To the Manager...   184-.

Sir,

I have engaged	....
Character	....
Where from	....
Age	....
Employment	....
Rate of Wages	....

                              Signed..Agent.

2   *Reports from the Commissioners, Mines*, 1846, p. 424.

APPENDIX 31

Specimen Receipts, Cwmavon Works Schools[1]

1. *Pupil Teacher's Receipt.*

Cwmavon Works,
September 20th, 1873.

Received of the Governor and Company of Copper Miners in England:
One Pound . . . Three shillings . . .and four pence for week's tuition as pupil teacher at the Boys' school due this day.
£1-3-4.   John Thomas.   Stamp.

2. *Receipts for cleaning school buildings.*

Four usual receipts for cleaning the following schools belonging to the Governor and Company of Copper Miners in England:
Cleaning Cwmavon Schools, 1862.
Cleaning Oakwood Schools, 1862.
Cleaning Bryn school and Tymaen Infants, 1862.
Cleaning Penycae schools, 1862.

3. Receipt for £10-7-9 for one month's service as master and mistress of Oakwood day and night schools, 1873.

4. Receipt of £1 from William Button for conducting Cwmavon Evening school up to this date. September, 1873, and April, 1862.

1 Cwmavon Works Schools, *Miscellaneous papers and documents.*

APPENDIX 32

Bryndu Ironworks School[2]

Established 1846. Promoter: H. A. Ford, Esq., Bryndu Works, near Bridgend.

Tenancy at will. Good building, no outbuildings. 60 x 18, 12 feet high. Insufficient furniture and apparatus in good repair.

143 on books, but 100 stay for less than one year.

Monitorial, 8 monitors.

No details of curriculum available. Religious instruction by teacher. Visitation by patron.

Master's age: 31. Began teaching at 28, Private gentleman.

Salary: £52-10-0. No school pence.

Stoppage of 1d. in the £ upon workmen of Bryndu Works.

Glamorganshire. Evening Schools at Tonmawr and Bryndu

Evening schools had started at Bryndu, but the master objected to the promoter's suggestion.

Tonmawr. 5 per fortnight. Reading, writing, arithmetic, etymology, geography, astronomy, singing.
12 pupils. Master is librarian in Mechanics Institute.

2 1847 *Reports*, p. 354, and pp. 70-3.

IRONWORKS SCHOOLS

APPENDIX 33

Tonmawr Ironworks School[1]

Established 1846. Promoters: Tonmawr Coal and Iron Co.

Resident Agent: Mr. Robert Parsons, Tonmawr, Near Neath.

Tenancy at will. Good buildings, no outbuildings. 9 feet high 33 x 15.

52 on books, and 52 attend less than one year.

Visitation by promoter.

Master's age: 18, commenced teaching at 15, single man.

Librarian to Neath Mechanics Institute: £5-5-0.

Salary: £54-10-0. School pence, £6-18-0.

Stoppage of 6d. per month on men's wages, and 3d. per month on boys' wages.

Tonmawr School, in Upper Baglan, 4 miles from Neath. 52 scholars. The works with which it is connected lie at the extremity of Cwmavon, and can hardly be said to have a road to them. There had been no school previous to the present master's coming a few months before. Among the scholars are five children of the agent of the works.

Those with whom I was most concerned, the working people's children, were hardly any further advanced, any of them, than being just able to read.

1   1847 *Reports*, Part 1, pp. 62-5.

IRONWORKS SCHOOLS

APPENDIX 34
SUMMARY OF GLAMORGAN IRONWORKS SCHOOLS (ATTENDANCES)

School	Numbers in attendance Year	Numbers
Dowlais	1828	110[1]
	1846	525[2]
	1855	642[3]
	1865	2,156[4]
	1877	1,568[5]
	1892	2,099[6]
Hirwaun	1846	55[7]
Georgetown (Merthyr Tydfil)	No details available	
Cyfarthfa (Merthyr Tydfil)	1854	295[8]
Penydarren (Merthyr Tydfil)	1877	200[9]
Plymouth (Merthyr Tydfil)	No details available	
Aberaman	No details available	
Neath Abbey	1846 (No registers kept for boys: 163 girls and infants)[10]	
Venallt (Glyncorrwg)	1846	72[11]
Ystalyfera (Girls)	1846	30[12]
Maesteg	1846	121[13]
	1854	183[14]
	1858	195[15]
	1868	208[16]
Llynfi	1846	143[17]
	1852	180[18]
	1866	252[19]
	1877	421[20]

1 *Minutes of Committee of Council*, 1844, p. 226.
2 ibid, 1847.
3 Notes on the Dowlais schools, *Copy of Memorandum*, 1892. This total excludes Roman Catholics.
4 *Report of the Pakington Committee, Minute* 3030.
5 *Minutes of Committee of Council* 1878, p. 279, this includes Roman Catholics.
6 Memorandum, 1892.
7 1847 *Reports*, Part 1, p. 54.
8 *Minutes of Committee of Council* 1856, p. 414.
9 ibid 1877, p. 411. This school is not mentioned before 1854.
10 1847 Reports, Part 1, p. 62; pp. 340-1.
11 ibid p. 63.
12 ibid pp. 56-7.
13 ibid Part 1, p. 352.
14 *Minutes of Committee of Council*, 1855, p. 250.
15 ibid 1859, p. 276.
16 ibid 1869, p. 669.
17 *Mines Commissioners*, 1846, p. 429.
18 *Minutes of Committee of Council*, 1853, p. 294.
19 ibid 1867, p. 641.
20 ibid 1878, p. 411.

IRONWORKS SCHOOLS

APPENDIX 34(a)

GLAMORGAN . . . cont.

School	Year	Numbers in Attendance Numbers
Tondu	1858 1865 1875	112[1] 139[2] 516[3]
Cwmavon	1846 1867 1877 1889	283[4] 261[5] 572[6] 1,057[7]
Oakwood (Cwmavon)	1846 1867 1877	130[8] 211[9] 204[10]
Bryn (Cwmavon)	1877	90[11]
Tymaen Infants (Cwmavon)	1880	250[12]
Aberavon	1854	240[13]
Bryndu	1846	143[14]
Tonmawr	1846	52[15]
Pentyrch		No statistics
Taff Vale		No statistics

1 *Minutes of Committee of Council*, 1859, Report by J. Bowstead, H.M.I. on British Schools for 1858, p. 337.
2 ibid 1866, p. 291.
3 ibid 1876, p. 214.
4 1847 *Reports*, Part 1, pp. 62-5; and pp. 70-3.
5 *Minutes of Committee of Council*, 1867, p. 669.
6 ibid 1877-78, p. 414.
7 ibid 1889-90, p. 561.
8 1847 *Reports*, Part 1, pp. 62-5 and pp. 70-3.
9 *Minutes of Committee of Council*, 1867, p. 669.
10 ibid 1878.
11 ibid.
12 ibid 1880-1, p. 732.
13 *Nefydd MSS, Journal for* 1854, entry for July 11th.
14 1847 *Reports*, pp. 70-73 and pp. 354-5. *Reports from Commissioners, Mines*, 1846, ibid, p. 430.
15 1847 *Reports*, Part 1, pp. 62-5.

IRONWORKS SCHOOLS

APPENDIX 35
SUMMARY OF CARMARTHENSHIRE AND BRECONSHIRE IRONWORKS SCHOOLS
SCHOOL ATTENDANCES

Carmarthenshire:

School	Year	Numbers in Attendance Attendance
Trimsaran ..	1846	42[1]
Gwendraeth	1865	60[2]
	1867	84[3]
	1874	96[4]
Amman ..	1863	115[5]
	1868	133[6]
	1871	200[7]

Breconshire:

Yniscedwyn ..	1854	200[8]
Clydach (Llanelly) ..	1844	180[9]

1 1847 *Reports*, Part 1, Appendix, pp. 6-9.
2 *Minutes of Committee of Council*, 1866, p. 410.
3 ibid 1868, p. 756.
4 ibid 1875, Appendix, Table D, p. 139.
5 Amman Ironworks British *School Logbook*.
6 ibid, entries for April 1st, and August 11th, 1868.
7 ibid entry for December 21st, 1871.
8 *Nefydd MSS, Journal for August* 1854, entry August 15th.
9 1847 *Reports*, Part 2, pp. 214-217.

CHAPTER IV

Sir John Guest's Education Scheme

FROM the standpoint of establishing schools for the education of the working classes, the Guest family of Dowlais, near Merthyr Tydfil was undoubtedly the most important and also the most progressive in the industrial history not only of south Wales, but of the whole of Britain during the nineteenth century. The Guest schools, the largest of their kind in the country, achieved as much fame as the Guest ironworks, and the Educational Scheme planned and implemented by the outstanding member of the family, Sir Josiah John Guest, M.P. (1785-1852), and his cultured wife, Lady Charlotte, was the most comprehensive and practical ever to be attempted during the last century, and for that reason warrants independent treatment and attention.

During the latter half of the eighteenth century four large ironworks were established in the Merthyr district at Dowlais, Cyfarthfa, Plymouth, and Penydarren, which became the largest ironsmelting centres on the south Wales coalfield during the nineteenth century. Dowlais, in particular, developed into a stupendous concern.[1] In 1815, six furnaces produced fifteen thousand tons of iron; in 1845, eighteen furnaces produced nearly seventy-five thousand tons, employing over seven thousand workers.[2] The Dowlais works covered an area of forty acres, ten of which were occupied by the works buildings. By 1852, it was estimated that no less than four thousand five hundred men, three thousand women, and three thousand children were dependent for subsistence on the Dowlais ironworks.[3]

Population figures for the first fifty years of the nineteenth century are even more striking. In 1801, Merthyr (including Dowlais) had a a population of 7,705 (or seven times the population of Cardiff in that year). In 1821, this had doubled, and by 1851 Merthyr's population had increased sixfold.[4] In 1839, Dowlais alone had a population of 12,000,[5] and, apart from Guest's original schools, there were but few others

---

1   M. Elsas, (ed.), *Iron in the making: Dowlais Iron Company letters*, **1782-1800**. Cardiff, 1960.
2   T. E. Clarke, *A Guide to Merthyr Tydfil*, 1848, p. 17.
3   C. Wilkins, *History of Merthyr Tydfil*, 1908, p. 218.
4   *Census Returns*, Glamorgan, 1801-1851.
5   *Reports from the Commissioners, Mines and Collieries*, 1846, p. 416.

available for the rapidly growing town. By 1846, little improvement had been made for the education of large numbers of young children: 'there were no schools of public institution except Sir John Guest's at Dowlais and the National schools at Merthyr. The tradesmen and shopkeepers of Merthyr naturally felt that they ought not to be called upon to contribute *pari passu* with the three great (iron) masters—Crawshay, Guest, and Hill of the place—to educate a population in the profits of whose labour the latter got the lion's share. Of the thirty-seven private schools which existed in Merthyr and Dowlais for the labouring classes, twenty-one were dame schools. Of the entire number, not more than three could be pronounced even moderately good; twenty-six were indifferent, and eight were very bad'.[1]

Guest had started one of his earlier schools in 1828[2] in an unpretentious building which was later converted into suitable stables to house the horses owned by his Company.[3] The original schools were for boys and girls, although the 1847 *Reports* said that only the girls' school existed in 1828[4] and sometime before 1844 an infants' school had been added. In that year the Rev. W. H. Bellairs, in his Report on Church schools said 'I visited schools for boys, girls, and infants, supported by the Dowlais Iron Company under the superintendence of Sir John Guest, Bart., and the history of these schools was as follows:—in 1828, a school was established on the National system supported by funds from the Dowlais Company. At that period, the attendance of the boys was from fifty to sixty; of girls, from forty to fifty. The payment was 1d. per week evenly spent on books and rewards'.[5] In 1843 and many years earlier Sir John and Lady Charlotte Guest[6] had made it known to Commissioners and Inspectors alike that they considered the Company's efforts for educating the labouring classes in the large village of Dowlais as being very meagre and unsatisfactory for a population of over twelve thousand,

1   1847 *Reports*, Part 1, p. 305.
2   In the files of the earliest *Letter Books of the Dowlais Iron Company* (Glamorgan County Record Office), one letter dated 1814 revealed that Guest had already opened a school for his workmen's children. The 1828 schools were therefore his second venture in elementary education.
3   *Notes on the Dowlais schools*, Education Office, Merthyr Tydfil.
4   1847 *Reports*, Part 1, p. 34.
5   *Minutes of Committee of Council*, 1845: Reports on 138 schools in the Western District by the Rev. W. H. Bellairs, February, 1845, p. 226.
6   In 1833, at the age of forty-eight, Sir John Guest (who was a widower) had married Lady Charlotte Elizabeth Bertie, of Uffington, Lincs. Henceforth this lady made it her business to provide every educational facility possible for the Dowlais workpeople and to this end encouraged and induced Sir John 'to do everything possible in the way of education'. Earl of Bessborough, *Diaries*, op. cit. William Edmunds: *Traethawd ar Hanes Plwyf Merthyr*, Aberdare, 1864, p. 47.

and were, moreover, greatly concerned with the long waiting lists for admission to the schools.[1] Accordingly they took the decision that new and larger schools must be built, and also decided that the 'instruction to be given in the schools was to be well-calculated to meet the wants of the labouring portion of the community, and to be of a quality, both from the religious and secular point of view, to leave a lasting impression of good on the minds of all who partook of it'.[2]

The Guests forthwith embarked on a most ambitious plan which envisaged the erection of entirely new schools on the most up-to-date lines. About this time, Lady Charlotte had persuaded her husband to buy Canford Manor, near Poole, Dorset, where she consulted the well-known architect, Sir Charles Barry (who was engaged at that time on plans for the new Houses of Parliament) to convert Canford Manor to her ideas while she herself furnished the mansion in the most sumptuous style.[3] Sir Charles was commissioned to design Guest's new schools which were opened in 1844, and a new infants' school was added in 1846.[4] This new venture inaugurated the second stage in the history of the Dowlais schools which lasted until 1855.

With the opening of the new schools, Guest entirely re-organized them and appointed a new staff.[5] The new headmaster, Mr. Mathew Hirst, a Yorkshireman[6] was assisted by two trained teachers from the Battersea Training School and several pupil-teachers.[7] The Boys' school was organized on a system of graded classes separated from one another by wooden partitions and curtains. This, in itself was an innovation of the greatest importance for that period, for separate classrooms, which became known as the Prussian or German system, was not introduced into this country until the London School Board adopted it after 1870 and became the standard pattern in elementary schools to this day.[8] The Boys' School also included a small laboratory properly fitted and well

1 *Reports from the Commissioners*, 1846, p. 416.
2 ibid
3 Earl of Bessborough: *Lady Charlotte Schreiber, 1853-1891, Second Volume of the Diaries of Lady Charlotte Guest*, John Murray, London, 1952, p. xi. Note also that Lady Charlotte promoted a school for the delicate children of Dowlais at Sully, Glamorgan, and at Poole, near Canford Manor, Dorset.
4 *Minutes of Committee of Council*, 1845, p. 226. 1847 *Reports*, Part 1, p. 34.
5 *Minutes of Committee of Council*, 1845. Also, C. Wilkins, op. cit., p. 222. These schools cost £7,000.
6 Mathew Hirst was at Dowlais for 48 years (1844-92).
7 *Minutes of Committee of Council*, 1845, p. 226. Battersea was Dr. Kay's (Kay-Shuttleworth in 1842) first Training College (see W. H. G. Armytage, op. cit., p. 114). Guest was one of the first to employ trained teachers.
8 Before 1870 elementary schools consisted of a large hall with tiered seats for classes, and a 'gallery' for infants, usually at the rear of the hall.

equipped with materials and apparatus for chemical experiments. The school was also abundantly furnished with the most recent apparatus, books, and maps.[1] The First Class was composed mainly of the sons of mechanics who were selected for a superior education to prepare them for the higher situations in the ironworks. They were taught algebra, arithmetic, mensuration, mechanics, etymology, music, reading, writing, drawing, Scripture history, English history, and religious knowledge.[2] In the Second Department the curriculum was more restricted and embraced mainly reading, writing, arithmetic, English history, Scriptural history, and the Church catechism. The Third Department confined its activities to elementary instruction. Throughout the school 'discipline and good order prevailed. The boys were clean and tidy in appearance and were much interested in their work. The Rector of Dowlais, the Rev. E. Jenkins, came to give religious instruction twice per week'.[3]

The Girls' School, in a separate building, was arranged in six classes, on the National system with a staff of one mistress, one assistant mistress, and twenty monitors. Each monitor was provided with a new suit of clothes every year.[4] The Girls' School also housed the Infants' Department (until 1846) and the small children, unless backward, were not retained later than six years of age. A separate enclosed playground was provided for the infants, equipped with circular swings.[5]

In the first few years of their existence the new schools rapidly established themselves and became the best of their type in Wales, if not in Britain. In 1845 Guest had also started the Workmen's Library which was described as one of the best and most attractive in the Principality.[6] The *Education Commissioners* in 1847 maintained that the Upper Boys' School 'had no parallel elsewhere'. It specialized in the teaching of science and mathematics, and later, logarithms and trigonometry were introduced. Mathew Hirst encouraged large numbers of young workmen to attend this school in the evenings to be taught mathematics, for generally speaking, boys were not allowed to remain at school after the age of fourteen.[7] This can be understood and appreciated when it is remembered that the Upper and Lower Boys' Schools were

1 *Minutes of Committee of Council*, 1846, p. 228.
2 ibid.
3 *Minutes of Committee of Council*, 1845, p. 228. *Reports from the Commissioners, Mines*, 1846, pp. 416-417.
4 ibid.
5 1847 *Reports*, Part 1, p. 306.
6 C. Wilkins, op. cit., p. 217.
7 This was quite an unusually high school-leaving age for the period when it was common for children to leave school around the age of 10.

always full to overflowing, though the boys in the Lower School were less able as compared with those in the Upper School.[1] Since the Upper School was so efficient and gave such a superior education, parents were in no hurry to remove their children.[2] It was precisely for this reason, viz. that boys were required to leave school at fourteen, that the Guests devised other means of continuing their education and, because of this need for further education, additional facilities were contemplated and later provided. By this time Lady Charlotte Guest seemed to be the mainstay of the educational side of the Dowlais works, and it is quite evident, judging from the numerous entries in her Diaries, that Sir John was in poor health and that she did most of the planning of what was to come in the way of additional educational facilities. One thing is quite certain—Sir John Guest started the day schools in Dowlais—but it was Lady Charlotte who developed them, secured new buildings, and envisaged a more liberal curriculum. It was most certainly her inspiration and vision that called into being the extensive and highly successful and popular evening schools which were the consummation of an elaborate and complete educational structure.

It was during this second phase of the Dowlais schools, 1844-1855, that the extremely ambitious and comprehensive Educational Scheme was evolved on the lines of a present day local education authority. No other works community could boast of anything approaching this scheme. By 1849, although there were already in existence three excellent schools for boys, girls, and infants, in addition to flourishing evening schools for adolescents, Lady Charlotte aimed at establishing nothing short of a complete educational ladder from the infant to the adult stage. It was without question the largest and most successful experiment in the field of elementary, and, to some extent higher education, during a century which was more concerned with the minima in educational attainment and school provision. The Guest Educational Scheme had a four-fold gradation carefully devised and planned: Infants' schools, Junior and Senior day schools, Adolescent evening schools, and Adult day and evening schools. Four successful Infants' schools existed at Dowlais, Gwernllwyn, Gellifaelog, and Banwen.[3] The Junior school consisted of the Lower Boys' and Girls' day schools: the Senior school comprised the Boys' Upper school. The daily average attendances for each department

---

1 *Minutes of Committee of Council*, 1850, Vol. II, p. 247.
2 ibid, p. 247.
3 ibid, 1849-50; 1850-51; Rev. H. Longueville Jones's Report on Church of England Schools, pp. 303-311. *Reports of Commissioners on the State of the Population in the Mining Districts*, 1850, Vol. XXIII, p. 417, ff.

SIR JOHN GUEST'S EDUCATION SCHEME

in this scheme (with the exception of the working men's day school) on 12 February 1849, were:[1]

Adult and Adolescent

Male Upper Evening School	23
Male Lower Evening School	93
Female Lower Evening School	127
	243

Junior and Senior

Boys' Upper School	45
Boys' Lower School	142
Girls' Day School	112
	299

Infants

Dowlais Infants	140
Gwernllwyn Infants	145
Gellifaelog Infants	131
Banwen Infants	51
	467

Total .. 1,009

The Adolescent and Adult schools consisted mainly of evening sessions corresponding to the various age-groups, of working men, boys, and girls. Lady Charlotte even went so far as to organize a successful day school for the workmen who worked alternate weeks at night.[2]

---

1 *Minutes of Committee of Council*, 1849-50: Statistics prepared by Rev. E. Jenkins, Rector of Dowlais.
2 Earl of Bessborough, op. cit., Vol. 1, entry for 1849, p. 224.

SIR JOHN GUEST'S EDUCATION SCHEME

PLAN OF THE GUEST EDUCATIONAL SCHEME

I
Adult Evening and Day Schools

- **Males** (Working Men)
  - Upper Evening School
  - Lower Evening School
  - Working men's Day School
- **Females** (Working Girls)
  - Evening School for older females

II
Adolescent Evening Schools

- Upper Evening School
- Lower Evening School
- Evening School for Young Girls

III
Junior and Senior Day Schools

- **Junior**
  - Lower Boys' School
  - Girls' Day School
- **Senior**
  - Girls' Day School
  - Upper Boys' School

IV
Infants' Schools

- Dowlais Infants
- Gwernllwyn Infants
- Gellifaelog Infants
- Banwen Infants

In October 1850, the Rev. H. Longueville Jones, H.M.I. had a complete list of attendances for all the schools in this Scheme. On 15 October, the highest total attendance was 1,141, and the lowest, on

28 October was 647, but this excluded evening schools.[1] In 1865, the total attendances, excluding evening schools, reached the figure of 2,156, which included the Roman Catholic school which Guest also promoted.[2]

The Upper Boys' School was Sir John Guest's particular interest where he drew freely on the older boys who were given jobs which required a good deal of technical knowledge and skill. Very often he would allocate a group of boys to watch and help the more experienced and older workmen engaged in highly skilled operations and also to the technicians who maintained and repaired the engines and other machinery. Just before he died, in 1852, he was considering a kind of day-release system from school for those boys who wished to specialize in the engineering departments, and had he lived to develop this idea no doubt he would have started some kind of technical school for this purpose.[3] Lady Charlotte made the evening schools, the girls' schools, and the infants schools her special interests. Since coming to Dowlais she had interested herself in the female population of the town, for it was a very 'remarkable transition' to her from a noble home and a wide circle of friends, to 'the cinder hole', as Dowlais was called. After a few years' residence there, she knew personally almost every child in the schools.[4]

In 1848-49 when the Educational Scheme was assuming definite shape and expanding, Lady Charlotte devoted a considerable amount of time to the various schools. In September, 1848, 'she was much engaged with the schools there for boys, girls, and infants, taking in from 500 to 600 children and she was also busy organizing a night school for the young females employed at the works'.[5] Throughout 1849, so enthusiastic was she in her educational schemes that she took to visiting some of her schools every day, and even from time to time gave lectures or lessons herself. Sir John found the extent of her school activities excessive, and

1 *Minutes of Committee of Council*, 1850-51: Report by H. Longueville Jones on Dowlais Schools attendances.
2 *Report of the Pakington Select Committee*, 1866, Minute 3030.
3 Earl of Bessborough, op. cit., p. 220.
4 ibid. p. 8. A note of her accomplishments is given concisely: 'her feat, in the midst of a very full and active life, in translating the Mabinogion, which involved not only a complete mastery of the Welsh language, but of the early mediaeval text in which these Welsh tales were written, as well as an immense amount of research, is an example of pertinacity and power of concentration, as well as intelligence, which alone could have made possible an achievement that must be regarded as very remarkable for an English woman to have performed. This great task took her eight years to accomplish. It was not her only literary effort for she wrote a book on the history of the iron trade, as well as pamphlets on technical iron processes.'
5 ibid, p. 222.

she undertook to limit her evening school visits to two a week.[1] Lady Charlotte's reforming spirit was kindled by another original idea. It was her usual practice when at her London residence to visit the City to purchase books and visual charts and maps for the schools and Workmen's library. She records in her diary that 'Merthyr (her usual reference to Sir John Guest) found the hawkers in the Dowlais market selling such trash that it occurred to us that we might be able to lead them to circulate something more solid and useful. For this purpose I have determined to put several volumes into their hands and entrust them for sale, giving them the benefit of a large commission. The object furthered was to collect books of good tendency and of a popular description, it being quite certain that if that class of literature should take with the people, the Hawkers would in future learn to supply themselves with it'!'[2]

By 1850 it was becoming evident that the accommodation provided in 1844 was getting too cramped, and in addition to the programme to which Lady Charlotte had committed herself, the school numbers were increasing year by year. One thing gave her lasting joy—her schools and projects were being appreciated by the Inspectors and other official enquirers, by many admirers on all sides, and above all, by the people of Dowlais itself. One admirer went so far as to give her all the credit for what was done 'for the mental and moral elevation of the Dowlais people, and if, after the lapse of many years, and the expenditure of vast sums of money, the results were not in harmony with her hopes, and the means employed, we must deem the ruggedness of the material operated upon as the cause'.[3]

The *Inspectors' Reports* for 1850 and subsequent years are full of commendation for the Dowlais schools, but showed some concern for the crowded accommodation. For 1850 it was reported that 'the Upper Boys' school has no parallel in any of the counties that come under my inspection. The tone, and the extent of education given there is much higher than in the schools of the agricultural districts. It is intended to train those acute engineers and miners, upon a proper supply of whom the prosperity of the great ironworks at Dowlais depends so much, and as no expense is spared, the object is readily attained'.[4] He referred to his *Tabulated Report*[5] for an account of the subjects taught in the school, and he

1 Earl of Bessborough, op. cit., p. 224.
2 ibid, entry for April 2nd, 1849.
3 ibid, p. 9.
4 *Minutes of Committee of Council*, 1850, Vol. II, Report by Rev. H. L. Jones on National Schools, p. 247.
5 ibid, for 1848-1850: Report for 1849, Appendix C.

promised a highly intellectual treat to any lover of education who had the good fortune to be admitted to witness the school in full operation.[1] Particular mention was made of the work of the schools in 1852, when it was observed that 'a good deal of individual teaching was being done in the Boys' and Girls' schools'.[2] Finally, the *Report* added 'did but the buildings correspond to the great work carried on within them, these schools might prove the envy of any town'.[3]

In consequence of the ever widening facilities offered in the schools and as the Educational Scheme continued to unfold, it soon became apparent to those concerned that yet another school-building programme would have to be inaugurated to cope with the rising tide of education for the 'increasing numbers of working class children' in Dowlais. After 1851, successive *Reports* continued to include adverse comments on the 'cramped accommodation' at the schools, and by 1854 it became quite obvious that if the schools were to develop further, new extensions or schools would be necessary for the boys' and girls' departments.[4] But Lady Charlotte was determined that the scheme should come to fruition, and although Sir John had died in 1852, she enlisted the aid of her new Works Manager, Mr. George T. Clark[5] who carried on 'with a number of new schemes for the welfare of the workers and their families, in addition to undertaking the intricacies of helping with the works management'. Clark proved to be the very person she was looking for and the fortunes of the Educational Scheme became as much a part of his life as Lady Charlotte's. One outcome of these 'new schemes' was the opening of the new schools in 1855 which inaugurated the third and final phase of the history of the Dowlais schools.[6]

1 *Minutes of Committee of Council,* 1850, Vol. II, p. 247.
2 ibid, for 1853, Rev. H. Longueville Jones's Report.
3 ibid.
4 ibid.
5 George Thomas Clark, 1809-1898. Engineer and archaeologist. Helped Brunel to construct the Great Western Railway. In 1843, went to India and started railways there, but returned to England on account of the climate. At the end of 1852 he became a Trustee of the Dowlais Estate and Ironworks under the will of Sir John Guest, Bart. For some time previously the works had carried on at a loss, but having procured the necessary capital, he induced Henry Austin Bruce (Lord Aberdare) to share with him the responsibility of the Trusteeship. Clark took up his residence at Dowlais and devoted all his energies to the development of the works, and the redemption of the estate. Under his regime Dowlais became a great training school which supplied similar undertakings elsewhere a much larger number of managers and leading men than any other iron and steelworks in the country. Was also an archaeologist and historian. Also did great work on the history of Glamorgan, especially the *Cartae et alia Munimenta quae ad Dominium de Glamorgan pertinent.* (D.N.B., Supplement, Vol. II, 1901).
6 Earl of Bessborough: *Lady Charlotte Schreiber,* p. xii. Lady Charlotte married Charles Schreiber, Tutor to the first Lord Wimborne, in 1855.

SIR JOHN GUEST'S EDUCATION SCHEME

The second and third parts of the Educational Scheme (which became a special feature of the schools between 1850-1855, and afterwards) were the adolescent and adult evening schools. Reporting on these in 1853, the Inspector said that 'the evening schools for adults and young persons employed in the works during the day were producing highly beneficial results. Everything pleased me—the earnestness of purpose shown by all engaged in them . . . the good behaviour, and cheerfulness of pupils and teachers . . . and the excellent progress achieved. But I ventured to throw out a hint for the consideration of the managers—that the teachers of the day schools should not be employed in evening classes: such severe labour would infallibly injure and diminish their powers of teaching in the day schools, which after all, are the most important'.[1] It is questionable whether the good and well-meaning Inspector's statement was true in that day and age when children were withdrawn prematurely from elementary instruction, and the twin evils of 'early withdrawal' and 'irregular attendance' such a characteristic feature of Victorian industrial society.[2]

The evening schools were attended by males and females. The female classes 'had the active aid in teaching and general superintendence of the ladies both of the clergy and of the principal persons in the ironworks'. Between seventy and eighty young women had attended the evening schools at a time, and were taught sewing, embroidery, including the more intricate arts of petit-point and point-devise, reading, and writing. The work achieved such a good standard in the embroidery classes that Lady Charlotte arranged exhibitions of their work.[3]

The third phase of the Dowlais schools from 1855 to 1892 was the most flourishing and successful one. The new buildings opened in 1855 had six hundred and forty-two pupils. The cost of the new schools (exclusive of those provided for Roman Catholics), comprising the ground, buildings, school fittings, etc., was borne by the Dowlais Iron Company to the extent of over £20,000, a very considerable sum of money in those days (equal to the first sum voted by Parliament in 1833 for elementary education for the whole of England and Wales!) and also at a time when the affairs of the Company were in an uncertain state financially. In addition, a very remarkable system of heating apparatus was employed, viz. large underground ducts connected the schools with the engine-house of the ironworks, and hot air was conducted through them to the various parts of the schools by special pumps.[4]

1 *Minutes of Committee of Council*, 1853, Rev. H. L. Jones's Report.
2 See Chapter X.
3 *Reports of the Commissioners, Mines*, 1850, p. 417 ff.
4 *Memorandum issued by the Trustee*, 1892.

The Catholic schools were maintained by a ½d. deduction from the wages of the Irish workmen and transmitted to the Catholic authorities who were also managers of these schools. One condition was strictly adhered to, namely, that the schools were to be inspected by government inspectors.[1] Two features characterized the new Dowlais schools after 1855. First, the schools were placed officially under government inspection in 1856 and thus became eligible for grants.[2] Nevertheless, when the income from grants and the poundage system on wages proved insufficient it was supplemented on a generous scale by the Dowlais Iron Company. In 1856 only £27. 10s. 0d. came from government sources, but in 1890 it had risen to £1,882.[3] Secondly, until 1855, the Dowlais schools had been conducted on the National system, the catechism was taught, and the 'visitations' were made by the Rector of Dowlais, Canon Jenkins. Henceforth, they were conducted on the unsectarian or 'neutral system'.[4] Here, as in similar industrial districts in Wales, Nonconformists formed a large proportion of the workmen. They made successful representations to Lady Charlotte and G. T. Clark, and were promised that the schools would henceforward be inspected by the British and Foreign School Society's Inspectors. The Roman Catholics, not to be out-done, requested and were granted their own schools, referred to earlier. In addition to the new Dowlais schools two others were opened in 1856 in the outlying villages of Pant and Pengarnddu, again promoted by the Dowlais Iron Company.[5]

It was during this third phase of the Dowlais schools that the Educational Scheme reached its fullest development and consolidation. The Junior and Senior day schools had already proved their worth before 1855 and the large numbers clamouring for admission had warranted the building of new schools. Lady Charlotte now turned her attention to the Infants' schools and also to other aspects of her evening schools. She employed more, specially trained, mistresses for the infants' and also equipped the schools with 'suitable materials and apparatus for young children' and made weekly visits to each school which were in separate buildings. Lady Charlotte was in complete accord with the nineteenth century view—and repeatedly stressed by leading educationists—that good infant schools, properly organized and staffed with competent

1 *Memorandum issued by the Trustee*, 1892.
2 Before 1855, the National Schools Inspector, the Rev. H. Longueville Jones, came at the express wish of Sir John Guest.
3 *Memorandum*, 1892.
4 *Report of the Pakington Committee*, 1866, Minutes 3233-3238. *Nefydd MSS*, Journal for August, 1856, entries for 13th and 14th August.
5 *Notes on Dowlais Schools*. Also, *Nefydd MSS*, 1856.

teachers, would do a great deal 'to improve the character of the preparative instruction in schools of this type, towards carrying on the education of young children by ten years of age to a higher point than was attained previously'.[1]

By 1858 there were over five hundred infants attending the 'admirably organized schools who received as useful a preparation for the work of the juvenile school as it was practicable to give them, care being taken on the one hand that the schools should not degenerate into mere playrooms, and on the other, that instruction should never be allowed to press too heavily upon the half-developed faculties of the infant scholars'.[2] Another aspect of infant school education was also relevant, as practised in the Educational Scheme. The Scheme had been planned to tackle the problem of early withdrawal from school—a feature, for reasons already given earlier—which was not so much a danger in the Dowlais community. Yet it was for this reason that Lady Charlotte devoted more attention to the infants' end (at the bottom) and the adult end (at the top). If the diagrammatic plan of the Educational Scheme is studied closely, it will be seen that more schools exist at the infants and adult levels than at the juvenile. In effect, the Scheme had aimed at the most favourable solution for this widespread evil, and it succeeded to a very satisfactory degree at Dowlais. Moreover, it was contended that the evil of early withdrawal could only be alleviated by holding out encouragements calculated to prolong education both before and after the ordinary school period— 'infants' schools should be zealously promoted on the one side and evening or adult schools on the other'.[3] Both were included in the Guest Scheme. The schools at Dowlais were not promoted merely for the sake of schooling and schools. At every stage they were planned with a purpose and sought to combat the prevailing ills of a society bereft of national guidance, or, indeed, experience of any precedent. The school system at Dowlais attempted to solve social problems by careful experiment and the provision of optimum conditions. Indeed, it could be said that the Scheme implemented at Dowlais contained many of the ideals and certainly the guiding philosophy which inspired the Education Act of 1944.

From 1855 onwards, judging from the comments of the Inspectors of Schools, the further education system of evening schools at Dowlais

1 *Newcastle Commission Report*, 1861, Vol. II, Report of J. Jenkins on The Mining Districts of Neath and Merthyr in South Wales, p. 479.
2 *Minutes of Committee of Council*, 1859, p. 311.
3 ibid.

were well conceived and organized and formed an integral and viable part of the Scheme. Attendances were most satisfactory, and more than three hundred and fifty names were on the registers with an average attendance of over two hundred in 1855. Two-thirds of this number comprised colliers' sons varying in age from eleven to twenty-six years.[1] The success of these classes stemmed from the personal interest shown by Lady Charlotte and G. T. Clark, and the practical value of a good elementary education was rewarded by the allocation of better jobs in the various departments of the works to those who had shown proficiency in reading, writing, and casting accounts.[2] In 1856, Mr. Joseph Bowstead, M.A., H.M.I., on his first visit as the Inspector of the British and Foreign School Society, conducted an examination at the evening schools and his report disclosed an average attendance for the winter session of four hundred and forty-three. He was very satisfied with the results 'considering that the candidates had done no previous written work'.[3] This was due in large measure to the efficient teaching staff which Bowstead acknowledged: 'These Dowlais night schools are almost the only thoroughly successful institutions of the kind with which I am officially acquainted, and their success is chiefly due to the peculiar circumstances[4] which have driven the managers to engage, at great expense, so many adult assistant teachers'.[5]

In 1862, although the headmaster deplored the early age at which many of the boys left school, he maintained that most of them even at ten years of age could generally 'read and write fairly, and would also be able to do the simple rules of arithmetic'. Hirst conducted a night school in the six winter months with an average attendance of one hundred and fourteen boys and an additional number of girls which made the total number up to two hundred, the boys ranging in age between ten and twenty years. In 1864, Hirst said in his evidence before the Commissioners how facilities were provided for the boys to continue their education: 'The younger boys generally came to night schools when they left the day school to go to work. They came pretty regularly during the weeks in which they worked on the day-turn. We used to have morning school from 9.30 to 11 for the boys who had been working in the night. We had to give up that class because it interfered with the day school. I found that the boys in the night school were very attentive and studious. The main

1 *Reports from the Commissioners, Mines*, 1856, p. 417.
2 ibid.
3 *Minutes of the Committee of Council*, 1857, p. 203.
4 ibid, p. 202. The 'peculiar circumstances' arose over the lack of pupil teachers at that time.
5 *Minutes of Committee of Council*, 1857, p. 203.

SIR JOHN GUEST'S EDUCATION SCHEME

object was to keep up what the boys had learnt and we found that many improved themselves considerably. The girls were not employed in the ironworks before the age of 16. There were many very respectable girls who came to our evening schools and the popular sewing-school from the works'.[1]

Undoubtedly, the chief reason for the success of the Guest schools was the efficient teaching staff, all of whom were trained teachers. In addition the schools had accepted government inspection for the purpose of maintaining high standards of efficiency, and grants for the augmentation of the teachers' salaries. At Dowlais, the monitorial had long been replaced by the pupil-teacher system, and the permanent staff received higher salaries than in other similar schools. This particular aspect of school organization was aptly described by the Assistant Commissioner in 1861 when he stated that 'The Dowlais schools were equally distinguished for their excellence, and for the munificence in all matters pertaining to education, of the Company, which established them. The teaching power was wholly supplied by a staff of able, trained assistants, at a scale of remuneration of course, greatly exceeding that which would be incurred by the employment of pupil-teachers, but securing at the same time for the scholars incomparably superior advantages to those which it would be possible to obtain with pupil teachers'.[2] This did not mean that no pupil-teachers were employed at Dowlais, but, that they were not employed at the expense of replacing trained teachers. In fact, the Dowlais schools were looked upon as a breeding-ground for these apprentice teachers—it was certainly the place which produced the finished article judging what they went through, from the evidence in the schools log-books. It is interesting to note that the log-books of more than one works school in other parts of south Wales contain references to the fact that they appointed teachers who had been pupil-teachers in the Dowlais schools. Indeed, this was a common occurrence in south Wales at this time—the constant mobility of trained pupil-teachers from one works school to another—i.e. pupil-teachers who had qualified as teachers sought appointments in other similar schools. In 1872, for example, a female pupil-teacher from Dowlais was appointed to the Miskin Infants' school (a branch of the Duffryn colliery schools in the Aberdare Valley);[3] in 1871, the Dowlais schools log-books confirm the appointment of a pupil-teacher from the

1 *Third Report of the Commissioners on Children's Employment, with Appendix*, 1864: Mr. F. D. Longe's Report, p. 395.
2 *Newcastle Commission Report*, 1861, p. 491.
3 *Duffryn Schools Logbooks*, Vol. 1, 1872, entry for July 15th.

SIR JOHN GUEST'S EDUCATION SCHEME

Llanelli copperworks school,[1] also the appointment of Mr. James Rosewarne Gray who completed his apprenticeship in the Foundry school at Hayle, Cornwall, in 1872,[2] and in 1876, the appointment of an ex-pupil-teacher from the Cwmavon works school.[3]

After 1860 the Dowlais schools reached their climactic—if it were only on a statistical basis. From six hundred and forty-two in 1855,[4] (day school pupils only) they expanded to two thousand, one hundred and fifty-six in 1865[5], and this total included Roman Catholics. In 1892, when the schools were transferred to the Merthyr School Board, the total number of scholars attending (excluding evening schools) was 2,492.[6] Lady Charlotte Guest's dream had come true, and long before this time Mr. W. Edwards, H.M.I., said in his Report of 1880: 'The children of Dowlais are educated in the fine schools of the Dowlais Iron Company, and the Merthyr School Board have so far been saved from any expenditure on behalf of this portion of their district'.[7]

This chapter is but a brief description of the educational scheme at Dowlais, and if all the information supplied by the Inspector of Schools, other Commissioners, and G. T. Clark to the *Newcastle Commissioners* in 1859 were included, it would embrace a respectable volume. Apart from describing the educational condition of the population at Dowlais during that period Clark included details of the works schools, their management and the attitude of the workmen towards them. Throughout the whole period of their existence the inspiration of Lady Charlotte and her indefatigable industry permeated not only the schools but countless generations of children from working class homes.

1 *Dowlais Schools Logbooks*, Vol. I, 1871, entry for April 3rd: 'David Gay commenced duties from Llanelli Copperworks school'.
2 *Dowlais Schools Logbooks*, Vol. II, entry for January 16th, 1872.
3 ibid, *Logbook for* 1876, Vol. 4, entry for January 26th.
4 *Minutes of Committee of Council*, 1856, p. 317.
5 *Report of Pakington Committee*, Minute 3030.
6 *Memorandum issued by the Trustee*, 1892, p. 4.
7 *Minutes of Committee of Council*, 1881, General Report for 1880, by W. Edwards, H.M.I., p. 305.

SIR JOHN GUEST'S EDUCATION SCHEME

APPENDIX 1
Dowlais Iron Works National Schools, 1846[1]

Promoter	Accommodation	No. of Children on books	Salaries
Sir J. J. Guest, Bart., Lady Charlotte Guest: Dowlais Iron Company	Boys' School 259	160	*Master:* £55 with coal and house rent free. *Assistant:* £45. P.T. £10.
Sir J. J. Guest, Bart., Lady Charlotte Guest: Dowlais Iron Company.	Girls' School 258	165	*Mistress:* £50, with coal, and house rent free. *Assistant:* £40. *Assistant:* £10 8s. 0d.
Sir J. J. Guest, Bart., Lady Charlotte Guest: Dowlais Iron Company	Infants School 172	200	*Master:* £60 with coal and house rent free.

Attendance in the three Departments in 1828: 110
Attendance in the three Departments in 1846: 525

[1] 1847 *Reports*, Part I, pp. 34-36.

APPENDIX 2
Report from the Commissioners, Mines and Collieries on the Dowlais Schools, 1846 [2]

The means of education for the labouring classes in the large village of Dowlais, with a population of about 12,000, were, in the autumn of 1839, very meagre and unsatisfactory. An important improvement was made in the Spring of 1844. A headmaster and two assistants were appointed from the Training establishment for teachers at Battersea, and the schoolroom was fitted up with desks, etc., according to the plans used at that establishment, which facilitate the labours of effective teaching. The number on the books is 150; the school is full, and there is a waiting list for admission. As long as there was little to be learnt at the school, the attendance remained scanty. The instruction is now well calculated to meet the wants of the labouring portion of the community, and is of a quality, both in religious and secular point of view, to leave a lasting impression of good on the minds of all who partake of it.
The First class have the opportunity of advancing in algebra, mechanics, and drawing, so as to qualify them for superior situations about the works. The progress in these branches, and in arithmetic was considerable. English, history, and instructive books of general information are read in the first classes, and a correct knowledge of language is imparted by means of etymology and grammar. The foundation is thus laid of a taste for reading, and a right direction given to the minds of the young. The incumbent, the Rev. Jenkins superintends the religious instruction of this and of the well-managed girls' school and infants school.

[2] *Report from the Commissioners, Mines and Collieries*, 1846, Vol. XXIV. Report of the Commissioner appointed under the provisions of the Act 5 and 6 Vict. c. 99, to inquire into the operation of that Act, and into the State of the population in the Mining Districts, 1845, with Appendix.

SIR JOHN GUEST'S EDUCATION SCHEME

It is understood, that if some contemplated arrangements take effect, additional church and school accommodation will be provided by the Dowlais Company for that populous district.

APPENDIX 3

COMMISSIONERS' REPORT ON THE DOWLAIS SCHOOLS FOR BOYS, GIRLS, AND INFANTS, 1846

'I visited these schools on the 29th March. The funds by which they are supported are derived out of a monthly stoppage of 4d. in the £ upon the workmen's wages. But the sum thus raised is also applied to provide medical assistance, medicines, and relief during sickness.

The girls and infants schools are held in an upper and lower room of the same building.

The boys' schoolroom is quite separate, in another place. The latter is divided into an Upper and Lower school.

The girls' schoolroom is well supplied with light and ventilated; it has the advantage of 3 adult teachers, 2 of them trained. I expected a great deal more proficiency in this school.

The infants' school is well supplied with apparatus—and the master appeared an efficient one. There is a small inconvenient room used as a classroom. The playground contained circular swings, and slag was on the ground as a covering.

Besides the stoppages upon wages, the children pay in the Infant, Girls, and Lower Boys' schools, 1d., and in the Upper Boys' school, 2d. per week.

The Upper and Lower Boys' schools occupy two unequal parts of a long room, well lighted and ventilated. The entrance is into the larger part, or Lower school, which is fitted with a gallery, running longitudinally, and divided, like the boxes of a theatre, into transverse sections by curtains. Each class has a section. The curtains can be drawn back, and two or more classes united for instruction.

The teacher of each class occupies the floor in front of its section of the gallery. Opening out of this, and partitioned off from it, is the Upper schoolroom, which in shape is nearly square, and also fitted with a gallery. It contains a piano; drawings from solid figures, done by the boys upon the walls; maps, and every kind of useful apparatus.

It is by far the best provided schoolroom which I have seen in Wales. I found 28 boys in it, receiving a singing lesson.

As a general rule, the boys are not allowed to remain in school after 14. The two schools are always full to overflowing and when this Upper School is once attained, it is considerably appreciated, and parents are in no hurry to remove their children. It offers the means of a thoroughly good, even superior education, which the master appeared well-qualified to give.

Attached to this school is a very well-furnished laboratory, of which use is made in lecturing. The master has an evening class of Adults—upper workmen who come to learn mathematics.

In the Lower School, I set the head class (27 boys) to write a few lines from dictation. Only six of the number could read tolerably; not one could be said to read with ease. In arithmetic they could do the simple and compound rules, but not readily and correctly. Finding the most advanced class in the lower school so very ignorant, it became important, in order to estimate the practical influence to the school, that I should ascertain from what part of the school the majority of boys leave it. No registers of admission or departure had been kept in the Lower school. I am indebted to the master of the Upper school for the subjoined particulars:

SIR JOHN GUEST'S EDUCATION SCHEME

Dowlais, April 5th.

Sir,

I have made a list, as correct as possible, according to the plan you desired when at Dowlais. I am anxious to state regarding the Lower school, that at present it labours under considerable disadvantage. Originally, there were two masters in it; but for a long time past, there has only been one—the place of the other that left never having been supplied. The second master has, therefore, had more to perform than he has been able to do efficiently. A third master has been now engaged, and he will shortly commence his duties.

I am, etc.,
MATHEW HIRST,
Headmaster.

R. R. W. LINGEN, ESQ.

32 boys were in the Upper school at the commencement; 56 have been taken from the Lower to the Upper school during the last three years.
56 have also left the Upper School.
32 of those who have left the Upper School are employed by the Dowlais Iron Company in the ironworks.
10 are apprenticed to various trades.
10 have left in consequence of their parents leaving the works.
2 are engaged as clerks in Merthyr Tydfil.

Note.—1 as an Assistant at *Sir John Guest's School in Poole.*
1 dead.
54 boys have left from the various classes of the Lower school during the last three years, without entering the Upper school at all.
20 of that number are from the first class alone (of the Lower school), consequently, upon the average the proportion of those boys who enter the Upper school from the first class of the Lower, to those who leave before entering the Upper School is nearly as 19 to 7; i.e. about 19 boys enter the Upper school for every 7 that leave from the First class of the Lower, without doing so.

MATHEW HIRST.

The result of this information is that of 110 boys who have left school during the last three years, nearly one half, 54, have not reached the Upper school, and more than one third, (54-20, is 34) have not attained even the first class in the lower school.[1]

APPENDIX 4
DOWLAIS GIRLS IRONWORKS SCHOOL [2]

Established 1828, by Dowlais Iron Company.
Tenancy at will. Good building, insufficient outbuildings. 86 x 18 feet, in bad repair.
Sufficient furniture in good repair.
165 on books; under 5, nil. From 5 to 10: 117. Over 10: 48.
Average attendance in last year: 110. 3 monitors.
Curriculum: Holy Scriptures; catechism; reading; writing; arithmetic; geography; English grammar; History of England; Vocal Music.
Religious instruction by teacher. School opened and closed with hymn and prayer.
Visitation by minister, patron, and promoters.
English books only.
Mistress aged 26. Assistant mistress aged 21
Mistress trained at Chelsea for 2 years.
Salary: £50 p.a. House and coals.
Assistant mistress: £40, house and coals.
Another assistant: £10. 8s. 0d.

1 1847 *Reports*, Part I, pp. 306-11.
2 ibid

APPENDIX 5

Dowlais Ironworks School, Boys [1]

Established 1844. Promoters: Sir John Guest and Dowlais Iron Company. Good building, insufficient outbuildings.

Lower School: 9 feet high, 64 x 18 feet.

Upper School: 9 feet high, 22 x 18 feet.

Sufficient furniture in good repair. 160 on books.

Average attendance in last year: 150. 2 monitors.

Curriculum as per Girls' school. In Upper school, algebra, mechanics and science.

Religious instruction by teacher. Visitation by minister. Patron also visits.

Age of master: 22; assistant master: 21.

Master trained for 3 years at Battersea.

Salary of master: £55. £10 from school pence.

Assistant Masters' salaries: £45 and £10 from school pence. House each with coals.

4d. in the £ stopped on all wages by the Dowlais Co. The sick fund as well as the school fund is covered out of this.

1   1847 *Reports*, Part I, pp. 306-11.

APPENDIX 6

Dowlais Infants School [2]

Established 1846 by Sir John Guest and Dowlais Iron Company. Good building. 9 feet high; 43 x 24 feet. Sufficient furniture in good repair. 200 on books. 14 monitors.

Average attendance last year: 60 boys, and 80 girls.

Note.—The bulk of pupils at school for only one year. Very few remain for more than three years (in the three schools).

No curriculum given. Religious instruction by teacher. Visitation by minister and patron.

Age of master: 28. At Cheltenham for four months.

Salary: £60 p.a. with house and coals.

Age of mistress: 19. At Westminster for 6 weeks.

Commenced teaching at 18.

2   1847 *Reports*, Part I, pp. 306-11.

SIR JOHN GUEST'S EDUCATION SCHEME

APPENDIX 7

GUEST EDUCATIONAL SCHEME, 1850

Weekly summary for October, 1850, of Junior and Senior day-schools [1]

Date	Boys' Upper School	Boys' Lower School	Girls' Day School	Total
1850 Oct. 7	41	95	117	253
8	39	102	129	270
9	42	97	134	273
10	41	98	125	264
11	39	93	121	253
14	40	101	124	265
15	43	100	135	278
16	42	103	131	276
17	42	90	132	264
18	41	91	137	269
21	40	104	134	278
22	44	108	143	295
23	44	113	141	298
24	43	106	139	288
25	40	101	135	276
28	42	100	123	265
29	40	136	131	307
30	41	132	159	332
31	43	129	152	324
Nov. 1	41	118	141	300
Total	828	2,117	2,683	5,628

1 *Minutes of Committee of Council for* 1850-1851: Report by the Rev. H. Longueville Jones, H.M.I.

SIR JOHN GUEST'S EDUCATION SCHEME

APPENDIX 8

GUEST EDUCATIONAL SCHEME, 1850

Weekly summary for October, 1850, of Infants' Schools [1]

Date	Gwernllwyn Infants School	Gellifaelog Infants School	Banwen Infants School	Total
Oct. 7	240	161	24	425
8	258	166	21	445
9	262	—	26	288
10	260	155	22	347
11	238	159	21	418
14	267	150	13	430
15	280	164	20	464
16	265	167	23	455
17	270	162	25	457
18	260	143	25	428
21	225	128	33	386
22	250	136	33	419
23	249	145	32	426
24	200	141	33	374
25	250	131	33	414
28	220	130	32	382
29	240	135	33	408
30	200	139	31	370
31	200	140	33	373
Nov. 1	191	121	27	339
Total	4,825	2,773	540	8,138

[1] *Minutes of Committee of Council*, 1850-51, Report by the Rev. H. Longueville Jones, H.M.I.

SIR JOHN GUEST'S EDUCATION SCHEME

APPENDIX 9

GUEST EDUCATIONAL SCHEME, 1850

Weekly summary of Adolescent Evening Schools [1]

Date	Evening School for working boys	Evening School for working girls	Total
Oct. 7	95	153	248
8	137	170	307
9	Church	172	172
10	169	177	346
11	Tea party	Tea party	—
14	205	170	375
15	215	184	399
16	Church	Church	—
17	217	201	418
18	174	170	344
21	193	191	383
22	203	197	399
23	Church	Church	—
24	156	175	331
25	154	136	290
28	Meeting	for Jews	
29	146	182	328
30	Church	Church	—
31	73	94	167
Nov. 1	99	128	227
Total	2,236	2,500	4,736

[1] *Minutes of Committee of Council*, 1850-51. Report by Rev. H. Longueville Jones, H.M.I.

SIR JOHN GUEST'S EDUCATION SCHEME

APPENDIX 10

DOWLAIS EVENING SCHOOLS: PAPERS SET IN EXAMINATIONS FOR PRIZES [1]

You are recommended to answer at least one question from each section.

Holy Scriptures
1. Write out the commandment which teaches you your duty to your parents.
2. How, and within what time, was the world created? Describe the creation of man.
3. Write out either The Parable of the Good Samaritan, or that of the Ten Virgins, and state what lesson is to be learnt from it.

Arithmetic
1. From 100,023 take 3,507.
2. Find the number of men in an army of 17 regiments—each regiment containing 1,012 men.
3. If a person who receives a legacy of £1,000 spent £457. 6s. 9d. in the first year, and half that sum in the second, how much will he have left at the beginning of the third year?
4. What would £2. 13s. 10½d. per week amount to in a year? Prove the correctness of your result by division.
5. If the diameter of a ½d. piece is 1⅛ inches, how many ½d's will reach 8¾ miles? Work this sum if you can, both by vulgar fractions and by decimals.
6. What would be the cost of a door 7 feet 6 inches high, and 3 feet 4 inches wide 2/3 per sq. ft.?

[1] *Minutes of Committee of Council*, 1850-51, ibid.

APPENDIX 11

Time Tables of Dowlais Upper and Lower Schools, 1847 [1]

Routine of the Upper School

Time	Monday.	Tuesday.	Wednesday.	Thursday.	Friday.
9 till ¼ past 9. ¼ past 9 till ½ past 10.	Hymn and Prayer. Slate and Mental Arithmetic.	Algebra.	Mensuration.	Slate and Mental Arithmetic.	Algebra.
½ past 10 till ¼ to 11. ¼ to 11 till ½ past 11. ½ past 11 till 12.	Recreation. English History. Grammar.	Drill. Geography. Etymology.	Recreation. Dictation. Tables, &c.	Drill. English History. Grammar.	Recreation. Geography. Etymology.
AFTERNOON:— 2 till ¼ to 3. ¼ to 3 till ¼ to 4.	Writing. Vocal Music.	Writing. Linear Drawing.	Writing. Experiments on Chemistry. Vocal Music.	Writing. Linear Drawing.	Writing. Vocal Music.
¼ to 4 till ½ past 4. ½ past 4 till 5.	Scripture. Hymn and Prayer.	Scripture.—Changing Library Books.		Scripture.	Scripture.

M. Hirst.

[1] 1847 *Reports*, Part I, p. 307.

SIR JOHN GUEST'S EDUCATION SCHEME

ROUTINE OF THE LOWER SCHOOL.

Daily Routine—1st Class.

Time.	Monday.	Tuesday.	Wednesday.	Thursday.	Friday.
9 till ¼ past 9. ¼ past 9 till ¼ to 10.	Hymn and Prayers. Church Catechism and Faith and Duty. Recreation. Slate Arithmetic.	Bible Lesson.	Reading New Testament. Slate Arithmetic. Recreation. English History—Spelling ditto. Examination.	Bible Lesson.	Examination ditto. Slate Arithmetic. Recreation. Pestalozzi.
¼ to 10 till ½ past 10. ½ past 10 till ¼ to 11. ¼ to 11 till ½ past 11.		Tables. Drill. Slate Arithmetic.		Tables. Drill. Slate Arithmetic.	
½ past 11 till 12.	Bible.	2nd Book Lessons.		Etymology.	Bible.
AFTERNOON:— 2 till ¼ to 3. ¼ to 3 till ½ past 3. ½ past 3 till ¼ past 4.	Writing. Pestalozzi. Drawing.	Writing. Mental Arithmetic. Bible.	Writing. Geography. Hullah's Music.	Writing. Mental Arithmetic. Reading New Testament.	Writing. Dictation. Geography.
¼ past 4 till ½ past 4.	Hymn and Prayers.—Dismiss.				

Daily Routine—2nd Class.

Time.	Monday.	Tuesday.	Wednesday.	Thursday.	Friday.
9 till ¼ past 9. ¼ past 9 till ¼ to 10.	Hymn and Prayers. Reading New Testament. Recreation. Slate Arithmetic.	Bible Lesson.	Reading New Testament. Recreation. Slate Arithmetic.	Bible Lesson.	Examination—Catechism. New Testament. Recreation. Slate Arithmetic.
¼ to 10 till ½ past 10. ½ past 10 till ¼ to 11. ¼ to 11 till ½ past 11.0 ½ past 11 till 12.0		Tables. Drill. Slate Arithmetic.		Tables. Drill. Slate Arithmetic.	
AFTERNOON:— 2 till ¼ to 3. ¼ to 3 till ½ past 3. ½ past 3 till ¼ past 4. ¼ past 4 till ½ past 4.	Writing. Reading 2nd Book. Spelling. Hymn and Prayers—Dismiss.	Writing. Reading 2nd Book. Spelling.	Writing. Drawing. Hullah's Music.	Writing. Reading 2nd Book. Spelling.	Writing. Mental Arithmetic. Writing on Slates.

PLATE 2   SIR JOSIAH JOHN GUEST (1785-1852).
PLATE 3   LADY CHARLOTTE GUEST (later SCHREIBER) (1812-1895).

PLATE 4   SIR THOMAS PHILLIPS (1801-1867).
PLATE 5   REV. DAVID REES, CAPEL ALS, LLANELLI (1801-1869).

All plates by kind permission of National Library of Wales.

ENGLAND AND WALES
Indenture of Pupil Teacher's Apprenticeship

This Indenture made the first day of August

18__ between Mary Ann Oliver of Dowlais, Merthyr Tydvil, Glamorgan of the first part, David Oliver of Dowlais Brother of the said Mary Ann Oliver of the second part, and George Thomas Clark of Dowlais House, Glamorgan, Trustees Henry Austin Bruce of Dyffryn, Aberdare Superintendents of the Dowlais school, of the third part; and Jane Oliver of Dowlais Mistress of the said Dowlais school, of the fourth part;

WITNESSETH that the said Mary Ann Oliver of her own free will, and with the consent and approbation as well of the said David Oliver as of the said George Thomas Clark and Henry Austin Bruce

doth hereby place and bind herself apprentice to the said Jane Oliver to serve her henceforth until the 31st day of December, 186_, (inclusive) in her business of a School Mistress in the Dowlais school aforesaid.

AND in consideration of the acceptance by the said Jane Oliver of the said Mary Ann Oliver into her service, and of the covenants on the part of the said Jane Oliver hereinafter contained, the said David Oliver doth hereby for himself, his heirs, executors and administrators, covenant and agree and the said Mary Ann Oliver doth promise and engage with and to the said Jane Oliver her executors, administrators and assigns, that the said Mary Ann Oliver shall at all times during the said term faithfully and diligently serve the said Jane Oliver in her business of a School Mistress in the Dowlais school aforesaid, and shall not, except from illness, absent herself from the said school during school hours, and shall conduct herself with honesty, sobriety, and temperance, and not be guilty of any profane or lewd conversation or conduct, or of gambling or any other immorality, but shall diligently and obediently assist in the instruction and discipline of the scholars of the said Dowlais school, under the direction of the Mistress, and apply herself with industry to the instructions which shall be given her by the Mistress, and shall regularly attend divine service on Sunday.

And for the considerations aforesaid the said David Oliver doth hereby for himself, his heirs, executors, and administrators, further covenant with the said Jane Oliver her executors, administrators, and assigns, that he the said David Oliver his executors and administrators, shall at all times during the said term provide the said Mary Ann Oliver with all proper lodging, food, apparel, washing, medicine, and medical attendance.

AND in consideration of the covenants and agreements hereinbefore contained on the part of the said David Oliver and Mary Ann Oliver she the said Jane Oliver doth hereby for herself, her heirs, executors, and administrators, covenant with the said David Oliver his executors, administrators, and assigns, and also as a separate covenant with the said Mary Ann Oliver her executors, administrators and assigns, that she the said Jane Oliver shall at all times during the said term, or so much thereof as she shall continue Mistress of the said school, to the best of her ability teach the said Mary Ann Oliver the business of a School Mistress as carried on in the said school, and afford her daily opportunities (Sundays and the usual school holidays only excepted), of observing and practising the art of teaching in the said school, under the superintendence of her the said Jane Oliver and devote one hour and a half at the least in every morning or evening, before or after the usual hours of school keeping (except as aforesaid), to the further personal instruction of the said Mary Ann Oliver in the several branches of useful learning usually taught in the said

---

Insert in the places where the undermentioned numbers occur particulars according to the following directions:—

No. 1.—The Name of the Pupil Teacher.
  2.—The Name of Father or Mother, or other relative or friend, who is a party to the Indenture.
  3.—The Names and Residences of a quorum of the Committee of Managers, if there be such a Committee; and if not, then the Names of the Trustees
  4.—The Name of the Parish or District, and the designation of the School, thus:—" Fulham National School," " Finsbury British School."
  5.—The Name of the Master or Mistress.
  6.—Here insert " Trustees" or " Managers" as the case may require.
  7.—Here insert " Master" or " Mistress" as the case may require.
  8.—Plural.
  9.—Here insert " Father," — " Mother," if a widow,—the degree of relationship of any friend.

N.B.—The Father, if alive, is to be a party to this Indenture. The Mother is to be a party only when the Father is dead; and another relative or friend only when the Apprentice is an orphan.

PLATE 6   PUPIL TEACHER'S INDENTURE (facsimile).

CHAPTER V

Works Schools of the Non-Ferrous Metal Industries

THE two important metallurgical industries which initiated industrial development in the western part of the south Wales coalfield were coppersmelting together with its allied manufactures and ironsmelting. The large-scale smelting of copper which became localized in the Swansea and Llanelli districts during the early years of the nineteenth century also created several important ancillary industries which were, in the main, juxtaposed to the parent copperworks. These included spelter, lead and silver, yellow-metal,[1] chemical (especially sulphuric acid), superphosphate, alkali, and brass works.[2] Two phases emerged in the evolution and expansion of the copper industry—each with its characteristic schools. An early phase, already noted in an earlier chapter, which was involved with the fortunes of Sir Humphrey Mackworth and his mines in north Cardiganshire, and with the early works charity schools associated with them. During the eighteenth century non-ferrous smelting works had spread into the lower Tawe valley around Swansea, where nine copperworks were in operation before 1800.[3] The later modern phase which started in the early years of the nineteenth century saw the establishment of copperworks at Swansea, Llanelli, Pembrey, Cwmavon,[4] Neath, and Taibach near Margam, Port Talbot. Each of these coppersmelting concerns, including the small smelting house at Crown copperworks, Neath, had its works school. Similar schools were connected with the Maesteg Spelter works, the chemical works at Pontamman near Ammanford, Carmarthenshire, and smaller schools associated with other non-ferrous smelting industries such as the lead and silver mines at

1 An amalgam of zinc and copper.
2 Vivian's (Swansea) works and collieries included the following: Hafod Isha Silver Works; Hafod Foundry and Engineering works; Hafod Copperworks; the White Rock Silver works; Hafod Superphosphate Manure works; Sulphuric Acid works; Spelter works at Clase, Morriston; Llythrid Alkali works at Parkmill; Margam Copperworks, and numerous collieries around Swansea and Skewen.
3 'Llangavelach', 1717; Gabriel Powell's Works, 1720; Taibach (Landore), 1727; Forest, 1727; White Rock, 1737; Middle Bank, 1755; Upper Bank, 1777; Birmingham (circa) 1791; Rose, 1795.
4 Cwmavon, another large integrated industrial concern, has been discussed in Chapter III. See also: Leslie Wynne Evans, Ironworks schools in South Wales, 1784-1860, *Sociological Review*, Vol. XLIII.

Ysbyty Ystwyth and Goginan in Cardiganshire, the lead mines at Rhandirmwyn in Carmarthenshire, and the lead and copper mines at Gloddaith, Llandudno, Caernarvonshire.

Two prosperous industrialists established two of the largest copper-smelting works in south Wales, the Vivians of Swansea and the Nevills of Llanelli. Their schools, the Hafod copperworks schools at Swansea, and the Heolfawr copperworks schools at Llanelli were the largest and the most important in the western part of the coalfield, being almost in the same category as the Guest schools at Dowlais. The commercial ramifications of Vivian and Nevill reflected a characteristic feature of Welsh industrial organization, namely, the integrated concern.[1] The two coppermasters owned and developed numerous collieries, smelted and produced lead and silver, brass and yellow-metal, zinc and spelter, and manufactured several by-products of the copper trade including sulphuric acid, alkali, and other commercial products. The copperworks schools catered for the workmen and families involved in all these industries, for all the early registers and account books of these schools were filled with the names of children whose fathers and brothers were employed in the copper and allied trades.[2] The development and growth of Swansea was intimately bound up with the rise of the coppersmelting industry—in fact, copper made Swansea. Its population in 1801 was only 6,091 but by 1851 it had swollen to 40,000.[3] In that year Swansea was acclaimed the copper centre of Britain and the copper mart of the world—the Swansea *Ticketings*, or weekly auctions of copper-ore attracted merchants from far and wide. The growth of the port reflected the magnitude of its copper trade: 'large and valuable cargoes of ore were continually arriving, with ships in long queues at the entrance to Swansea docks, from every country in the world where copper-mining was pursued. In 1814 only four vessels traded with foreign ports but in 1849 this number had increased to 771, the greater proportion of them directly engaged in the copper trade'.[4]

The first copperworks school in the Swansea district was associated with the White Rock, Upper, and Middle Bank Copper Companies. It was promoted by the two proprietors, Pascoe St. Leger Grenfell of Maesteg House, St. Thomas, Swansea, and John Freeman, and classes started in

---

1 A. H. John, op. cit., p. 137.
2 *Admission Registers, Account Books, and Logbooks* of Hafod Copperworks Schools, Swansea, and the Llanelli Copperworks schools.
3 *Census Returns, Part I*, 1801, *Abstract of Answers and Returns*, Swansea, p. 479; for 1851, p. 438.
4 *Chambers' Edinburgh Journal*, 1852, p. 234.

1806.[1] It was built by the proprietors and maintained by stoppages of a 1d. per week from the workmen employed in the three copperworks. The girls, for some unknown reason, paid separately at the works offices.[2] This school was later converted into a Boys' department and a new school for girls was opened in 1842. This initial venture was so successful that the coppermasters decided to turn their attention to the infants' side. In 1839, John Freeman presented another site which Grenfell used, to build the new Kilvey Infants' school which had over 200 attending in 1846.[3] The three Grenfell schools became the Kilvey Copperworks schools which were considerably enlarged in 1850 to serve an extensive area from St. Thomas to Pentrechwyth.[4] Pupils were admitted whose parents were not employed by the Company provided there was accommodation for them, and that they paid at a higher rate.[5]

From the outset Grenfell paid particular attention to the quality of his teaching staff, and among other things was insistent that all teachers in his schools should be fully trained and also inspected annually. To this end he applied for, and obtained grants from the Committee of Council in order to supplement teachers' salaries, train pupil-teachers and to procure suitable equipment. He was wise enough to ascertain the views of his workmen concerning the religious aspects of the schools. As in other areas the majority were Nonconformist, and although Grenfell was a Churchman he acquiesced to their request that the schools be conducted on an unsectarian basis. Grenfell was fortunate in his choice of headteacher, for under the guidance of Richard Gwynne the schools were rated as one of the best and most efficient in the Swansea district.[6]

The equivalent of the Guest schools in the eastern part of the south Wales coalfield were those of the Vivian family in the western part. The Hafod copperworks schools launched by this family and centred at

1 1847 *Reports*, Part I, p. 330: 'the site was given by Freeman and the cost of erection defrayed by Messrs. Grenfell'. *Miscellaneous Papers*, Education Department, Guildhall, Swansea. See Appendix 1.
2 *Education Inquiry*, 1833, Vol. III, Glamorgan, p. 1284: 'Two schools, one whereof containing 40 males and 10 females is partly supported by the White Rock etc. Co. who allow 13/4 weekly for instructing the boys of their workmen. The girls are paid for by their parents.'
3 See Appendix II. Also, 1847 *Reports*, Part. I, p. 330.
4 *Reports from the Commissioners (State of Population in the Mining Districts)*, 1850, Vol. XXIII, Monmouth, Brecon, and Glamorgan, p. 307: 'The Grenfell Company has erected spacious school buildings and a church for the population collected near their smelting works.' See Appendices 3 and 4.
5 *Miscellaneous Papers*, Education Department, Guildhall, Swansea.
6 ibid, Richard Gwynne was 'postmaster turned schoolmaster'. He was the father of Howell Gwynne, editor of the London *Morning Standard*, and of Bishop Gwynne, Khartoum.

Trevivian, Hafod, between Swansea and Landore, were among the outstanding schools of their type in the nineteenth century. Not only did they rank as one of the largest, numerically and structurally, but were conducted and organized on an extremely efficient basis, and from the commencement were staffed with fully trained teachers. In addition, the pupil-teacher system was given particular attention, for John Henry Vivian believed in efficiency—in teacher and pupil, in gaffer and workman, in management and boardroom—for he himself was a very remarkable man in more than one direction, as will be shown later on. One word appeared with unfailing regularity in the annual *Reports of Inspectors of Schools* from 1850 to 1903, the *Reports of Inspectors of Factories*, and the evidence of numerous Commissioners who visited Hafod during the nineteenth century, and that word was efficiency—often coupled with excellence.

The Vivian family arrived in the Swansea district in 1800, when John Vivian, of Truro, Cornwall, representing the Associated Miners of Cornwall, came to ascertain the prospects of coppersmelting in the area.[1] Vivian had some connection with a coppersmelting house on the south side of the Loughor river and in Gower, originally known as the Kenthouse Lead Works which were later converted to coppersmelting. The Association of Cornish Miners had reason to believe that they were not getting maximum value for their ores from the smelters of south Wales and decided to erect their own copperworks at Penclawdd. John Vivian was one of the managing partners, success crowned their venture, and convinced that the district possessed potential advantages for further developments, Vivian brought his family to settle in Swansea.[2]

John Vivian was a shrewd and far-seeing business man who, in order to ensure that the copper industry connected with his family started off on the right foot, sent his son John Henry Vivian to study the theory and practice of coppersmelting at various mining schools in Germany and Moravia. After spending several years abroad he returned to Swansea in 1810, his father acquired a parcel of land at Hafod from the Duke of Beaufort and the Earl of Jersey, in the names of his sons—John Henry and Richard Hussey Vivian—and built the North and South Works which were named Hafod Copperworks. Nearby, in 1847, the Hafod copperworks schools were erected.[3]

1 H. Hamilton, *The English Brass and Copper Industries to* 1800, 1926, pp. 213-236.
   E. Phillips, *History of the Pioneers of the Welsh Coalfields*, 1925, p. 46.
2 H. Hamilton, op. cit., p. 213.
3 The school was originally opened in 1846, but in temporary buildings.

WORKS SCHOOLS OF THE NON-FERROUS METAL INDUSTRIES

Richard Hussey Vivian, one of the original partners, had no truck with coppersmelting, made the Army his career, and at the end of the Peninsular War was created a Baron, with the title of Lord Vivian. John Henry Vivian, on the other hand, became the driving force behind the Hafod industrial machine. Having had a sound and expensive technical education, and practical training in all the complicated processes of coppersmelting including leadsmelting and the extraction of silver, he had gained a specialized knowledge of metallurgy in German smelting works and towns. He became the acknowledged authority on coppersmelting during the nineteenth century, contributed authoritative papers to the *Annals of Philosophy*, was elected a Fellow of the Royal Society, and was on intimate terms with the leading scientists of the day including Sir Michael Faraday and Sir Humphrey Davy.[1] In 1832 he was elected Member of Parliament for Swansea and remained so until his death in 1855. The management of the copper trade passed into the hands of his son, Sir Hussey Vivian, who also became M.P. for the same constituency and was later created the first Lord Swansea.

Long before the building of the Hafod schools, J. H. Vivian and his wife had interested themselves in the provision of schools in Swansea, being 'constantly deeply conscious of the almost complete lack of educational facilities in the Swansea district'. The efforts of the Rev. E. B. Squire, the Vicar of Swansea, to provide National schools for the town were considerably enhanced by the practical support shown by Vivian who 'subscribed most liberally towards their maintenance' every year.[2] But Vivian had also started his own schools on a small scale with his wife as 'a tireless supporter'. Realizing that something had to be done for the large masses of working-class children, Mrs. Vivian started a small school of forty girls in the parish of St. John in 1825[3] and also a Model Dame School in the grounds of their residence at Singleton Park.[4]

1 *Chambers' Edinburgh Journal*, p. 235: J. H. Vivian's standard works on metallurgy were, with some modifications, re-written by Drs. Ure and Lardner, the nineteenth century metallurgical authorities.
2 *Minutes of Committee of Council*, 1848, Mr. H. Longueville Jones's Report on Wales
3 *Education Inquiry*, 1833, Vol. III, p. 1281.
4 *Minutes of Committee of Council*, 1848-49. Appendix to J. Fletcher's Report: 'The Cottage Dame School had accommodation for 25 boys and girls occupying a pretty Swiss cottage in the grounds of J. H. Vivian, M.P. This is a Model Dame School for children of both sexes . . . who receive individual instruction from an excellent matron in reading, writing and arithmetic, with knitting for the boys and both knitting and sewing for the girls, and form at the same time a picture for a painter'. Note: What a continuity of academic tradition we have here—from Swiss Cottage and Dame School to University College! Vivian's (Lord Swansea) residence became the original nucleus of University College, Swansea, founded in 1920, developing into the imposing modern campus around the mansion in Singleton Park today.

Although these efforts were commendable, and effective within their limits, the major problem of educating large numbers of workmen's children still remained, for, compared with the schools already in active commission through the efforts of his neighbour, P. St. Leger Grenfell, Vivian's ventures were somewhat limited. But within a few years J. H. Vivian's best work was yet to come. His fellow Member of Parliament and friend was Sir Josiah John Guest who already had achieved a reputation for establishing more than one school for his workmen's children at Dowlais. There is no reason to doubt that Vivian had discussed this matter with him and had also visited Guest's earlier schools. Both industrialists had heard the Reform Parliament discussing and voting the sum of £20,000 for educational purposes in 1833 and the setting up of the *Committee of Privy Council on Education*; both had witnessed the industrial unrest and Chartist outbreaks in 1839, and had heard the rejection in the House of Sir James Graham's controversial Factory Bill of 1843 with its insidious proposals regarding education.[1] Withal, in March, 1846, both had heard the clarion call—the long but stirring oration of William Williams, M.P.—demanding an inquiry into the state of education in the Principality.[2]

Some significance might be attached to the opening of the Hafod copperworks schools in February, 1847,[3] although they were not established directly as a result of the *Commission of Inquiry*, for the *Reports* did not appear until the latter part of that year. However, Vivian had been visited and interviewed by the Assistant Commissioners and was sensitive about his meagre contribution. He had also, no doubt, concluded that it would be a long time before schools could be established by the State, and the rejection of Graham's Bill had confirmed his view. The religious issues inherent in the Bill had repercussions on Vivian's school activities in Swansea regarding the 'conduct' of the schools, i.e. whether they were to be conducted on the National or British system. He gave this matter very careful thought for he was aware that the majority of his workmen were Nonconformists and when the Hafod schools were opened he decided to conduct them on an undenominational or "neutral" basis, and by this action endeared himself to his employees. Thus the schools became British and were inspected by the inspectors of the British and Foreign School Society.[4]

1 D. Salmon, The story of a Welsh Education Commission, 1846-7, *Y Cymmrodor*, Vol. XXIV, p. 189. Frank Smith, op. cit., pp. 194-5.
2 *Hansard's Parliamentary Debate*, 1846, 10th March.
3 Education Department, Guildhall, Swansea: Register of Boys, Hafod Schools, 1854-94, with Notes by W. G. Williams, teacher at the School. See Appendices 5 and 6.
4 *Report of Pakington Committee*, op. cit., p. 197, Minutes 3931-36.

The Hafod schools were built in three stages at a cost of between two and three thousand pounds.[1] It was thought at first that one building would suffice as a mixed school, and for this purpose a wooden partition was erected along the length of the schoolroom with boys on one side and girls on the other. But this arrangement proved unsatisfactory, for the schoolroom soon became overcrowded because children were flocking to the school.[2] The original schoolroom was given over to the girls, a new boys' department was added and in 1848 a new Infants' schoolroom completed the first Hafod scheme. Again the additional accommodation proved totally inadequate and the schools were crowded once more although preference was given to children whose parents were employed in Vivian's undertakings.[3]

From their inception the schools enjoyed the services of fully trained teachers and a careful search was made in the various Model and Training schools for suitable ones. In 1848, for example, a few weeks before the opening of the new Infants' school, Vivian and his son paid a special visit to the Home and Colonial Institution in London to choose a suitable mistress who had been trained in the Pestalozzian methods. They appointed a Mrs. Finlay who started a long association with the Hafod schools and her work was continued by her daughter until the Infants' school was closed in 1903.[4]

Children attending the school were of two types. The works children were the sons and daughters of Vivian's workmen who had the first right of admission, were instructed free of charge but their parents contributed a 1d. per week from their wages. The 'pay' children were admitted, but only if there were vacancies, since their parents were unconnected with the works. Payment varied between 1d. and 2d. per week according to the number in each family.[5] The schools attracted pupils from the out-lying districts as far as Pontarddulais, Llangyfelach, Birchgrove, Sketty and Cockett.[6] Two registers were kept—for works and 'pay' pupils—and the headteachers were enjoined to adhere strictly to this distinction. Between 1847 and 1852 no registers were kept but attendances were transmitted as a weekly return to the works offices. The first name of interest on the

1 *Reports from Commissioners, Mining Districts,* 1850. Vol. XXIII, *Minutes of Committee of Council,* 1847-48, Vol. II, p. 298 ff. John Lewis, *The Swansea Guide,* W. M. Brewster, 1851, p. 50.
2 Anon, *A Brief History of the Hafod Copperworks School from its Foundation, Swansea,* 1905, p. 4. This pamphlet unfortunately contains only very general information.
3 *Notes* by W. G. Williams.
4 *A Brief History,* p. 7.
5 *Admission Registers, Hafod schools.*
6 ibid.

1852 register was that of Walter Hogg who eventually became an inspector of schools. The 'works children' register contained the names of children from 1852 to 1894, after which year no school payments were exacted.[1]

From 1847 to 1854 the Hafod schools paid their way without grants from any source, the school pence of the 'pay' pupils covering the cost of books and apparatus.[2] The teachers' salaries, payments to pupil-teachers and building maintenance 'were derived wholly from the liberality of Mr. Vivian and the poundage levy. The teachers and pupil-teachers were young, active, well instructed, and of the most recent training at the London Borough Road Schools.'[3] In 1857 the schools underwent a fundamental change in many directions. With the aid of grants from the Committee of Privy Council they were 'extensively renovated and extended, classrooms were added, more pupil-teachers were recruited, and the last remains of the old monitorial system gave way to class instruction by trained teachers'.[4]

The progress and development of the schools are set out in great detail in the school logbooks from 1862. Day to day progress is faithfully recorded, the Inspector's *Report* is appended at the close of each school year, together with staffing and pupil-teacher establishment. In 1864, for example, at the boys' school, the headteacher, Mr. J. M. Carr had two qualified assistants and four pupil-teachers, and in 1874, four qualified assistants and six pupil-teachers. Other entries refer to Mrs. Vivian's weekly visits when she always listened to the reading and dictation lessons and saw that everything generally was in order.[5] It remains to mention briefly the main characteristics of the Hafod schools. They started with 350 pupils in 1847 and this number had risen to 521 in 1865, and by 1893 there was a school roll of 1,114, with an average attendance of 889. The schools were purchased and taken over by the Swansea School Board in 1898.[6] In 1849 they were described as 'three large schools erected by Mr. Vivian for the use of his workpeople, which rival in size those of Sir John Guest at Dowlais'.[7] In 1859 the Inspector's *Report* referred to them as 'excellent and efficient schools, and at the head of the list of the

1 *Admission Registers, Hafod Schools.*
2 *Minutes of Committee of Council*, 1847-48, Vol. II, Appendix, p. 29.
3 ibid.
4 *Report of the British and Foreign Schools Society*, 1858, p. 86.
5 *Hafod Copperworks Schools Logbooks*, 1863-1900.
6 G. J. Jones, Winning poem on the Hafod Schools, Morriston Eisteddfod, 26 September 1854. *Minutes of Committee of Council*, 1865-66. Tabulated Reports on Wales, Rev. B. J. Binns. Tabulated Reports for 1895, p. 289; Vivian *MSS and Papers*, 1840-1923, D/DGV, 36. *Glamorgan County Record Office.*
7 *Minutes of Committee of Council*, 1848-49: Appendix to J. Fletcher's Report.

best schools in Wales'.[1] Vivian also promoted and subscribed to two other schools—one at his Court Herbert Colliery at Skewen, and the Sketty National School.[2]

Before concluding this survey of Vivian's educational efforts two other matters are of interest. Swansea, in common with other industrial areas in south Wales, experienced the problem of 'the works versus the works school', i.e. the works always attracted more boys than the school because employment was readily available and offered quick rewards, but the higher classes in such schools suffered from low attendances. Vivian did his utmost to counteract this evil by introducing evening classes which were however not a successful feature of his schools. The other matter concerned an aspect of the voluntary system known as the 'pure voluntaryists' who were against any form of State aid in education and also comdemned employers of labour for assuming responsibility for educating working-class children.[3] The Rev. David Rees, an Independent minister in Llanelli, and the leading protagonist of the Voluntaryists, praised and condemned the Swansea coppermasters in the same breath: '... y mae ysgolion J. H. Vivian, Ysw., A.S., ac ysgolion Foxhole (Kilvey) dan ofal P. St. Leger Grenfell, Ysw., Maesteg House, yn ardal Abertawe. Y mae'r ddau foneddwr uchod yn ddynion rhyddfrydig eu barn wleidiadol, ac yn sefyll yn y rhes flaenaf fel meistri. Cadwant eu gweithiau ymlaen yn gyson; rhoddant gyflogau da i'w gweithwyr, a chant fyned lle y mynnent i bwrcasu cynhaliaeth. Y mae hyn yn wir ganmoladwy, a thrueni fod brycheuyn mor ddu a'r ysgolion hyn ar eu cymeriadau'.[4]

Llanelli, at the beginning of the nineteenth century was mainly concerned with coalmining and ironsmelting and had a population of just under 3,000.[5] In 1804, Charles Nevill of Birmingham, who was in charge of a coppersmelting house at Swansea, went into partnership with three other smelters, moved to Llanelli and started coppersmelting.[6] He

1 *Minutes of Committee of Council*, 1858-59: Report on British Schools by Joseph Bowstead.
2 J. Bowstead, *Letters concerning education in Wales (South) suggested by a recent charge of the Bishop of St. David's*, 1861. Printed by W. Partridge, Stroud, p. 21.
3 See Chapter 12. See also Leslie Wynne Evans, Voluntary Education in the Industrial Areas of Wales before 1870, *N.L.W. Journal*, Vol. XIV, No. 4, 1966, pp. 407-23.
4 Rev. David Rees: *Y Diwygiwr*, Rhif. 216, Gorff. 1853, Cyf. XVIII, p. 223: 'The schools of J. H. Vivian and P. St. Leger Grenfell, near Swansea, are in the hands of two gentlemen whose political views are Liberal and are in the foremost ranks of good proprietors of works. They keep their works in constant operation, pay good wages to their workmen and allow them to purchase their food wherever they wish. This is most praiseworthy, but it is deplorable that these schools are such a black stain on their characters.'
5 *Census Returns* for 1801 and 1821: population in 1801, 2,972; in 1821, 5,649.
6 Leslie Wynne Evans, *History of Carmarthenshire*, Vol. II, pp. 361, ff. Messrs. Daniel, Saville and Guest.

became the copper 'king', and the Nevill family, like the Vivians at Swansea, played a leading role in the industrial development of Llanelli for the next hundred years and promoted and established schools for their employees. Charles Nevill died in 1813, and his son, Richard Janion Nevill entered the partnership with Druce,[1] and along with other prominent industrialists of the town such as Pemberton, Raby, and Warde, became an ardent supporter of the Llanelli Free schools mentioned earlier.[2] The only other schools in the town were the numerous private adventure and dame schools which did a thriving business in instructing 'principally workmen's children, the children of mechanics, and the children of labourers, mariners, coppermen, and colliers'.[3]

By 1840 the population of Llanelli had increased very rapidly, copper smelting became prosperous, and Nevill and his Company were also engaged in developing many new industries associated with lead and silver, yellow-metal and brass, and numerous new collieries appeared in the vicinity of the town.[4] At that time Llanelli had no National or British school and Nevill realised that something more was required than the small Free schools and the numerous private ones. In his evidence before the *Commissioners of Inquiry* in 1846, Nevill gave an account of the educational state of the town and urged that something should be done to 'improve and extend the system of education in the rapidly expanding parish for boys and girls'. By that time Nevill had made preliminary moves to open new schools in connection with his Company, and without disclosing this information to the Commissioners, said that 'considerable efforts to that end were being made in Llanelli'. He was of the opinion that if every married man could be induced or compelled to contribute towards the education of his children, there would be some inducement to send them to school.[5] Nevill, some years before, had already played with the idea of establishing a school in connection with his Company, for sometime before 1846 an experimental kind of copperworks school was carried on at the 'Barracks'—a store room in the copperworks yard. At the end of 1846 school buildings for boys and infants were started[6]

1 In 1823, the partners were Daniel, Nevill, Druce & Co.
2 Chapter 1. See also Leslie Wynne Evans, Colliery schools in South Wales in the Nineteenth Century, *N.L.W. Journal*, Vol. X, No. 2, 1957, p. 137.
3 1847 *Reports*, op. cit., Part 1, pp. 36, 213, and 380.
4 Leslie Wynne Evans, *History of Carmarthenshire*, Vol. II, p. 364
5 1847 *Reports*, op. cit., Part 1, Appendix, p. 486: Evidence respecting the mining and manufacturing districts, Carmarthenshire, 6th April, 1847. *Nevill MSS:* Letter dated 4th March, 1839, shows that Nevill was a keen educationist, and also his son James had been to school at Bridgnorth with Dr. Rowley, and Oriel College, Oxford; another son, Henry, was with Dr. Arnold at Rugby.
6 1847 *Reports*, op. cit., Part 1, Appendix, p. 209.

and came into commission in 1847.[1] In 1848, 'comfortable teachers' houses were added to the copperworks schools'[2] and in January, 1852, the schools were completed by the addition of a girls' department.[3] The primary function of these schools was to serve the needs of children whose parents were employed by the Copperworks Company which had a variety of interests comprising the Copperworks, Lead works, Silver works, the Old Lodge Ironworks, the Wern Foundry, numerous collieries, and the 'Pilots'—the Nevill Dock and Wharf Department, including the shipbuilding yard.[4] Nevill also admitted the children of other working-class parents not employed at the works. In addition to the contributions made by the workmen from their wages, all children were required to pay school pence, the fees being carefully graded for children coming from the same family, while the children of other workmen not employed by Nevill had to pay 1d. per week extra. Any deficit at the end of the year in the cost of maintaining the schools was defrayed by the Company, but this was never excessive and lasted only a few years until eventually the schools cost nothing.[5]

Nevill was extremely fortunate in his choice of headteachers and the development of the schools can be reviewed briefly in two stages up to 1894 corresponding to their periods of stewardship. The first period from 1847 to 1863 had David Williams as headteacher, a ruthless disciplinarian of the benevolent kind, who made the school so successful that it was recognised as 'one of the best in Wales'. He had been trained at Brecon and knew 'how to teach and to drill a school'.[6] In 1862, the year before he left to take up duties as the South Wales Agent for the British and Foreign School Society (succeeding the Rev. William Roberts (Nefydd)) the Inspector's annual *Report* stated that 'reading, writing, and arithmetic, and all the ordinary subjects were admirably taught in

---

1 *Minutes of Committee of Council*, 1847–48, Vol. II, p. 300.
2 ibid, 1848-49, Report of J. Fletcher, Appendix, 11th June, 1848.
3 *Minutes of Committee of Council*, 1852. General Report by Mathew Arnold, H.M.I. on British, Wesleyan, and other Denominational schools inspected in the Midland District of England and Wales. See Appendix 15.
4 *MS letter*, undated, '*Reminiscences re Copperworks School, Llanelli*,' addressed from Beaumont House, Goring Road, Llanelli, Llanelli Public Library.
5 ibid.
6 *Nefydd MSS, Journal for* 1854, entry 16th August, 1854.

the schools. The attendances were more numerous than heretofore, and in every respect highly efficient and successful'.[1]

It was during J. E. Jones's period as headteacher that the Llanelli 'Heol-Fawr' school made a name for itself. During his reign, 1863-1894, the number of pupils doubled, new extensions were built and new classrooms added.[2] Jones was assisted by four pupil-teachers[3] and being deeply interested in scientific and technical subjects worked incessantly to qualify himself for the advanced certificates of the Science and Art Department, Kensington,[4] and in 1867 was awarded First Class certificates in Plane and Solid Geometry, and Mechanical and Machine Drawing. 'Jones Heolfawr' was beloved by all, particularly by his pupil-teachers and pupils. Following his example, his pupil-teachers worked hard for additional qualifications and easily obtained teaching posts all over south Wales. By 1874, Jones had introduced practical and inorganic chemistry to the upper school curriculum, the only school in Wales to attempt such courses.[5] Many of his pupils were employed as assayers in the laboratories of the copper and silver works. Chemistry and other scientific subjects became one of the main attractions of the school. He initiated and personally conducted a whole variety of evening classes at the school—perhaps the most significant and successful feature of his work. Among the successful candidates in the Science and Art Department examinations, and a former pupil at the school, was Alfred Daniel the eminent chemist, who became a Freeman of Llanelli.[6] Jones also conducted classes in navigation for the local sailors who wished to take the examinations for their mate's or master's tickets, for at this time the copperworks had its own docks and built its own vessels which were

1 *Logbook, Llanelli Copperworks Schools, August,* 1862. When David Williams resigned, the Inspector's Report said: 'The instruction is thoroughly sound, far advanced and well graduated. The discipline appears to me to be faultless. The school is in all respects in a condition of efficiency which cannot be too highly praised. Mr. David Williams . . . is about to resign in order to take a situation under the B. & F.S.S. in which I am happy to say his valuable services will still be devoted to the cause of education in the district.' D. Williams became Vice-Principal of Swansea Training College in 1872.
2 *MS letter,* op. cit., *Llanelli Copperworks Schools Papers.*
3 August 11th 1864: Edwin Daw, P.T. 3rd year; Edwin D. Pryor, P.T. 2nd year; J. J. Morris and Sam. J. Williams, P.T.s of 1st year. August 8th 1866: John Trehearne, P.T. 5th year; E. D. Pryor, P.T. 4th year; David Gay, P.T. 1st year; Thomas Job, P.T. 1st year. See Appendices 18 and 20.
4 *Llanelli Guardian,* 4 December 1867.
5 *Logbook, Llanelli Copperworks school.* Also, *Minutes of Committee of Council,* 1874, p. 136.
6 *Llanelli Guardian,* 22 August 1867. Alfred Daniel of Hendre, who gained 1st Class Queen's Prize, Inorganic chemistry.

manned mainly by local mariners.[1] Jones left the school after thirty-one years' service to become the first headmaster of the new Llanelli Higher Grade school in 1894. In the meantime the copperworks schools were 'remodelled and greatly enlarged' and were eventually absorbed by the Llanelli School Board.[2]

W. H. Nevill, another member of the family who lived at Llangennech Park near Llanelli was one of the founders of the Llangennech National school and was mainly responsible for its maintenance.[3] After R. J. Nevill's death in 1856, Messrs. W. H. and C. W. Nevill carried on his work and were equally keen educationists. The educational work done in the town by R. J. Nevill was duly recognised in 1864 when the Nevill Memorial Hall was erected with the following eulogy: 'He elevated his workpeople socially and morally, and liberally supported all institutions tending to improve the conditions of the masses. The establishment of the copperworks schools, which ranked as one of the first of their class in the Principality was a practical exemplification of his zeal for the diffusion of education'.[4]

At Pembrey, a few miles west of Llanelli, coppersmelting was a later development. In 1846, Messrs. Mason and Elkington, who hailed from Birmingham and London, built the copperworks.[5] In 1855, the Company erected the copperworks school 'for the children of the workers employed in its copperworks, collieries, and brickworks'. Other children were admitted if there were vacancies. The buildings cost £1,700 and the entire sum was contributed by the Company who also gave £270 for its upkeep.[6] The schools had several interesting features. For the first few years a 'tax on the workmen's wages for educational purposes was made at the works office'. Thereafter workmen's children paid the following rates: girls and boys 2d. or 1d. per week; infants, 1d. per week; children of persons not employed at the works, 3d. per week, and infants 1d. or $1\frac{1}{2}$d. per week. Children of workmen who earned less than £1 per week were educated free of charge.[7] No preference was shown to children who had been educated in the copperworks schools in supplying vacancies at the works—such promotions depended entirely on ability and skill. The

---

1 *Llanelli Guardian*, 8 April 1869.
2 *Logbook*, Vol. II, 1894. *Minutes of Committee of Council*, 1897, Report by A. G. Legarde, p. 289.
3 *Letters concerning Education in South Wales*, p. 21.
4 *Llanelli Guardian*, 21 June, 1864.
5 Leslie Wynne Evans, *History of Carmarthenshire*, Vol. II, p. 367.
6 *Reports from Commissioners, Inspectors of Factories*, op. cit., 1868-69, p. 232.
7 ibid.

majority of pupils at the school were 'outside' children, e.g. in 1868, 265 outsiders attended against 214 of the workmen's children.[1] The school was entirely undenominational in character and ministers of religion of all denominations interested themselves in its activities. The original building was designed to accommodate about 500 children, boys, girls, and infants, including living accommodation for the teachers. A reading room and library were also included.[2] In 1874 the school was described as 'one of the most efficient in the Inspector's District'.[3]

The Margam copperworks school, for boys and girls, at Taibach, was established by the Margam Copperworks Company in 1830 (Patron: the Hon. Captain Lindsay),[4] which was later acquired by Vivian of Swansea, and managed by his son, Pendarves Vivian.[5] As the school grew rapidly in numbers an infants' department was added and in 1858 was described as 'one of the outstanding schools in the West Glamorgan and Carmarthenshire Prize Association, when seven pupils carried off substantial prizes for regular attendance, and achieving the cardinal accomplishments of the elementary schools'.[6]

The Crown Copper and Spelter works at Neath, mentioned twice in the *Reports of* 1847, probably had some kind of school although it is not mentioned again in any *School Returns* of the nineteenth century. In his survey of day schools at Neath in February, 1847, the Assistant Commissioner said that 'Miss Williams's school was at the Crown Copper works'[7] but in the *Parochial Table of Day Schools* listed for Cadoxton, Neath, it is described as a private school conducted by Miss Williams near the Crown copperworks, established in 1841 and attended by thirty boys and girls.[8]

Two other schools were established in connection with the non-ferrous metal industries in the western south Wales coalfield, at Maesteg and Pontamman, near Ammanford. The Spelter works school at Maesteg was first mentioned in the *Returns of the Committee of Privy Council* in

1   *Reports from Commissioners, Inspectors of Factories*, 1868-69, p. 232.
2   *Y Diwygiwr*, Medi, 1855, Rhif. 242, Cyf. XX, p. 314: Penbre, Sir Gaerfyrddin, gan y Parch. H. Evans, Penbre.
3   *Minutes of Committee of Council*, 1874: Report by Rev. S. Pryce: Appendix, Table D. p. 139. See Appendix 23.
4   1847 *Reports*, Part 1, p. 70.
5   C. Wilkins, op. cit. p. 60.
6   *The Cambrian*, Swansea, 6th August, 1858: These were: reading audibly and properly; writing legibly and neatly; working sums in arithmetic correctly, and well trained in the habits and elementary truths of Christianity.
7   1847 *Reports*, Part 1, p. 338,.
8   ibid, p. 62.

1854,[1] the proprietors erecting the school without the aid of a building grant, but receiving grants for the training of pupil-teachers. In 1866, the average attendance was only 48, but this had risen to 227 in 1878.[2] The Pontamman Chemical works school was established in the 1850s by a Mr. Morris, the proprietor, and Messrs. Brodies who later took over the works and maintained the school. Nefydd wrote almost contemptuously of the school in his *Diary*: 'Pontamman: there is a small mixed school in this place established by Mr. Morris, proprietor of the chemical works. There are 40 children, but the young woman that is the schoolmistress is not at all adapted to the work. She is the daughter (21 years of age) of the schoolmistress at Cross Inn, Miss Edwards. She only gets of Mr. Morris £10 per annum. It is only the name of a school, and I thought of seeing Mr. Morris, but he was away from home. I will visit again and urge him to establish a good school'.[3] In spite of the Agent's *Report* the school persisted until 1882 and also qualified to receive grants from the Committee of Council.[4] The School was open to all children, and those parents who could afford nothing, sent their children free of charge.[5]

The remaining schools associated with the non-ferrous industries were in rural Wales far removed from the industrial regions. In Cardiganshire, not far from Esgair Hir, where Mackworth had established a school in the eighteenth century, two schools were promoted by proprietors of lead and silver mines at Ysbyty Ystwyth and Goginan. The Ysbyty Ystwyth Miners' school was established in 1842 by the Level Fawr Leadmining Company. It started its life in a temporary building but in 1846 a school was built. It was 'a good stone building 63 by 15 feet, the accommodation at six square feet—157 . . . there were 60 children attending, but the schoolmaster was not too competent and he received a salary of £25 per annum'.[6] Henry Penry who visited the place on 19 November 1846 said: 'I examined the day school. The building in which it is held was erected by the Lefel Fawr Leadmining Company whose works are close by it. It is a long narrow building, four times as long as it is broad. It is well lighted and ventilated, and would be more convenient for two rooms, for a master and assistant, or two masters, better than for one. The school is conducted upon no system, nor has the master been trained, but the principal persons connected with these works are anxious that the master should be able to teach efficiently. They

1 *Minutes of Committee of Council*, 1854, p. 250, Rev. H. L. Jones's Report.
2 ibid for 1878, Tabulated Reports, Glamorgan. See Appendix 26.
3 *Nefydd MSS, Journal for* 1856, entry for 21st September, 1856.
4 *Minutes of Committee of Council*, 1882, p. 770. See Appendix 27.
5 Information given by J. Jenkyn Morgan, Esq., Glan Berach, Glanamman.
6 1847 *Reports*, Part 2, p. 31.

therefore wish him to go to see other schools at Aberystwyth and elsewhere, that he may improve his own. The reading of the highest class was tolerable. Two or three of the girls, daughters of some of the Agents connected with the works, read very well, and the knowledge of Scripture evinced by these scholars was more correct and extensive than what was manifest in other schools . . . and the only things aimed at seemed to be reading the Bible and spelling long columns of words'.[1] This school carried on in association with the mines until December, 1877, when the land was purchased, and the school was transferred to the local School Board as a public elementary school.[2]

The Goginan mines producing lead and silver were leased to the Mine Adventurers in 1700 for a period of ninety-nine years and worked intermittently throughout the eighteenth century. In 1760 the property was bought by Pryse of Gogerddan, but after 1785 Sir Thomas Bonsall obtained the lease of the mine.[3] In the early part of the nineteenth century the mining company of Messrs. J. Taylor developed the mine.[4] and this Company—the Goginan Lead and Silver Mining Company—promoted a school by renting the schoolhouse from one of 'the Dissenting congregations' situated near the mine. The first headteacher, although 'of considerable talent as a preacher and orator, was a very bad character whom the Company subsequently dismissed'! His successor, a very young man, was an untrained teacher. The pupils were drawn from the miners' families and the children 'of the captains and Superintendents of the works who were all Cornishmen and consequently the first class consisted chiefly of English children'.[5] The master received a salary of £10 per annum and school fees. 'Mr. Fossett, the intelligent Agent of the Company was desirous of improving the school and of rendering the master efficient by sending him to be trained, but wished to see what the Government would do'.[6] The description of local conditions and the remuneration of the schoolmaster given by two different people revealed some discrepancies. The Commissioner maintained that the yield of the lead and silver mines was very large, that the works were carried on without intermission and that the people as well as the proprietors were very prosperous, but inconceivably ignorant. The Rev. Owen Owen, a local resident, stated that the people were poor and that the schoolmaster could not be expected to be efficient in return for what he received as his remuneration. He said

1 1847 *Reports*, Parochial Returns of schools, Part 2, p. 173.
2 *Ysbyty Ystwyth School Deeds*, Education Offices, Aberystwyth.
3 A. Francis, *History of the Cardiganshire Mines*, p. 49.
4 1847 *Reports*, p. 37.
5 1847 *Reports*, Part 2, p. 158.
6 ibid.

that most of the schoolmasters received gratuities in the form of food mainly, from the farmers and shopkeepers 'who paid in kind for trifling services, and not infrequently for teaching their sons to read, cipher, or write'.[1] The total income of the Goginan schoolmaster was £28, receiving only £10 from the Mining Company, and his comment to the Commissioner was 'I give them quite as much instruction as they give me payment for'.[2] In 1877 the Goginan land was bought for the Melindwr School Board and passed into the Board's hands.[3]

It is uncertain whether a school was provided by the Leadmining company at Rhandirmwyn, Carmarthenshire, but 180 workers at the lead mines were enthusiastic enough to remunerate a schoolmaster to teach their 30 children who 'cleaned the ores at the works'.[4]

In north Wales a small school had a brief existence at Llandudno, in connection with either the Gloddaith Lead mines or the Great Orme Copper mines.[5] According to the Rev. Dr. John Prichard, a celebrated Baptist minister of that time, 'an English school came to Llandudno promoted by the proprietors of the mine'—'pan oeddwn o bedair-ar-ddeg i bymtheng mlwydd oed, daeth ysgol Saesoneg i Landudno, yr hon a gynhelid gan mwyaf gan berchenogion y gwaith mwn. Cefais yma ddechrau dysgu y Saesoneg: weithiau bod yn yr ysgol drwy y dydd ac weithiau yn y prydnawnau wedi y deuwn oddiwrth fy 'stems' o'r mwnglawdd—dim yn gyson. Cyn ymadawiad John Rees, athraw yr ysgol, gallwn ddarllen ychydig yn y Beibl, ac ysgrifennu rhywfaint. Yn y flwyddyn 1811, yn ol a allaf gofio, ymadawodd John Rees a Llandudno, a chydag ef bob gobaith i mi am ychwaneg o ysgol'.[6]

1   1847 *Reports*, Part II, p. 31.
2   ibid.
3   *Goginan School Deeds*, Education Offices, Aberystwyth.
4   1847 *Reports*, Parochial Returns, Carmarthenshire, Part 1, p. 225: Parish of Cilycwm: 'The mining district of Rhandirmwyn near Llandovery. There are employed in the Lead mines: 180 men and 30 boys and girls cleaning ores . . . their education has been greatly neglected in consequence of which they have no taste for reading any books or newspapers . . . except the Bible. The inhabitants have tried to get education by subscribing a small sum to remunerate an inefficient schoolmaster to teach the children the rudiments of learning, without which they would be wholly unprovided.'
5   Parch Owen Davies: *Cofiant y Parch. Dr. Prichard, Llangollen, Caernarfon*, 1880, p. 14.
6   'When I was 14 or 15 years of age an English school came to Llandudno, maintained mainly by the proprietors of the mine. Here I started to learn English; sometimes I attended school all day, sometimes in the afternoons, having returned from my 'stems' in the mine—but not regularly. Before John Rees the schoolmaster left, I could read the Bible a little, and also write a little. In 1811, so far as I recollect, John Rees left Llandudno, and with him all further hope of schooling for me.' ibid, p. 14.

APPENDIX 1

KILVEY JUVENILE WORKS SCHOOL (COPPERWORKS) [1]

Established 1806. Promoters: The White Rock (Messrs. Freeman and Co.); and Upper Rock (Messrs. Grenfell and Co.) Copper Companies.
Indifferent buildings; no outbuildings. 15 feet high, area 26 x 17.
Insufficient furniture and apparatus in bad repair.
36 on books, 9 for less than one year; 15, from one to two years; 7, two to three years; 4 remain from 3 to 4 years.
Under five years: nil; 5 to 10: 2 girls, 24 boys; over 10, 1 girl and 9 boys.
Average attendance in last year: 14 girls, 36 boys. Monitorial; 5 monitors.
Religious instruction by teacher. Visited by minister and promoter.
English books only; Welsh spoken to explain.
Master's age: 75. Started at 34. Mason previously.
Salary: £31–4–0. House and coals.
1d. per week stopped from the men's wages.

APPENDIX 2

KILVEY INFANTS (COPPERWORKS) SCHOOL [2]

Not connected with a religious organization.
Established 1839. Promoters as before.
Tenancy at will. Good building, insufficient outbuildings, but good. 15 feet high, 30 x 53.
Sufficient furniture and apparatus in good repair.
200 on books. No admission book kept.
Under 5 years: 35 girls, 29 boys.
5 to 10 years: 96 girls, 45 boys.
Over 10 years: 5 girls, No boys.
Average attendance in last year: 90 girls, 50 boys.
No curriculum given. Religious instruction by teacher.
Visited by minister and promoter.
English books only. Welsh spoken to explain English books.
Master's age: 25. Trained at Grays Inn Road Model School, 6 months in 1841; and at Norwood, 6 weeks, 1841.
Commenced teaching at 19. Compositor before.
Salary £60. No school pence. House and coals.
1d. per week from each workman of White Rock, Upper Rock, and Middle Bank Copperworks.

1   1847 *Reports*, Part 1, p. 330.
2   ibid.

WORKS SCHOOLS OF THE NON-FERROUS METAL INDUSTRIES

APPENDIX 3

Commissioner's Report on the Kilvey Infants and Juvenile Copperworks Schools [1]

These schools are supported by stoppages upon the wages of the men employed in the copperworks of Messrs. Grenfell and Sons, and Messrs. Freeman and Co. The cost of accommodation is borne by the employers.

Mr. Grenfell told me that he had it in contemplation, after a time (he had but recently resided in the neighbourhood), to admit no young people into his works who could not read and write, or at least to make such, at extra hours, attend school. Just before my visit, five young men in his employ, aged from 18 to 22 years, had all signed an agreement, respecting their work, *with marks*.

Infant school:

I visited this school on the 17th February. The building is commodious and furnished in the usual manner. The site was given by Messrs. Freeman and Co. and the cost of erection defrayed by Messrs. Grenfell and Sons.

I heard a gallery lesson given. There was a stand with a frame into which prints could be fixed. Each Scriptural lesson was illustrated by a Scriptural print.

The girls were much older than the boys: the latter were drafted off into the juvenile school. There is no similar school for girls. They sew with the mistress in the afternoons, and members of Mr. Grenfell's family attend twice per week to teach them writing. Beyond this their daily instruction is confined to the routine of the infants' school. Almost all the answers came from the girls. Among others they repeated the number of miles which the sun is distant from the earth, etc. This school appeared to be efficiently conducted.

Juvenile school:

I visited this school on the 17th February. It is held in a dingy, dilapidated building I found the old master (a mason disabled 41 years ago) sitting stick in hand. The 12 senior boys present were reading the Epistle of St. James.

The writing was middling. The books were not very clean. The master complained that the children could not come early in the morning, because they had to take their parents' breakfast to the works, and that they were removed at a very early age from school.

A list of attendance is sent in weekly to the Companies whose workmen support the school.

1   1847 *Reports*, Part 1, p. 331.

APPENDIX 4

Summary of Kilvey Copperworks Schools, 1858-1894

Category:—British School.

1858–59 Grants of £73 for the augmentation of the salaries and pensions of certificated teachers.

£38–2–0 grant for pupil teachers.

£10 grant for books and apparatus.[1]

1865–66 Average attendance: 326 in day school; 42 in evening classes. Annual grant: £212–1–8.[2]

1867 Average attendance: 333 in day school; 51 in evening classes.[3]

1868 Special comment in the Inspector's Report on its non-denominational character and excellence of schools.[4]

1877 Average attendance: 448; Annual grant: £301–17–0. Two school Boards 'advancing in Swansea, but not complete'.[5]

1882 Accommodation for 608. Average attendance: 486. Annual grant: £354–4–0.[6]

1888 Due mainly to the works schools, no accommodation problem at Swansea.[7]

1889 Accommodation: 649. Average attendance: 537 at day school (Grant £477–6–9). Evening school: 65 (Grant £32–8–0).[8]

1894 Listed as Board School. Accommodation, 842. Average attendance, 634. Grant: £536–10–6.[9]

1897 'After considerable delay, the School Board of Swansea has settled down in earnest, not only to meet the demands of a growing population, but also to substitute new and improved buildings for old ones unsuitable and condemned. New schools will be built, especially at St. Thomas, to contain 1,200 scholars and to supply the place of the old Kilvey Copperworks schools, which when opened at the beginning of the century were thought to be equal to anything of the kind in the country.[10]

1 *Minutes of Committee of Council*, 1858-59: Reports on British schools by J. Bowstead.
2 ibid, 1865, Report by B. J. Binns.
3 ibid, 1867, p. 669.
4 ibid, 1868-9, p. 280.
5 ibid, 1877-78, p. 453.
6 ibid, 1882, p. 776.
7 ibid, 1889, p. 691.
8 ibid, 1890, p. 455.
9 ibid, 1895, p. 1084.
10 ibid, 1898, Mr. Monro's Report, p. 289.

WORKS SCHOOLS OF THE NON-FERROUS METAL INDUSTRIES

APPENDIX 5

St. John's Swansea
Hafod Copperworks, School [1]

Established 1847. Promoter: J. H. Vivian, Esq., M.P., Singleton Hall, near Swansea.

Tenancy at will. Good buildings; sufficient outbuildings in good condition, 20 feet high; 60 x 30 feet.

Sufficient furniture and apparatus in good repair.

119 on books. Newly opened school. 119 stay for less than one year.

Under 5 years nil; 5 to 10 years, 41 girls, 50 boys. Over 10 years, 13 girls, 15 boys.

Monitorial, 20 monitors.

No religious instruction. Subjects include reading, writing, arithmetic, grammar, geography, history.

Religious instruction by teacher.

English books only; English grammar.

Master aged 19. Trained at Borough Road for 6 months in 1846.

Started teaching at 19. Joiner before.

Salary £85, with house, coal, and candles.

1d. per week from men, and ½d. from the children employed at the Hafod Works.

APPENDIX 6

Hundred of Swansea. Parish of St. John's, near Swansea [2]

This parish includes the northern suburbs of Swansea, and extends up the eastern bank of the Tawe (opposite to Llansamlet on the western) until it joins the parish of Llangyfelach. The aspect of it differs little from Llansamlet. The principal feature in it is the Copperworks at Hafod, belonging to J. H. Vivian, Esq., M.P. His agent informed me that about 500 persons were employed in them of all ages and sexes, of which number 100 might be children, and 30 women.

No boy was then employed who was under 12 years of age. As to wages, calciners were getting 14/- ro 15/-; furnacemen, 21/- to 25/-, and occasionally 30/- (extra hours) per week, besides fuel gratis and a two-room cottage built by Mr. Vivian, at 1/4 per week. As a class they were not intemperate, but improvident, relying on constant employment. They were mostly Welsh, with few English or Irish among them. The Agent recollected no instance of a man who had risen from a workman to be a clerk; he considered them better off than any other class of workmen in the kingdom. The district was not unhealthy.

The Copperworks school is maintained by each man's wages being stopped 1d. per week, for which he has the privilege of sending all his children (however many) to school. In general, they were apathetic about education. The only intellectual resource of the adult population is the chapel, whether used for preaching or a Sunday school: such as do not frequent the chapel pass their leisure time in the beer-house. They are all

---

1 1847 *Reports*, Part I, pp. 74-7.
2 ibid, pp. 359-60.

Dissenters. A great improvement was said to have taken place in the manners of the district. This was attributed to the Sunday schools: they were introduced about 27 years ago: at that time the population was left wholly without spiritual care. I took down verbatim the following statement from a sort of clerk or overseer, apparently a man of 50 or 60 years old:

> 'At that time an Independent minister came to look after us—if he had been Baptist, Churchman, or anyone else to have drawn the net, he would have had us all.'

The present excellent and conspicuous building has been erected at the expense of J. H. Vivian, Esq., M.P., and other rooms are about to be built in a short time for the separate accommodation of girls and infants. The present room has a floor sloping upward from the dais, on which stands the master's desk. The parallel desks are divided down the centre by a partition, so that when the children are in the desks, either to write or receive simultaneous instruction, the boys and girls are separated. When the school is in drafts, they occupy opposite sides of the room.

The master, who appeared a superior man, had arrived only the day before my visit, and was wholly engaged in the process of organization. Indeed, the carpenters were still at work, and the apparatus not fixed.

APPENDIX 7

Report by Joseph Fletcher, H.M.I. on the Hafod Schools, 1848 [1]

5th June, 1848: Hafod, Swansea, British School. Boys: 185; Girls: 167; Infants, 202. These schools have been raised and are maintained on a scale of the greatest munificence, chiefly for the children of the men employed in the neighbouring copperworks, by J. H. Vivian, Esq., M.P., on the principles, with regard to religious instruction, of the British and Foreign School Society, viz. that the authorised version of the Scriptures but no catechism shall daily be used in the instruction of the children. The boys' and girls' schools are under teachers trained by that Society, and the Infants' school under a female teacher trained by the Home and Colonial Infant school Society. The boys' school has not made during the past year the progress that could have been desired, although reading, without spelling and interrogation, is taught mechanically on the text of Scripture cards in the lower part of the school, which likewise receives a course of excellent collective secular lessons, as well as lessons in elementary arithmetic, devised by the master, and given chiefly by a pupil teacher, paid by the patron, though sometimes also by the master himself. In all, except these secular lessons, the school is not above the average, and in several important particulars is below it.

The writing is in good style, and the arithmetic on a good system; but for want of a spirit of accuracy, of neatness, and I think, also of duty, the results are inferior. Again the interrogatory exercises upon the draft reading lessons, entirely omitted in the lower part of the school, are conducted in a spirit of offhand indolence and inaccuracy in the upper: and as this is a most important part of the training of the upper body of the school, the defects which hence arise, combined with a general looseness in the reading exercises, entail an unclearness in the reading of the master's own class, and a want of alert and dutiful correctness in it, which is inconsistent, after every possible allowance, with his own attainments and abilities, and with the amplitude of the means placed at his disposal. Even the express intellectual culture of the lower half of the school is very defective, in being totally dissevered from the reading lessons, except at the brief visits of the master to each draft, and the effect throughout is a want of that order in the operations and coherence in the results, for the exhibition of which the school offers a very favourable opportunity.

1 *Minutes of Committee of Council*, General Report for 1848-9, by Joseph Fletcher H.M.I. on British and Denominational Schools. Appendix.

The general plan of the girls school is similar to that of the boys', and the lowest section appears to take part in the secular gallery lessons given to the lowest section of the school. Some of the monitors were working at spelling exceedingly well, writing the words down on the blackboard as they were orally spelt, if any difficulty arose; but the methods generally were not such as to secure a real collectiveness of attention, as they ran into individual instruction on the one hand, or simultaneous answering on the other, where interrogation was at all practised, in the few upper drafts. As a whole, therefore, while this school has made a much greater progress in cleanliness, neatness, order, and general tone than the boys', it shows an analogous want of a consistent and pervading correctness in the attainments of the children, as far as they have gone, and of a more vigorous cultivation of the habits by which alone it can be attained. The Infant School is in a condition of neatness, order, discipline, and complete organization, which under the circumstances of a rude neighbourhood, in which the vernacular tongue is almost wholly Welsh, is very creditable to its matron teacher; whose large gallery, however, contains too great a number for her to keep the whole in effective operation, learning at once to use the English language as well as their own faculties, as they must.

To meet this deficiency, she requires several pupil teachers or a select double set of paid monitors from the girls' school, to enable her to have at work several sections between that of the babies and the one held by herself for collective instruction, which, by this means, would always be kept to a moderate number.

APPENDIX 8 [1]

Report on Hafod Copperworks Schools for 1850-51
by Joseph Fletcher, H.M.I.

Hafod Copperworks, Swansea. Inspected 10th September, 1850.
Excerpts from Report:
185 boys; 167 girls; 202 infants.
Boys' School: British; good furniture. Books and apparatus good. Monitorial organization, good. Good discipline. Good methods. Zealous and qualified teachers.
Girls' School: ditto.
Infants School: One large gallery, and numerous forms. A second smaller gallery required. A fairly qualified matron.
This school supported entirely by Messrs. Vivian, has changed teachers since my last visit, and is now in thoroughly sound condition, as a monitorial school on the general plans of the British and Foreign School Society, with an enlarged top class, well grounded by the master himself. The organization, plans, methods, etc. of the school are all good, but require to be carried out with greater energy and completeness than is exhibited by the mere boy-monitors employed under the teacher, and yet the progress recently made in the habits, manners, language, and intelligence of the children, is, under the circumstances, quite satisfactory.
The girls' school also has changed teachers, but with far less happy results: for though it is in good mechanical order, while under the general command of its teacher, the methods pursued in its classes are so defective as to sustain the attention imperfectly to a very moderate course of instruction; while the general tone of the management is harsh and repulsive.
The infant school, which retains its former teacher, has made excellent progress in English, order, and cleanliness, and wants only a little adult or adolescent assistance to make its sectional teaching thoroughly good in three different portions, and become an exemplary institution. Its success is already sufficient to decide the value of this class of schools in the struggle against the peculiar difficulties of language especially, which lie in the way of the instruction of the poorer classes in Wales.

[1] *Minutes of Committee of Council*, for the year 1850. Joseph Fletcher's Report on British, Wesleyan, and other Denominational Schools.

WORKS SCHOOLS OF THE NON-FERROUS METAL INDUSTRIES

APPENDIX 9

Hafod Copperworks School, Swansea. Note by W. G. Williams, (one of the teachers at Hafod Council School, 1933), on the first page of an old register of the school).

Note: Some of these details are not correct, e.g. the statement that the children did not pay school pence.

1. When this school was first opened, and for quite 40 years afterwards, children of parents who worked under Messrs. Vivian and Sons had preference over other children as regards admission. Children of parents employed by Vivian did not pay school money, as their parents paid a certain small sum through wage deductions. For these reasons it was necessary to keep separate 'Admission Registers'. This admission register was used for 'Works' children as they were called, and children admitted to the school, whose parents were not employed under Vivian were entered into another 'Admission Register'.
2. When, however, all elementary education became free, the differentiation between such children ceased, and this admission register was discontinued. Thus this register contains the names of Works children from 1854 to 1894. From 1894, to the opening of the new Hafod schools, all children were placed on the same register.
3. The Hafod Copperworks school was first opened on the 11th February, 1847, but it appears from other sources of information that such books as admission registers were not used. This will account for the first name on the register being entered in 1852.
4. This book was found among some rubbish in the old school building, and returned to the Hafod Council school by one of the teachers, namely, W. G. Williams, who has entered these notes for the guidance of others.

June 1933.

APPENDIX 10 [1]

Specimen Page of First Admission Register, 1852
Hafod Copperworks School

1852.

Date of Entry	From what school	No.	Name	Age	Residence	Father's No. in Works Register	Class on Entering	Class on Leaving	Date of Leaving	Remarks
—	—	1	Walter Hogg	14	Trevivian	19	—	—	—	Very good boy

1. Some remarks in the last column included: Father in silver works; Uncle in silver works; Father in Spelter works; Father in lead works, etc.
2. The ages of admission varied from 6 to 14 years.
3. For the years 1852-1860 the records were poorly kept. Most of the pupils left to work in one of Vivian's works.
4. Children came up from the Infants school at 7 years of age.

[1] *Admission Register, Hafod Copperworks school.* The above notes appear on the inside of the cover page.

WORKS SCHOOLS OF THE NON-FERROUS METAL INDUSTRIES

APPENDIX 11 [1]

CERTIFICATE OF ADMITTANCE TO HAFOD COPPERWORKS SCHOOL

Memorandum

From: W. Morgan,
Vivian and Sons,
Hafod Sulphuric Acid Works,
Swansea.
July 27th, 1855.

To: Mr. Carr,
Headmaster.

Please admit William Henry, and Albert Hughes, children of Samuel Solt, to the Boys' Schools, and pass Jane, daughter of the above into the Infant School.

APPENDIX 12 [2]

EXCERPTS FROM HAFOD COPPERWORKS SCHOOL, LOGBOOK, 1863-1900

Note.—For most days, the phrase 'ordinary progress' appeared as the comments for the day.

1863.

Page 1. June 1st: The pupil teachers all in good time this morning: a full school, 156 boys present, and I think a good day's work done. J. M. Carr, Headmaster.

Page 2. June 10th: A boy named Fudge left school today to work in the Tinworks, Landore. Age: 9 years.

Page 3. July 1st: Pupil teachers left school for an hour or two in order to get their money from Post Office.

Page 4. July 2nd: Few children in school today because of the Swansea Wool Fair.

Page 5. August 10th: Swansea Boat Races. Very few children present.

Page 6. August 20th: Mrs. Vivian and Mr. Graham Vivian, visited the school today.

Page 6. Sept. 3rd: Very wet morning, new supply of books and slates from Borough Road, London.

Page 7. Sept. 10th. Mrs. Vivian visited the school.
Sept. 16th. Mrs. Vivian visited the school.

Page 10. Oct. 13th. Mrs. Hussey Vivian visited the school this evening: 175 boys present.

Note.—Mrs. Vivian seemed to visit the school weekly, and always listened to reading and dictation lessons.

1864.

Page 24. Average attendance for past year: 152.
No. presented for examination: 114.
Amount of Grant for boys' school: £73–1–4.

---

[1] *Admission Register, Hafod Copperworks Schools.*
[2] *Hafod Copperworks School Logbook.*

WORKS SCHOOLS OF THE NON-FERROUS METAL INDUSTRIES

Page 25. The school establishment consists of:
1. John M. Carr, Certificated Master, Headteacher.
2. Gethyn Davies, pupil teacher close of 4th year.
3. David Morgan, pupil teacher close of 1st year.
4. John Jenkins, pupil teacher close of 1st year.

1867. *Joseph Bowstead, H.M.I., 20/6/64.*

Page 102. School Report for 1867: 'As a school connected with Works, this Department has many good points and is satisfactory on the whole. But the boys ought to do their work more accurately, especially in ciphering'.

Total amount of grant for 1866: £266 –1–6
Total amount of grant for 1867: £293–16–6

Increase: £27–17–0

School Establishment: John Carr, and four pupil teachers.

Page 172. 1870: An evening class of 39 young men has passed a creditable examination.
Page 226. 1874: School Establishment: John Carr, 1st class Cert.
J. John, Asst. 3rd Class Cert.
6 Pupil teachers.

APPENDIX 13
Summary of Hafod Copperworks Schools, Swansea, 1846-1894

Year	No. on Books	Average weekly Attendance	Government Grants
1846	350	Not given	—[1]
1848	316	223	—[2]
1850	554	Not given	—[3]
1854	Schools received £97 grant for Pupil Teachers, but no building grant.[4]		
1855	£140–10–0 for Pupil Teachers and gratuities to teachers for instructing them.[5]		
1865	Not given	521 (day) 38 (evening)	£266–16–3[6]
1873	Boys .. 361 Girls .. 341 Infants 476 Total .. 1178	Not given	Not given[7]
1877	Not given	809	£585–18–0[8]
1882	1,038	787	£662–7–0[9]
1889	1,042	923	£882–4–0[10]
1894	1,114	889	£860–4–0[11]
1898	Schools taken over by Swansea School Board.[12]		

1 *Minutes of Committee of Council*, Vol. II, 1847-8: Appendix to Mr. Fletcher's General Report.
2 ibid
3 ibid, 1850-1: Tabulated Reports for 1850 by J. Fletcher.
4 ibid, General Report on Schools aided by grants, 1854, p. 250.
5 ibid, 1854-5: Detailed statement of grants, Wales, 1855.
6 *Minutes of Committee of Council*, 1865-6; Tabulated Reports for Wales, Rev. B. J. Binns, M.A.
7 *Parliamentary Papers*, Vol. LIX, 1873, p. 410.
8 *Minutes of Committee of Council*, 1877-8, Tables for Glamorgan by B. J. Binns.
9 ibid, 1882: Tabulated Reports, p. 776.
10 ibid, 1889: Tabulated Reports, Part IV, Appendix, p. 691.
11 ibid, 1894: Tabulated Reports, p. 289.
12 Vivian Collection, MSS and Papers, 1840-1923, D/DGV, 36. Glamorgan County Record Office, Cardiff.

WORKS SCHOOLS OF THE NON-FERROUS METAL INDUSTRIES

APPENDIX 14

Summary of Llanelli Copperworks Schools, 1847-1894

Year	No. on Books	Average weekly Attendance	No. present at examination
1847	223	160	150[1]
1848	150 boys: 100 girls & infants	Not given	Not given[2]
1850	120 boys; 80 girls & infants	Not given	Not given[3]
1852	164 boys; 68 girls	Not given	Not given[4]
1854	(No statistics of pupils, but a £91-13-4 grant for Certificated teachers, and £284 for pupil teachers.)[5]		
1858	393 boys & girls	219	Not given[6]
1864	265 boys	Not given	Not given[7]
1865	Not given	352 boys and girls	Not given[8]
1867	Not given	366	Not given[9]
1871-2	Not given	491 (Average)	636[10]
1874	Not given	535 (Average)	605[11]
1877-8	Not given	589 (Average)	Not given[12]
1880	699 (accom.)	625 (Average)	Not given[13]
1882	740 (accom.)	721 (Average)	Not given[14]
1885	723 (accom.)	730 (Average)	Not given[15]
1889	741 (accom.)	741	Not given[16]
1890	741 (accom.)	733	Not given[17]
1894	741 (accom.)	743	Not given[18]

1 *Minutes of Committee of Council*, Vol II, 1847-8, Appendix, p. 298.
2 ibid 1848-9: Appendix, Report for June 11th, 1848.
3 ibid 1850-1: Tabulated Reports by J. Fletcher, 11 September, 1850.
4 ibid 1852: Report by Mathew Arnold on Midland District.
5 ibid 1854: General Report by H. Longueville Jones, p. 250.
6 *Return to an Address of the House of Commons*, 25th July, 1861: printed, 28th April, 1862. Letter from R. Goring Thomas, Esq., Junr. to the Secretary of the Committee of Council on Education, 10th July, 1858 (written from Iscoed, Kidwelly).
7 *Llanelli Guardian*, November 3, 1864. Letter from J. E. Jones, Headmaster.
8 *Minutes of Committee of Council*, 1865, Report by B. J. Binns, Carmarthenshire.
9 ibid, 1867, p. 669.
10 *Minutes of Committee of Council*, 1874; Appendix, Table D. p. 139.
11 ibid.
12 ibid, 1877-8.
13 ibid, 1880, p. 732.
14 ibid, 1882, p. 770.
15 ibid, 1885, p. 631.
16 ibid, 1889 p. 678.
17 ibid, 1890: List of schools aided by grants, Appendix, Part IV.
18 ibid, 1894: p. 1076.

APPENDIX 15

Excerpts from Inspectors' Annual Reports on the Llanelli Copperworks Schools for 1850 and 1852

11*th September* 1850: Inspected by Joseph Fletcher, H.M.I.
Boys: 120. Pupil Teachers: 3. Girls and Infants: 80, P. T. 1.

Since my last visit to these schools built and supported on a liberal scale by Messrs. Nevill, the master of the former has been for 2 months at the Church Normal School at Carmarthen and there obtained his certificate: and an entire change appears to have come over the spirit of his work, which is now carried on in the best tone and with equal vigour throughout the school, alternately in monitorial drafts and in three large sections of nearly equal numbers and progress: the former for the more and the latter for the less technical branches of instruction.

I can have no hesitation therefore in recommending this school for pupil teacher training.[1]

1852:
Llanelli Copperworks, Boys. 128. Desks and furniture modified for collective teaching and good; books and apparatus good; Organisation in three sections for collective and small classes for monitorial instruction. Good. Methods good. Certificated teacher zealous and improving.

This school has made a very satisfactory year's progress, and the improved neatness, intelligence, and general ability of the children are very obvious. The writing may yet be made an occasion of cultivating habits of superior nicety of hand, etc., yet the school in its present condition is a model for the surrounding districts.

Llanelli Copperworks, Girls. 85. Details as above boys'. Methods fair; Mistress improving—though little trained. This school has undergone a change of teachers in the course of the year. It is in excellent discipline and tone and shows great progress in the neatness and improved demeanours of the children. Its class methods want more vigour however; and the present teacher, if she enjoyed some opportunities of training, would be qualified to supply the deficiency.[2]

APPENDIX 16

Llanelli Copperworks School

Pupil Teacher Agreement Form[3]

Memorandum of Agreement between:

Charles Wm. Nevill, Esq., of Westfa, and William Henry Nevill, Esq., of Llangennech, and John Evans of Marine Street, Llanelly, hereinafter called the Managers, on behalf of the Managers of the Llanelli Copperworks British School,

AND

Thomas Jones of Railway Terrace, Llanelli, the father of Thomas J. Jones, hereinafter called the Pupil Teacher.

Receives £10 per annum 1st year, and increased by £2–10–0 per annum each subsequent year. Period of engagement (serving under a Certified Teacher): 1868-1873.

1 *Minutes of Committee of Council*, 1850-1: General Report for the year 1850, by Joseph Fletcher, H.M.I. on British, Wesleyan, and other Denominational Schools.
2 ibid for 1852-3.
3 *Nevill MSS.*, 516, N.L.W.

APPENDIX 17

Llanelli Copperworks School[1]

Statement of Accounts for the year 1864

1864	Income			Totals
	School Pence	Govt. Grant	Other Sources	
Boys	£112–9–1½			
Girls	62–0–8			
Infants	53–15–3			
Total	£228–5–0½	£190–17–2	£92–10–1½	£511–7–4

Expenditure

	Salary of teachers	Salary of Assts.	Bks. & App.	Fuel &c.	Repairs	Rent	Other Exes.	Total
	£	£	£	£	£	£	£	£
Boys	126-5-0	107-9-7	17-6-9	6-0-0	1-18-0	8-15-0	4-12-3	272-6-7
Girls	64-0-0	30-15-3	8-18-0	3-9-0	1-0-2	4-7-0	2-6-2	114-15-7
Infants	45-16-8	58-18-7	8-8-10	3-9-0	0-19-0	4-7-0	2-6-1	124-5-2
Total	£236-1-8	£197-3-5	£34-13-7	£12-18-0	£3-17-2	£17-9-0	£9-4-6	£511-7-4

APPENDIX 18(a)

Excerpts from the Diary or Logbook of Llanelli Copperworks School.

Two volumes: August 25, 1862—June 6, 1873; and June 9, 1873—November 4, 1910. Vol. I. 1862-1873.

August, 1862, Summary of Inspector's Report: 'Reading, writing and arithmetic, and all the ordinary subjects are admirably taught in this school. It is more numerously attended than heretofore, and in every respect highly efficient and successful.'

August 3rd, 1863: School examined under the Revised Code by S. Joyce, Esq., H.M.I. David Williams Headteacher.

September 14th, 1863: John E. Jones, succeeded Mr. David Williams as Headmaster. School full.

December 23rd, 1864: Scriptural examination conducted by C. W. Nevill, W. Morgan, H. Hammond and the Master.

Vol. II. June 9, 1873.

School fairly full. The half-timers (under the Factory Act) coming to school so irregularly were required to pay a full fee of 8d. per week.

May 18th, 1874: School full. Mr. John Dodd, ex pupil teacher of the Bryndu Colliery School, Glamorgan, came to act as an Assistant Master.

January 17th, 1876: Total children in Boys' school: 289. Paying 8d.: 1; 6d. 4; 4d. 120; 3d. 118; 2½d. 15; 2d. 25; 1d. 6. Free—none. Total, 289.

22nd October, 1878: Sent list of irregular children of parents working at Copperworks and lead works to C. W. Nevill, Esq., with a view of getting the workmen to send them more regularly.

30th March, 1882: Pupil teachers and candidates receive their stipends at the Copperworks Office.

1 Llanelli Copperworks Schools, Miscellaneous Papers and Account Sheets.

APPENDIX 18(b)

LLANELLI COPPERWORKS SCHOOLS

Results of the examinations of the classes in connection with the Science and Art Department, London.

Subject I.	Plane, Descriptive, and Solid Geometry. Mr. J. E. Jones, Headmaster, Copperworks school. 1st Class certificate of competency.
Subject II.	Mechanical and Machine Drawing: Mr. J. E. Jones, Headmaster, Copperworks school. 1st Class Certificate of competency.
Subject IV.	Elementary Mathematics: E. D. Pryor, Copperworks school; 3rd class, Queen's Prize. Francis M. Lewis, New Road; Thomas Charles, Bryn Terrace; and William Ll. Thomas, Seaside, were awarded Honourable mentions. Thomas Jones, Llewellyn St., Daniel Stephens, Vauxhall, and William V. James, received 5th classes.
Subject VI.	Theoretical Mechanics: A. R. Mollison, Swansea; 2nd class, Queen's Prize. Thomas Griffiths, Burry St., 3rd Class, Queen's Prize. David Roberts, Wern; John Rees, Marine St., Henry Davies, Dillwyn St., and Thomas Job, Seaside, received 5th classes.
Subject VII.	Applied Mechanics: A. R. Mollison, 2nd Class, Queen's Prize.
Subject VIII.	Acoustics, Light, and Heat: A. R. Mollison, 1st Class, Queen's Prize.
Subject IX.	Inorganic Chemistry: Alfred Daniel, of Hendre: 1st Class, Queen's Prize.
Subject XX.	General Navigation: Richard Norman, Felin Voel. (Honourable mention). Edward Mainwaring, 5th Class.
Subject XXIII.	Physical Geography: Mrs. Jones, Copperworks school, M. A. Hughes, Thomas St., M. Moses, Infant school, E. D. Pryor, Copper Works school, received 1st class certificates of proficiency and Queen's Prizes. M. A. Hammond, Copperworks school, 3rd class Queen's Prize.

Freehand, Model, and Geometry.
This examination was one of the Day scholars', and was conducted like the preceding, but the time allowed was 40 minutes. Samuel Daw, David Randell, Thomas Vaughan, John Williams, David Rees, George Richmond, William Owens, Simon Dunstan, Thomas Jones, Thomas Owens, Henry Davies, and E. D. Pryor, were awarded excellent, and will receive prizes. Over 50 more gave evidence of satisfaction and proficiency in the examination, and will receive certificates recording their success.

Llanelli Guardian, August 22nd, 1867.

APPENDIX 19

MEASUREMENTS OF HEOLFAWR LLANELLI (COPPERWORKS) SCHOOL FOR STATISTICS JUNE, 1871[1]

Tabulated Returns of Statistics calculated on measurements taken by Mr. Moseley, H.M.I., June, 1871

	Area Principal Room and Classroom	Max. Attend. allowed for 8 sq. ft. per child	Cubical cont. of Principal Room	Max. Attend. permitted at 80 cu. ft. per child	Last year's aver. attend.	Last quarter's aver. attend. on July 28
Boys	1687 5/6	211	23,000	287	211.7	216
Girls	1055 25/72	132	12,950 7/27	167	145.1	200
Infants	1107 1/4	138	12,925 11/12	162	134.3	195.6

1 Llanelli Copperworks Schools, Miscellaneous Papers, and Accounts.

APPENDIX 20 [1]

Llanelli Copperworks School, November 30, 1893

Scale of Salaries

Boys' School

1. W. D. Smith, Headmaster. Particulars of qualifications, length of service, and former salary already given. £75 p.a.
2. Tudor J. Thomas, assistant, do. do. £69 to 1st September, £74 from.
3. Rees G. Thomas, do do. £42 to 1st September, £52 from.
4. David Evans, and Joseph James, Pupil teachers to be at £13, £16, £19, £22, for each year of service respectively. Pupil Teachers in 2nd year had been paid by Nevill, Druce, and Co., to March 31st, at £15 per annum.
5. Thomas Francis was a candidate for P.T., has now left paid at £5 p.a. to 31st March —left 13th October.
6. Wm. E. Davies is a candidate for P.T. as above.
7. Wm. E. Rowlands, do. from October 13th.

Girls' School.

1. Sarah A. Samuel. Certificated Assistant, not trained took 2nd year papers, Christmas, 1890—passed 2nd class, 3rd Division. Had her parchment February, 1893. Been in service 7 years. Present rate £45 p.a. to be £50 from September 1st.
2. Andrena M. Davies, Assistant, 2nd Class Queen's Scholarship, 1890. Been assistant 3 years, present rate £30 p.a. £42 from 1st September
3. Mary A. John, assistant, passed 3rd class scholarship, 1892, to be at £40 p.a.
4. Sarah Davies, P.T. in third year, from February 1st, paid by Nevill, Druce and Co., at rate of £14 p.a. £15 as from March 31st.
5. Sarah J. Phillips, P.T. in second year, from February 1st paid by Nevill, Druce and Co., at rate of £12 p.a. To be £13 p.a.
6. Annie J. Morgan, P.T. in 1st year, from February 1st, paid by Nevill, Druce and Co., at £10 p.a. to be £11.
7. Helena Jones, do. do. do. do.

Infants.

1. Ellen Belt, Cert. Asst. untrained, cert. exam. Xmas, 1888. 3rd class 2nd Div. Parchment, February 1891. Asst. from August 1888, to be £50 from 1st September.
2. Rose Thomas, asst. 4 years, not passed Queen's scholarship. £40 from 1st Sept.
3. Margretta Evans, P.T. in fourth year from 1st February, paid by Nevill, Druce and Co., to be £17.
4. Annie Morris, P.T. in 3rd year as Sarah Davies above, £15.
5. Annie Vaughan as S. J. Phillips, above, £13.
6. Mary Hallam, candidate for P.T. from June 19th, 1893.
7. Kate Evans, do.

[1] Llanelli Copperworks Schools, Miscellaneous Papers and Accounts.

APPENDIX 21

Pembrey Copperworks Schools [1]

Place where the Works & schools are established	Name of Proprietor	School rooms, size of in feet	Total cost buildings incl. teachers' houses	Amount given by Privy Council or any other body
Pembrey, near Llanelly	Messrs. Mason & Elkington	Boys 62 x 20. Girls do. Infants: 30 x 24	£1,700	—

WORKS SCHOOLS OF THE NON-FERROUS METAL INDUSTRIES

Average annual cost of schools to the proprietor: £270.
The parents are at perfect liberty to send them to school or not.
Has the principle of a small tax on workmen's wages for educational purposes been at any time adopted? Yes, but now abandoned.
Is any kind of preference given to children who have been educated in the school in supplying vacancies in the works, or after they have obtained employment? No.
How long have the schools been opened? 13 years (i.e. 1855).
Are the rules of the schools regarding regularity of attendance and cleanliness, etc., enforced? Yes.
Does the school provide slates, books, etc., or do the parents supply them? The school.
How many children attend whose fathers earn less than £1 per week? Cannot say.
Are any scholars free? How many and under what circumstances? 1.
Teachers' Grade of Certificate: Boys: 3rd; Girls: 3rd; Infants: 3rd.
Fees paid by children of workpeople: Boys: 2d. and 1d.; Girls, 2d. and 1d.; Infants, 1d.; Evening, 0.
Fees paid by children of other people: Boys: 3d. and 2d.; Girls, do. Infants: 1½d. and 1d. Evening: 0.
Number of children of workpeople in school: Boys, 69; girls, 86, infants, 59. Other people: boys, 94; girls, 97; infants, 74.
Average age of children in various classes: 10 years.
No one working under the half-time system attends the schools.

1   *Reports from Commissioners, Inspectors of Factories*, 1868-9, p. 232.

APPENDIX 22

PEMBREY COPPERWORKS SCHOOLS [2]

Description of schools by the Rev. H. Evans, Independent Minister, present at opening:

Penbre, Sir Gaerfyrddin. Ymgasglodd tyrfa luosog yn y lle uchod ar yr achlysur o agoriad ty-ysgol newydd a hardd wedi ei adeiladu gan Mason ac Elkington, Ysweiniaid, yn hollol ar eu traul eu hunain, ac yr ydym yn sicr ei fod yn un o'r adeiladau mwyaf ardderchog adnabyddus yng Nghymru.
Ei fesuriad: 63 x 40 o droedfeddi o fewn i'r muriau. Y mae wedi ei addurno a'r paentwaith harddaf, ac a'r darluniau (maps) o'r fath orau . . . a chyflawnder o lyfrau o bob dosbarth . . . anghenrheidiol i blant ddysgu darllen, rhifyddiaeth, celfyddyd, a chân. Adeilad yn ddigon helaeth i gynnwys o 400 i 500 o blant.
Y mae y boneddigion hefyd wedi bod mor garedig a darparu ystafell ddarllen (reading-room) yn y pen deheuol i'r adeiladaeth, ac addewid o lyfrgell heaeth a gwerthfawr. Am 6 o'r gloch y dydd uchod, galwyd ar y gweithwyr a'i gwragedd i gyfranogi o'r wledd a ddarparwyd gan y Cwmni, sef Mason ac Elkington yn hollol ar eu traul eu hunain, pan y cyfranogodd o bedwar i bum cant o de a theisen flasus. Wedi i bawb gael eu digoni, agorwyd drws yr ystafell arall perthynol i'r un adeiladaeth, pan y cododd Chas. Williams, Ysw. i fyny, ac y cynygodd Apsley Smith, Ysw., i gymeryd y gadair, ac eiliwyd ef gan y dorf . . . rhoddodd gynghorion gwerthfawr hefyd i'w weithwyr, etc.
Yna galwyd ar y canlynol i siarad: Parch. H. Evans (A); Parch. R. Hancock (A. Seisnig); Parch. Mr. Morgans (B); J. H. Rees, Cilymaenllwyd, a C. W. Coombs, Gwaith Llestri, Llanelli.
Mae y gweithwyr a'r ardal yn gyffredin yn teimlo yn wresog iawn at y boneddigion uchod am y dull rhydd a di-bartiaeth sydd yn perthyn i'r ysgol yn ei chychwyniad cyntaf. Nid yw yn perthyn i'r un enwad yn fwy na'r llall. Rhyddid i'r plant fynd i'w capeli ar y Sul, a dim un catechism i'w ddysgu yno.
Y mae gan y perchnogion waith copr eang, gweithau glo, a gwaith priddfeini. Telir y gweithiwr ag arian bob pythefnos,—dim 'truck' yma o gwbl.

2   *Y Diwygiwr*, Medi, 1855, Rhif. 242, Cyf. XX, p. 314.

APPENDIX 23

Summary of Pembrey Copperworks Schools

Year	Average Attendance	Accommodation	Grant
			£ s. d.
1858	210		2 0 9 (*Appar. & Books*)
			68 2 6 (*Certif. Teachers*)
			93 0 0 (*Asst. Teachers*)
			49 6 0 (*P.T's*)[1]
1865	221		108 17 4[2]
1867	231		Not given[3]
1874	School listed among three of the most efficient schools in the H.M.I.'s District.[4]		
1882	370	493	312 19 0[5]
1889	443	509	387 12 6[6]
1890	452	509	395 10 0[7]
1894	475	509	549 19 1[8]

APPENDIX 24

Margam Copperworks School[9]

Boys. Church

Established 1830. Promoters: The Margam Copperworks Company.
Resident Director: Hon. Capt. Lindsay, Taibach, Glam.
Tenancy at will. Good building with sufficient outbuildings.
In good condition. Area: 30 x 18.
Insufficient furniture and apparatus in good repair.
140 on books.
Duration of attendance not available.
Under 5: 40 boys. From 5 to 10: 80. Over 10: 20.
Method: Monitorial, with 60 monitors (including girls school).
Subjects: Holy Scriptures; catechism; reading; writing; Rel. Instr. by teacher. Visited by patron.
English books only; English grammar.
Master's age: 30. Starting teaching at 30. Accountant.
Salary: £55, with house, coals, and candles.
Married to mistress in Girls' School.
Stoppage on the men's wages at the Copper works of 1½d. per week from those who are married and householders; 1d. per week from unmarried men who are not householders.

1 *Minutes of Committee of Council*, 1858-9: Report by Rev. H. L. Jones, Tabulated Reports.
2 ibid, 1865-6: General Report by Rev. B. J. Binns, Tabulated Reports.
3 ibid for 1867: p. 670.
4 ibid, 1874: Appendix, Table D. p. 139.
5 ibid for 1882: p. 770.
6 ibid for 1889: General Report by W. Williams on the Welsh Division, p. 679.
7 ibid for 1890: Tabulated Reports, Carmarthenshire.
8 ibid for 1894: Carmarthenshire, p. 1077.
9 1847 *Reports*, Part 1, p. 70.

WORKS SCHOOLS OF THE NON-FERROUS METAL INDUSTRIES

APPENDIX 24(a)

MARGAM COPPERWORKS SCHOOL[1]

Girls

Established 1830. Details as for boys' school.
Area 30 x 18. 95 on books. Attendance not ascertained.
Under 5 years: 30 girls; from 5 to 10: 30; over 10: 35.
Monitorial. 60 monitors including boys' school.
Subjects: Holy Scriptures; Catechism; reading; writing. Other details as for boys' school.
Age of Mistress: 27; Married woman, joint salary with master of the boys' school.
Stoppages as for boys' school.

APPENDIX 25

SUMMARY OF MARGAM COPPERWORKS SCHOOLS

1861: 150 boys.[2]

1877: 'The Margam Copper works infants school has been enlarged to double its size'.[3]

1880: Accommodation 537.
   Average attendance 404.
   Annual grant £289–13–8.[4]

1890: Accommodation 704.
   Average attendance 558.
   Annual grant £488–5–0.[5]

1894: Accommodation 704.
   Average attendance 552.
   Annual grant £474–10–0.[6]

---

1 1847 *Reports*, Part 1, p. 70.
2 *Newcastle Commission Report*, 1861, Vol. II, Appendix E, p. 636.
3 *Minutes of Committee of Council*, 1877. Reports of schools in Glamorgan by Rev. B. J. Binns, M.A.
4 *Minutes of Committee of Council*, 1880: p. 733.
5 ibid 1890: Tabulated Reports of Schools, Glamorgan.
6 ibid 1894: Tabulated Reports of Schools, Glamorgan, p. 1084.

APPENDIX 26

Maesteg Spelter Works School

Summary

1854 Grant of £43–15–0 for Pupil teachers. No building grant.[1]

1859 Grant of £43–15–0 for Pupil teachers. No building grant.[2]

1866 Average attendance 48. Annual grant: £19–19–6.[3]

1867 Average attendance 107. Not given.[4]

1878 Average attendance 227. Annual grant £165–9–0[5]

1880 Accom. 236 Average attendance 218. Annual grant £126–14–0[6]

1890 Accom. 312. Average attendance 242. Annual grant £211–15–0[7]

1894 Accom. 312. Average attendance 261. Annual grant £228–7–6[8]

APPENDIX 27

Pontamman Chemical Works School

Summary

1877–78   Average attendance 38
         Annual Grant £25–18–0[9]

1880   Accommodation for 57
         Average attendance 34
         Annual Grant £24–8–0[10]

1882   Accommodation for 57
         Average attendance 50
         Annual Grant £34–10–0[11]

---

1 *Minutes of Committee of Council*, 1854. p. 250.
2 ibid 1859: Report by J. Bowstead on British Schools.
3 ibid 1866: Tabulated Reports by Rev. B. J. Binns.
4 ibid 1867: p. 669.
5 ibid 1878: Tabulated Reports, Glamorganshire.
6 ibid 1880: p. 733.
7 ibid 1890: Tabulated Reports, Glamorganshire.
8 ibid 1894: Tabulated Reports, Glamorganshire.
9 *Minutes of Committee of Council*, 1878. Tabulated Reports, Carmarthenshire.
10 ibid 1880: p. 732.
11 ibid 1882: p. 770.

CHAPTER VI

Tinplate Works Schools

DURING the nineteenth century, for historical reasons, the tinplate industry became located in the western part of the south Wales coalfield in a region which had already established itself as the metallurgical sector of the coalfield, a triangle whose base extended from Port Talbot to Burry Port, with its apex in the region of Ystradgynlais.[1] In 1891, the peak year of the tinplate industry, this industrial triangle, in addition to a few isolated tinplate works in Glamorgan and Monmouthshire, contained 71 tinplate works of which there were 20 in Carmarthenshire comprising 119 mills, and 51 in Glamorgan with 277 mills. There were 11 tinplate works with 86 mills in Monmouthshire. North Wales had no tinplate works.[2]

Schools associated with tinplate works were few in number for three reasons. In the first place, the majority of the early tinworks of the first half of the nineteenth century were attached to ironworks, and were often described as 'appendages to the iron forges'.[3] In such circumstances where ironworks had schools connected with them the children of the tinworkers attended those schools. Again, there were many examples of large Companies owning or controlling a group of different manufactories or other industrial concerns in a particular place, i.e. the parent Company and its ancillary industries. For example, the English Copper Company at Cwmavon owned copper, iron, tinplate, and chemical works in addition to several collieries, all in the same area, and the Company's schools catered for the children of all the employees, irrespective of their kind of work. Secondly, for technical reasons, the tinplate industry did not fully expand until after 1875 when steel supplanted iron in the manufacture of tinplate, and large tinplate works developed in and around Llanelli, Swansea, and Port Talbot with other less important ones in other parts of Glamorgan and Monmouthshire. Thirdly, the tinplate era coincided with the period after the Education Act of 1870 when School Boards were set up to supply deficiencies in school provision so that on a chronological basis schools associated with the tinplate industry were much

---
1 There were several tinplate works in operation during the eighteenth century but only Melingriffith had a school.
2 Lane Bowen, *The Rise of the Tinplate industry*, Llanelli, 1892, p. 37.
3 Bar-iron was rolled into iron sheets and coated with tin.

fewer in number than those connected with the older metallurgical industries.

The tinplate works schools fall naturally into two groups, corresponding roughly with the two phases in the development of the industry in the nineteenth century, i.e. before and after 1850. Four regions contained tinplate works schools: Carmarthenshire, Swansea Valley, Glamorgan, and Monmouthshire. In Carmarthenshire, at Carmarthen, 1844,[1] Dafen, near Llanelli, 1850,[2] New Dock School, Llanelli, 1866,[3] Hendy Higher Grade school, 1886,[4] and Brynamman, 1868.[5] In the Swansea Valley, at Pontardawe, 1846,[6] Ystalyfera, 1850,[7] and at Ynyspenllwch (Glais), 1860.[8] Glamorgan's tinworks schools were at Melingriffith, 1808,[9] Margam, 1829,[10] Aberdulais, 1842,[11] and Melincrythan, 1868.[12] The sole representative in Monmouthshire was Tydee (Rogerstone), 1860.[13]

TINPLATE WORKS SCHOOLS 1800–1850

The earliest school associated with tinplate works in south Wales was promoted by the Harford family, of Quaker stock, at Melingriffith, Whitchurch, Cardiff. This family also promoted other activities for their workmen directed towards social improvement which included a medical and sick fund.[14] Some kind of school was in operation in the eighteenth century, for the works' accounts for 1786-7 showed that workmen were engaged in 'effecting repairs to the school at Melingriffith' but it did not seem to have a long life.[15] However, in 1807, the Harfords invited Joseph Lancaster to address a meeting at Melingriffith to arouse interest in the establishment of a British school there. As a result, a committee was appointed forthwith with the object of setting up a day school on Lancasterian principles and the sum of £19–5–0 was promised. The school was opened in 1808,[16] and although directly connected with the tinworks,

1 1847 *Reports,* Part 1, p. 293.
2 *Reports from the Commissioners, Factories,* 1868-9, p. 232.
3 *Llanelli Local Board of Health, Minutes,* February, 1867.
4 *Minutes of Committee of Council,* 1887, Report for 1886, p. 340.
5 *Amman Ironworks British School Logbook.*
6 1847 *Reports,* Part I, p. 326.
7 ibid, p. 490.
8 *Minutes of Committee of Council,* 1868-9, p. 280.
9 E. L. Chappell, *Historic Melingriffith,* Cardiff, 1940. p. 48. *Education Inquiry* 1833, Vol, III, p. 1285.
10 1847 *Reports,* Part 1, pp. 70-71. *Education Inquiry,* 1833, Vol. III, p. 1285.
11 1847 *Reports,* Part 1, pp. 64-65.
12 *Minutes of Committee of Council,* 1870, Report for 1869, p. 671.
13 ibid.
14 E. L. Chappell, op. cit.
15 ibid.
16 Cardiff Central Library, *MS* 4.999, Whitchurch School, Melingriffith, *Subscription book,* 1807.

was also maintained by public subscription. The subscription book gives many interesting details. All types of people, many of them unconnected with the works, subscribed sums varying from 6d. to £1. John and Samuel Harford headed the list with their contributions of £5–5–0 each. There were also collective subscriptions from several departments in the works, e.g. 6 sawyers, 6/-; 7 scalers, 15/-; 7 tinmen, 21/-.[1] The total sum collected amounted to £53–3–3 and in January, 1809, a further subscription list was opened. Boys and girls came to the school from Whitchurch, Eglwysilan, and Pentyrch, special admission tickets being issued to each pupil.[2] During 1809, 62 children attended, but no information is available after that date.[3] Later in the nineteenth century, Thomas W. Booker who owned the Pentyrch and Melingriffith works did not provide a school but carried on the tradition by subscribing liberally towards the National schools.[4]

In 1829, the tinworks school in the parish of Margam (at Taibach, near Aberavon) was opened. At that time the population of the parish was 2,902 with four schools 'one whereof . . . contained 50 males and 40 females, partly supported by the Margam Tinworks Company and partly by small weekly payments from the workmen'.[5] The workmen paid 9d. per month deducted from their wages at the works office. Messrs. Roberts and Smith who built the tinworks in 1822 previously owned the Carmarthen tinworks, and on moving to Margam brought many of their old employees with them from Carmarthen and also a number from the Llechryd tinworks near Cardigan.[6] The first school at Margam was held in a room attached to the tinworks, but in 1833 two schools were in use for boys and girls with 65 and 106 pupils respectively on the school books.[7] In addition to the day schools connected with the works the parish also had two Sunday schools one of which was Anglican and supported by C. R. M. Talbot, Esq., who contributed £5–5–0 per annum. The other was the tinworks Sunday school originally started for adults but later extended to children of all ages capable of being taught, chiefly in the Welsh language. It consisted of from 180 to 190 males and females, carried on at the expense, and superintendence of Mr. Robert Smith, proprietor of the tinworks since 1810.[8] After 1860 the Margam Tinworks

1 *MS* 4,999. Also see Appendix 3.
2 *Melingriffith MSS*, ibid, *Admission Tickets*, 1808. See Appendix 2.
3 ibid for 1809.
4 *Minutes of Committee of Council*, 1874. Report for 1873 by the Rev. B. J. Binns on Glamorgan, p. 75.
5 *Education Inquiry*, 1833, Vol. III, p. 1285.
6 E. H. Brooke, op. cit., p. 55.
7 1847 *Reports*, Part 1, pp. 72-3. See Appendices 4, 5, and 6.
8 *Education Inquiry*, 1833, ibid.

schools were amalgamated with the National school, the number of pupils exceeded 300 and 'the boys' tutor was Mr. Edward Owen, former master at the tinworks school. Miss Mary Richards of the National school became the girls' tutor'.[1]

Not far from Margam, at Aberdulais in the Neath valley the tinworks had a school in 1842.[2] John Miers had built a forge there in 1785, and in 1830, William Llewellyn of Aberavon, who had already promoted two schools in that town, took over the tinplate works[3] and opened the Aberdulais tinworks school which had 50 pupils of both sexes and the workmen contributing 2d. per week towards its maintenance.[4]

In 1844 a small school was established in connection with the Carmarthen tinworks. One of the earliest works of its kind in south Wales, it was started by Robert Morgan in 1748.[5] The tinworks passed into the hands of successive owners and in 1846 were described as 'a tinworks where about 200 persons are employed, being the only large manufactory in Carmarthen, but that did not give to it the character of a manufacturing town'.[6] The school was held in a room of the master's house who had formerly been a clerk at the tinworks. It was maintained partly by the proprietors and partly by a levy of 1d. per week on the men employed at the works.[7] The school is not mentioned in any government returns or Inspectors' reports after 1847.[8]

In the Swansea valley two tinworks schools existed at Pontardawe and Ystalyfera. Established in 1846, the one at Pontardawe, conducted on the National system, was promoted by W. Parsons, proprietor of the tinworks.[9] At Ystalyfera the proprietor of the iron and tinplate works, Mr. J. Palmer Budd, had two schools. Mrs. Palmer Budd had already opened the Wern ironworks schools for Girls in 1842, and Palmer Budd started the tinworks school for boys in 1850 on the National system. Unfortunately for Budd this proved quite unacceptable to his workmen. They were mainly Nonconformist and resented having to contribute out of their wages for the support of a National school. Within a short time, rather than submit to Budd's system the workmen built their own school

1 Margam Tinworks school *Logbook*, 1863.
2 1847 *Reports*, Part 1, pp. 62-3.
3 E. H. Brooke, op. cit., p. 46. *Nefydd MSS*, July 11th, 1854.
4 1847 *Reports*, Part 1, pp. 62-3. See Appendices 7 and 8.
5 Leslie Wynne Evans, *History of Carmarthenshire*, p. 331.
6 1847 *Reports*, p. 284.
7 ibid, p. 293, also, Parochial Returns, Carmarthen Borough, p. 30.
8 Night schools were held on 5 evenings a week free of charge for the workmen and their children, 15 persons attended, 7 of whom were children. They were taught reading, writing, and arithmetic. See Appendix 9.
9 1847 *Reports*, Part 1, pp. 54-5. See Appendix 10.

on the British system with the aid of grants from the British and Foreign School Society.¹ But deductions continued to be made from their wages thus compelling them to contribute to two kinds of schools. Similar schools under the same circumstances were erected at Abercrave and Ystradgynlais, the only examples for the whole country where workmen built schools for themselves.²

Just before 1850 Llanelli began to assume some importance in the manufacture of tinplate, when several ironworks went over to this kind of work. One of the earliest tinworks in the town was started at Dafen by Messrs. Motley and Winkworth in 1846, but later were taken over by Messrs. Phillips, Nunes, and Company.³ The tinworks school was opened in 1850 and conducted on the National system. Built at a cost of £500, wholly borne by the Company, it had accommodation for boys, girls, and infants. The Company also contributed £20 annually towards its maintenance and deducted 2½d. in the £ from each workman's wages. The school had an average attendance of 198⁴ and received the highest praise in the Inspector's annual *Reports*.⁵

Tinworks Schools after 1850

Between 1850 and 1870 many new tinplate works were established in the Llanelli and Swansea areas and, with one exception, all the remaining tinworks schools were opened in the decade 1860-70. By this time the intense concentration of the metallurgical industries in these parts had given rise to a tremendous increase in population, but after 1878 the question of school accommodation had almost completely devolved upon the newly elected School Boards.⁶ Omitting Dafen (an outlying village at that time) it is rather surprising to find that Llanelli the tinplate town had no 'real' tin-works school, i.e. no school specifically built by a tinplate concern. In 1851 the Morfa Tinplate works were erected, to be followed by several others in rapid succession in the following years, but it is not clear whether the school nearby was connected in any way with these tinworks. However, the school was in existence in 1866, called the New

1   *Minutes of Committee of Council*, 1868-9, Mr. Bowstead's General Report for 1868, p. 281.
2   ibid, pp. 281 ff.
3   E. H. Brooke, op. cit., p. 62.
4   *Reports from Commissioners, Factories, Parliamentary Paper*, XIV, Reports of sub-Inspectors for 1868, p. 232.
5   *Minutes of Committee of Council*, 1850-1890. See Appendices 11 and 12.
6   School Boards were very late in being convened in many places, but they were formed in quick succession after 1878 especially in the industrial areas. *Parliamentary Papers, Accounts and Papers*, Vol. LII, 1873. Returns from all School Boards up to 30th September, 1872, pp. 200-8., ibid Vol. LVIII, *Education*, 1875, pp. 490-3.

Dock British school and attended mainly by tinworkers' children.[1] When the school was replaced by a larger one in 1873, two local tinplate manufacturers, Messrs. J. S. Tregoning and E. Morewood contributed £100 towards its cost.[2]

In the Amman valley, the Amman Iron Company erected a three-mill tinworks in 1872 and in the same year the tinworks school at Brynamman was opened. The committee of management advertised for a master and a young student fresh from Bangor Normal College was appointed. He was Henry Jones, later Sir Henry Jones who succeeded Edward Caird in the Chair of Moral Philosophy in the University of Glasgow.[3] The Brynamman Tinworks school continued as a works school until 1893 when it was sold by the proprietors to the Llandeilo Fawr School Board.[4] Of the remaining tinworks schools established after 1860, namely the Glais School in the Swansea valley connected with the Ynyspenllwch tinplate works, the Melincrythan tinworks school, the Hendy Higher Grade school near Pontarddulais, and the Tydee tinworks school near Rogerstone in Monmouthshire, scant information is available apart from a few statistics in the Reports of the Committee of Council. The last school of this type to be erected was the one at Hendy, and the only entry available regarding this school is in the Minutes of 1887: 'A Higher Grade Elementary school has been started at Hendy, Pontarddulais in connection with the tinworks in that place'.[5] There was a particularly large school at Melincrythan in 1894, after it had been absorbed by the local School Board, with accommodation for 773 and an average attendance of 724.[6]

---

1 *Minutes of Committee of Council*, 1868, p. 641.
2 *Llanelli Local Board of Health, Minutes*.
3 Henry Jones, *Old Memories*, 1923. p. 101. See Appendix 13. Amman Ironworks British School Logbook, 1872-3. Henry Jones started duties in 1873.
4 *Minutes of Committee of Council*, 1894, p. 1084.
5 ibid, 1887, p. 340. See Appendix 14.
6 ibid 1895, Tabulated Reports.

TINPLATE WORKS SCHOOLS

APPENDIX 1

Tabulated List of Tinworks Schools

1.	Carmarthen			1844
2.	Llanelli Area:	Dafen Tinworks		1850
		New Dock		1866
		Hendy (Pontarddulais)		1885
3.	Brynamman			1868-1872
4.	Swansea Valley:	Pontardawe		1846
		Ystalyfera		1850
		Ynyspenllwch (Glais)		circa 1860
5.	Glamorgan:	Melingriffith–Pentyrch		1808
		Margam		1833
		Aberdulais		1842
		Melincrythan		circa 1872
6.	Monmouthshire:	Tydee, Rogerstone		circa 1860

APPENDIX 2

Admission Tickets to Melingriffith (Whitchurch) School [1]

No 1 Fourth Quarter, 1808.

To the master of Whitchurch School:

Please to admit the bearer Charles Gibbon, son of Thomas Gibbon, of the Parish of Whitchurch to a quarter's schooling from the 1st of October, to the First of January following.

Melingriffith, Robert Rowlands,
October 1st, 1808. Treasurer to the School Committee.

[1] *Melingriffith MSS*, 4.999.

APPENDIX 3 [2]

Subscription List towards establishing a school in the Parish of Whitchurch, October, 1807. Established 1808.

First two entries, October 1807:

October 25th:	John Harford	£5–5–0
	Samuel Harford	£5–5–0

About 114 others contributed sums varying from £5–5–0, £1, 10/-, 2/6, 1/-, 6d., etc.

6 sawyers: 6/-; 7 scalers, 15/-; 7 tinmen, £1–1–0.

Total subscribed: £53–3–3.

Second Year of Establishment, 1809.

School for Boys and Girls.—S. and J. Harford £5–5–0 each.

Total subscribed: £14–0–6.

[2] *Melingriffith MSS*, 4,999.

APPENDIX 4

Margam Tinworks School, Boys. Church [1]

Established 1833, by Margam Tinworks Company, Taibach, Glams. Area 36 x 21.
65 on books.
Duration of attendance not ascertained.
106 girls on school books in girls school.
60 attend for less than one year.
20 attend from 1 to 2 years.
17 attend from 2 to 3 years.
12 attend from 3 to 4 years.
62 attend from 4 to 5 years.
Under 5 years: 9 boys; 5 to 10 years: 36 boys; over 10 years: 20 boys.
Average attendance last year: 40 boys.
Monitorial: 18 monitors (joint).
Subjects: Holy Scriptures, reading, writing, etc.
Master's Age: 40. Started at 35, Master Mariner.
Salary: £56.
9d. per month stopped on workmen's wages.

1   1847 *Reports*, Part 1, pp. 70-71.

APPENDIX 5

Margam Tinworks School, Girls [2]

Established 1833; Promoters as for boys' school.
Area: 26 x 13 feet. 106 on books. Attendances as before, joint.
Ages: Under 5, 30; from 5 to 10, 50; over 10, 26.
Average attendance in last year: 55.
Monitorial, 18 monitors, joint as before.
Subjects: Holy Scriptures, Catechism, reading, writing.
Age of mistress: 46. Started at 36, widow.
Salary: £36–8–0.
9d. per month deducted as before.

2   1847 *Reports*, Part 1, pp. 70-71.

APPENDIX 6

Report of the Commissioner on the Margam Tinworks School, 1847 [3]

Tinworks school (Close to Aberafon):
I visited this school on the 4th of March. In the boys' school at twenty minutes past nine, only 14 children were present. The schoolroom lies above the stables of the works. It is in the shape of a gnomon; ill-furnished, and ill-calculated for a schoolroom. The master appeared intelligent but untrained. I visited the girls' school while a muster was being made of the boys. On my return I heard 13 read (from one of Chamber's school-books) about Creation . . . the girls' school contained no furniture but benches. I heard six girls read viii St. Matthew, all very ill; they could answer hardly any questions.

3   1847 *Reports*, Part 1, p. 353.

TINPLATE WORKS SCHOOLS

APPENDIX 7

Aberdulais Tinworks School [1]

Established 1842. Promoters: Messrs. W. Llewellyn, and Sons, Aberdulais Tinworks, near Neath.

Tenancy at will. Good building. Outbuildings sufficient and in good repair. 9 feet high, 25 x 18 feet. Insufficient furniture and apparatus in good repair.

50 on books. Less than one year: 4; from 1 to 2 years, 17; from 2 to 3 years, 6; from 3 to 4 years, 20; from 4 to 5 years, 3.

Ages: under 5 years: 12 girls and 6 boys; from 5 to 10 years: 7 girls and 9 boys; over 10: 8 girls and 8 boys. Average attendance in last year: 70 girls and 25 boys.

Method: Monitorial with 10 monitors.

Religious instruction by teacher. Visitation by minister.

English books only.

Master's Age: 50. Started at 48. Grocer.

Salary: £39, with house and coals.

2d. per week deducted from workmen's wages.

1   1847 *Reports*, Part 1, pp. 64-5.

APPENDIX 8

Summary of Margam and Aberdulais Tinworks Schools

Margam Tinworks.

1889.	Accommodation for 168. Average attendance 124.	Annual Grant: £103–7–2.[1]
1894.	Accommodation for 253. Average attendance 141.	Annual grant: £130–5–0.[2]

Aberdulais Tinworks.

1882.	Accommodation for 150. Average attendance 50.	Annual Grant: £40–12–0.[3]
1889.	Accommodation for 150. Average attendance 65.	Annual Grant: £60–5–6.[4]
1894.	Accommodation for 150. Average attendance 83.	Annual Grant: £ not given.

1   *Minutes of Committee of Council*, 1890. Tabulated Reports.
2   ibid 1895.
3   ibid 1883.
4   ibid 1890.

APPENDIX 9

CARMARTHEN TINWORKS SCHOOL [1]

Borough of Carmarthen. Tinworks. Established 1844. Good building. Insufficient outbuildings, but good.

School 9 feet high, 16 x 10 feet. Insufficient apparatus. Furniture in good repair.

55 on books. Under 5, 12 girls and 9 boys; from 50 to 10, 10 girls and 13 boys; over 10, 7 girls and 4 boys. Average attendance in last year: 29 girls and 24 boys.

Teacher instructor, no monitors.

Scripture, English, and writing, reading.

English books only; Welsh spoken in explanation of English books. Grammar of Welsh.

Age of master: 31; commenced teaching at 29; clerk at the tinworks.

Salary: £27–16–0. School pence: £7–16–0.

1d. per week from men employed in the tinworks.

Tinworks Day School Carmarthen: This school is held in a room of the master's house which was far too small to contain the number present—40, although generally attended by 50. The master has been brought up in a superior manner, and seemed well-qualified to discharge his duties. From what I saw and heard, his scholars were making great progress under his instruction, but an undue proportion were in the junior classes. Several of the best scholars had lately been taken away from school. Their writing was good and some answered questions readily on what they had been reading.

1   1847 *Reports*, Part 1, p. 293. Parochial Returns, Appendix, p. 30.

APPENDIX 10

PONTARDAWE TINWORKS SCHOOL. NATIONAL [2]

Established 1846. Promoter: W. Parsons, Esq., Tinworks, Pont ar Dawe, near Swansea. Tenure in trust. Bad building with insufficient outbuildings. Dimensions: 8 36 x 21. Accommodation at 6 square feet: 126. Insufficient furniture in bad repair.

Number of Children on books: 65.

65 attended for less than one year. 4 boys under 5 years; 11 boys between 5 and 10 years; 35 girls above 10 years; 15 boys above 10 years.

Instruction by teacher only, no monitors.

Religious instruction by teacher. Visitation by minister.

English books only. Grammar of English.

Master's age: 25. Commenced at 24. Mineral Agent before.

Salary: £50 p.a. £4 from school pence. £50 from subscription.

Age of mistress: 25. Commenced at 24. Married.

2   1847 *Reports*, Part 1, pp. 54-57.

TINPLATE WORKS SCHOOLS

APPENDIX 11

Dafen Tinworks School, Llanelli, Carmarthenshire [1]

Proprietors: Messrs. Phillips, Nunes, and Co.
Promoters: Messrs. Phillips, Nunes, and Co.
Schoolrooms, size of, in feet: Mixed School, 60 x 20. Infants: 30 x 20. Classrooms: 15 x 10. Total cost of buildings: £500.
Amount contributed by Privy Council or any other body: nil.
Average annual cost of schools to proprietors: £20.
The parents are at perfect liberty to send their children to school or not.
Small tax on workmen's wages for educational purposes employed.
Preference given to children who have been educated in the school when supplying vacancies at the works.
School established in 1850. School provides all equipment.
About 20 children attend whose parents earn less than £1 per week. $2\frac{1}{2}$d. in the £ deducted from workmen's wages. 4d. per week paid by the children of other people, and also for evening school.
Number of children belonging to workpeople: Boys—60; Girls—59; Infants—79.
Number of children belonging to other people: Boys—2; Girls—2; Infants—5.
Average age of children in various classes:

Boys: Class 1:	13;	2, $10\frac{1}{2}$;	3, $10\frac{1}{2}$;	4, $8\frac{1}{2}$;	5, 8;	6, —.
Girls:	13;	$10\frac{1}{2}$;	$10\frac{1}{2}$;	$8\frac{1}{2}$;	8;	—.
Evening:	17;	14;	13;			

1 *Reports from Commissioners*, Inspectors of Factories, 1868-69: p. 233.

APPENDIX 12

Dafen Tinworks National School, Carmarthenshire

Detailed statement of Annual Grants, 1855.[1]
1 In augmentation of Certificated teachers' salaries, and in retiring pensions: £15–0–0.
2 In stipends to apprentices and gratuities to teachers instructing them: £49–10–0.
3 Name of apprentice and year of apprenticeship:
Boys: J. Morris, 3rd year; R. Davies, 2nd year; D. Griffiths, 1st year.

Summary of Dafen Tinworks school, 1866-1894.

1866. Average attendance 161. Annual grant: £108–6–3 [2] Evening: 42.
1874. This school was one of the three most efficient schools in the Inspectors District, Average Attendance, 210.[3]
1882. 283 on books. 225 average attendance. Grant of £189–9–8. 30 attend evening school.[4]
1885. 283 on books. 213 average attendance. Grant of £187–5–0. 20 in evening school.[5]
1889. 194 average attendance. 7 in evening school. Grant of £157–17–6.[6]
1894. 234 average attendance. Grant: £250–2–5.[7]

1 *Minutes of Committee of Council*, 1856, Appendix.
2 ibid 1866. Tabulated Reports.
3 ibid 1875, Appendix, Table D, p. 139.
4 ibid 1883, p. 770.
5 ibid 1886. Tabulated Reports.
6 ibid 1889-90. Tabulated Reports.
7 ibid 1895. List of Board Schools, p. 1076.

TINPLATE WORKS SCHOOLS

APPENDIX 13

EXCERPTS FROM BRYNAMMAN TINWORKS SCHOOL LOGBOOK

(Sir) Henry Jones, Headmaster from 21st April, 1873 to 7th May, 1875. Later, Professor of Moral Philosophy at Glasgow University.

April 21st, 1873: Henry Jones takes charge. Average attendance for week not entered—about 190. Lateness almost universal—conveying food to fathers at works.

November 14th: School examined by Mr. Legge and Mr. Davies from the Works Office.

Inspector's Report for 1873: Large attendance of children of which many were mere infants. The present master seems to be an efficient and energetic teacher, and at present he works under some disadvantage. When the Infants Dept. is opened, and the classroom made more private, he will doubtless be able to produce better results.

May 7th, 1875: Henry Jones finishes, and Mr. Gibbs takes charge.

1878: Mr. Strick, Proprietor of Tinworks distributes prizes and Certificates.

Report for 1893: The grant is paid for the 7 months during which the school has been in possession of the School Board.

APPENDIX 14

PENTYRCH, MELINCRYTHAN, AND TYDEE TINWORKS SCHOOLS

1. *Pentyrch.*
    1878. Average attendance: 177. Grant: £148–6–0.[1]
    1889. Accommodation: 332.
    Average attendance: 176. Grant: £157–1–3.[2]
    1894. Accommodation 332.
    Average attendance: 164. Grant: £147–4–0[3]

2. *Melincrythan.*
    1894. Accommodation 773.   Average attendance: 724.[4]

3. *Tydee.* One Department, Boys.
    1866. Average attendance: 62.   Grant: £29–12–8.[5]
    1876. Average attendance: 83.   Grant not given.[6]
    1877. Average attendance: 93.   Grant not given.[7]

1 *Minutes of Committee of Council:* 1879. Tabulated Report.
2 ibid 1890.
3 ibid 1895.
4 ibid.
5 ibid 1867.
6 ibid 1877.
7 ibid 1878.

CHAPTER VII

Colliery Schools

IT HAS already been noted that the characteristic feature of the industrial evolution of south Wales during the first half of the nineteenth century was the growth and expansion of the ferrous and non-ferrous metallurgical industries. Their prosperity depended essentially upon the availability and supply of cheap coal and it was for this reason that most of the larger iron and copperworks had their own collieries.[1] Therefore, collieries in this category had no schools, since the colliers' children attended the iron or copperworks schools, for example, at Llanelli and Hafod (Swansea) copperworks schools, the Rhymney, Dowlais and Neath Abbey ironworks schools and many others.[2]

The real colliery school was the one promoted or established by the owner of a colliery or a colliery company. Sometimes a school in a mining community was maintained partly by fixed annual donations from colliery owners or companies. Such schools were primarily for colliers' children, but, as in other works schools, children of other workpeople took advantage of such educational facilities, provided there were vacancies or 'places' in these schools. Over forty such colliery schools were promoted in the South Wales Coalfield during the nineteenth century. The North Wales Coalfield had no colliery schools.

The establishment of colliery schools in south Wales followed very closely the various phases of coal-mining. During the eighteenth century Sir Humphrey Mackworth's Charity School at Neath for his miners' children[3] and R. J. Nevill's Free Schools at Llanelli[4] in the first decades of the nineteenth century were the earliest. The second phase, roughly from 1820 to 1860, corresponded with the development of the heavy industries which necessitated the sinking of large numbers of new pits to meet the high fuel demands. A few small colliery schools were beginning to appear during this period, before monetary grants began to flow from government

1 A. H. John, op. cit., p. 36.
 David Williams, *Modern Wales*, J. Murray, 1950, p. 215.
2 *Newcastle Commission Report*, 1861, Reports of Assistant Commissioners, Vol. II, Appendix E.
3 T. Shankland, *Seren Gomer*, 3, XXIV, 1903: Appendix I, p. 145.
4 *Returns of the Llanelli Free Schools*, 1818-1823.

sources through the Voluntary Societies. Between 1840 and 1860 however, others were established when (*a*) grants were forthcoming from the Committee of Privy Council, (*b*) the Voluntary Societies became more active, and (*c*) when several government Commissions produced *Reports on the State of Education in the Mining Districts*.[1] The final phase from 1860 to the end of the century was associated with the rapid development of the central Glamorgan coalfield, especially the steam coal deposits of the Rhondda valleys for export purposes. This region, by 1900 became one of the most densely populated parts of Britain.[2] This third stage in the development of the coalfield inaugurated a whole succession of new colliery schools most of which were located in the two Rhondda valleys whilst many others appeared in other colliery districts. Measured in terms of years however, the life of most of these schools was brief for they appeared too near the first Education Act of 1870. It is surprising moreover to find that colliery schools continued to be opened well on into the 1880s. Eventually, their subsequent history became intimately bound up with the establishment of local School Boards which finally absorbed them.

COLLIERY SCHOOLS 1820-1860

For historical reasons the colliery schools of this period are divided into two groups: those established between 1820-1840, and 1840 to 1860. In the first period before 1840, the few colliery schools which were established represented the efforts of individual proprietors and private subscribers to provide some kind of educational facilities in the mining areas before parliamentary grants were available. Moreover, although the two Voluntary Societies, the National and British and Foreign School Societies, had been formed in 1811 and 1814 respectively, very few schools were promoted by them in the mining areas in the first three decades of the nineteenth century. This deficiency in the provision of schools in the mining areas became the main topic of the Reports of the Minutes of

---

1 i. *Reports from the Select Committee on the Act for the Regulation of Factories, with Minutes of Evidence*, 1840, X; 1841, XI.
   ii. Report of R. J. Saunders, ibid, February, 1842, 1843, XXVIII.
   iii. *First Report of the Commissioners, Mines*, 1842, XV.
   iv. *Reports and Evidence of Sub-Commissioners*, ibid, XVI, XVII.
   v. *Second Report of Commissioners*, ibid, 1843, XIII.
   vi. *Annual Reports of the Commissioners on the State of the Population in the Mining Districts*, Annually, 1844-1859.
   vii. *Six Reports of the Commissioner on the operation of the Mines Act*, 1844-1849.
2 In 1861, the population of the old parish of Ystradyfodwg was 3,857. In 1901, the population of the modern Rhondda Urban District Council was 113,735.

Committee of Council after 1840 and was the subject of more than one government inquiry—long before the Blue Books of 1847 appeared.[1]

The colliery schools which existed before 1840 were wholly dependent on the benevolence of colliery proprietors coupled with the income derived from the poundage levy on the colliers' wages. The first colliery school of the coalfield was established at Hirwaun in 1820—at that time one of the most desolate places in Glamorgan with a population of about 2,000.[2] Here, there were two schools connected with the ironworks—one of the few examples of an undertaking which had a separate school for its colliery—the Colliers and Miners School, and the Furnace or Firemen's School. The Colliers' School, located 'in a room over a stable' was packed with fifty boys and girls and confined itself to the teaching of the three R's. The Commissioner said that 'the children read better than many children whom I have met with . . . and they were able to add simple figures with extreme activity'.[3] This school was promoted by F. Crawshay of Treforest, Pontypridd, and maintained by a weekly 'stoppage' of a $\frac{1}{2}$d. in the pound from the colliers' wages. But the entire management of the school was in the hands of the workmen—an arrangement which produced constant friction and inefficiency.[4] In addition, the majority of the workmen at Hirwaun, as in other places, were Dissenters which produced the usual situation of rebellion against the catechism and visitations by Church clergy. This discontent reached boiling-point in 1846 when the fractious workmen, like their compatriots at Ystalyfera, decided to build their own school on the British system. This action cost them nearly £300 in 1849 and they were still compelled to submit to deductions from their wages to subvent the National school.[5]

Roberts, the British Agent, attended a committee of the workmen at Hirwaun in December, 1853. He was very concerned to learn that although the workmen had collected some hundreds of pounds since 1849, this

---

1 i. *Minutes of the Committee of Council on Education*, 1840-41: 1842-1846.
   ii. *Parliamentary Papers, Accounts and Papers on Education*, 1839, Vol. XLL.
   iii. *Parochial Returns made to the Select Committee on the Education of the Poor*, 1819, XI.
   iv. *Education Inquiry*, 1833, Vols. II and III.
   v. *Report from the Select Committee on the Education of the Poorer Classes in England and Wales*, 1834, IX: 1835, VII; 1837-38, VI.
   vi. *Abstract of Answers and Returns relative to the State of Education in England and Wales*, 1835, XLI, XLII, *and* XLIII. *Reports of the Commissioners, Mines, from*1846.
2 1847 *Reports*, Part 1, p. 54, and pp. 333-4.
3 ibid.
4 ibid, See Appendix II.
5 *N.L.W.: Nefydd MSS* 7096, 7106, 7132 *E*, The Journals of the Rev. William Roberts (Nefydd) of Blaina, Mon.: Journal for 1853, entry for 1 December.

money had been expended in maintaining the teachers and furnishing the school, and that the committee was £220 in debt 'on account of the building' which had to be closed, and 150 children were affected. He persuaded the workmen to re-open the school and promised to send Mr. Joseph Bowstead, H.M.I. to visit them with the object of securing a government grant.[1] When the Inspector visited the school in 1855 he found that the Marquis of Bute's lawyer was dilatory in granting an extended lease for the site and Bowstead could promise no government grant.[2] Roberts made further enquiries in 1856 but the school was still in 'great financial trouble and difficulties' the committee informing him that the school could no longer continue without some kind of external aid. In May, 1857, Roberts went to Hirwaun and 'conferred with some leading men with the object of putting the case to Crawshay Bailey to try and get government aid'. The deputation was successful, they obtained grants through the British and Foreign School Society and the school was saved.[3]

In the parish of Llangyfelach in the western part of the coalfield near Swansea, the Llewellyn's of Penllergaer promoted the Llangyfelach Church school in 1822,[4] another at Penllergaer in 1834,[5] and a boys' and girls' school at Gors Eynon (Gorseinon) in 1846. The two latter schools were entirely maintained by this family which owned extensive collieries in the district.[6] The Marquis of Bute, liberal sponsor of new Church schools in several places in east Glamorgan, was the chief promoter of two schools at Aberdare—the Aberdare 'Free' schools in 1830, and another at the same place in 1850.[7]

The first colliery school of the Rhondda valleys was at Dinas, in the parish of Llantrisant, established by the pioneer colliery proprietor Walter Coffin of Llandaff, Cardiff. He first of all sank the Dinas Lower Pit and in 1832 the Dinas Middle Pit, and from an indenture drawn up on 29 September 1829, an Agreement was made 'Between Morgan David (owner of the local Graigddu and Gwaunadda farmland) and Walter Coffin (Rhondda coal pioneer who held mortgages on this land) and

---

1 *Nefydd MSS, Journal for* 1855, entry for 27 December.
2 ibid. *Journal for* 1856, entry for 18 December: This difficulty of obtaining sites arose very often in south and north Wales where British schools were built. According to the regulations of the Committee of Council grants could not be given for the building of school rooms unless the sites were freehold. The land in most cases belonged to church landowners. See Chapter XII.
3 ibid, entry for 11 March: *Journal for* 1857, entry for 14 May, See Appendix 3.
4 1847 *Reports*, Part 1, p. 50. See Appendix 4.
5 ibid, p. 54. See Appendix 5.
6 ibid, p. 326. Llewellyn also contributed to the school at Cilybebyll, ibid, Part I, p. 62.
7 Cardiff Central Library. *Bute Documents, MS*, 4.1034, X 8, and X 2/3: *Abstracts of Payments and Receipts for the late Marquis of Bute's Executors and Trustees.*

Moses Rowlands, Schoolmaster, for 600 square yards of Gwaunadda land . . . for 999 years, at the yearly rent of 10/-, first payment to be made September 29th, 1830'.[1] This evidence suggests that the Dinas schools started in 1830, a much earlier date than the one found in the 1847 Reports where it is stated that the Dinas Girls' and Boys' schools were opened in 1838 and 1845 respectively.[2] However, the later Dinas schools were at Tai (Dinas) and may have been moved to that place on the dates mentioned in the Reports. Another source mentions that the original Dinas schools were housed in a colliery storehouse,[3] moved from there to the vestry of a Methodist chapel and finally to Tai where they were known as the elementary schools.[4]

A small colliery school at Cilybebyll (Crynant) served the children of colliers employed in the Ynys y Geinon, Waunycoed, and Primrose collieries. The schoolroom was erected and presented by Howell Gwyn, Esq., of Duffryn, Neath, in 1839.[5] This completes the initial phase of colliery schools as individual institutions. But these were not the only collieries in operation—there was an impressive number up to 1840— most of them owned by well-established smelting companies, and the children who lived in the vicinity of such collieries were able to attend the schools built by the parent Company of the colliery.

COLLIERY SCHOOLS 1840-1860

This second phase in the establishment of colliery schools is given separate consideration in the period 1820-1860 because it was dominated by one of the most distinguished and colourful personalities in the field of Welsh industry and education in the nineteenth century, namely, Sir Thomas Phillips, Q.C. (1801-1867), and his work and influence merit more than ephemeral notice. Born at Ynysgarth, Clydach, in the parish of Llanelly, Breconshire, he later moved with his parents to Trosnant, near Pontypool, Monmouthshire, and became a solicitor in Newport. He was mayor of the town in 1838, and for the part he played in quashing the Chartist outbreak in Newport in 1839 was invited to stay with the Queen at Windsor Castle for a week, secured a knighthood and subsequently admitted a Freeman of the City of London. Later he became a

---

1   Moses Rowland(s), 1790-1837, a native of Caio, Carmarthenshire, first schoolmaster of Dinas schools; elementary education enthusiast of the period.
2   1847 *Reports*, Part 1, p. 58.
3   Information from Mr. Harry Harris, Rosebank, Ystrad, Rhondda, retired schoolmaster and local antiquary.
4   See Appendices 8 and 9.
5   *Newcastle Commission Report*, 1861, Appendix: Evidence of Howell Gwyn, Esq., of Duffryn. 1847 *Reports*, Part 1, p. 343.

barrister attached to the Chancery Division and was also one of the governors of King's College, London.[1]

It was as an educationist that Sir Thomas left his most durable and conspicuous mark. He owned several collieries in Monmouthshire and it was in connection with one of his collieries at Courtybella that he started his educational work. Well-versed in the educational deficiencies of the mining districts, closely acquainted with the social and working conditions of the populations in the industrial areas, and wounded in the Chartist disturbances in his own home district, he was conscious of 'a great and presssing need of an elementary system of popular education as exhibited by the recent outrages'.[2] It is not surprising therefore to find that in 1840 he took steps 'to further the material and moral welfare of those who were brought into close connection with himself'. He established a colliery school at Courtybella 'a locality distinguished as a seat of disaffection in 1839',[3] together with a lending library and also built a new church. In addition he gave lectures to his workmen, set up a cooperative store in connection with the colliery, and promoted a sick fund.[4] The story of his efforts to establish this school and several others which he promoted and endowed, made him one of the leading figures in the sphere of elementary education within the National Society, and a champion of the cause of education not only for the working classes of Monmouthshire and the coalfield but for the whole of the Principality.

He may be regarded as the pioneer colliery owner, who, in spite of the lack of interest displayed by his fellow proprietors, opened the first colliery school in the county. For several years, without any measure of success he endeavoured to get together other colliery owners to establish schools, but his earnestness of purpose and pertinacity in his cause prevailed to such an extent that eventually he enlisted the sympathy and obtained the assistance of the other iron and colliery proprietors of the two counties of Monmouthshire and Glamorgan in the promotion of similar schools.[5] It is important to remember that Sir Thomas was an ardent churchman and Sunday school teacher, and numbered among his closest friends the Rev. Thomas Phillips, Association Secretary of the Bible Society, and the two Bishops, Copleston and Ollivant. In his role as educational reformer it is pertinent to pose a number of important questions. Was Sir Thomas Phillips motivated to provide schools merely

1 *Y Bywgraffiadur Cymreig hyd* 1940, Ail argraffiad, Caerdydd, 1954, p. 717.
2 J. Morgan, *Four Biographical Sketches*, London, 1892, p. 170.
3 *Reports from the Commissioners, Mines*, 1846, p. 416.
4 J. Morgan, ibid.
5 ibid, p. 171.

to combat educational destitution and to ameliorate the condition of the labouring populations, or did his educational aims and activities have a much deeper significance? Bearing in mind his own background and religious integrity, including his concern for the public weal, were his schools meant to be merely places of catechetical instruction with some proficiency in the three R's? He had great admiration for the work of Thomas Charles and his Sunday schools for the Welsh 'gwerin'[1] which were so successful during the lifetime of Sir Thomas, both in the rural and industrial areas.[2] Is it unreasonable to assume that he envisaged a similar crusade in the guise of day-schools on the National System as a panacea for discontent among the working classes? In short, was his motive for founding schools based on the fear of anarchy or of subversive elements which might flourish among an illiterate proletariat? In fact, Thomas Charles was a fervid disciple of the law of subordination[3] for in his 'Rules' for the Sunday schools he lays specific stress on manners or submissiveness 'to one's elders and to the public authorities', and other writers on education during the same period emphasized moral conditioning, including M. J. Rhys, the 'Radical' Baptist.[4] Similar references to 'the morals of the population' abound in the annual reports of the two Voluntary Societies, and in more than one government inquiry before 1840.

In 1839, the Committee of the Privy Council on Education was set up and 'entrusted with the application of any sums which might be voted by parliament, through the two Voluntary Societies, for the purposes of education in England and Wales'[5] and in the same year the first *Minutes* of the Council contained the 'gloomy' Report by H. S. Tremenheere on the Mining Districts.[6] On 25 March 1840, the Committee of Council sent a Circular Letter to the twenty-nine mining proprietors in Monmouthshire deploring the lack of educational facilities in the county 'and realized that few schools existed . . . and had little effect on the labouring populations'.[7] This Circular had as its object an offer of help in the erection of schools on a 50 per cent grant basis provided that the promoters of

1 A difficult word to translate: the peasantry or 'ordinary people'.
2 See Chapter IX.
3 Thomas Charles (of Bala), *Rheolau i ffurfio a Threfnu yr Ysgolion Sabbothawl*, R. Saunderson, Bala, 1813. Although Charles asserted that 'the salvation of souls is the only point we have in view' his 'Rules' are quite specific about the 'formation of manners'.
4 J. J. Evans, *M. J. Rhys a'i Amserau*, Liverpool, 1935. p. 85.
5 *Parliamentary Papers, Accounts and Papers*, 1839, Vol. XLI, Papers on Education, 4th February, 1839, p. 255.
6 *Minutes of Committee of Council*, 1839-40, p. 415.
7 ibid, 1840-41, p. 28.

schools secured the services of a teacher trained in a Normal School of the National or the British and Foreign School Society. Sir Thomas Phillips had, in the meantime, written to the Committee of Council stating that his fellow colliery proprietors were not very interested in establishing schools although there were many thousands dependent on the collieries in the districts of Bedwellty, Mynyddislwyn, Machen, and Risca.[1] He furthermore implored the Council to grant money to build a school 'in order to show them up' and his letter ended with the plea 'your memorialist therefore humbly solicits from your Lordships a liberal grant for the erection of buildings so that proprietors might imitate'.[2] His wish was granted on 13 November 1840, when the Council promised to pay, through the National Society, 50 per cent of the expenses of his school. This was the first of the *works schools* in Wales to be aided by a parliamentary grant. The Courtybella colliery school in the parish of Mynyddislwyn, Monmouthshire, was opened in 1842. The initial estimate of the cost of erection was £900 of which Sir Thomas had to pay £450 in addition to a fixed annual sum for its upkeep and the poundage money from the men employed in his collieries.[3] But when the school was finally completed the actual cost was £1,400 of which Sir Thomas contributed £700.[4] This sum included the cost of the school buildings and the master's house which were described as 'handsome buildings'.[5]

The funds for the maintenance of the school were raised in the following manner: 'In 1843 Sir Thomas Phillips contributed £90. 5s. 2d. and his workmen contributed a 1d. in the £ to the school funds in return for which their children were educated'.[6] The children of parents not in the employ of Sir Thomas were admitted on payment of a small weekly sum. The school had accommodation for 300, and an adult school was conducted on two evenings a week.[7] In addition to the Courtybella school he supported another Church school at Llanellen, near Abergavenny, contributed generously to other schools in Monmouthshire and to the Monmouthshire Diocesan School Board.[8] In his evidence to the Pakington

1 *Minutes of Committee of Council*, 1840-41, p. 28. Copy of letter from Sir Thomas Phillips.
2 ibid.
3 ibid, p. 118. Also Appendix 2, p. 48.
4 ibid for 1844, Report by Rev. H. W. Bellairs, Feb. 1845, p. 224.
5 *Reports from Commissioners, Mines*, 1846, p. 416.
6 *Minutes of Committee of Council*, 1844. Also see Appendices 10, 11, 12, 13 and 14.
7 *Minutes of Committee of Council*, 1844, p. 224.
8 *Results of the Returns to the General Inquiry made by the National Society into the State and Progress of schools*, 1846-47, published 1849: Monmouth, p. 7. *Annual Reports of the Monmouthshire Education Board*, Published by T. Farror, Beacon Office, Monmouth. Trustees of Sir Thomas Phillips: William Graham and Co., Midland Bank Chambers, Newport, Mon.

Select Committee[1] he referred to his frequent visits to the proprietors of other works in Monmouthshire who had followed his example by establishing schools with government assistance since 1850.[2] Sir Thomas was a member of the national committee of the National Society and also of its Welsh Education Committee, and his other main work in the provision of schools for the mining areas was through the latter committee. He was mainly responsible for the organization of the Education Fund of the Welsh committee which he inaugurated in 1846 for the extension of Church instruction throughout the industrial districts.[3] He also enhanced the work of the National Society in Wales in another typical and practical manner. As organizer of the Welsh committee of the Society he made a circuit throughout the Principality and was largely instrumental in establishing two Welsh Training Schools, one at Caernarvon and the other, Trinity College, Carmarthen, which resulted in the production of good teachers, and the erection of new schools in north and south Wales—especially south Wales.[4]

Sir Thomas did not permit the national character of his work to dim his enthusiasm for more local work in his own county. In addition to keeping one eye on the rest of the country he promoted and managed other schools in the hilly and Welsh districts of Monmouthshire.[5] In short, Sir Thomas was the main driving force behind the National Society in Wales during the period when the rival British and Foreign School Society had two full-time Agents in North and South Wales.

Another side of his work should be mentioned. In common with other industrialists he was fully aware and particularly concerned about the early age at which large numbers of young children left school to go to work. Several methods were employed to entice children to remain at school for a longer period including the provision of evening classes for them after working hours. Sir Thomas Phillips organized a successful Prize Scheme in Monmouthshire and later persuaded his fellow industrialists in south Wales to form themselves into a committee which was

1 At the Inquiry he was in company with the two British Agents, the Revs. John Phillips and William Roberts (Nefydd); Mr. J. Bowstead and the Rev. B. J. Binns (Inspectors of the British and National Societies); Sir Hugh Owen, and the Rev. Thomas Gee.
2 *Report of the Pakington Select Committee*, Minutes 5459, ff.
3 ibid, Minute 5459-60.
4 ibid, Also 1847 *Reports*, Part III, p. 35: 'Some landed proprietors subscribe to the church schools. Large sums were being raised among the proprietors and clergy chiefly by the exertions of Sir Thomas Phillips of Newport for a common fund to promote popular education in Wales in connection with the Church of England.' The Caernarvon Training College was later moved to Bangor as St. Mary's College.
5 *Report of the Pakington Select Committee*, Minute 5461.

afterwards known as The Iron and Coalmasters Association of which he was secretary and treasurer.[1] Finally, it is worth recording that this energetic industrialist found time to accomplish work in more permanent form. He had been most disturbed by 'the partisan and exaggerated statements' contained in the Blue Books of 1847, about the moral and social conditions in Wales, and decided to examine the question for himself by travelling the length and breadth of Wales and compiling a whole mass of information. In 1849 he published his book on Welsh education as a reply to the scathing Commissioners' Reports.[2]

In the Swansea district colliery schools were established at Llansamlet, Cwmllynfell, and Cwmtwrch. At Llansamlet, C. H. Smith the coal proprietor started a small school in 1841, and in 1845 procured a new site from the Earl of Jersey and erected a new National colliery school, which was maintained by the deduction from the wages of his colliers.[3] Two colliery proprietors in the upper Swansea valley, Messrs. James and Aubrey of the Cwmllynfell colliery and Moira Crane, Esq., of Cwmtwrch colliery also established schools.[4]

In 1844, the Marquis of Bute promoted a Church school at Rhigos in the parish of Ystradyfodwg[5] and also contributed fifty guineas annually towards the maintenance of National schools in the parish of Llantrisant[6]. The Bute family never established a colliery school but wherever they had industrial interests in Glamorgan always supported Church schools.[7] A little attention has already been given to educational efforts among the colliers at Hirwaun, especially the fortunes of the British school. In 1856 a new school was opened on the British system 'in connection and for the benefit of the colliers and miners under R. Crawshay, Esq., of Hirwaun. The movement originated entirely among the colliers, and they were afterwards aided in their efforts by the committee of Hirwaun British school'.[8] The colliers obtained a suitable room from Crawshay, who also gave his consent to apply a 1d. in the £ of their wages for its maintenance, instead of supporting the inefficient National school at Hirwaun.[9]

1   *Report of the Pakington Select Committee*, Minute 5462. See Appendix 15.
2   Sir T. Phillips, *Wales*. He also wrote the *Life of James Davies, Devauden* (1765-1849).
3   1847 *Reports*, Part I, p. 330.
4   ibid, Part I, p. 329.
5   ibid.
6   ibid.
7   The Bute family also supported the Pentyrch works school.
8   *Nefydd MSS*, 1856.
9   ibid, entry for April 3rd.

COLLIERY SCHOOLS

In the 1850s a small school was established in connection with Insole's collieries at Cymmer, Porth, but the accommodation was poor and the school had an inefficient and untrained master.[1] Between 1855 and 1860 many new pits were sunk in the Rhondda Fawr valley and although no colliery school was opened in the area until 1860, Nefydd wrote in 1858 stating that 'most of the new colliery owners in Ystradyfodwg were very anxious to have a good school for the colliers, and wanted me to deliver a Welsh lecture on education to their workmen in the collieries'.[2] The remaining colliery schools established before 1860 included the Bryndu (Pyle) school, 1846,[3] and the Llanfabon colliery school in the parish of Gelligaer, 1846.[4] The colliery Steward, Benjamin Daniel, at the large Bryndu colliery owned by H. H. Ford, described them as 'schools built for boys and girls when our works began three years ago. The men earn 21/- to 25/- per week and some 30/- yet they threaten to strike for higher wages. We have much trouble with them. The schools are likely to be well attended; there are already 100 boys in the boys' school, and the master was obtained from Bristol'.[5] The parish of Gelligaer contained several collieries, the majority of the colliers living at Llanfabon. Three colliery companies supported the colliery school at that place—Duncan and Co.'s colliery at Llancaiach promised £50, Powell's colliery at Gelligaer, £60, and Mr. Cartwright, proprietor of Tophill colliery, £30.[6]

COLLIERY SCHOOLS 1860-1890

Before 1860 the old parish of Ystradyfodwg showed few signs of industrial development. Comprising the two Rhondda rivers and the area between them, the parish extended on the western side (the Rhondda Fawr) from Rhigos and Blaenrhondda on the north, down to Porth, including Treherbert, Treorchy, Pentre, Ton, Gelli, Ystrad, Llwynypia, Penygraig and Trealaw. The eastern boundary (the Rhondda Fach) extended from Porth north-eastwards to Ynyshir, Tylorstown, Ferndale, and Mardy. This parish had a population of 3,857 in 1861; by 1891, the new Rhondda Urban District had grown to 88,351, and at the turn of the century in 1901 had 113,735 inhabitants. Other parts of the coalfield, hitherto undeveloped, were exploited after 1860, particularly the Aberdare, Ogmore and Garw valleys, Maesteg, Clydach Vale, and several places in Monmouthshire. The anthracite coalfield of the west was not developed

1 *Nefydd MSS, Journal for February*, 1857, entry for 3rd February.
2 ibid, for 1858, entry for 4th August.
3 1847 *Reports*, Part I, p. 70.
4 ibid, p. 302.
5 *Reports from Commissioners, Mines*, 1846, p. 430.
6 1847 *Reports*, Part I, p. 302.

to any great extent until the last decade of the century, but by that time the Local School Boards had come into operation to provide schools for that area.

In the early years of the nineteenth century the Rhondda was described by one traveller as 'the glorious green valley'[1] and even in 1847 it had only two day schools, described by the assistant Commissioner in that year:—'Parish of Ystrad—Tafodog: visited this parish 27th February and the 5th and 16th March, 1847. It is a long narrow strip extending from Hirwaun across the centre of the county to Dinas in the parish of Llantrisant. It contains Rhigos and Penrhin collieries, and the mine-patches of Hirwaun ironworks. I found the following day schools—Penrhin school near Pont Walby, and Rhigos school'.[2]

Before 1860 not a single day school was under government inspection within the parish of Ystradyfodwg, though collieries had been sunk at Treherbert (1851-55), and Bodringallt (Ystrad) in 1858. The first colliery schools to be opened were Treherbert British school in 1860, Bodringallt in 1861, and a year later the National school was built at Treherbert with a building grant of £494 from the Privy Council.[3] The colliers employed at the Bute collieries in the vicinity of Treherbert which included the Dunraven, Tynewydd, and Ynysfeio collieries, contributed weekly sums deducted from their wages for the maintenance of the Treherbert British school which a few years later received an annual grant through the British Society.[4] The financial accounts for this school covering a period of four years from 1868 to 1872 show the detailed poundage sums transferred from the colliery accounts to the school.[5] Other information includes the headings of expenses for coal, school books, window cleaning, and a payment of 20/- per week to Mr. M. O. Jones, schoolmaster.[6]

The Rhondda valleys developed rapidly between 1860 and 1870, a development which continued up to the first World War. New collieries were sunk in rapid succession and with them the establishment of many new colliery schools. The Voluntary Societies became more active among the growing populations and several new schools were opened through

1 B. H. Malkin, *The Scenery, Antiquities and Biography of South Wales*, 1807. Reprinted S. & R. Publishers, Wakefield, Yorks, 1970. (mentions a school at Ystradyfodwg, kept in the Church). C. F. Cliffe, *Book of South Wales*, 1848.
2 1847 *Reports*, Part I, p. 336. See Appendices 16 and 17.
3 M. O. Jones, *A History of the Parish of Ystradyfodwg*, 1902, p. 125, MS 4383D, N.L.W.
4 ibid, p. 127.
5 MS 12.628A N.L.W. Treherbert British school Account from 10th February. 1868 to May, 1872. The account was kept by Mr. Aaron Cule, Grocer, Treherbert See Appendix 18.
6 ibid.

their renewed efforts. The Treherbert and Pentre National schools were opened in 1862 and 1864 respectively,[1] and the Tonypandy National school in 1870.[2] Further colliery schools in association with the British and Foreign School Society were established at Llwynypia, 1865;[3] United Collieries, Treorchy, 1866;[4] Dunraven and Blaenycwm, 1863; Pentre, 1875;[5] Ton, Ystrad, 1869;[6] Penygraig, 1869; Ferndale, 1869;[7] Cwmparc, 1871;[8] and Clydach Vale, 1872.[9] The Glamorgan Coal Company under the direction of Archibald Hood who came to the district from Scotland in 1860 established the Llwynypia colliery school.[10] Started in temporary buildings in 1865 it became so popular within a year that it became necessary to build a new school 'for the education of children and adults, and children only of labouring, manufacturing, and other poorer classes in the parish of Ystradyfodwg, and for no other purpose'.[11] Nearby, at Treorchy, the Ocean Coal Company (David Davies) was actively engaged in opening up several new pits and at the same time promoted a group of colliery schools which were maintained partly by the Company and partly by the weekly contributions by the colliers out of their wages. The accounts and wages books of these collieries show how the various schools were financed by these deductions.[12] The United Collieries school at Treorchy was maintained by the colliers employed at the Dare colliery;[13] the Ton colliery school by the colliers at Maindy colliery;[14] and joint contributions from the Park and Dare collieries maintained the Cwmparc colliery school.[15]

1 *MS* 4383 *D*, p. 126.
2 ibid, p. 127.
3 ibid, p. 126.
4 ibid.
5 *Logbook, Pentre British school*, 1875, entry for 12th March 'Pentre National school broke up last Monday. Children came flocking here.'
6 *MS* 4383*D*, p. 127.
7 ibid, Also: *Education Records*, Council Offices, Pentre, Rhondda.
8 ibid.
9 See Appendix 20 and 22.
10 C. Wilkins, *The South Wales Coal Trade*, op. cit., pp. 137-9.
11 *Three conveyances*, 1869, 1876, *and* 1884, conveyed to Mr. Archibald Hood and Mr. Robert Duncan. Council Offices, Pentre, Rhondda.
12 Ocean Coal Company's Office, Treorchy: *Wages Books of the Maindy, Park, and Dare Collieries*. See Appendix 19.
13 ibid, *Dare Colliery Wages Books, Nos.* 1, 5, *and* 6; 2d. in the £ poundage for Treorchy and Cwmparc schools. See Appendix 19.
14 ibid, *Maindy Colliery Wage Books, Nos.* 1 *and* 6; *Eastern Colliery Wages Books, Nos.* 1, 2, 3, *and* 4; 1d. in the £ poundage for Ton schools from the collieries.
15 ibid, *Park Colliery Wages Books, Nos.* 1 *and* 6; *Dare Colliery Wages Books*, ibid, *Nos.* 1, 5, *and* 6.

The Cwmparc school started some years before 1871 had an interesting story.[1] In 1860, Cwmparc was a new mining village of about two hundred families employed in the two new pits sunk by David Davies in the narrow valley, and who later formed the Ocean Coal Company. The first managing director of the Company, William Jenkins, of Ystradfechan House, formed a committee with himself as Chairman and recruited his colliery officials and six working colliers as members. The original school which was opened in a large loft over the colliery stables had one class of pupils whose ages ranged from 8 to 18. The Ocean Coal Company contributed a certain sum annually and the pupils paid 1d. per week. In 1871 a British school was built, the Company continued its financial support and a poundage on the colliers' wages met the additional expenses.[2]

The Blaenycwm colliery school was originally connected with the earlier Dunraven colliery which was in operation in 1856. The owner of this colliery, T. Joseph, a staunch Baptist, hailed from Heolyfelin, Aberdare, and many of the first colliery workers came with him from that place and lived in small cottages built for them in Blaenselsig, the original name for Blaenycwm. Starting as a Sunday school in 1859, the Blaenycwm school was opened in 1863 and was maintained fully by Joseph. Later, the Dunraven school was built at Tynewydd, maintained by grants from the colliery proprietors and the usual poundage.[3]

The Ocean Coal Company owned collieries outside the Rhondda area, in the Ogmore and Garw valleys, and at Ynysybwl. The wages books of the Western colliery at Ogmore Vale show no deductions from wages in support of any school,[4] but the books of the Garw and Lady Windsor collieries, at Blaengarw and Ynysybwl respectively, show poundage deductions of 1d. in the £ for the maintenance of the Blaengarw (1883), and Ynysybwl (1886) schools.[5]

It has already been noted that the National Society with the help of the Marquis of Bute had opened schools in the Aberdare valley as early as 1830, and also that Crawshay Bailey had been hesitant in opening a school, although the British and Foreign School Society had been ready to help him with grant aid.[6] However, the most important schools in

1 *Education Records*, Council Offices, Pentre, Rhondda.
2 ibid.
3 Information from Mr. S. Nicholas, Treherbert, late Headteacher of Dunraven school.
4 *Wages Books Western Colliery, Nos. 1 and 5*, Ocean Coal Co., Treorchy, Ltd.
5 *Wages Books of the Garw Colliery, Nos. 1, 2, and 4*. and *Lady Windsor Colliery, Nos. 1, 2, and 5*, Ocean Coal Co., ibid.
6 *Nefydd MSS, Journal for 1857*, entry for 16th April.

that valley were established by another group of colliery owners. In the late 1850s the Rt. Hon. Henry Austin Bruce, later Lord Aberdare,[1] who became one of the leading Welsh educationists of the latter years of the nineteenth century, was one of the promoters of schools for the new colliery populations, and the Duffryn colliery schools served at least six large collieries in the Aberdare valley. Most of these collieries were in operation after 1860, and although the Duffryn schools were opened in 1857[2] they are included here for that reason. The schools were conducted on the National system and the children came from the collieries of Lord Aberdare, Powell Duffryn, and Nixon.[3] The original schools built in 1857 were for boys, girls, and infants, but as the population of the district increased and new collieries were sunk, additional schools were provided at Mountain Ash for very young children. By the middle of 1872, there were three Infants' schools at Mountain Ash—Cwmpennar,[4] Miskin, and Newtown[5] which supplied the Boys' and Girls' Junior schools at Duffryn.[6] The schools were managed by a committee with Lord Aberdare as chairman together with colliery officials, other colliery proprietors, and workmen's representatives[7] and all meetings were held at Duffryn House.[8] Lord Aberdare was a frequent visitor to the schools and nothing was done, no appointment was made and no decisions were taken on any matter without his advice and personal consent.[9]

The Duffryn schools resembled very closely the Educational Scheme devised by Sir John and Lady Charlotte Guest at Dowlais. This is not surprising when it is remembered that Lord Aberdare became one of the Trustees of the Dowlais works on the death of Sir John in 1852, and was

1 Henry Austin Bruce of Duffryn, Aberdare (1815-1895), First Lord Aberdare Educated abroad and Swansea Grammar School. Barrister, Stipendiary Magistrate, Merthyr Tydfil and Aberdare. Succeeded Sir John Guest as M.P. for Merthyr in 1852, and one of the Trustees of the Dowlais Ironworks. Vice-President of the Committee of Privy Council for Education, and one of the Charity Commissioners. In 1873, President of the Privy Council and Baron. Elected an F.R.S. in 1876. In 1880, Chairman of the Departmental Committee on Intermediate and Higher Education in Wales and Monmouthshire, which produced the Aberdare Report of 1881 which recommended Welsh secondary schools and University Colleges. First Chancellor of the University of Wales.
2 *Duffryn National Schools Logbooks*, 4 *Vols*., Vol. I, 1863-1885, entry for March 10th, 1879—22nd anniversary of opening of schools.
3 ibid, entry for 24th November, 1876.
4 ibid, entry for 17th February, 1874.
5 ibid, entry for 28th October, 1872.
6 ibid.
7 ibid, Vol. 1, entry for 2nd February, 1880.
8 This is now Mountain Ash Comprehensive, formerly, Grammar School.
9 Vol. I of the Logbooks is full of references such as 'Mr. Bruce was consulted on all matters and payments'.

well acquainted with that elaborate school system.[1] The new Dowlais schools had been opened in 1855 and some significance may be attached to the fact that the Duffryn schools were built two years later. Using the information contained in the detailed logbooks of the schools the following scheme was followed at Duffryn:

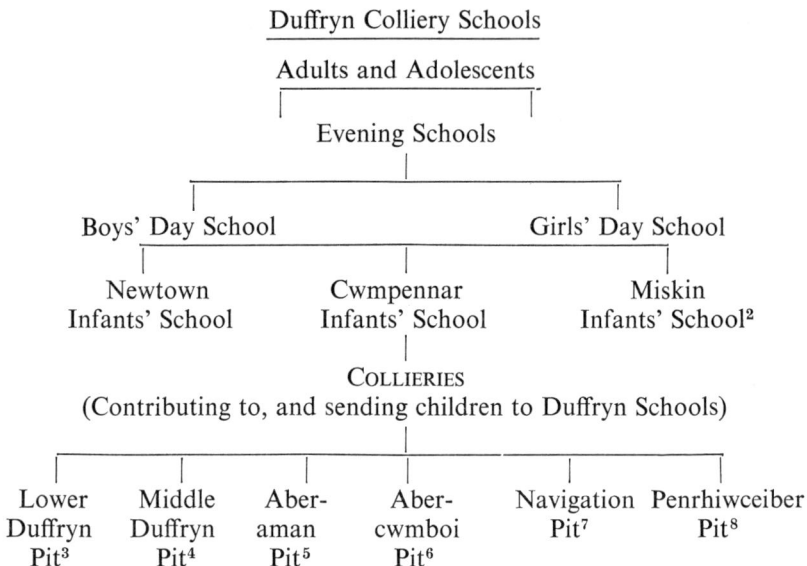

Among other interesting details in the school logbooks are the references to 'the large number of boys between 10 and 12 years of age who were sent from the collieries in conformity with the new Mines Regulations Act'. The school managers also kept the colliery officials informed of the progress of the youths who attended evening schools.[9] A regular entry in the records was the strict attention paid to the 'Colliery Lists' which

1. Bruce had paid frequent visits to Dowlais before Sir John's death.
2. *Logbooks*, Vol. I, entry for 15th July, 1872: 'This school was opened today. I, Esther Thomas, formerly a pupil-teacher in the Dowlais Ironworks schools entered on my duties as mistress this morning.'
3. ibid, entry for 2nd February, 1880.
4. ibid.
5. ibid, entry for August 5th, 1873.
6. ibid, entries for 13th, 24th November, 1874; and November, 1876.
7. ibid.
8. ibid, entry for March (undated) 1878, and Note on p. 478. See Appendix 21.
9. *Duffryn school Logbooks*, Vol. I, entry 6th January, 1873.

contained the names of colliers' children from each of the six collieries eligible to attend the schools. These lists were sent regularly to the schools by the chief clerk at the Colliery office.[1] It seems that a colliery could decide for itself whether or not it desired to agree to the poundage system for educational purposes. An entry dated 24 November 1876, stated that the 'clerk from Abercwmboi colliery called at the school today to inform me that the men had decided to adopt the poundage system of payment, and that from this day the children of parents employed in that colliery are to be admitted on the same footing as those from the Powell Duffryn and Messrs. Nixon's collieries'.[2] The management committee also allowed the pauper children from the parish of Llanwonno to attend the schools on payment by the parish clerk of a special fee.[3] Two other colliery schools are mentioned in the Minutes of Committee of Council after 1870, viz. Llanwonno Navigation and Cwmaman, Aberdare schools.[4]

In the Maesteg area numerous collieries were started after 1860 (an area already served by three ironworks schools promoted by the Maesteg and Llynfi Iron Companies) including the Oakwood, Garth, Duffryn, and Coegnant pits.[5] Schools were established at the Garth and Coegnant collieries, and later at the Merthyr (Maesteg) colliery.[6] The Merthyr colliery school had a somewhat precarious existence, being closed periodically due to strikes at the pit, but after 1877 it was reopened and housed 'in more commodious and newer buildings'.[7] The Infants' school at Coegnant pit started its life in the colliery engine room but was later moved to a proper school building.[8]

The remaining colliery schools after 1870, listed in the parliamentary publications were scattered in distribution on the coalfield. In Monmouthshire the sole representative was at Varteg Hill colliery.[9] In Glamorgan, colliery schools existed at Gilfach Goch,[10] Clydach Vale,[11]

1 *Duffryn School Logbooks*, entry for 22nd May, 1873.
2 ibid, entry for 24th November 1876.
3 ibid, 9th May 1873 'Received cheque for £4-0-4 from parish of Llanwonno in payment of school fees of pauper children attending these schools.'
4 *Parliamentary Papers*, Vol. LIX, p. 406. One informant states that the Cwmaman school was once known as the George Elliot school. In 1864 Sir George Elliot who had started life as a door-boy in a Durham pit, acquired Thomas Powell's pits and formed the Powell Duffryn Company.
5 C. Wilkins, op. cit., p. 146.
6 *Minutes of Committee of Council*, 1874, p. 75; 1880, p. 732.
7 ibid, 1880-81, p. 86.
8 Information from Thomas Bevan, Workmen's Institute, Blaengwynfi.
9 *Minutes of Committee of Council*, 1880-81, p. 732.
10 ibid, 1870, p. 621. Also, *Parliamentary Paper*, Vol. LII, 1873, p. 404.
11 *Minutes of Committee of Council*, 1880-81, p. 644.

Tynewydd (Wyndham colliery), Nantymoel,[1] Resolven,[2] Court Herbert Colliery, Skewen (owned by J. H. Vivian, Swansea),[3] Dyhewid (Llantwit Faerdre), Pentre Bach (Merthyr Vale), Kenfig Hill,[4] Pits (Ebbw Vale),[5] and the Yard School (Charles Pit Colliery), Llansamlet.[6]

Carmarthenshire and Pembrokeshire had no colliery schools. Reference has already been made to this western part of the South Wales Coalfield mainly composed of anthracite coal which did not play an important part in industrial development for smelting purposes, although due to certain technical discoveries it was utilised on a very limited scale after 1838 for ironsmelting. It has also been noted that there were two reasons for the absence of colliery schools in the western region. In the first place, the large-scale exploitation of the anthracite coalfield did not occur until after 1890 when a vigorous export trade was developed. Secondly, educational provision was met by the machinery of the local School Boards which by that time had been set up in every part of the country.

1 *Minutes of Committee of Council*, 1880-81, p. 644.
2 ibid, 1874, p. 76.
3 ibid, 1880-81, p. 732.
4 *Kenfig Hill school logbook*.
5 *Minutes of Committee of Council*, 1889-90, p. 94.
6 *Education Records*, Education Department, Guildhall, Swansea.

COLLIERY SCHOOLS

APPENDIX 1

Evidence of Howell Gwyn, Esq., of Dyffryn, regarding the schools at Bryncoch and Cilybebyll.[1]

'In this neighbourhood (Dyffryn Clydach) we are peculiarly situated as it respects the school (Bryncoch), as the workmen belonging to the colliery near the school subscribe to the Neath Abbey School which belongs to the colliery proprietors, and some of the children are sent there.

The average attendance at the Bryncoch school is about 80. In aother school, which I have erected at Kilybebyll, we are similarly situated to Bryncoch, as there are other schools in the neighbourhood. The remarks I make extend only to the manufacturing districts with which I am connected as a landowner.

In the Swansea Valley, where I have property, they are generally very well off for schools, some of which are on a large scale.

The population connected with the works are rather improvident in their habits. I do not think that the parents appreciate the value of education for their children, more particularly in the working districts. Some time since, Mrs. Gwynn introduced needle-work into the school for the purpose of enabling the girls to be more useful at home.

The great drawback on educational improvement in this district is, that the parents care for nothing so much as the immediate reward of money. As soon as a boy can make 10d. or 1/- a day, he is removed from school.'

1 *Newcastle Commission Report*, 1861, Appendix.

APPENDIX 2

Hirwaun Miners' and Colliers' Works School[2]

Established 1820. Founder: F. Crawshay, Esq., of Treforest, Pontypridd.

Tenancy at will. Good building, no outbuilding. 9 feet high. 21 x 14 feet. Accommodation at 6 square feet: 49. Insufficient furniture in good repair.

50 children on books. Duration of attendance: 5 for less than one year; 5, from 1 to 2 years; 15, from 2 to 3 years; 15, from 3 to 4 years; 10, from 4 to 5 years.

Admission: children not admitted under 6 years of age. From 5 to 10 years: 14 Girls and 24 boys. Over 10 years: six girls and six boys.

Average attendance in last year: 20 girls; 30 boys.

Instruction by teacher and monitorial: 3 monitors.

Subjects: Holy Scriptures, reading, writing, arithmetic.

English books; English grammar; Welsh to explain same.

Visitation by Trustees and committee.

Master's age: 60. Commenced vocation at 18. Previous Occupation: In school. Salary: £36–8–0.

Stoppage of $\frac{1}{2}$d. in the £ upon the men's wages.

2 1847 *Reports:* Part 1, pp. 54-57.

COLLIERY SCHOOLS

APPENDIX 3

Extracts from the Journals of the Rev. William Roberts, Blaina (Nefydd), referring to the Hirwaun Works schools

Journal for December, 1853: Entry for December 1st.
Attended a committee at Hirwaun (between Merthyr and Swansea) with a view to aid them in establishing the school, and to obtain government aid towards paying off the debt upon the building, which was erected in 1849, costing near £300. They collected some hundreds of pounds from time to time, which sum was spent in maintaining the teachers, furnishing the schools, etc. The Committee is now in £220 debt (on account of the building, etc.). Population 4,000: children once in school—150. The school had been closed for some time, but now will be re-opened. Mr. Bowstead will visit it in August.

Journal for 1855: entry December 27th.
Hirwaun: In consequence of two schools being supported in connection with the works in this place, and that the workmen are obliged to pay towards the support of the very inefficient teachers that are in them out of their wages, it is impossible for the British school to succeed.
In consequence of the delay of the Marquis of Bute's lawyer to give the lease here and in Aberdare, they can have no aid from the Committee of Council towards re-fitting the school. It is deplorable that in many instances men of wealth, who ought to do most for facilitating the education of the people are the readiest to mar all the efforts in its favour.

Journal for 1856: Entry for March 11th.
Hirwaun: I made enquiries re the state of the British school and found that the miserable schools connected with the works in this place are still great obstacles in the way of the British school, so that it is kept entirely inefficient. The workmen are obliged to pay out of their wages towards the support of schools, one superintended by a drunken man who is in the habit of cursing and swearing the children.
The population of this place being almost entirely under the influence of the manager of the works, who is quite careless about the education of the people, causes the few individuals who went to £300 expense in 1849 in building a British school, £230 of which is now unpaid, to be in great trouble and difficulties.

Nefydd MSS.

APPENDIX 4

LLANGYFELACH NATIONAL SCHOOL[1]

Established 1822. Promoter: J. D. Llewellyn, Esq., Penllergaer, Near Swansea.
Tenancy at will. Bad building, no outbuildings. 10 feet high; 28 x 14 feet. Insufficient furniture in good repair.
53 children on books. Under 5 years: nil. From 5 to 10 years: 1 girl, and 34 boys. Over 10 years: 8 girls and 10 boys.
Average attendance in last year: 9 girls and 50 boys.
Instruction by teacher.
Subjects: Holy Scriptures; catechism; writing, reading, English grammar, Vocal music. Religious instruction by teacher and minister. Visitation by minister.
English books only; English grammar.
Master's age: 40. Newport, Pem. 3 months in 1828.
Commenced teaching at 20; Farmer's son.
Salary: £22. School pence: £13. House and garden rent free.

1   1847 *Reports*, Part 1, p. 50.

COLLIERY SCHOOLS

APPENDIX 5

Gors Eynon National School [1]

Established 1846. Promoter: J. D. Llewellyn, Esq., Penllergaer, Near Swansea.
Tenancy at will; good building, good outbuildings. 8 feet high. 14 x 12 feet. Insufficient furniture in good repair.
37 on books; 37 remain for less than one year. under 5: 1 boy. From 5 to 10: 19 boys; over 10, 17 boys.
Monitorial: 5 monitors.
No curriculum given. Religious instruction by teacher.
Visitation by minister. English books only.
Master's age: 54. Trained at the National Central school for 6 months in 1816. Commenced teaching at 23. Previous occupation: clerk.
Salary: £40 from donations and subscriptions. Nil from school pence. Coals, House and garden rent free.

1   1847 *Reports*, Part 1, p. 50-54.

APPENDIX 6

Aberdare Free School Boys [2]

Established 1830. Promoter: The Marquis of Bute, Cardiff Castle.
Tenure in trust. Good building, sufficient outbuildings in good condition.
11 feet high; 31 x 16 feet. Insufficient apparatus and furniture in good repair.
110 on books. 20 less than 1 year; 60 from 1 to 2 years; 30 from 2 to 3 years.
Under 5 years of age: nil. From 5 to 10: 92; Over 10, 18. Average attendance in last year: 66. Monitorial: 16 monitors (alternate).
Subjects: Holy Scriptures; catechism; Reading, writing, English grammar, geography, History of England, Vocal Music.
Religious instruction by teacher and minister.
Visitation by trustee and minister.
Master's age: 36. Started teaching at 33, Carpenter.
Salary: £60. House and garden rent free.

2   1847 *Reports*, Part 1, pp. 56-59.

APPENDIX 7

Aberdare Free School Girls [3]

Established 1830. Promoter: The Marquis of Bute.
Same remarks as per boys' school. Dimensions: 15 feet high; 14 x 16 feet.
60 on books. In school: 5 for less than 1 year; 35 from 1 to 2 years; 20 from 2 to 3 years.
Ages of children: Under 5 years, 5; from 5 to 10 years, 47; over 10 years, 8.
Average attendance in last year: 45.
Teacher instruction.
Subjects: Holy Scriptures; catechism; reading; writing; arithmetic; History of England; Vocal Music.
Age of Mistress: 32. Commenced teaching at 29. Married.
Salary as per master of Boys' school (bracketed).

3   1847 *Reports*, Part 1, pp. 56-9.

COLLIERY SCHOOLS

APPENDIX 8
Llantrisant: Dinas Colliery School, Boys [1]

Established 1845. Promoter: Walter Coffin, Esq., Llandaff, Cardiff.
Tenancy at will. Bad building, no outbuildings. 8 feet high; 21 x 15 feet.
Insufficient furniture and apparatus in bad repair.
40 on books.
22 stay for less than 1 year. 18 from 1 to 2 years.
Ages of children: under 5 years, 8; from 5 to 10 years, 32; Over 10, nil.
Average attendance in last year: 40.
Instruction by teacher. No curriculum given.
English books only. Welsh spoken to explain same.
Master's age: 30. Commenced teaching at 29. Baptist Minister.
Salary as Baptist Minister: £40. As schoolmaster £30.
1d. in the £ stopped upon men's wages at colliery.

1   1847 *Reports*, Part 1, p. 58.

APPENDIX 9
Llantrisant: Dinas Colliery School, Girls [2]

Established 1838. Promoter: Walter Coffin, as before.
Tenancy at will. Good building, no outbuildings. 8 feet high; 15 x 15 feet.
Insufficient furniture and apparatus in good repair.
40 on books.
Attendance: 4 less than one year; 30, from 1 to 2 years; 6 from 2 to 3 years.
Ages of children: under 5 years, 11 girls; from 5 to 10 years: 21; over 10 years: 8.
Average attendance in last year: 45.
Instruction by teacher. No curriculum given.
Religious instruction by teacher. English books only.
Age of Mistress: 62. Commenced teaching at 40. Married woman.
Salary: £18–4–0 with house and coal.
1d. in the £ stopped on the men's wages at the colliery.

2   1847 *Reports*, Part 1, p. 58.

APPENDIX 10
Courtybella National School [3]

Established 1842. Tenancy in trust for ever.
Good building and sufficient outbuildings in good repair.
Dimensions 45 x 20 feet. Accommodation at 6 square feet: 150.
Sufficient furniture and apparatus in good repair.
Number on books: 134. 32 stay for less than one year.
62 for more than 1 year and less than 2 years.
16 for more than 2 years and less than 3 years.
7 for more than 3 years and less than 4 years.
17 for more than 4 years and less than 5 years.
Ages: Under 5: 16 boys, 18 girls; from 5 to 10 years: 43 boys, 42 girls; Over 10 years: 13 boys, 2 girls.
Average attendance: 63 boys, 60 girls.
Monitorial: 6 monitors.
Religious instruction by master and minister.
Visited by Committee, Patron and Minister.
Age of Master: 38. Mistress: 38. Master for 3 months and Mistress for 6 months at Central National school in 1827.
Both commenced teaching at 18. Joint salary: £90 with house and garden rent free. £15–16–7 from school pence.

3   1847 *Reports*, Part 2, pp. 316-319.

COLLIERY SCHOOLS

APPENDIX 11

Commissioner's Report, 1847 on Courtybella School[1]

'I visited this school on the afternoon of March 31st, accompanied by the Rev. Mr. Hughes, of Mynyddislwyn. It was established and is chiefly maintained by Sir Thomas Phillips, who has large coalmines in the immediate neighbourhood.

The exertions of this truly benevolent man in the cause of education are well known, and this school is worthy of its author. It is a handsome building standing on the bank of the deep ravine which skirts the tramroad to Tredegar.

It consists of three spacious rooms, of which the two outer ones contain galleries. Neither the master nor the mistress were in the school when we entered; they both came shortly, and the two first classes were marshalled in one of the galleries for examination.

They read indifferently, but the first class and a few of the second class answered questions in Scripture history and doctrines remarkably well. They also acquitted themselves very fairly in arithmetic and geography. I was not able to examine the lower classes, but I believe that they were not nearly so proficient. The master appeared to me to be a person of considerable ability.'

1   1847 *Reports*, Part 2, p. 285.

APPENDIX 12

Courtybella, in the Parish of Mynyddislwyn in the County of Monmouthshire[2]

The school was erected in 1842 at an expense of £1,400, one half of which was contributed by Sir Thomas Phillips, the other half by the Committee of Council. The funds of the school are raised in the following manner: Sir Thomas Phillips contributed in 1843, £90–5–2. His workmen are required to contribute 1d. in the £ of their earnings to the school fund in return for which their children are educated.

An adult school is open two evenings in every week for men and boys employed during the day. Children of parents not employed by Sir Thomas Phillips are allowed to send their children on payment of a small weekly sum. The contribution of the workmen as above and the weekly payments amount to £29–19–2. The salary of the master and mistress per annum is £90; coals, rewards, books, etc. are £30–4–4. The average attendance is 124. The number on the books is 136.

On the day of my visit, there were present 137, in age from 4 to 10 years, arranged in 5 classes under the management of a master, mistress, and 5 monitors. Children were clean and neat; discipline and instruction were good, and the general intelligence of the children satisfactory. All subjects taught satisfactorily.

Parish of Mynyddislwyn is 7 miles from Pontypool (population 6,000) chiefly employed in mining.

2   *Minutes of Committee of Council*, 1844. Report on 138 schools in Western District, by Rev. H. W. Bellairs, February, 1845. p. 224.

COLLIERY SCHOOLS

APPENDIX 13

Courtybella School: Statistics of application for aid from the Parliamentary Grant.[1]

APPLICATION:

November 13th, 1840: To obtain aid in the erection of a schoolhouse at Courtybella. Two clergymen and one gentry as Trustees.

Population of district from which children will assemble is 2,000.

Accommodation to be provided for: 303.

Estimated expense of school buildings.

Site: £30. Schoolrooms and fittings: £550. Fences: £100. Master's House: £220. Total expenses: £900.

Sir Thomas Phillips intends to contribute one-half of the expenditure.

It is intended to require the men employed in the collieries to contribute towards its support.

1 *Minutes of Committee of Council*, 1840-41. Appendix II, pp. 48-9.

APPENDIX 14

H. S. Tremenheere's Report on Courtybella School, 1845[2]

Courtybella:

At Courtybella, in the neighbourhood of Blackwood in Monmouthshire, a locality distinguished as a seat of disaffection in 1839, Sir Thomas Phillips, at that time Mayor of Newport, has contributed largely towards the building and support of a large and handsome school and a master's house.

The school is conducted by an able master, mistress, and 3 paid monitors. The average attendance is about 50 boys and 50 girls. As the school is partly supported by a small sum stopped from the wages of the men employed in Sir Thomas Phillips's collieries, an evening school is opened for them, of which, however very few take advantage.

The Sunday school is attended by about 120 more children, and in the absence of a curate for that part of the parish, the master reads a portion of the church service.

A church will probably soon be built for this portion of the parish of Mynyddislwyn.

2 *Reports from Commissioners, Mines and Collieries*, Vol. XXIV, 1846, p. 416.

COLLIERY SCHOOLS

APPENDIX 15

Table handed in by Sir Thomas Phillips, 8th May, 1866.[1]

Results of the Monmouthshire Prize Scheme, so far as regards the Prizes for Religious Subjects.

Description	From Church Schools	From Works Schools	From British Schools
Proportion per cent of the candidates sent up from each class of schools, who obtained prizes during 8 years from 1858-1865, inclusive	43	31	18
Proportion per cent as above for the last 5 years from 1861-1865 inclusive	40	26	12
Average number of marks obtained by each child examined during 1861-5	10.2	7.2	5.7
Average number as above for years 1861-62 ...	10.5	8.2	6.5
Average number as above for 1863, 64, and 65 ...	9.5	6.2	4.9
Average value in marks, of each prize obtained during the 5 years from 1861-65 inclusive	15	11	11

1 *Report of Pakington Committee*, 1866: Appendix 4, p. 312.

APPENDIX 16

YSTRADYFODWG. RHIGOS SCHOOL, CHURCH[2]

Established 1844. Promoter: Marquis of Bute.
Tenancy at will. Good building, no outbuildings.
Dimensions: 9 feet high. 18 x 15 feet and gallery.
Insufficient apparatus and furniture in good repair.
13 on books. Attending for 1 year and less: 2; from 1 to 2 years: 5; from 2 to 3 years: 6.
Ages of children: Under 5: 1 boy; from 5 to 10 years: 1 girl and 4 boys; over 10 years: 3 girls and 4 boys. Average attendance in last year: 6 girls and 14 boys.
Teacher instruction. Holy Scriptures, catechism, reading, writing.
Religious instruction by teacher.
English books only. English grammar.
Master's age: 58. Started at 38. Grocer and draper before.
Salary: £16–10–0. School pence: £10–0–0.

2   1847 *Reports*, Part 1, pp. 58-61.

COLLIERY SCHOOLS

APPENDIX 17

Rhigos British School: from the Journal of the Rev. Wm. Roberts (Nefydd).

April 3rd, 1856: *Rhigos:*
This is a new school opened not many months ago, in connection, and for the benefit of the colliers and miners under R. Crawshay, Esq., of Hirwaun, whose population is increasing. Crawshay's preparation towards educating the children of his Fire workmen and mechanics is miserably attended to (as I reported to you lately) that it is worse than if it was neglected altogether.

This Rhigos school is about 1½ miles distance, where the colliers and miners dwell· The movement originated entirely among themselves. They were afterwards aided in their efforts by the committee of Hirwaun British School. They obtained a suitable room to commence from R. Crawshay, Esq., and also his consent to apply 1d. per £ of their wages towards the support of this instead of supporting those that are in Hirwaun.

They have obtained an untrained young man as a master in whom some of the leaders have much confidence. We had no teacher to offer them from the Borough Road, neither would the salary they can give at present be acceptable to a competent one, being only £40. There are from 60 to 70 children already in the school.

Nefydd MSS, Journal for April, 1856.

APPENDIX 18

Extracts from the Financial Account of the Treherbert Colliery British School, where the late, well known M. O. Jones was headmaster. The account was kept by Mr. Aaron Cule, Grocer, Treherbert.

Salary: M. O. Jones, 20/- per week. Mrs. Jones, 12/6 per week.

February, 1868:
Receipts		Expenditure.
per D. Richards	9/6	Salaries weekly at £1 and 12/6 respectively.
Tynewydd Colliery	6/-	2 loads of coal, 8d.
Ynisfeio Colliery	£1–15–4.	

Poundage from collieries to the school.
June, 1868. Grants: £72–9–2.
  Dunraven Colliery: £2–13–6.
  Tynewydd Colliery: £2–7–9.
  Ynisfeio Colliery: £2–17–4.

Specimen page of poundage: April–July, 1869.
April 3rd.   Tynewydd Colliery: £3–1–6.
              Ynysfeio Colliery: 7 weeks, £2–6–10.
April 24th.   Dunraven Colliery: £3–16–3.
May 8th: Ynysfeio Colliery: £1–3–2.
May 22nd: Tynewydd Colliery: £3–17–0.
June 17th: Ynysfeio Colliery (two pays) £2–18–6.
July 24th: Dunraven Colliery: £3–9–0.

MS 12,628*A*, *N.L.W.* Treherbert British School Account Book from February 1868—May 1872.

COLLIERY SCHOOLS
APPENDIX 19
Ocean Collieries, Rhondda, School Fund
Colliery Wages Books: Deductions from Colliers' Wages

Colliery	Date	No. of Book	Title of Wages Book	Amount of 4 weekly deductions	Rate of deductions	School which benefited
MAINDY	1869	1	Maindy Colliery Wages Book	£8–2–4	1d. in £	Ton
PARK	1867	1	Park Colliery Wages Book	£1–18–5	1d. in £	Park
	1876	6	Park Colliery Wages Book	£9–7–0	1d. in £	Park
DARE	1871	1	Dare Colliery Wages Book	£3–15–3	1d. in £	Park
	1879	5	Dare Colliery Wages Book	£9–12–5	1d. in £	Park (£6–8–4) Treorchy (£3–4–1)
	1879	5	Dare Colliery Wages Book	£15–2–7	2d in £	Shown as school fund
	1880	6	Dare Colliery Wages Book	£17–15–1	2d. in £	Park £14–34– Treorchy £3–11–9
	1881	6	Dare Colliery Wages Book	£18–18–10	2d. in £	Park (£16–8–10) Treorchy £2–10–0)
EASTERN	1873	1	Eastern Colliery Wages Book	£–8–0	1d in £	Ton
	1879	2	Eastern Colliery Wages Book	£12–0–0	2d. in £	Ton
	1880	3	Eastern Colliery Wages Book	£8–2–6	1d. in £	Ton
	1882	4	Eastern Colliery Wages Book	£15–7–9	1d. in £	Ton
GARW	1883	1	Garw Colliery Wages Book	nil	nil	nil
	1886	2	Garw Colliery Wages Book	£2–3–11	1d. in £	Blaengarw
	1890	4	Garw Colliery Wages Book	£7–2–10	1d. in £	Blaengarw
LADY WINDSOR	1886	1	Lady Windsor Colliery Wages Book	nil	nil	nil
	1887	2	Lady Windsor Colliery Wages Book	£3–13–0	1d. in £	Ynysybwl
	1890	5	Lady Windsor Colliery Wages Book	£14–8–11	1d. in £	Ynysybwl

Ocean Coal Company, Treorchy, Wages Books (as numbered).

APPENDIX 20

SCHOOLS IN THE PARISH OF YSTRADYFODWG IN 1870[1]

School	Date of Estab.	Teachers	Government Grant 1867-68	Average attendance	Pupil Teachers
Treherbert Colliery (Brit.)	1860	M O Jones, M Jones	£60	105	3
Bodringallt Colliery	1861	John Rees, M. A Rees	£69–18–8	117	2
Treherbert (Nat.)	1862	J. Pollard, M. A. Davies	£29–17–6	68	–
Pentre (Nat.)	1864	J. Fry, C. Bunting	£34–16–8	95	–
Treorchy United Collieries	1866	J. Pope, Mrs. Pope	£53–0–4	101	3
Dunraven Colliery	1867	Mary Williams	£23–14–5	54	–
Ton Ystrad (Brit.) Colliery	1869	W. G. Howell	—	—	–
Penygraig (Brit.) Colliery	1869	L. T. Morgan		not given	
Ferndale (Brit.) Colliery	1869	Miss Austin		not given	
Llwynypia Colliery	1865	J. Gumbley		not given	

All above schools were under government inspection and receiving annual visits from H.M.I.

1870: National School at Tonypandy; 1871: Cwmparc Colliery School.

1 *MS* 4383*D*, *N.L.W.*, ibid, pp. 126-7.

COLLIERY SCHOOLS

APPENDIX 21

EXTRACTS FROM THE DUFFRYN COLLIERY NATIONAL SCHOOLS, LOGBOOKS
4 VOLUMES. VOLUME 1, 1863-1885

NOTE:

Duffryn National Schools received parcels of school books and apparatus at frequent intervals from the National Society, London.

The schools were visited regularly by H. A. Bruce (Lord Aberdare) and family.

'Mr. Bruce' was consulted on all school matters and payments of accounts.

October 5th, 1863: Mr. Evans refused to pay for his son on plea that his son (aged 14) works in coalpit. I gave him 2 weeks to consider. Received a reply from Mr. Bruce stating that Evans has no right to send his children to school without paying.

January 13th, 1864: Night school attendance very low because the overmen at the different works are not sufficiently particular in enforcing the Act of Parliament (Mines Act of 1861). Wrote to Mr. Brown, Manager of the Navigation Colliery about it, and spoke to Mr. Wilkinson, Manager of Mr. Powell's pits.

April 14th, 1864: School visited by Rt. Hon. H. A. Bruce.

June 5th, 1871: In consequence of a strike among the colliers, great numbers of the lads belonging to the works attended the schools today, and will continue to do so during the continuance of the strike. The numbers will be stated each day.

June 6th, 1871: Attendance at school: 290; workboys, 60.

June 15th, 1871: Attendance at school: 278; workboys, 103.

June 19th, 1871: The strike among the colliers still continues and the workboys still attend, but the numbers of the day scholars are falling off, through their parents leaving the place to look for work elsewhere.

July 18th: Strike still goes on. Received today the under-mentioned notice from Managers to all the teachers employed by them in these schools:

'In consequence of the strike, I am requested by the Managers of the Duffryn Schools to give you 6 months notice from the above date, July 18th, that your services will not be required by them as teachers at the Duffryn schools after the 19th January next'.

Signed for the managers,
D. MORGAN.

August 24th: The colliers have this day returned to work, but many have left the place and the attendances are low.

October 28th, 1872: Received 3 drafts of boys from Duffryn Infants, Newtown Branch, and Miskin Branch.

May 12th, 1873: Received 7/- from Aberaman works for fees of children whose parents work in that colliery.

August 5th, 1874: Received 10/9 from Aberaman Colliery for school fees, which were sent on to the Secretary.

November 13th, 1874: Made up list of children whose parents are employed at the Abercwmboi Colliery, and sent same to Lord Aberdare.

24th November, 1876: Amount received from Abercwmboi Colliery as from 18th November, 1876: £2–11–9.

February 9th, 1877: 86 children received from Abercwmboi Colliery.

September 10th, 1878: List of children received from the Penrhiwceibr Colliery.

March 10th, 1879: 22nd Anniversary of the opening of Duffryn Schools (i.e. opened in 1857).

February 2nd, 1880: Two workmen's representatives on the school committee visited the schools today.

COLLIERY SCHOOLS

Summary of Duffryn Colliery Schools

1872: 400 boys, 340 girls, and 490 Infants paid by poundage.[1]
1877: Average attendance: 864.
1880: Number of scholars accommodated: 1,190. Average attendance: 1,002. Amount of Grant for improvements: £1,482. Annual Grant: £876–15–0.[2]
1894: Listed as a Board School. Accommodation for 1,121; Average attendance: 669. Annual Grant: £630–14–0.[3]
1873: Miskin Duffryn Branch (Infants), Mountain Ash: 76 paid by poundage; 3 at 1d. Newtown Duffryn Branch (Infants), Mountain Ash: 141 paid by poundage, 3 at 1d.[4]

APPENDIX 22

Summary of Rhondda Colliery Schools

Dinas Colliery School
1858: Grant for books: £3–15–0½.[5]
1865: Average attendance 121; Evening school: 7. Grant for improvements: £158–2–6. Annual Grant: £82–11–11.[6]
1867: Average attendance 124 (day); 16 (evening).[7]
1872: 111 paid at a 1d.; 74 at 2d. Employment at colliery determined different rate of payment.[8]
1877-78: Average attendance 215. Grant: £147–19–9.[9]
1880: Average Attendance 247. Grant for improvements: £158–2–6. Annual grant: £190–7–0.[10]

Dunraven Colliery School
1868: Average attendance: 54 (day); 14 (evening).
1870: Average attendance: 154. (day); 14 (evening).
1878: Average attendance: 261. Grant: £227–6–3.
1880: Average attendance: 370. Grant: £268–1–0.
(References as above).

Ferndale Colliery School
1867: Average attendance: 84 (day); 35 (evening).
1873: 177 paid by poundage; 92 infants paid by poundage.
1880: 630 average attendance (day); 123 (evening). Grants: £551–16–0 (day school); £61–2–0 (evening school).
'In 1880, the Ferndale schools under the Llanwonno School Board, raised the sum of £343–7–11 by the poundage tax, and £36–11–0 was paid by the children of tradesmen; the rates were not called into requisition at all.' (*Minutes of Committee of Council*, p. 310.)
1883: Average attendance: 683. Grant: £601–0–10.

1 *Parl. Papers, Accounts and papers*, Vol. LIX, *Education*, 1873: p. 402.
2 *Minutes of Committee of Council*, 1880-81, p. 732.
3 ibid 1894: p. 1084. Listed as Board schools in 1894.
4 *Parl. Papers*, 1873.
5 Minutes of Committee of Council, 1859, Tabulated Lists.
6 ibid for 1866.
7 ibid for 1868.
8 *Parl. Papers*, 1873 p. 404.
9 *Minutes of Committee of Council*, 1878.
10 ibid for 1881, p. 732.

COLLIERY SCHOOLS

APPENDIX 22—*continued*

SUMMARY OF RHONDDA COLLIERY SCHOOLS—*continued*

Treorchy United Collieries School:
1867: Average attendance: 83.
1877: Average attendance: 281.
1880: Average attendance: 694. Grant: £480–6–10.

Llwynypia Colliery School
1878: Average attendance: 458. Grant: £444–5–0.
1880: £315 grant for improvements. 456 average attendance. Annual grant: £395–12–0.
1889: Average attendance: 724. Grant: £706–10–0.

Pentre Colliery School
1878: Average attendance: 387. Grant £330–3–1.
1883: Average attendance: 550. Grant £470–14–10.

Bodringallt Colliery School
1872: Average attendance: 207 (day school; 40 (Evening).[1]
1877: Average attendance: 204 (day school).[2]
1880: Accommodation for 472; average attendance: 439. Annual grant: £362–8–0.[3]
1883: Accommodation for 472; average attendance: 544. Annual grant: £487–0–0.[4]

Cwmparc Colliery School
1880: Accommodation for 228; average attendance: 255. Annual grant: £205–17–0.[5]
1883: Accommodation for 410; average attendance: 284. Annual grant: £284–5–4.[6]

Penygraig Colliery School
1877: Average attendance: 347; Annual grant: £355–8–9.[7]
1880: Accommodation for 523; Average attendance: 480. Annual grant: £397–6–0.[8]

Treherbert Colliery School
1877: Average attendance (two departments): 242.[9]
1880: Average attendance 141. Grant: £44–10–6.[10]

---

1 *Minutes of Committee of Council*, 1873, p. 374.
2 ibid 1878, Tabulated lists of schools.
3 ibid 1880-81, p. 732.
4 ibid 1884, p. 753.
5 ibid 1880.
6 ibid 1884.
7 ibid 1878.
8 ibid 1880.
9 ibid 1878.
10 ibid 1880.

APPENDIX 23

Summary of Other Colliery Schools

Courtybella Colliery School
1866: Average attendance: 166. Grant of £700 for improvements. Annual grant: £66–10–3.
1870: Average attendance: 180.
1877: Average attendance: 173 (day school); 3 (evening).
1880: Average attendance: 112 (day school); 39 (evening).

Varteg Hill Colliery School
1880: Number of scholars: 225.
1890: Accommodation: 290; Average attendance: 196. Annual grant: £175–3–3.

Cwmaman (Aberdare) Colliery School
1872: 231 boys paid by poundage. 204 infants paid by poundage.

Gilfach Goch Colliery School
1873: Average attendance: 96. In 1872, 180 were paid for by poundage, and 6 at 2d.
1880: Accommodation for 314. Average attendance: 191. Annual grant: £152–10–0.

Clydach Vale Colliery School
1872: Average attendance: 95.
1880: Accommodation for 247; Average attendance: 109. Annual grant: £74–16–0.

Merthyr Colliery School, Maesteg
1880: Average attendance: 123.
1881: Average attendance: 112. Grant: £79–8–0.
1890: Accommodation for 301. Average attendance: 256. Annual grant: £226–11–0.
1894: Accommodation for 304; average attendance: 259. Annual grant: £205–7–0.

Coegnant Colliery (Infants), Maesteg
1880: Accommodation for 162; Average attendance: 99. Annual grant: £61–0–0.

Court Herbert, Skewen, Colliery School (National) Vivian's
1880: Accommodation for 586. Average attendance, day school 436; evening school: 74. Grants: £361–5–4; £26–3–6. Grant for improvements: £423–0–0.
1894: Accommodation: 524; Average attendance: 558. Grant: £488–5–0.

Navigation Colliery School
1877-78: Average attendance: 71. Annual grant: £69–8–0.
1880: 110 scholars. Average attendance: 60. Grant: £48–4–0.
1893: Board school. Accommodation: 322. Average attendance: 280. Annual grant: £259–10–0.

Tynewydd, Wyndham Colliery School
1880: Accommodation for 190; Average attendance: 187 in day school; 17 in evening school. Grant: £140–4–0 and £5–3–0 respectively.

References as for Appendix 22: *Minutes of Committee of Council.*

COLLIERY SCHOOLS

APPENDIX 24

BRYNDU COLLIERY SCHOOL, PYLE, NEAR BRIDGEND

REPORT OF MR. H. LONGUEVILLE JONES, H.M.I., 1852-53

Bryndu Colliery School, Mixed

95 present at examination; 40 left this year; 160 admitted this year; 100 in ordinary attendance.

Desks and furniture fair; books and apparatus very fair; Organization: one master, six classes. A woman should be employed to teach the younger children their letters, etc., and she might teach sewing to the girls in the afternoon. Instruction as good as could be carried into effect during the short time the school has been erected; discipline good; methods good.

The room is well-kept and in cleanly condition; it requires however more space for so many children, and the managers are going to make the requisite improvements. The children are well-clothed.

Summary of Bryndu Colliery School

1853: Grant of £2-10-0 for pupil teachers. No building grant.[1]

1854: In augmentation of teachers' salaries: £20. In stipends to apprentices, and gratuities to teachers instructing them: £29.[2]

1858: Grants to Cert. Teachers and pensions: £10-11-8¼. Grants to pupil teachers: £63.[3]

1867: Average attendance: 275 (day school); 4 (evening).[4]

1877-78: Average attendance: 289. Grant: £248-8-3.[5]

1880: Accommodation for 348; Average attendance 323. Grant: £282-12-6.[6]

1889: Number of scholars, 348. Average attendance, 254. Annual grant: £222-5-6.[7]

1894: Board school: This might also have been called the Kenfig Hill Colliery school. Accommodation: 476. Average attendance: 296. Grant: £285-12-0.[8]

1 *Minutes of Committee of Council*, 1854. Tabulated lists.
2 ibid 1855.
3 ibid 1859.
4 ibid 1868.
5 ibid 1877-78.
6 ibid 1880-81, p. 732.
7 ibid 1890.
8 ibid 1894, p. 1084.

CHAPTER VIII

Slate Quarry Schools and the Voluntary Societies in Industrial North Wales

THE PROVISION of education by employers of labour in the industrial areas of north Wales during the nineteenth century was, apart from one region almost entirely absent. For special reasons industry in north Wales did not provide that sequence of activities in mining and smelting which was so characteristic of south Wales with its large iron and other metallurgical industries together with coalmining on an enormous scale. Consequently, the provision of schools for the industrial populations of north Wales—apart from the slate quarrying region, some financial support from industrialists on the coalfield, and limited efforts by proprietors of small textile factories—was met by the Voluntary Societies. In this situation it would be wrong to confine attention merely to schools promoted by slate quarry owners without considering in some degree the part played by the National and British Societies, particularly the latter.

Except for two industrial patches on its magnificent mountainous landscape north Wales enjoyed an almost rural environment at a time when south Wales contained a motley complex of industries associated with the vigorous exploitation of its natural resources. But north Wales also bore the scars of economic activities, with the familiar piles of discarded debris from mining, smelting, and quarrying operations together with large concentrations of urban living. These however were the visible signs of industrial enterprise on a more diffused pattern linked with the general quickening of economic life that constituted the first phase of the Industrial Revolution, before the era of concentration set in.[1] In short, the Industrial Revolution in north Wales had almost played itself out by the time that the real Industrial Revolution was beginning in south Wales. Moreover, the North Wales Coalfield was a very minor version of its south Wales counterpart, poised on the periphery of the north-east corner of the Principality—a borderland coalfield—embodying parts of the two counties of Flint and Denbigh with small extensions into north Shropshire and the Wirral.

---

1 A. H. Dodd, *The Industrial Revolution in North Wales*, University of Wales Press, 2nd ed., 1951, p. vii. This volume covers the period 1750-1850.

The other major industrial region was in the western part of north Wales which comprised the slate quarries of Caernarvonshire and Merioneth, ensconced among the mountain fastnesses of the Snowdonia National Park—an area which developed along different lines from the coalfield. Its remoteness discouraged the immigrant but preserved the vernacular and evolved a vigorous native culture which made slate-quarrying the most Welsh of Welsh industries.[1] It was an industry in a truly rural setting devoid of belching smoke and tall industrial chimneys but in its decline bequeathed vast accretions of waste slate which rivalled the grandeur of Eryri itself.

The remainder of north Wales shared a whole variety of other industries including lead and copper mining, cotton and linen manufacturing, which were so dispersed that they seldom marred the countryside. The river valleys of Montgomeryshire and Merioneth boasted a long tradition of woollen manufacture which, apart from centres such as Llanidloes, Welshpool and Newtown, never interfered with the rural environment, employed local labour, and was wholly Welsh in character.

Educationally, the major problem was the lack of schools for the labouring populations in the two industrial complexes and the rural areas. The remedial measures initiated were similar to those adopted in south Wales and from a practical standpoint were easier to implement. The National Society had bestirred itself after 1837, and by 1846 had made splendid progress in school provision although much remained to be done.[2] The main religious denomination in north Wales, the Calvinistic Methodists, adopted a less belligerent attitude towards government subvention and the British and Foreign School Society was warmly embraced by the Dissenting working-class populations after 1843. Perhaps the most significant and disappointing feature of all was the role of employers of labour in the provision of schools as compared with the industrialists of the south. In the North Wales Coalfield not a single works proprietor established a school, and only a few contributed to, or supported them. As in south Wales immigrant English capitalists developed the coalfield which was easily accessible across the border, but they were more concerned with the workman's hands than with his mind. On the other hand the quarrymen of the west were blessed with solicitous proprietors who built schools and were not averse to other aspects of 'good works'. Unfortunately, in some instances the appreciation

1 A. H. Dodd, op. cit., p. 203.
2 Sir Thomas Phillips, *Wales,* op. cit., p. 397 ff. W. E. Davies, *Sir Hugh Owen, his life and life-work*, 1885, p. 67.

displayed by some Dissenting communities did not always match the good intentions and liberality of their benefactors since the majority of such schools were organized on the National system and the bitterness of religious controversy could not be quelled. Their hostile attitude towards the Anglican Church produced more than one British school.

Here, as in south Wales, the provision of schools was dictated by religious issues. Dissent was in the ascendant in the two dioceses of St. Asaph and Bangor (roughly the six counties of north Wales), and the National Society had already started the school-building race and was moving along quickly. Church schools, bitterly resented by the Nonconformists, stirred up deep feelings coupled with a yearning for British schools. They had no organizing machinery and were in dire need of a prophet to lead them to the promised land of unsectarian schools. This is the story of the British and Foreign School Society in north Wales. Its remarkable success was due in large measure to the support which came from the Calvinistic Methodists and the indefatigable efforts of one energetic person. No account of education in north Wales nor for the whole of the Principality for that matter can be understood or appreciated without reference to the part played by Sir Hugh Owen.

Any evaluation of his work must be related to the educational condition of north Wales in 1843. According to the census returns of 1841 the population of the six north Wales counties of Anglesey, Caernarvon, Denbigh, Flint, Merioneth, and Montgomery was 396,320.[1] There was little likelihood that any significant educational change took place between 1843 and 1846, so that if the two available sources are examined for the latter year some idea of the educational scene can be gained. The *Reports of the Commissioners* in 1847 showed the existence of 578 schools attended by 32,033 children.[2] A short while after the appearance of the *Reports*, Sir Thomas Phillips compiled a detailed personal survey of schools in Wales which was based on the returns collected and classified with great care and labour by the National Society in the years 1846-47, which received substantial confirmation from the tables appended to the *Reports of the Commissioners*.[3] In brief, it was shown that the Established Church had made quick progress in the provision of schools between 1837 and 1846. His statistics revealed that by 1846, out of a population of 396,320, districts containing 317,215 had been provided with 402 National schools, with 20,917 children attending,

1 1847 *Reports*, Part III, p. 1.
2 ibid.
3 Sir Thomas Phillips, *Wales*, op. cit., p. 375.

but for districts with a population of 79,105 the Church had made no provision.[1] The numbers attending non-Church schools totalled 13,271 made up as follows: schools connected with other denominations, 755; schools united to the British and Foreign School Society, 4,979;[2] other schools for the poor, including workhouse schools, 2,189; private adventure and Dame schools, 5,348.[3] Two observations are relevant. In the first place, Phillips's figures are at variance with the 1847 *Reports* for he showed that 34,188 children attended all types of schools.[4] Secondly, Sir Hugh Owen's biographer is completely misleading in his interpretation of Sir Thomas Phillips's tables and omits the numbers attending the 31 new British Schools and those schools in union with the British and Foreign School Society which were 4,979.[5] Considering north Wales as a whole and accepting the calculation adopted by the Education Department that one-fifth of the whole population should be found in elementary schools, the result is disheartening since the figure should be 79,264. Less than fifty per cent attended school and the majority were the children of Nonconformists. The reason was not the lack of schools, but since they were Church schools the Nonconformists kept their children away.[6]

In the first Annual Report of the Bangor Normal College it was stated that prior to 1843 only two British schools existed in North Wales[7] but 4,979 children attended unsectarian schools 'united to the British Society' in 1846, and also by that year many new British schools had been opened.[8] The facilities for establishing British schools circulated by the Society were not generally known to the Nonconformist populations. In north Wales, geography did not help, for large numbers of Nonconformists were often in remote areas out of touch with the rest of the world. Moreover, they were responsible for building and maintaining their own chapels and paying their ministers. For them, building and maintaining a school was no mean enterprise, and those who ventured often burnt their fingers.

1 W. E. Davies, op. cit., p. 67.
2 Several unsectarian schools were in union with this Society, and also 31 new British Schools had been established.
3 Sir Thomas Phillips, op. cit., p. 376.
4 ibid.
5 W. E. Davies, op. cit., p. 68. Is it possible that he wanted to show the poor strength of unsectarian education? His figures are quite misleading, e.g. he gives 40 as attending schools of other religious bodies, but this was only for the diocese of Bangor; there were also 715 in the diocese of St. Asaph; he omits 4,979 attending other unsectarian schools, and the total of north Wales children attending schools was 34,188 and not 28,494.
6 ibid, p. 69, ff.
7 Idwal Jones, op. cit., p. 90, ff.
8 Sir Thomas Phillips, op. cit.

The chapel was the social focus and the Sunday school the strongest intellectual and cultural force in their lives. For them, secular education in day schools seemed an unattainable ideal until 1843. In that year salvation came unexpectedly, and the prophet arrived, not from Wales, but from London.

Sir Hugh Owen, born in 1804 at Y Foel farm on the Menai Straits, Anglesey, arrived in London at the age of 21 having attended Evan Richardson's school at Caernarvon. He was proficient in shorthand, and keen on studying law. After a few years in solicitors' offices he had a clerkship in 1836 in the offices of the Poor Law Commission, where he remained for the rest of his life as a senior civil servant.[1] In 1839 he became associated with a group of persons who were establishing a British school in Denmark Terrace, Pentonville—his first introduction to educational work and the British and Foreign School Society. The school was opened in 1842 and realising that such advantages were possible in Islington he saw no reason why they should not be available in Wales. Knowing that the Welsh people on the whole were ignorant of the details of procedure, and that few applications had been received by the Society from the Principality, he addressed a letter to the Welsh people which was circulated freely in the Welsh press urging them to erect British schools to counteract Church control in education. The letter, headed 'Day Schools: To the Welsh people', dated 26 August 1843, was meant to arouse action through denominational fears, and the right chord was struck in the opening sentences: 'Dear Fellow-Countrymen, You feel the necessity of giving education to your children, and you love liberty of conscience: in order to provide the children with education, you must have schools: in order to secure liberty of conscience, you must have schools which shall not be identified with any particular religious denomination'.[2] He then defined his scheme in detail[3] and the letter ended with a dramatic directive which brought a spate of applications to the office of the British and Foreign School Society: 'I believe that this path is so easy that every district in Wales may, by following it, secure an efficient school, with due regard to perfect freedom of conscience. An oppressive yoke has been already placed upon the neck of several districts

---

1 W. E. Davies op. cit. for the details of his life.
2 ibid. pp. 76-78. Also it should be mentioned that in the context of events in 1843 associated with Sir James Graham's controversial Factory Bill and its educational clauses which seemed to favour the Church, the British Society became alert to the danger and was considering extending its agency throughout the country.
3 See Appendix 1.

through the instrumentality of schools; the same yoke is being prepared for others; and the only way to escape it is by erecting your own schools according to the system of the British School Society'.[1]

The administrative machinery was quickly set in motion. In December 1843, the Rev. John Phillips was appointed organizer for north Wales[2] and by 1846 '31 new schools had been established since the commencement of his labours . . . with provision for the daily education of at least 4,000 children . . . and twelve other schools are proposed'.[2] In August of the same year the Cambrian Education Society was formed, with Sir Hugh Owen as honorary secretary 'to promote the establishment of Day Schools in Wales on the Principles of the British and Foreign School Society'.[3] Although independent of the British Society it was a useful auxiliary, and in many ways served as the Welsh branch. From 1846 to 1854, the busiest period of Phillips's Agency, the annual Reports of the British and Foreign School Society showed that British schools had been established in rapid succession, e.g. of the 92 listed in 1850, 42 were on the Flint and Denbigh coalfield at such places as Wrexham, Rhos, Acrefair, Rhosymedre, Ruabon, Brymbo, Bagillt, and Flint. By 1854 there were 105 schools with the following numbers in the four industrial counties: Denbighshire, 29; Flintshire, 20; Caernarvonshire, 30; Merioneth, 19.[4] A great part of Sir Hugh Owen's Islington dream had come true and his letter to the Welsh people had borne abundant fruit. His deft lieutenant, the Rev. John Phillips, had made full use of his propaganda through the Calvinistic Methodist Connexion Meetings, and his work received the denomination's accolade at the Annual Assembly at Bala in June, 1848: 'That the cordial thanks of this Assembly be presented to the British and Foreign School Society for the kind and effectual notice which it has taken of Wales. And in order that the acknowledgement of the Society's labours in the Principality be not in words only, it is hereby required that a public collection be made this year by all the congregations which are in connexion with the Assembly throughout north Wales and the towns of Liverpool and Manchester towards the income of the Society'.[5] Owen had led the Calvinistic Methodists *en bloc* into the fold of the British and Foreign School Society—even inducing the denomination to pass resolutions and collect funds! How different was the attitude of the denominations

1 W. E. Davies, op. cit.
2 *Annual Report of the British and Foreign School Society*, 1846.
3 Idwal Jones, op. cit., p. 88.
4 *Annual Reports of the British and Foreign School Society*, 1846-54.
5 ibid, for 1849, p. 4. Also 'the sum of £170. 6s. 11d. has already been received from this source (irrespective of the congregations in Liverpool and Manchester).'

in south Wales—where the Voluntaryists had attempted to combat educational destitution and had failed.¹

The Calvinistic Methodists in north Wales took the keenest interest in education at all levels, elementary, secondary, teacher training, and university. The interest of this denomination in the field of elementary education in the slate quarrying districts of Caernarvonshire demands closer attention. The work already accomplished by the Rev. John Phillips was taken up on a denominational basis by the Calvinistic Methodists after he left to become the first Principal of the new Bangor Normal College in 1863.² In August 1866, the North Wales Association at its Bangor meeting set up a standing Education Committee to watch the interests of education in Wales and to report to the Association. In August 1869, acting upon a resolution passed at the Association meeting at Denbigh in June of that year, every Monthly Meeting and Presbytery appointed an education committee of its own to further the interests of education within its own area. Immediately upon the passing of the Education Act of 1870 the North Wales Association took steps to bring its provisions home to the people of Wales and urged the people to avail themselves of the Act to the greatest possible extent. The South Wales Association did likewise.³ But before School Boards were established, the Calvinistic Methodists of the slate quarrying region of Caernarvonshire, the Arfon District which included Dinorwic, Waunfawr, Carneddi (Bethesda), Llanllechid, and Llanrug had spent nearly £8,000 on the erection of school buildings, and between 1844 and 1873 twenty-three British schools had been opened.⁴ The same district contributed £3,371 or one-third of the cost of the new Bangor Normal College buildings⁵ and also collected large sums of money for the establishment

---

1   See Chapter XII. The Rev. William Roberts (Nefydd) was appointed South Wales Agent in 1853.
2   *Y Bywgraffiadur Cymreig*, op. cit., p. 715.
3   *Royal Commission on the Church of England and other Religious Bodies in Wales and Monmouthshire*, 1910, 1911. H.M.S.O., Vol. VII, 1911, Appendix XXVIII, pp. 125-7, Question 25497, answer submitted by the Rev. John Owen, Bowydd, Blaenau Ffestiniog.
4   ibid, p. 126. Also see Appendix 2 to this chapter.
5   In the year 1862, the buildings of the Bangor Normal College were erected at a cost (including site, furniture, etc.) of £13,004. Of this amount Wales contributed £11,520, nearly a third of this being subscribed in the Arfon District, viz. £3,371. Of this £3,371, the Calvinistic Methodists of Arfon contributed £3,105, leaving a remainder of £266 to be contributed by the other nonconformist denominations and the Church of England. For the maintenance of the College, collections to the amount of £830 had been made in the Sunday schools and congregations of the denomination.

of the six new County (Secondary) schools in the area at Bethesda, Bangor (boys), Bangor (girls), Penygroes, Llanberis, and Caernarvon.[1] Finally, when the University College was opened at Bangor in 1884 'a remarkable collection for the building fund was made in the Penrhyn quarries, Bethesda'.[2]

In 1846 when the Commissioners were roaming the Principality collecting their material for the Blue Books, and John Phillips was busily engaged in addressing hundreds of meetings for the establishment of British schools, educational conditions in the Flint and Denbigh coalfield were rather dismal. Every district which contained large concentrations of population were lacking in good day schools, except for the small number of British schools which were just beginning to appear. In some centres like Rhosllannerchrugog, Rhosymedre, and Wrexham, the Calvinistic Methodists, Baptists, and Wesleyans had established British schools in the absence of any efforts on the part of employers of labour.[3] The social conditions were as bad here as in any similar district in south Wales. Denbighshire, with a population of 88,866 in 1841 had the largest number of people of any county in north Wales.[4] The ironworks and coalmines in the districts of Wrexham, Ruabon, Rhosllannerchrugog, Rhosymedre, and Brymbo 'had collected a dense and increasing population which, in respect of ignorance and social depravity were more degraded than those of any district in north Wales'.[5] The Rev. P. M. Richards, incumbent of Rhosllannerchrugog, and formerly curate at Merthyr Tydfil in south Wales, stated that although Merthyr Tydfil was usually considered the most depraved and uncivilized locality in Wales, yet 'he never met with so much poverty, so much social and moral degradation as in Rhosllannerchrugog'.[6] Similar conditions were found in the other industrial districts including Bagillt, Holywell, and Flint.[7]

1 *Royal Commission*, op. cit., pp. 126-7. See also Appendix 3 to this chapter.
2 ibid. £1,341. 11s. 0d. was collected from 2,907 subscribers of whom 876 were Calvinistic Methodists, and their contributions amounted to £615. 5s. 6d.
3 1847 *Reports*, Appendix A, Part III, p. 46 ff.
 NOTE: The work of the National Society and its attempts to combat educational destitution in South Wales through its active personality, Sir Thomas Phillips has been referred to earlier. Sir Hugh Owen in North Wales achieved for the Dissenters and the British Society precisely what Sir Thomas aimed for in the industrial districts of the South, through the National Society. These two men were the spearheads of their respective Voluntary Societies in Wales. Both knew every part of the country; both established Welsh Committees, and were members of the National Committees, and both were mainly instrumental in establishing the first Training Colleges for teachers in Wales.
4 1847 *Reports*, Appendix A, p. 46.
5 ibid, p. 65 ff.
6 ibid.
7 ibid, p. 85 ff.

Chirk possessed the only school established and supported by an employer of labour. The entire 1,611 inhabitants of the parish 'were all dependent upon Colonel Myddleton Biddulph, of Chirk Castle for their employment'.[1] Chirk Charity School, established in 1820, was built by a former resident of Chirk Castle and 'Colonel Biddulph supported the boys' school, and required all his labourers to send their male children to school, care being taken by his agent to ascertain the circumstances of those who could not afford to pay, in which case they were taught free. No religious test was required; the Bible was employed, but no catechism enforced'.[2] Two schools had been established in Rhosllannerchrugog, the National school in 1844, and the British school in 1846 'by the Dissenters in the village, held in a Calvinistic Methodist Chapel, with a committee of 13 persons selected from the different denominations of Dissenters, who have guaranteed the master a salary of £50'.[3] The Commissioners were obviously impressed by the exertions of the local workmen and stated 'even now, although great and praiseworthy efforts are being made by the different religious bodies for the spiritual improvement of the people, no attempts are made by the employers of labour to improve their social condition, to remove the flagrant institutions and customs which make social degradation inevitable, or even to set before their operatives a higher standard of civilisation'.[4]

At Brymbo and the adjoining industrial townships of Broughton, Stansty, Minera, Nant, and Bersham, it was stated that 'the Company who conduct the extensive ironworks at Brymbo would willingly assist towards the erection and support of a school upon the liberal basis as regards religion, which is prescribed in the directions of the Court of Chancery and that the rate of wages is at present so high, owing to the success of the works, that the people could well afford to pay 1d. per week towards education'.[5] But the willing assistance of the Company never materialised, for in his evidence before the *Pakington Select Committee* in 1866, W. H. Darby, the Quaker ironmaster of Brymbo admitted that his firm promoted no specific school but maintained that 'his Company were the largest ratepayers, employed the most men of anybody in the district, were the largest subscribers to the National school, and also subscribed to the Dissenting schools'.[6]

1   1847 *Reports*, Part III, p. 48.
2   ibid.
3   ibid, p. 77.
4   ibid, p. 76.
5   ibid, p. 82.
6   *Report of the Pakington Committee*. Minutes 4773-4796; 4287-4288; 4875-6.

Flintshire, the smallest Welsh county but the most densely peopled of any county in north Wales, had a population of 66,919 in 1841.[1] Most of the schools available were National, and those at Caerwys and Whitford were supported by Lord Mostyn, the Hon. E. M. Lloyd Mostyn and Viscount Feilding.[2] The British schools were at Licswm, Pentre, Mold, Talacre.[3] Bagillt, Flint, Pentremoch, Mancott, Mostyn, Tremeirchion, Holywell, Newmarket, Brynhyfryd, Ffynongroew, Lock, Whitford, Carmel, Trelogan, and Prestatyn.[4] In the Commissioners' *Report* of 1842, two schools were mentioned in connection with industry —one mine-owner in the Halkin district subscribed to the local school, and a brickworks proprietor at Buckley provided an evening school for his young workmen.[5]

In the slate quarrying districts of Caernarvonshire and Merioneth many schools were established by quarry proprietors on the National system—in a land of strong Dissent. H. Vaughan Johnson, one of the Commissioners of 1847, said that 'the condition of the quarrymen in the large quarries of Caernarvonshire was unequal. Where attention was paid to their wants by the proprietors, who derive immense revenues from the labour of the operatives, the cottages are cleaner, neater, and the general social condition is higher than among any other class. Elsewhere they remained in the state of degradation of the quarrymen in the parish of Llandwrog'.[6] However, when the testimony of Mr. Joshua Williams the schoolmaster of Llandwrog is examined, little evidence can be found of Johnson's allusion to degradation. In truth, all the schoolmaster tried to make clear was the fact that the quarryman usually had a large family and was so poor that he could ill-afford school pence for his children's education. Moreover, a good deal of information was given about the quarryman's children. Unlike smelting and coalmining, the craft of the quarryman was carried on mainly out of doors and also needed a high degree of practical skill to cut and split slabs of slate to required sizes. Children were sent to the quarries before they were ten years old to be apprenticed to the quarry business, which took three or four years. During this period the children earned no money and they attended school

1 1847 *Reports*, Part III, p. 85.
2 Lord Mostyn and the Hon. E. M. Lloyd Mostyn owned the Mostyn ironworks. At Whitford, Lady Emma Pennant supported a girls' school, and Viscount Feilding later built and supported a girls' school.
3 Talacre school was supported by Sir Pyers and Lady Mostyn.
4 *Annual Reports of the British and Foreign School Society*, 1846-60.
5 *Report of Royal Commission on Children's Employment*, 1842: North Wales, by H. Herbert Jones, XVIII, pp. 423-5.
6 1847 *Reports*, Part III, p. 64.

only during the winter months when it was too cold for them in the open quarries. Nevertheless, when the evidence of John Jones, one of the Assistants to the Commissioners, is examined with reference to the parish of Ffestiniog in Merioneth he stated that 'the children were employed at a very early age in the quarries, of which there were five in the parish; that at 7 or 8 years old they began to make themselves useful by splitting blocks of slate, and earned in this way, 5/- per month. Boys under 10 years of age could earn 25/- per month. This operated as an inducement to the parents to withdraw them from school'.[1]

Perhaps the most interesting feature regarding the provision of schools by the proprietors of quarries was the fact that most of them were in operation before 1840 and were mainly National schools. This was the period before Graham's Factory Bill, before the publication of Sir Hugh Owen's letter, and before the Rev. John Phillips's peregrinations in north Wales on behalf of British Schools. The Dissenting labouring classes had attempted to establish and maintain their own schools which were held usually in Nonconformist chapels.[2] Where this was not possible the proprietors' schools were accepted as a mixed blessing, for the quarrymen were too poor to pay for education. In many respects the workmen of the quarry districts were in the same position as their fellow-workmen in the north Wales coalfield where the industrialists did not provide schools. After 1843 when the means became available, British schools appeared in rapid succession in the slate quarry areas.[3]

Some quarry proprietors built or maintained schools whilst others might present the land only, and the general practice was to place such schools under the control of the local clergyman for the National Society under the name of National schools. In fairness to the wealthy quarry owners it should be borne in mind that some of them were in sympathy with their workmen's grievances, for example, the Penrhyn family gave a

1 1847 *Reports*, Part III, p. 64. Also Appendix A, p. 120.
2 ibid, p. 6: 'Dissenting chapels, which are far more frequently employed as schools, are equally inconvenient for the purpose. The promoters of Church schools belong to the wealthy class of inhabitants, and having influence with the proprietors of land, who are all members of the Established Church, are able to procure sites, and, by the aid of government grants to erect sufficient schools. Whereas Dissenters, and those who establish British and other schools without tests or restrictions in matters of religion belong to the middle ranks and labouring class, who have neither funds for the erection of a schoolroom, nor sufficient influence to procure a site for the purpose.'
3 *Annual Reports of the British and Foreign School Society*, 1844-50. *Minutes of Committee of Council*, 1848-9. Report by Joseph Fletcher, H.M.I., on British Schools, Appendix, 24 July, 1848.

plot of land for a British school,[1] and Samuel Holland established a British school in Penrhyndeudraeth for his quarrymen.[2] Other examples will arise when dealing with particular districts. The proprietors concerned with schools were the Oakeley family of Blaenau and Llan Ffestiniog; Samuel Holland, Liverpool merchant and quarry proprietor of Ffestiniog, and Col. Pennant (Lord Penrhyn). Many of the schools are not mentioned in the *Reports* of 1847 where the quarrymen of Caernarvonshire at Llanberis and Llanddeiniolen were described as 'having been left to educate themselves, unaided by their employers'.[3] The extensive Dinorwic quarries at Llanberis were owned by G. W. Duff Assheton Smith who contributed nothing towards his workmen's education. But in 1844 the quarrymen took the initiative and set up undenominational British schools with aid from the British and Foreign School Society.[4] One of them was built at Dinorwic where 'the inhabitants of Llanberis and Llanddeiniolen are, for the most part employed upon the extensive slate quarries of Mr. Assheton Smith, which give employment to 1,600 men. 400 families have established themselves near the quarries, and formed the new village of Dinorwic where a British school was established in 1844. The building was erected by the quarrymen, unaided by the gentry or clergy, upon a piece of land belonging to a Dissenting congregation, and lying near the top of the mountain. It appears to be supported by the children's pence and payments exacted from the quarrymen in return for the right of presentation to the school. No other school has been provided for the poor of Llanddeiniolen and Llanberis, amounting to 5,226'.[5] However, other quarry owners provided schools at Llan and Blaenau Ffestiniog, Maentwrog, Penrhyndeudraeth, Tanygrisiau, Tremadoc, Bethesda, Llandegai (Bangor), and Nantlle.

THE OAKELEY SCHOOLS

The Ffestiniog district of Merioneth was fortunate in having its quarry proprietors in sympathy with the religious views of their employees. William Griffith Oakeley and his wife, of Plas Tan y Bwlch, were probably the first to establish schools for the quarrymen of this area although another source states that 'it was Mr. Turner, the quarry proprietor who made the first move towards providing elementary education at Ffestiniog

1 A slate tablet on the old British School at Bangor (built 1848 and still in use) states that the land was donated by Col. Pennant, owner of the Penrhyn quarries.
2 ibid.
3 1847 *Reports*, Part III, p. 20.
4 *Annual Reports, British and Foreign School Society*, 1845-48.
5 1847 *Reports*, Appendix A, p. 36.

VOLUNTARY SOCIETIES IN INDUSTRIAL NORTH WALES

in the early years of the nineteenth century'.[1] Mr. Turner's identity has been easily traced but the contribution he made to education in the district is still a mystery. William Turner and the brothers Casson came to Ffestiniog from Lancashire at the turn of the nineteenth century and acquired the Diphwys quarry, called later the Diphwys Casson quarry.[2] The accredited authority on the local history of Ffestiniog makes no mention of Turner's move although the old schools of the parish are treated in some detail, going back to Evan Rolant's school in the old parish church between 1780 and 1790. After referring to several other schools in the district, unconnected with slate quarries, he mentions the first school established by W. G. Oakeley: 'Yn y flwyddyn 1829 agorwyd Ysgol Genedlaethol y Pentref, sef Llan Festiniog, a adeiladwyd gan Mr. Oakeley.'[3] Samuel Holland, a fellow-quarryowner who was at the official opening of this school, described it as 'the first school for Festiniog village, opened on the 27th May, 1829'.[4] The school was called Pen yr Allt Goch National school whose first headteacher, Mr. J. W. Thomas (Arfonwyson), came from Bangor and later went to London where he obtained a post at the Royal Observatory, Greenwich, eventually becoming its Superintendent.[5] Mrs. Oakeley had built a church in the St. David's district of Blaenau Ffestiniog[6] and in 1840 paid for the school buildings at Llwynygell.[7] The first headteacher was a Mr. Jones, formerly a shoemaker, who was followed by Mr. Ellis Roberts—afterwards the Rev. Ellis Roberts, Llangwm—(Ellis Wyn o Wyrfai), and Mr. Robert Roberts who was manager of Oakeley's Middle quarry.[8] Before 1835 two other schools had been established by the Oakeleys at Maentwrog and Gellilydan (Tynant school) for the children of their tenants and workmen.[9]

1 *North Wales Gazette*, 4 June, 1812.
2 F. J. North, *The Slates of Wales*, 3rd edition, National Museum of Wales, 1946, p. 94. Also A. H. Dodd, op. cit., p. 211.
3 G. J. Williams, *Hanes Plwyf Ffestiniog o'r Cyfnod Boreuaf*, 1882, Hughes a'i Fab, Wrecsam, p. 143.
4 MS. 4983, *N.L.W.*, 'The Autobiography of Samuel Holland (1803-1892), a pioneer of the North Wales Slate Industry, etc.,' pp. 43-44: 'The first school for Ffestiniog village was opened below the village near the Ralltfawr. The Oakeleys, Cassons, the Rector, and others, as well as myself, attended, 27th May, 1829.'
5 G. J. Williams, op. cit.
6 1847 *Reports*, p. 120. 'District of St. David's. This ecclesiastical district has been formed in the centre of the thickest part of the population employed upon the slate quarries. A church and schools have been erected there by Mrs. Oakeley, Plas Tan y Bwlch.' The date given here is 1836, Appendix B. p. 234; Williams, supra, states 1840.
7 1847 *Reports*, Part III, p. 120.
8 ibid.
9 Information by the Rev. M. J. Daniel, Maentwrog Rectory.

When W. G. Oakeley died in 1835, several poems appeared in the Welsh periodical 'Y Gwladgarwr' which referred to his educational work:

> 'Mae gwaedd plant ymddifaid yn rhwygaw fy mron,
> Collasom ein Noddwr haelfrydig!
> Pwy drefna i'n addysg—pwy'n gwisga ni'n llon?
> Rhag oerni ein bryniau uchelfrig?'[1]

Another member of the Oakeley family, Mrs. L. J. Oakeley, established a National school at Penrhyndeudraeth in 1859, but there is no further reference to this school in the Casson records.[2] Mrs. W. G. Oakeley was also active in other good works, particularly her 'Juvenile Clubs' both at Llan and Blaenau Ffestiniog. Children were encouraged to contribute 1d. per week and Mrs. Oakeley gave an additional 1d. so that at the end of the year every child had enough money to purchase sufficient material for clothing—but were expected to wear their new outfits on a special Sunday and march to church.[3] For some time after the new National schools had been built at Llan Ffestiniog children were required to attend the parish church at least once very Sunday. This caused considerable discontent among the quarrymen and many of the quarry agents, who decided to establish a British school in 1846.[4] For some time it was held in a chapel schoolroom but in 1847 'the united resources of the Dissenters enabled them to erect a proper schoolroom and master's house, on a site given by Lord Newborough with aid from the Committee of Council . . . and in the meantime they have employed one of the best teachers in the county, formerly a master at the Dolgellau British school.'[5] This was the Dinas or Ffestiniog Slate Quarries British school[6] and here again, to her credit, appeared the name of Mrs. W. G. Oakeley 'as one of the school's supporters and active patrons'.[7]

---

1 *Y Gwladgarwr*, 1836, p. 212-16: Marwnad fuddugol gan Gruffydd Jones, Ysgolfeistr, Llansanffraid Glan Conwy. I am indebted to the late Mr. Bob Owen, M.A., Croesor, for this and other poetic references. A footnote appears to this verse: 'This alludes to the schools erected and established by Mr. Oakeley both at Ffestiniog and Maentwrog, where not only the charges of the poor children's education, but also that of their clothing in a great measure was defrayed by this excellent man and his highly valuable lady.'
2 B.J.C. Index No. 603, *Records of Messrs. Breese, Jones and Casson.*
3 G. J. Williams, op. cit. p. 143.
4 *Minutes of Committee of Council*, 1848-49, Report by J. Fletcher, H.M.I.
5 ibid.
6 ibid, 1851: Report on British schools by J. Fletcher, H.M.I.
7 ibid.

VOLUNTARY SOCIETIES IN INDUSTRIAL NORTH WALES

Two other industrialists promoted schools in this district, Samuel Holland and William Alexander Madocks.[1] Holland and his wife built schools at Tanygrisiau and Penrhyndeudraeth. At Tanygrisiau, Holland records 'I erected a small school-house at this place which was supported by the people, but as other schools were established, I converted mine into five cottages'.[2] Later, Mrs. Holland supported a small infants' school at the same place.[3] Holland also built a school at Penrhyndeudraeth in 1835, one of the few quarry schools organized on the British system. In his report on the school for 1848, Mr. J. Fletcher, H.M.I., stated that 'the premises were rather confined but were about to be reconstructed on a new site'.[4] It housed two departments, boys' and girls', with 54 on the registers and staffed by one master and one pupil teacher.[5]

William Alexander Madocks was a remarkable personality 'who spent a whole fortune on public works and left the fruits to others'.[6] He was the creator and planner of the village of Tremadoc together with the harbour and town of Portmadoc. His model village had a perfect lay-out plan of streets and buildings which included a church and Town Hall. He also intended to erect a school for which a piece of land was set aside, but it never materialised. Instead, in 1810 he opened a school in the Town Hall on the Lancasterian (British) system. The first headteacher was Owen Williams from Anglesey who was succeeded by several others including D. M. Williams of Pwllheli, under whom the school prospered so well that it became the most noted school in north Wales at that time. In 1827 it was moved to another site, accommodated in new buildings and continued on the British system.[7]

In Caernarvonshire the chief promoter of schools for his quarrymen was Lord Penrhyn who owned the Penrhyn quarries at Bethesda. Before dealing with his work it should be noted that other quarry proprietors gave land for the building of schools on the National system. In 1872, Col. W. A. Darbishire, owner of the Penmaenmawr granite quarry, gave the site for the National school at that place for the children of his work-

1 A. H. Dodd, op. cit., p. 42 ff. W. A. Madocks, a Denbighshire man, educated at Oxford, inherited a considerable fortune from his father, and 'acquired some notoriety in Parliament where he sat for Boston as a member of the dwindling group of Foxites.'
2 *MS.* 4983, *N.L.W.*
3 *Minutes of Committee of Council*, 1877: Report by Rev. E. T. Watts, H.M.I., for 1876, Merionethshire, p. 637.
4 ibid, 1848-49: Appendix to General Report, 7 August, 1848.
5 ibid.
6 A. H. Dodd, op. cit.
7 R. I. Jones, (Alltud Eifion), *Y Gestiana, sef Hanes Tre'r Gest, etc.* Tremadoc, 1892, t. 184-5.

men. The conveyance was between Darbishire and the Vicar, and the school was 'used for education in union with the National Society'.¹ A similar executive act was made by Lord Penrhyn in 1872 in connection with the Gerlan school. Gerlan, originally a farm, was used as a site for quarrymen's houses and was situated in the parish of Llanllechid, a district of Bethesda—five miles from Bangor—which had become a populous slate quarrying region. By deed, dated 1872, Lord Penrhyn conveyed to the vicar and churchwardens of Glanogwen land, part of Gerlan farm and a field called Gardd Las, together with a school house upon trust to use the same as a school and residence.[2] It has already been noted earlier that Lord Penrhyn also gave the site for a British school at Bangor.

THE PENRHYN SCHOOLS

Lord Penrhyn (Col. Pennant) and his wife established schools at Llandegai, near Bangor (referred to as two Charity schools for boys and girls in the 1847 *Reports*), the school at Ty'ntwr, unsectarian, and also subscribed to the Church schools at Llanllechid. These schools were popularly known as 'Ysgolion Col. Pennant'.[3] The Llandegai National schools were built for the children of the Penrhyn estate workmen whilst the Gerlan school was for quarrymen's children, and a tablet on the old school house (still in use) at Llandegai states that it was built by Lady Penrhyn in 1810. In 1847 they were described as 'three schools provided for the poor, supported by the Hon. Col. Douglas Pennant, M.P., of Penrhyn Castle. Two were situated in the village of Llandegai at the northern extremity of the parish, and the third at Ty'ntwr in the immediate neighbourhood of the quarries'.[4] The Llandegai schools for boys and girls, were in separate buildings staffed by a master and mistress, and instruction was free.[5] In addition to the usual basic subjects the curriculum included geography and linear drawing, the girls were taught needlework and the

1 *Deeds, Trusts, and Endowments of schools in Caernarvonshire*, EA5/18f.25 1872, County Record Office, Caernarvon: 'A conveyance between W. A. Darbishire and others of the first part, Mary Darbishire of the second part, and Murray Gladstone and the Rev. David Jones, Vicar of third part, of land on which the Penmaenmawr National school formerly stood. In 1874 an Order of the Charity Commissioners vested the school site and building in the vicar and churchwardens in trust for use for education in union with the National Society.'
2 ibid, *EA5/18f.66*.
3 'The schools of Col. Pennant': *Y Cymro*, Treffynnon, Awst 20, 1851; ibid, Ebrill 23, 1852. 1847 *Reports*, op. cit., Part 3, Appendix B, pp. 186-9. Dates of schools: Llandegai 1810 and 1844; Ty'ntwr, 1830; Llanllechid, 1828.
4 ibid, Appendix A, p. 36.
5 ibid.

boys had instruction 'in the management of a garden which adjoined the school and set apart for that purpose'.[1] The school buildings included accommodation for the master and mistress—although neither was trained—and all apparatus for teaching purposes 'had been well selected and furnished in abundance by the patron' who also provided the children with footwear and cloaks.[2] In 1846 the boys' and girls' schools had average attendances of 76 and 90 respectively[3] and in 1865, 129 boys and 161 girls attended.[4]

The Ty'ntwr undenominational school was established in 1830 on a site given by Col. Pennant but maintained by subscription from Lord Willoughby and the quarrymen employed in one of the largest of the Penrhyn quarries—Chwarel y Cae (Field Quarry).[5] This school had an entrance fee of one shilling and thereafter one penny per week. In 1846, 143 children attended but the report on the school was not too encouraging and the patron was most anxious that it should be rendered efficient for 'considering the income which the master derived from the school—£90 per annum with a house and garden rent free—the subjects which he professed to teach were very limited, and the progress made in the few subjects professed to be taught were very inadequate, 64 pupils having attended for more than two years and 44 for more than three years'.[6] In 1865, 148 boys and 144 girls attended.[7]

At that time most of the population of Llanllechid (4,957) were employed at the Penrhyn quarries, and the National school was supported by the Penrhyn family. 122 children attended and the school was often visited by the Dean of Bangor who was the incumbent of the parish.[8] Evening classes were held twice per week, 26 persons attended and were taught English, arithmetic and writing.[9] For many years the Llandegai schools were free for the estate workers' children but school pence had to be paid after 1870.[10] The 'schools of Col. Pennant' did not lack social and recreational facilities. Port Penrhyn, near Bangor, and the slate-carrying vessels were often visited by the children. School trips were made along

1   1847 *Reports* Part III, Appendix A, p. 36.
2   ibid.
3   ibid, Appendix B, p. 187.
4   Hugh Derfel Hughes: *Hynafiaethau Llandegai a Llanllechid*, Bethesda, 1866, t. 110.
5   ibid.
6   1847 *Reports*, Appendix A.
7   Hugh Derfel Hughes, op. cit.
8   1847 *Reports*, Appendix A, p. 41: the celebrated Dean Cotton.
9   ibid, Appendix D, p. 320.
10 *ES/1, Llandegai* 2, County Record Office, Caernarvon.

the coast to Caernarvon and beyond, complete with brass band on board: 'Ysgolion Colonel Pennant; Wrth borthladd y Penrhyn yr oedd dros tri chant o blant ysgolion Llandegai, Llanllechid, a Ty'ntwr yn myned am drip i Gaernarfon gyda llong y "Fairy" (Mr. Pritchard) gyda seindorf ar fwrdd y llong'.[1] It is also recorded that scholars and parents numbering about nine hundred went by rail to Mold, Flintshire, starting at 7 a.m., returning to Bangor at 2 a.m., and accompanied by the Bethesda Quarry Band![2]

Two other slate quarrying districts in Caernarvonshire were not so active in the provision of schools. Although Assheton Smith of the Dinorwic quarries did nothing for the education of his quarrymen one reference states that he owned the National school buildings at Llandinorwig in 1902.[3] Another National school is mentioned for the slate quarrying districts in the parish of Llandwrog—the Nantlle and Moeltryfan quarries.[4] Bron y Foel school centrally situated between these quarries was associated with the Cilgwyn Company which supplied the building materials and the slates for roofing the school. It started in the 1820s and a Mr. John Wynne, schoolmaster, Caernarvon, is mentioned. The *Reports* of 1847 refer to it as 'The mountain school' which was established in 1844 and it is quite probable that the first school like many others started in a vestry or other room connected with the quarry.[5]

The Welsh Granite Company at Trevor, Llanaelhaiarn, had a lease of land in 1875 which was to be used exclusively for the building of a school.[6] It had a reading room as well as a library, and in 1885 there were 139 attending the day school and 19 in the evening school.[7] In 1894 it was listed as a Board school.[8]

The quarrying districts of Caernarvonshire, like the coalfield of Flint and Denbigh, had their quota of British schools after 1843. Reference has been made to the quarrymen of Dinorwic who established their own British school in 1844. This was to be followed by a whole series of others in the quarry districts, and between 1844 and 1854 British schools existed at Talsarn, Rhiwlas, Cwmyglo, Llanberis, Rhostryfan, Dolbadarn,

1   *Y Cymro*, ibid, 1851.
2   ibid, 1852.
3   *EA/5/18 f*.14 County Record Office, Caernarvon.
4   Leslie Wynne Evans, Bron y Foel school, *Transactions of the Caernarvonshire Historical Society*, 1955.
5   *MSS* 27499, 27494, 27496, *Cilgwyn Papers, Porth yr Aur Collection*, U.C.N.W. Library, Bangor.
6   *E*.259, *County Deeds and Leases*, County Record Office. Caernarvon.
7   *Minutes of Committee of Council*, 1886, Tabulated lists, p. 633.
8   ibid, 1895, p. 1078.

Bethel, Llanllechid, Talybont, Penmachno, Portmadoc, Rowen, Caernarvon, Bangor, Carneddi, and Waunfawr.[1]

The remaining schools associated with industry in north Wales were in connection with textile factories. Textile mills and factories came within the purview of the early Factory Acts but these applied to apprentices and cotton mills only. However, under the Act of 1833, which covered children in cotton, woollen, hemp, flax, and linen mills, mill owners were required to make some provision for the education of their young employees for two hours per day.[2] Two cotton mills in Flintshire, at Holywell and Mold, made some effort to this end. At Holywell, Christopher Smalley, owner of the cotton mills, provided a Sunday school long before the Factory Acts. Smalley employed parish apprentices extensively, and in 1795 there were three or four hundred of these as well as local children. He accommodated them in two 'commodious houses' for boys and girls, supplied them with clothing and workhouse fare, and held regular Sunday schools—but apparently time was too precious on week days to educate them in day schools.[3] The Mold Cotton Mill Company (Messrs. Samuel and Knight who hailed from Lancashire) used a room in the factory for some kind of school in 1834 at which very few children attended—and not without cause if the report drawn up by Abraham Thomas, an assistant to the Commissioners of 1847 had any foundation. He visited the factory on 2 March 1846, and found 'a school for boys and girls taught together by a master in a room in the factory . . . Subjects taught: the Bible, Church Catechism, and reading. Master's salary: £20 . . . I arrived an hour after the time when the school professed to assemble, and therefore at a time when all should have been engaged with their studies, but I found only three children assembled. At length, nineteen were summoned . . . they got no instruction in writing, arithmetic, or any higher subject . . . the schoolroom would only accommodate twenty-six children. It was intensely hot and filthy in the extreme'.[4]

In mid-Wales although the owners of woollen factories in Montgomeryshire made some provision for education, they did not bother to provide schools. At Llanidloes, Messrs. David Davies and Edward Hughes, owners of the flannel factories, sent 'from 30 to 40 children employed in their factories to a day school in the town in which they are taught the

1 *Annual Reports, British and Foreign School Society*, 1845-1855.
2 3 *and* 4 *Will. IV. c.* 103.
3 T. Pennant, *Parishes of Whiteford and Holywell*, London, 1796, pp. 115-116. A. H. Dodd, op. cit., p. 362.
4 1847 *Reports*, Appendix A, p. 103; Appendix B, pp. 226-229.

English language'.¹ Similarly, at the small woollen factory at Garth, Machynlleth, the proprietors hired a woman to teach in the mill 'rather than waste the children's time by sending them to the National school in the town a mile away'.² The Independent congregation at Llanidloes established a Sunday school at the Glyn Factory in 1838. Expenses were defrayed by collections and instruction was given in reading, English, and scriptural geography, lasting from two to four and a half hours. 40 small children under the age of fifteen, and 43 over that age attended.³ A Sunday school promoted by the Calvinistic Methodists was in operation at a 'workshop' in Rhosbeiro, near Amlwch in Anglesey.⁴ If Shrewsbury is included in mid-Wales, this town possessed the only real factory school in the textile trade of that area. T. Jones Howell, the Inspector of Factories, in his Report on the effects of the educational clauses of the Factory Act of 1833, published in March, 1839, stated: 'In the flax mill of Messrs. Marshall and Company of Shrewsbury, there is a Factory school exclusively for the children employed in the mill, about 100 in number, who are taught reading, writing, and arithmetic upon Dr. Bell's system by a competent master'.⁵

1 *Reports by the Four Factory Inspectors on the effects of the educational clauses of the Factories Act, March,* 1839, Report of T. Jones Howell, Esq.
2 *Parliamentary Paper,* 1840, XXIII, *Factory Inspectors' Reports,* p. 51.
3 1847 *Reports,* Appendix C, p. 314.
4 ibid, p. 272.
5 *Reports by the Four Factory Inspectors,* op. cit., *March,* 1839. This school was one of the twelve instances in T. Jones Howell's District where factory schools had been established.

APPENDIX 1

DAY SCHOOLS

To The Welsh People
8 Coles Terrace, Islington,
London, 26th August, 1843.

Dear Fellow-Countrymen,

You feel the necessity of giving education to your children, and you love liberty of conscience: in order to provide the children with education, you must have schools: in order to secure liberty of conscience, you must have schools which shall not be identified with any particular religious denomination. In order to attain this end, I offer the following scheme for your consideration:—

1. That a British school shall be established in every district. The plan adopted in British schools is entirely consistent with freedom of conscience, and is excellently effective in the conveying of instruction.

2. That a society shall be formed in every county, to be called 'The British School Society of the County of . . . '. The work of the society to be carried on by a committee with the assistance of a treasurer and secretary. The Committee to be composed of fit and proper persons chosen from among the members of the various religious denominations in the county. The objects of the society shall be: to collect a fund for the assistance of poor neighbourhoods in the erection and maintenance of schools; to help in the formation of local committees; and to advise as to the best sites for schools, and upon the plans for their erection and their size; to point out the means for obtaining money for the execution of the work; to choose teachers, etc.

3. That in every district where a school shall be required a committee be formed, to consist of about twelve persons, with a treasurer and secretary. The members of this committee (which I will call the local committee) to be chosen from among the various religious denominations in the district, but they need not of necessity be professed members of their respective bodies. The objects of the local committee shall be: to find a site for a school; to secure its conveyance to trustees; to provide plans; to select an architect; to seek the assistance of the neighbourhood in building the school and in its subsequent maintenance; to secure a teacher; and, lastly, to see that the school shall be efficiently conducted.

I would further call your attention to the aid which Government offers for the provision of teachers and for the support of the schools.

Government Aid: Every man ought to know that the Government contributes about thirty thousand pounds annually towards the erection of schools, and that Dissenters enjoy full liberty to obtain part of this sum for the erection of British Schools. As an ordinary rule, a grant of ten shillings is made for every child which the school will accommodate; that is to say, one hundred pounds would be granted towards the erection of a school intended to accommodate two hundred children. The dimensions of a school for that number of children to be about 48 feet in length and 26 feet in width. The officials of Government will prepare, should that be necessary, specifications as well as plans free of expense.

I think I am advantageously situated for rendering my fellow-countrymen assistance in this matter, and I am willing to do it gratuitously to the full extent of my power. If therefore anybody, in any part of Wales, feels himself impelled to make a move in the direction of establishing a British School in his district, let him write to me, and I shall be glad to place his case before Government and to send him the necessary information to enable him to carry out his intentions.

Local Aid: I anticipate that the grant which the Government can make will be nearly sufficient, in a country like Wales, where labour and building materials are so cheap, and especially where so much help will be given free of cost in the haulage of building materials, to build the school. But to make up any deficiency, help should be asked from neighbouring landlords.

Teachers: It would never be worth entailing the cost and trouble of erecting the schools unless care be taken to secure for them efficient teachers. It is not always he who possesses knowledge himself that can convey it to others; learned men find it a task of extraordinary difficulty to give instruction to children, and it is a task which no one ought to undertake without special training. There is in London a school for the Instruction of Teachers in the method of the British schools, viz. the Normal School of the British and Foreign School Society. Eligible young men from Wales can obtain free admission to this school. They would have to remain there for some months in order to make them efficient in their calling.

The Support of Schools: After securing a school and a teacher, provision will have to be made for their support. This should be done in the following way: Let every landowner and every ratepayer in the district be asked what sum he will annually subscribe towards the schools. Every subscriber of five shillings to be entitled to send one child (his own or that of another) to school on payment by him or the child of three-halfpence per week. Every subscriber of ten shillings to be entitled to send one child to school without having to make any further payment. Every annual subscriber of twenty shillings to be entitled to send two children to the school free of further payment; and so on. Children of others than subscribers to pay a school fee of threepence per week.

I believe that this path is so easy that every district in Wales may, by following it, secure an efficient school, with due regard to perfect freedom of conscience. An oppressive yoke has been already placed upon the neck of several districts through the instrumentality of schools; the same yoke is being prepared for others; and the only way to escape it is by erecting your own schools according to the system of the British School Society.

                    I am, your obedient servant,
                           HUGH OWEN.

We entirely approve the above-written letter of our friend Mr. Hugh Owen, we are grateful for the patriotic offer which it contains, and we would urgently desire our fellow-countrymen in Wales to give it, without delay, the attention it deserves.

                          JAMES HUGHES,
                          Jewin Crescent, London.
                          GRIFFITH DAVIES,
                          Guardian Assurance Office,
                          London.

APPENDIX 2

THE ESTABLISHING AND MAINTAINING OF BRITISH SCHOOLS IN THE ARFON DISTRICT

Between 1844 and 1873 twenty-three British Schools were opened in the Arfon District. At Dinorwic the school building cost about £400. The site was given, the school building was erected, and the school was maintained (apart from grants received from the Committee of Council for Education) by the Calvinistic Methodist Church.

At Waunfawr the Calvinistic Methodist church built a school house on a piece of land attached to the Chapel at a cost of £150 which sum was taken by the church as a debt on the chapel. Later a classroom was added at a cost of £55. The chapel Treasurer's books show that during 1853-1870 the sum of £294 18s. 0d. was paid out of the pew rents towards the maintenance of the school.

VOLUNTARY SOCIETIES IN INDUSTRIAL NORTH WALES

At Carneddi, Bethesda, the Calvinistic Methodist church took upon itself the entire cost of building the school premises which amounted to £400. In 1876 a new Head-teacher's house was added at a cost of £316 which the four Calvinistic Methodist Churches of the district took upon themselves. These four churches also undertook to meet any deficit which might occur in connection with the maintenance of the school. The minute books show that the following sums were paid by the churches named, from the commencement up to the time when the school was transferred to the County Education Authority:

	£	s.	d.
Carneddi C.M.	733	2	0
Jerusalem C.M.	566	1	2
Gerlan C.M.	229	0	8
Brynteg C.M.	138	9	3
Ty'nymaes C.M.	2	1	3
	£1,668	14	4

At Llanllechid the Calvinistic Methodist church alone undertook to defray all cost of erecting the school building and Head-teacher's house. The initial cost amounted to £370. This church, moreover, contributed £30 per annum towards cost of maintenance. Many additions and alterations were made from time to time, and in 1880 the enlarging of the school building involved an expenditure of £300 for which the Calvinistic Methodist church alone became responsible.

In 1903 the Carneddi School and the Llanllechid School were transferred to the County Education Authority, in consideration of that Authority becoming responsible for the debt then existing, viz. £500 on the Carneddi school and £300 on the Llanllechid school, this debt forming but a small proportion of the money value of the buildings At Llanrug out of a total cost of £885 the Calvinistic Methodist church took upon itself the sum of £500 and merged it in its chapel debt.

Royal Commission, op. cit., 1911, Vol. VII, Appendix XXVIII.

APPENDIX 3

THE COUNTY SCHOOLS IN THE ARFON DISTRICT

There are six County Schools in the Arfon division, viz. Bethesda, Bangor (boys), Bangor (girls), Penygroes, Llanberis, and Caernarvon.

The school buildings at Bethesda cost £4,671. A considerable portion of this amount was covered by the generous donations of Lord Penrhyn, the late Mr. William Rathbone, at one time M.P. for Caernarvonshire, and Sir Henry Tate. The various religious denominations of the district collected between them the sum of £894 and of this amount £449. 12s. 0d., just a little over one half, was contributed by the Calvinistic Methodist churches. This contrasts favourably with the amount of £13. 15s. 0d subscribed by the Church of England, that Church being, in that locality, rather a large body.

Out of a total number of 88 Nonconformists who subscribed towards the Bangor Boys' School, 62 were Calvinistic Methodists, their contributions amounting to £378, out of a total of £521 subscribed by Nonconformists. Out of a total number of 162 Nonconformists who subscribed towards the Bangor Girls' school, 113 were Calvinistic Methodists, their contributions amounting to £822 out of a total of £1,048 subscribed by Nonconformists. In these figures Nonconformist subscribers from outside Bangor itself are not included.

In the Penygroes County school district the Calvinistic Methodist churches contributed towards the erection of the Penygroes County School, the sum of £568 out of a total of £776 contributed by the Nonconformist churches. The Church of England contributed £23. 10s. 6d.

In the Llanberis district the various religious bodies contributed £820. 3s. 10d. towards defraying the cost of the Llanberis County School. Of this amount the sum of £799 was contributed by Nonconformist churches, and £21 by the Church of England. Of the £799 contributed by Nonconformists the Calvinistic Methodists contributed £618.

At Caernarvon the contributions were much more evenly divided between Churchmen and Nonconformists, the former contributing £723 and the latter £845. Of the £845 contributed by the Nonconformists the Calvinistic Methodists accounted for £641. Where bazaars were held all sections of the community worked together.

A large number of ministers and laymen of the denomination kept private schools at which a considerable number of its prominent men were educated: Mr. Jenkins's school at Chester; Mr. John Evans' at Menai Bridge and later at Oswestry; Mr. Edwin Jones's at Towyn; Mr. Owen Owen's school at Oswestry;[1] Mr. T. J. Jones Lewis's at Menai Bridge; Mr. R. M. Jones's at Holyhead; Mr. Llewellyn Edwards's at Aberystwyth; Eben Fardd's at Clynnog; Mr. Josiah Thomas's at Bangor; Mr. J. Hughes's at Wrexham; Mr. Thomas Lloyd's at Abergele; the Holt Academy; Mr. John Jones's at Llansannan. Prof. Hugh Williams, D.D., now of Bala College at one time kept a private school at Menai Bridge.

Royal Commission, op. cit., 1911, Vol. VII., Appendix XXVIII.

1 Owen Owen left Oswestry in 1896 to become the first Chief Inspector of the new Central Welsh Board.

APPENDIX 4
FFESTINIOG NATIONAL SCHOOL[1]

Established 1829. Promoter: W. G. Oakeley, Esq., of Plas Tan y Bwlch, Merionethshire.
Tenure at will. Good building, with sufficient out-buildings in bad repair. Dimensions: 15 x 40 feet. Accommodation at 6 square feet, 100. Sufficient apparatus in good repair.
Number of children present: 73. Number of children on books: 87.
32 stay for less than 1 year; 7 stay for more than 4 years. Average attendance in last year: 25 girls, and 35 boys.
Method: in classes; 5 monitors; simultaneous instruction.
Subjects: Holy Scriptures, catechism, reading, arithmetic, geography, vocal music.
Religious instruction by master. Visited by trustees and minister.
Master's age: 54. Shoemaker previously. Salary £30.
£18 from school pence. House and garden rent free, also fuel.
School privately supported.

1 1847 *Reports*, Part III, Appendix B, pp. 234-7.

APPENDIX 5
ST. DAVID'S CHURCH SCHOOL (LLWYNYGELL), BLAENAU FFESTINIOG[2]

Established about 1836. Promoter: Mrs. W. G. Oakeley, of Plas Tan y Bwlch, Merionethshire.
Tenure at will Good building, sufficient outbuildings in good repair. Dimensions: 33 x 21 feet. Accommodation at 6 square feet, 115. Sufficient furniture in good repair.
40 children present, 83 on books.
Method: in classes, 6 monitors; simultaneous instruction.
Holy Scriptures, catechism, reading, writing, arithmetic.
Religious instruction by teacher. Visitation by minister.
Master's age: 26. Commenced teaching at 23. Previously shoemaker. Salary £40.
House and garden rent free, also fuel.
Privately supported.

2 1847 *Reports*, Part III, Appendix B, pp. 234-7.

APPENDIX 6
Maentwrog Church School [1]

Established before 1835. Promoter: W. G. Oakeley, Esq., Plas Tan y Bwlch, Merioneth.
Tenure at will. Good building, with sufficient outbuildings in good repair. Dimensions: 30 x 18 feet. Accommodation at 6 square feet: 90. Sufficient furniture and apparatus in good repair. 55 children present; 70 on books.
Average attendance in last year: 25 girls, 35 boys.
Method: in classes, 5 monitors, simultaneous instruction.
Holy Scriptures, catechism, reading, writing, arithmetic.
Religious instruction by master and minister. Visitation by minister, and Patron.
Master's age: 58. Started teaching at 28. Mariner before.
Salary £40. House and garden rent free. Income from school pence: £2. 5s. 0d.
Privately supported.

1   1847 *Reports*, Part III, Appendix B, pp. 238-241.

APPENDIX 7
Llandegai Charity School, Boys [2]

Established 1844. Promoter: Colonel Pennant, Penrhyn Castle, Bangor.
Tenure at will. Good buildings with insufficient outbuildings in bad repair.
Dimensions: 52 x 17 feet. Accommodation at 6 square feet: 147. 97 children on books. 150 present (boys and girls). Average attendance in last year: 76 boys.
Method: in classes, 21 monitors. Simultaneous instruction.
Holy Scriptures, catechism, reading, writing, arithmetic, geography, English grammar, vocal music, linear drawing.
Religious instruction by master and minister. Visitation by minister.
Master's age: 42. Commenced at 32; shoemaker before. Holds an Office in the Cathedral, income £20. Salary £65. Income from school pence: £25. House and garden rent free. Also coals.
Privately supported.

2   1847 *Reports*, Part III, Appendix B, pp. 186-189.

APPENDIX 8
Ysgolion Colonel Pennant [3]

Y Wyddgrug: Mawrth Pasg ymwelodd plant yr ysgolion uchod a'r Wyddgrug, Bwriadodd Ysgolion Llandegai a Llanllechid ynghyd a'r rhieni fyned gyda hwy, a chynullasant yn ymyl y Relwe oddeutu 6.30 yn y bore i'r perwyl. Golwg hyfryd ar y plant, dim calon drom yn eu mysg ar bod yno tua 600 o blant, ac o 200 i 300 o rai mewn oed.
Cychwynnodd y tren yn cynnwys 24 o gerbydau tua 7.0. Croesawyd hwynt yn yr Wyddgrug yn y farchnadfa. Ymdeithasant drwy'r dre; canwyd clychau rhagorol yr Eglwys. Blaenorid gan Band Bethesda i fyny i Fryn y Beili. Difyru eu hunain drwy dreiglo i lawr ei ochrau.
Annerchiadau gan Andreas o Fôn, wedyn John Williams, Warden Llanllechid; Eryr Arfon, etc. Ymadael a chyrraedd y Rhyl yn ddirwystr lle digwyddodd anffawd i un o bibellau y peiriant. Gwariwyd peth amser yno, ond cyrhaeddasant Bangor rhwng 1 a 2 o'r gloch y bore Mercher yn holl iach.

3   *Y Cymro*, Treffynnon, Ebrill 23 ain, 1852.

APPENDIX 8
Bronyfoel School: Summary of Tabular Reports [1]

Llandwrog Parish: Bronfoel School

Church School. Established in 1844. Tenure in Trust for ever. Good building with sufficient outbuildings, in bad repair. Dimensions 27 x 16, 27 x 16. Accommodation at 6 sq. ft.: 144. Sufficient furniture and apparatus in good repair.

Number of children present: 38. Number of children on books: 75. 42 attend for less than 1 year; 10 more than 1 year and less than 2; 23 more than two years and less than 3. 5 girls and 6 boys between 5 and 10 years of age; 2 girls and 25 boys above 10 years of age.

Average attendance in last year: 30. Method: in classes; there are 4 monitors.

Religious instruction by master or mistress. School opened with a hymn or prayer. Visitation made by Trustees, Minister, and Patrons. English is the language of instruction.

Master's age: 40. Mistress: 18. Trained at Borough Road for 6 months in 1844. Master commenced vocation at age of 25. His previous occupation: printer. Is now Methodist preacher. Salary: £47, no house or other emoluments.

Annual income of school: From subscriptions £23; From school pence £17. From endowments: nil.

1   1847 *Reports*, Part 3, Appendix B, pp. 186-189.

APPENDIX 9
Bronyfoel School or The Mountain School [2]

A School for boys and girls, taught respectively by a master and mistress in separate rooms of a building erected for the purpose. Number of children, 75. Number employed as monitors, 4. Subjects taught: the Holy Scriptures, reading, writing, arithmetic, and, to the boys, the elements of grammar and geography.

I examined this school December 1. Of 75 children only 38 were present. Of these none could read with ease, and only 14 could make out words of two syllables. Of Holy Scripture they were very ignorant, although attempting to read the most difficult passage in the Epistle to the Galatians, upon which subject the master assured me they could answer questions. It would be profane to detail the mistaken answers which were given.

Although grammar and geography are professed, nothing was known of either subject. The master did not appear to detect the blunders which his scholars committed: 'Brethren' he admitted to be the singular number, and the word 'child' was stated to be the singular number of the plural 'women.'

In geography, I was told that Wales is to the east of England, and Ireland to the east of Wales.

The questions were put in Welsh as well as in English.

The only attainment of the school appears to be arithmetic. 16 were learning arithmetic, and of these 10 could apply compound rules, and 5 of the 10 could work a sum in the Rule of three.

The master appears to have had very few opportunities of receiving instruction. He speaks broken English. He asked such questions as these: 'How many Gospels are?' 'How many apostles are?', etc.

The mistress is a girl of 18 years of age.

John James, *Assistant*

2   1847 *Reports*, Part 3, Appendix A, p. 38.

APPENDIX 10
Welsh Granite Quarry School, Trevor, Llanaelhaiarn, Caernarvonshire

1880-81: Number of scholars, 166. Average attendance 148.[1]
1882: Number of scholars, 166. Average attendance, 141. Annual Grant: £86–11–0[2]
1833: Number of scholars: 166. Average attendance, 148. Annual grant: £97–15–0[3]
1885: Number of scholars: 166. Average attendance, 139. Annual grant: £112–13–6. Evening school attendance: 19. Grant (evening school), £10.[4]
1889-90: Number of scholars: 166. Average attendance, 145. Annual grant: £118–15–0[5]
1894: Listed as a Board School. Number of Scholars: 166. Average attendance: 130. Annual grant: £108–1–0.[6]

1 *Minutes of Committee of Council*, 1880-81, Tabulated Lists of schools aided by grants.
2 ibid 1883.
3 ibid 1884, p. 753.
4 ibid 1886, p. 633.
5 ibid 1890, Appendix, Part IV.
6 ibid 1895, p. 1078.

APPENDIX 11
Rhosbeiro Sunday School

A workshop, connected with the Calvinistic Methodists. Established in 1820. Dimensions 18 x 18 feet. Bad premises, bad furniture. Used as a workshop. Expenses defrayed by collections. Number on books under 15: 18. Over 15: 29. Number who attend a day-school: 10. Instruction in Welsh by laymen teachers.
Subjects: Scripture and Scriptural geography.
School hours: 9.30-11.30; 1.30-3.30.[1]

Glyn Factory Sunday School, Llanidloes

Connected with the Independents. Established in 1838. Dimensions 30 x 27 feet. Good premises, good furniture.
Ordinarily a dwelling house. 8 teachers. Expenses defrayed by collections.
40 attend under 15; 17 over 15. 7 attend a day-school. Instruction by minister and laymen in English. Scripture and Scriptural geography.
School hours: 2 to 4.30 p.m.[2]

1 1847 *Reports*, Part III, Appendix C, pp. 272-3.
2 ibid, pp. 314-315.

APPENDIX 12
Mold Cotton Mill Company's School[1]

A Factory school established in 1834. Tenure at will. Indifferent building; indifferent outbuildings which are insufficient. Dimensions 13 x 12 feet. Accommodation at 6 square feet: 26. Insufficient apparatus in bad repair.
Number of children present: 19; number on books: 30. Average attendance in last year: 12 girls, and 12 boys.
Method: Individual, in classes.
Holy scriptures and reading.
Religious instruction by master. Master's age: 66. Commenced vocation at 53. Formerly a carrier. Salary: £20.
£20 from subscriptions.

1 1847 *Reports*, Part III, Appendix B, pp. 226-229.

CHAPTER IX

Nonconformity and Sunday Schools in the Industrial Areas

SOCIOLOGICALLY, the three main characteristics of Welsh life and culture in the industrial areas of Wales in the mid-nineteenth century were the rapid growth and florescence of Nonconformity, a successful and popular system of Sunday schools for all age groups staffed by voluntary teachers, and the use and preservation of the Welsh language by large masses of native immigrants from contiguous Welsh counties, which from 1860 onwards were reinforced by strong detachments of Welsh workers from north Wales to the rapidly developing Rhondda valleys of the mid-Glamorgan coalfield. When Mr. Joseph Bowstead, M.A., Her Majesty's Inspector of Schools, was compiling his report on the British, Wesleyan, and other Denominational schools in the Southern Counties of England and Wales for the Committee of Council for the period between the Great Exhibition and the Crimean war, he was constrained to make a 'particular and extended reference to one portion of his District which was so differently circumstanced from any other part of the country with which he was acquainted'.[1] It seemed to him a duty to endeavour to bring its peculiar features, viewed in relation to their influence upon the education of the labouring population, to their Lordships' notice in a somewhat special manner. That District was South Wales including under that term not only the six southern counties of the Principality, but also the English county of Monmouth which was bound up with the adjacent Welsh shires by the ties of a common industry, a simultaneous development of similar resources and characteristics, and the use of the same language for colloquial intercourse among the working classes.[2]

The 'peculiar features' encountered by Bowstead on his inspectorial tours of south Wales which, he said 'exercised an undoubted influence upon its school economy' were not exclusive to the phenomenal growth of population and industry, although that part of his report deplored the lack of day schools on the British System—and incidentally it should be borne in mind that the south Wales agent of the British and Foreign

1 *Minutes of Committee of Council*, General Report for 1854, p. 635.
2 ibid.

School Society had only just been appointed.[1] Rather, the observant inspector was contemplating the most fundamental 'feature', the overwhelming numerical superiority of Nonconformity in the coalfield as compared with the Established Church, among the labouring classes. He would have been equally impressed by the north Wales counties with their proliferation of Calvinistic Methodist congregations, day schools and Sunday schools. It has already been shown that the Calvinistic Methodists had taken kindly to government aid since 1843, but Bowstead was reporting on a region where Independents and Baptists with their uncompromising attitude towards parliamentary grants and their impregnable Voluntaryism had obstructed the establishment of British schools up to 1854—the year of his report.[2] Nevertheless it is fascinating to study his statistics on the religious side. He came to the conclusion that the proportion of Churchmen among the trading and working classes of south Wales did not exceed one to every five. In Monmouthshire, after 'a minute and personal investigation' of one of the valleys he found that 'whilst the Church claimed twenty families within a given area, the Protestant Dissenters claimed three hundred, and with the numerical strength of the Dissenting population was linked the whole question of secular and religious schooling'.[3] On this question Bowstead submitted a true and honest observation to 'My Lords'. After all, was he not inspecting a south Wales possessed of a chapel-based Welsh society at a time when Dissenting Sunday schools were flourishing? His submission was conclusive: 'South Wales must be recognised as a land of Dissenters and the schools intended for its benefit must be such as to command the confidence of men who hold nothing so precious as perfect religious freedom. The Welsh abandon so much denominational teaching in the day school not due to indifference, but due to the Sunday school. The same district which sent only 65,137 children to day schools in 1851, was filling its Sunday schools with 163,033 scholars, and whilst the day schools reached only 8.7 per cent, the Sunday school was brought home to 21.7 per cent of the population. The working classes attach the highest value to the Sunday school, and the day school is wanted for another purpose'.[4]

---

1 The Rev. William Roberts (Nefydd), Baptist minister of Blaina, Monmouthshire, was appointed Agent for an experimental period of twelve months from the 1st December, 1853, at a salary of £60. He relinquished this post in 1863.
2 See Chapter XII.
3 *Minutes of Committee of Council for* 1855, p. 638. Bowstead also noted that 'it is notorious that in the neighbourhood of not a few iron and coal works, the Church is numerically by far the weakest of the sects'.
4 ibid, p. 642.

Historically, the Welsh Sunday school had its roots in a series of philanthropic voluntary efforts to provide religious instruction for the poor of Wales, extending in point of time from the Welsh Trust of 1674 to the labours of Thomas Charles in 1785. It would be invidious here to enter into any detailed statement concerning the evolution of Welsh Sunday schools for that has been accomplished in standard works and has also undergone re-appraisal by recent Welsh historians.[1] What is important to bear in mind at this juncture is the fact that this typically Welsh institution emerged from the Welsh Circulating Schools of Griffith Jones, and later, from the Charity Schools of Thomas Charles. The latter schools were succeeded by his Sunday schools which spread very rapidly from 1789 onwards and before his death in 1814 had already begun to supersede his original schools.[2] This new development happened to coincide with the birth of a new Nonconformist body in Wales, the Calvinistic Methodists, which was to throw the balance of power decisively against the Establishment.[3] They were originally Methodist Sunday schools and in north Wales where the initial expansion occurred they served to cement the new denomination together and subsequently made it the Calvinistic Methodist stronghold of the Principality. After 1800 the Sunday schools swept through south Wales, flowed along every denominational channel, and by 1840 far outnumbered those of the Established Church. Moreover, the Bible Society, known later as the British and Foreign Bible Society, was expressly formed to meet the need for Welsh Bibles which the Sunday schools created. These schools were universal, democratic in organization, and brought into being a reading public and a literate nation in a period before the establishment of a national system of elementary education.[4]

Again, during the first half of the nineteenth century Sunday schools more than satisfied the emotional and intellectual interests of workers on the land and in industry—the Welsh 'gwerin' in general. But they brought

1 *Pioneers of Welsh Education*: Four Lectures, published by the Faculty of Education, University College, Swansea, Session 1961-62: The first two lectures were Griffith Jones, Llanddowror (1683-1761), by Glanmor Williams; Thomas Charles (1755-1814), by Ieuan Gwynedd Jones.
2 ibid, p. 48. Also see Appendix 1. A Charity-cum-Sunday School was established at Harwood, near Wrexham, in September 1789 for 'the children and others belonging to the Lead, Coal, Furnace and other Businesses residing at Rhos Llannerch Rugog, Minera, The Furnace and Harwood'. *Sunday School in Wales, etc., with a Report of the Sunday School at Harwood. Chester*, 1789.
3 *Wales through the Ages*, ed. A. J. Roderick, Christopher Davies (Publishers, Ltd.), Llandybie, 1960, Vol. II, p. 109.
4 M. G. Jones, op. cit., p. 321.

forth something far more dynamic and far-reaching in their wake. Welsh society whose king-pin was the Sunday school proclaimed the supreme importance of the individual within the Nonconformist fold. Its adherents became experienced in the working of democratic institutions and self-expression which helped to produce the political transformation of Wales during the last half of the nineteenth century. Welsh radicalism, the boisterous child of Welsh Nonconformity, aroused a national awakening in Wales after the elections of 1868 which had important repercussions in the fields of politics, religion, and education.[1]

In the rural areas of Wales Sunday schools rapidly became an integral part of the life and organization of Nonconformist chapels, especially in north Wales, where, after 1811 they appeared hand in hand with the new Calvinistic Methodist congregations and the other denominations.[2] The same was true of the industrial areas of south Wales so far as their popularity and basic function was concerned. Nevertheless, a closer study of this institution in that part of the Principality reveals certain distinctive features of some significance. The best method of approach is to look at the three main industrial regions separately. The first region extended roughly from Hirwaun in north Glamorgan, along the north-eastern rim of the coalfield down to Pontypool in Monmouthshire. This area produced the first phase of the general industrial development of south Wales which was dominated by the iron industry between 1750 and 1850. The second region can be described as the 'industrial triangle' of the western part of the South Wales Coalfield whose base extended from Port Talbot to Pembrey with its apex at Ystradgynlais in the upper Tawe valley—the non-ferrous metallurgical and anthracite area.[3] The third region was the mid-Glamorgan coalfield or the Rhondda valleys which emerged and developed so dramatically after 1860. In each of these regions the Sunday school, considered as an educational and religious institution was, at least up to 1870, the shining star of the working man's firmament, his educational highway, and the light which lightened his darkness. It was his main link between things temporal and spiritual, and satisfying to an extent which relegated any day school provision to second place. It was both elementary school and the free-way to eternal salvation for the working classes. Nevertheless, the three regions had

[1] Kenneth O. Morgan, op. cit., 1963, p. v.
[2] Adroddiad Ysgolion Sabbothol y Methodistiaid Calfinaidd yng Nghogledd Cymru: *Cofnodau Cymdeithasfau Llanrwst, Rhagfyr* 26, 1827, *a Ionawr* 1, 1829, *ynghyd a Hanes byr o'r Ysgolion.* Caerlleon, J. Parry, 1829. *Yr Ysgol Sabbathol A'r Oes, gan y Parch.* David Griffith, Bethel, Sir Gaernarfon. Hughes a'i Fab, Wrecsam, 1858.
[3] Just outside this triangle is the anthracite area of the Gwendraeth valleys.

different sociological backgrounds which the Sunday school reflected in more than one respect.

The function of the Sunday school in these industrial regions, considered from the viewpoint of urban sociology in the nineteenth century needs to be re-interpreted thanks to recent researches by geographers in the field of urban geography.[1] In our first region, when the ironmasters moved east from Merthyr Tydfil to exploit the resources of the heads of the adjacent valleys they came into districts devoid of existing settlements: 'In the initial period of development the nucleus of the settlement was the ironworks or the mine. These were the economic causes of settlement and the cottages of the workers were built around them. At this period the nascent towns were fundamentally manufacturing or mining camps which can be compared without exaggeration with the early mining camps of the American West'.[2] These cottage nuclei around the works were characteristic of such places as Tredegar, Nantyglo, Ebbw Vale, Blaenavon, and Rhymney, etc., as well as Merthyr Tydfil, Dowlais and Hirwaun. The ironworkers were a heterogeneous group composed not only of Welsh people from the surrounding districts but also of large numbers of non-Welsh immigrants from nearby English counties and the south-west of England, supplemented by generous drafts of Irish workers, the result of successive Irish famines between 1817 and 1846.[3] This was the period of intermittent economic adversity which beset the country as a result of almost a quarter of a century's warring with France. These were the places of working class industrial unrest and discontent, of recurrent rioting between 1805 and 1840, and a region which generated Chartism and mobilised its political militia for the historic march on Newport in 1839. Withal, this region attracted some of the most undesirable elements of the population and it was as easy for a 'wanted' character to lose his identity in the ironsmelting region of those days as it is for a similar one to get lost in London today.[4] The locational factor was all-important, for the geographical isolation of this area demanded that those responsible for the population agglomerations—the employers—had to provide almost everything for the workmen—the shops, churches, and schools.

1   Harold Carter, op. cit. Also, R. E. Dickinson, The Scope and Status of Urban Geography, *Land Economics*, XXIV, 1948.
2   Harold Carter, op. cit., p. 309.
3   David Williams, op. cit., p. 229. Also, Philip N. Jones, Some aspects of immigration into the Glamorgan Coalfield between 1881-1911, *Trans. Cymm. Soc.*, Session 1969, Part 1, 1970.
4   1847 *Reports*, Part II, p. 271: 'The mining communities are chiefly swollen by immigration and are, in fact, the receptacle and refuge of nearly all the unemployed labourers whom crime or want have induced to travel thither, lured by the golden harvest with which report invests mineral adventure and the wages it dispenses.'

Is it any wonder, considering the nature of this society in its squalid and often isolated urban settings, that the employers welcomed with open arms and offered every facility for the activities of Sunday schools? It was in this type of industrial district that the Welsh Sunday School, in one respect, resembled its English counterpart. Robert Raikes of Gloucester who initiated the English Sunday School movement maintained that ignorance and neglect were the cause of indiscipline among the younger elements of the population, and his Sunday schools sought to inculcate discipline as well as religion.[1] In this part of Wales, the Welsh Sunday school combined both—the predominent religious motive being the means whereby good behaviour and morals could be attained. This region, so different from the other two, also produced its own type of Sunday school not found in any other industrial area in Wales (except Harwood, near Wrexham)—the works Sunday school.

Before dealing with this particular institution, the Nonconformist tradition in this part of the country is worthy of passing reference. Monmouthshire, which contained so many ironworks, was the home of Welsh upper-class Nonconformity in the seventeenth century with many early Dissenting congregations in the industrial parts such as Llanwenarth, 1650; Blaenau Gwent (Abertillery), 1660, and Pontypool, 1729.[2] This tradition was continued in the first half of the nineteenth century by the appearance of numerous working class Nonconformist places of worship, but these chapels were not built for some time until the Welsh immigrants had fully settled down. It was during this intervening period that the works Sunday schools operated on a denominational basis which later on became the nuclei of new chapels. Thus in the new townships of the ironsmelting region the Sunday schools appeared before the places of worship. Here, compared with Nonconformity, the Established Church was in a sorry plight. It lacked militancy and vigour up to 1850 due in large measure to the poverty of the diocese of Llandaff.[3] In truth, almost all the new Anglican churches in this area were built by proprietors of works (who had already established schools) at Tredegar, Rhymney, Ebbw Vale, and Beaufort. Even Sir John Guest, himself a Methodist, built two churches for his Anglican workmen at Dowlais.

To return to the works Sunday schools. It has already been mentioned that Dissenting Sunday schools often existed before the chapels were

1 Frank Smith, op. cit., p. 49.
2 Thomas Rees, *History of Protestant Nonconformity in Wales*, 1861, pp. 286-293. R. T. Jenkins, *Hanes Cymru yn y Ddeunawfed Ganrif*, 1930, pp. 48, ff. E. G. Bowen, Bedyddwyr Cymru tua 1714, *Trafodion Cymdeithas Hanes Bedyddwyr Cymru*, 1957.
3 E. T. Davies, *Religion in the Industrial Revolution in South Wales*, Cardiff, University of Wales Press, 1965, (The Pantyfedwen Lectures, 1962) pp. 22, ff.

IN THE INDUSTRIAL AREAS

built and one has merely to refer to the various denominational annual handbooks or diaries to confirm this. One ironworks in particular illustrates this point. The proprietors of the Rhymney ironworks had provided facilities for Nonconformists of every denomination to conduct Sunday schools: three Baptist, four Independent, two Wesleyan, one Calvinistic Methodist and one for the Established Church.[1] In the ironworks region thirteen ironworks had Sunday schools attached to them, containing thirty-three in all, in the following denominational order: nine Baptist, seven Independent, six Wesleyan, four Calvinistic Methodist, four Established Church (of which two were at the Guest Ironworks at Dowlais), and three undenominational or 'neutral'. Compared with the Established Church the Nonconformist Sunday schools in this region were far ahead. By selecting specimen industrial parishes which contain ironworks Sunday schools[2] the following figures show a remarkable contrast:

	Church Sunday schools	Nonconformist Sunday schools
Total number attending under the age of fifteen	1,882	9,792
Total number attending over the age of fifteen	1,463	6,950
Total	3,345	16,742[3]

---

1 1847 *Reports*, Appendix C, p. 246; Appendix B, p. 328.
2 The parishes of Aberystruth, Bedwellty, and Panteg in Monmouthshire; Merthyr Tydfil, Michaelstone-super-Avon, Margam, and Glyncorrwg in Glamorgan, and Llanelly in Breconshire.
3 1847 *Reports*, Parts I and II, Tabulated lists of Sunday schools.

The following table shows the allocation of Sunday schools, by denominations, to the various ironworks:

County	Ironworks	Bapt.	Ind.	Wes.	Est. Ch.	Cal. Meth	Unden.	Total
Monmouth	Blaina	2	–	–	–	–	–	2[1]
	Tredegar	1	–	–	1	–	–	2[2]
	Sirhowy	–	–	–	–	1	–	1[3]
	Rhymney	3	4	2	1	1	–	11[4]
	Ebbw Vale	–	1	1	–	–	–	2[5]
	Victoria (Ebbw Vale)	1	1	1	–	–	–	3[6]
	Panteg (Blaendare)	1	–	–	–	–	–	1[7]
	Total for Monmouthshire							22
Glamorgan	Dowlais	–	–	–	2	–	–	2[8]
	Cwmavon	1	1	1	–	1	1	5[9]
	Oakwood	–	–	–	–	–	1	1[10]
	Bryndu	–	–	–	–	1	–	1[11]
	Blaengwrach (Glyncorrwg)	–	–	–	–	–	1	1[12]
	Total for Glamorgan							10
Brecon	Clydach (Llanelly)	–	–	1	–	–	–	1[13]
	Total for Breconshire							1
	Total for South Wales							33

1 1847 *Reports*, Part II, Appendix B, p. 328.
2 ibid.
3 ibid, Appendix C, p. 246.
4 ibid.
5 ibid.
6 ibid.
7 ibid, p. 332.
8 ibid, Part 1, p. 164.
9 ibid, p. 178, also p. 343.
10 ibid, p. 180.
11 ibid, Part 1, p. 352.
12 ibid, p. 178.
13 ibid, p. 244.

IN THE INDUSTRIAL AREAS

Functionally, Sunday schools in this region had one main purpose in mind—religious instruction. This meant not only receiving religious knowledge but also learning to read. This is clearly shown in the tabulated Reports, and the majority of ironworks Sunday schools, apart from those in Dowlais, Merthyr Tydfil, and Cwmavon, used Welsh as the medium of instruction. For the majority of the population in these new 'camps' or townships, starting life from scratch as it were—other attainments seemed unnecessary. The children, in any case, could obtain the other educational 'frills' such as writing and numeracy in the works day school. Nearly all the dame and private adventure schools which abounded in the older towns like Pontypool and Merthyr Tydfil were almost non-existent before 1840 so that for the greater part of the first half of the nineteenth century Sunday schools and works schools did most of the educational catering. Of these two institutions it must be emphasized that the Sunday school held the day as the main mechanism of instruction and was far more popular than the day school. Another important feature found only in this industrial region, which again demonstrates the functional aspect, was the amount of time spent in the Sunday school per session, e.g. at Rhymney Ironworks Baptist, six hours; at Rhymney Ironworks Independent, Tredegar Ironworks Baptist, and Victoria Ironworks (Ebbw Vale) Wesleyan, four hours; the other ironworks Sunday schools varied between two and three-and-a-half hours.[1] The Blaengwrach Sunday school of the Venallt Coal and Ironworks near Glyn Neath in the parish of Glyncorrwg, incidentally the only one of its kind in the anthracite coalfield, was an exceptional institution. It was a combined day and Sunday school on an undenominational basis held in a Unitarian chapel. Instruction was given through the medium of Welsh and the subjects of study as listed in the tabulated Reports for the Sunday school side showed a strong secular curriculum. In addition, to religious knowledge and reading, other subjects offered were arithmetic, writing, geography, and astronomy! This Sunday school did not displace the day school for it is recorded that of the 45 boys and girls attending, 22 of them also went to the day school. The Sunday school session lasted for five hours and one of the proprietors of the works always acted as Superintendent.[2]

Bowstead's observation 'that the working classes attached the highest value to Sunday schools', and Horace Mann's comment that 'Sunday schools took precedence in the educational race' rang true.[3] For the same

1 1847 *Reports*, Appendix B, p. 329.
2 ibid, Part 1, pp. 178-9. It was stated that no register was kept at the Sunday school, the attendance was irregular, and few under 15 years of age attended.
3 Horace Mann: *Census of Great Britain*, 1851, Report and Tables, published 1854, p. xv.

census year of 1851 the *Minutes of Committee of Council* recorded for south Wales that 'the public day school was no popular institution of the mining and manufacturing districts generally, but only the public Sunday school, for which edifices are raised sufficient to accommodate the whole population of the school-going ages during one day in the week, to remain during the remainder of it, either unoccupied, or tenanted only by some poor and unskilled teacher, permitted to assemble his few private pupils amidst its waste of dusty desks and benches'.[1]

Statistics again show the ascendancy of the Sunday school over the day school in the following analysis of the same specimen industrial districts for 1847:

County	Specimen Industrial Parish	Pop'n. 1841	No. attending Day Schools	No. attending Sunday Schools	No. of Day Schools	No. of Sunday Schools
Monmouth	Aberystruth[2]	11,272	616	(a) 1,402 (b) (2,331)	10	18
	Bedwellty[3]	22,413	1,236	2,863 (4,842)	16	32
	Panteg[4]	2,171	—	294 (389)	—	4
	Total	35,856	1,852	4,559 (7,562)	26	54
Glamorgan	Merthyr Tydfil[5]	34,997	2,301	4,290 (6,902)	41	36
	Michaelstone super Avon[6]	2,531	323	839 (1,350)	2	8
	Margam[7]	3,526	765	597 (927)	8	9
	Glyncorrwg (Blaengwrach)[8]	634	72	45 (128)	1	2
	Total	41,668	3,461	5,771 (9,307)	52	55

Brecon	Clydach (Llanelly)[9]	7,366	634	1,451 (2,398)	Not given
Total population of above parishes in 1841				..	84,890
Total number attending day schools ..			..	..	5,947
Total number attending Sunday Schools:					
(a) under 15 years of age			..	.. ..	11,781
(b) all age groups ..	..	..	..	..	(19,267)

The figures in the table include the total number of Sunday schools and attendances (a) of children under fifteen years of age, and (b) all age groups for all denominations and the Established Church. It should be noted firstly, that apart from Merthyr Tydfil which had thirty-eight small private adventure schools out of a total of forty-one day schools[10] all parishes had more Sunday schools than day schools. Secondly, with the exception of the parishes of Margam (which contained four large works schools) and Glyncorrwg,[11] more than twice the number of children went to Sunday schools in the under 15 age group, i.e. 11,781 as compared with 5,947. Thirdly, if all age groups are included, over three times the number went to Sunday schools. Finally, the over-all picture is still more striking for out of a total population for all the parishes of 84,890, 19,267 or almost twenty-five per cent attended Sunday schools.

In brief it can be said that the new townships of the ironsmelting region had the normal denominational Sunday school and an exclusive kind of similar school attached to the various coal and ironworks, which, with two exceptions, was not found in the industrial triangle of the west. The ironworkers regarded the Sunday school as the main educative

1 *Minutes of Committee of Council*, 1850-51.
2 1847 *Reports*, Part II, p. 273.
3 ibid.
4 ibid.
5 ibid, Part 1, p. 46. Out of the 41 day schools, 38 were small private adventure.
6 ibid, p. 48.
7 ibid; the parish of Margam contained 4 large works schools, with 7 departments.
8 ibid.
9 ibid, Part II, p. 9.
10 There were only two National schools for boys and girls in Merthyr Tydfil, and the Guest Ironworks schools (for boys, girls and infants) in Dowlais.
11 Margam had four works schools: Margam Copperworks, Margam Tinworks, Oakwood Ironworks, and Bryndu Ironworks. Blaengwrach was in the parish of Glyncorrwg. It is the only example of a secular Sunday school.

instrument whose purpose was primarily instructional and whose popularity compared with the day school was unquestioned.

The second region, the industrial triangle of west Glamorgan and south-east Carmarthenshire, had a long tradition of industry going back to the sixteenth century especially around the Neath area.[1] However, its real industrial metamorphosis occurred after 1800 with copper as the central feature linked with the development of many other ancillary industries including the smelting of iron. This went on apace so that by 1850 it became apparent that this region had a long course of industrial development yet to come. It was during this period that Swansea emerged as the regional metallurgical capital and became the acknowledged copper centre of the world.[2] After 1850, Swansea, Neath, and Llanelli, together with the Swansea, Neath, Amman, and Gwendraeth valleys, developed very rapidly in terms of population and industry, and by the end of the nineteenth century the copper, chemical, tinplate, steel, and anthracite coal industries were dominant in this area. Moreover, the anthracite coalfield developed differently from its neighbours in Glamorgan and Monmouthshire for this type of coal did not play any significant part in the industrial processes, and its export phase did not begin until the last decades of the nineteenth century.[3] This region, although it developed in a somewhat spectacular way, did so in a much more steady and exclusive manner. The main centres of industry had historical backgrounds associated with castles and abbeys and they assumed the industrial cloak more gracefully than other settlements which lacked municipal experience and tradition. This sector of the south Wales coalfield never depended on one or two major industries like coal and iron for its industrial mainstay. The motto emblazoned on its industrial crest was diversity of industry. Its working class personnel were different, for they were involved in highly technical and skilled processes in the smelting and refining of copper, silver, and lead; the distillation of chemicals; the manufacture of tinplate, and later of steel. The Commissioner when he reported in 1847 noted the difference in the two regions between the copper and the iron works: 'The former are situated at the bottom of valleys near the sea, because the ore is imported from Cornwall or Cuba. The latter are situated at the further end of the valleys because the ore is native, and is most accessible in those positions. Hence the men engaged in the Iron works are much more isolated from the casual influences of civilisation than those engaged

1 S. W. Rider and A. E. Trueman, *South Wales*, Methuen, 1929, pp. 77, ff.
2 ibid.
3 Leslie Wynne Evans, The Anthracite Coalmining Industry, *History of Carmarthenshire* Vol. II, p. 385, ff.

in the Copper Works. It was in the Ironworks that John Frost found his followers. The population in the Copper works has a greater tendency to become permanent; in the Ironworks it is always fluctuating'.[1]

Diversity of industry meant less fear of unemployment and periods of depression and this assurance of economic stability tended to produce less working class political activity and industrial unrest. Here, Chartism had its counterpart in the Rebecca risings, a protest against agricultural poverty due to population growth which had disrupted an old social pattern. But the riots—sparks from adjoining militant rural areas—only appeared spasmodically in the industrial centres of Llanelli, Gwendraeth and Pontarddulais, associated with two colourful figures who had migrated here from Merthyr and Tredegar.[2] At Llanelli, the workmen among the manufacturing population were commonly small freeholders or leaseholders, and the Commissioner described the Swansea region as being more superior to Merthyr Tydfil, and as a class, the workmen in the former region were not intemperate but improvident—relying on constant employment. They were mostly Welsh—a copperman was almost always the son of a copperman: 'They are all Dissenters and the intellectual resource of the adult population is the chapel whether used for preaching or a Sunday school'.[3] The same description could be applied to the tin-worker in Llanelli and the Swansea valley. In this region employers of labour were not faced with the problem of providing everything for their workmen such as shops, houses, churches, and chapels, although most of them did provide schools. Day schools of a sort abounded in Neath, Swansea, Llanelli, as well as in the Neath and Swansea valleys which included private adventure schools, dissenting schools held in chapels, and representatives of the old 'Free' and Charity schools.[4] Swansea boasted an endowed grammar school and twenty-one superior schools with 319 scholars at an average charge for daily instruction of £4. 12s. 2d. per annum. It is apparent that we are here dealing with a superior type of population which could afford such sums to educate their children.[5]

On the religious side this region became the mecca of working-class Nonconformity in the nineteenth century, predominated by two large denominations, the Baptists and Independents. The former had deep roots associated with the Rev. John Myles and the first Baptist cause at Ilston

1 1847 *Reports*, Part I, p. 13.
2 David Williams, *The Rebecca Riots*, Cardiff, 1955, p. 246 ff. John Jones, (Shoni Sgubor Fawr) and David Davies (Dai'r Cantwr). Jones, had been employed by R. J. Nevill, the Llanelli copper smelter.
3 1847 *Reports*, Part I, p. 209.
4 ibid, p. 373.
5 ibid, p. 41, pp. 1-95.

(a few miles from Swansea, in the Gower peninsula) in 1649, together with a second 'mother' church at Felinfoel, Llanelli, in 1709.[1] From these two centres scores of Baptist chapels were established throughout the area. Here, likewise, the Independents became firmly ensconced especially in the Llanelli district which grew into the empire of 'Independia Fawr' (the 'Congregational' centre) in all its glory. The presiding genius within this territory was the Rev. David Rees, minister of Capel Als—the dynamic divine, founder of churches, militant educationist, the king-pin of Voluntaryism, and the arch-enemy of British schools and government aid.

It is against this background, quite a different land from our first region, with its staid yet fervent Nonconformist population, its variety of industrial occupations, and its proliferation of day schools that we must judge the role of the Sunday school. To all outward appearances it formed part of the national pattern, but here, as in the ironsmelting region of the east, there were important regional differences. Firstly, apart from the two works Sunday schools in connection with the Margam tinworks[2] and the Unitarians at Blaengwrach in the Neath valley, there were no others connected with industry in this industrial triangle. Secondly, Sunday schools in this area grew naturally with the chapels and were devotional as well as instructional. They were rather, the meat-in-the-sandwich of the Nonconformist three-session Sunday pattern, i.e. morning service, afternoon school, evening service. Thirdly, the Sunday school session rarely lasted longer than two hours—very often one hour.[3] Fourthly, Sunday schools were not the main educative instrument in the lives of these people. Although reading was taught when necessary, they assembled for religious knowledge and discussion, and later in the nineteenth century the Sunday school became the Sabbatic social focus for young and old. Many contained good lending libraries, Sunday school banks, and the 'cold water armies' of the Temperance Movement. Fifthly, in some places, e.g. Llanelli, the Rev. David Rees organized his large Sunday school at Capel Als on the lines of a denominational day school and laid great emphasis on the training of teachers.[4] His chapel was the pivot of the Voluntaryist movement and if it was too expensive to establish and build

1 *Undeb Bedyddwyr Cymru a Mynwy, Cyfrol Goffa, Seion, Llanelli*, 1928, p. 18.
2 *Education Inquiry*, 1833, Vol. III, p. 1285: 'Margam Tinworks, two Sunday schools, one supported by C. R. M. Talbot, Esq., Established Church, who allows £5. 5s. 0d. per annum. The works Sunday school was originally for adults, but is now extended to children of all ages capable of being taught, chiefly in the Welsh language. It consists of from 180 to 190 males and females, and has been carried on at the expense, and under the Superintendence of Mr. Robert Smith, the proprietor, since 1810.'
3 1847 *Reports*, Part 1, Appendix, Tabulated Parochial Sunday schools.
4 *Undeb yr Annibynwyr Cymraeg, Llawlyfr Cyfarfodydd Llanelli*, 1929, p. 21.

IN THE INDUSTRIAL AREAS

a denominational day school he was determined on the next-best prototype. His stand against any form of State aid for establishing British schools postponed activity on the part of the British and Foreign School Society in this district up to 1854, so that Sunday schools were more popular in Llanelli than at Swansea or Neath—as the statistics indicate below. Sixthly, apart from Llanelli, there was little difference in the numbers attending the day and Sunday schools, in marked contrast with the first industrial region. Finally, at Swansea, Neath, and Llanelli, day schools outnumbered Sunday schools. The following figures speak for themselves and it should be noted that only children under fifteen years of age are included:[1]

Specimen area	Population 1841	Number attending day schools Noncon. and Church	Number attending Sunday schools Noncon. and Church	Number of day schools	Number of Sunday schools
Borough of Swansea and Llangyfelach	34,697	3,423	3,320	79	55
Town of Neath	4,970	536	757	13	8
Town of Llanelli	11,155	976	1,918 (140 in Church S. School)	20	13
Total	50,822	4,935	5,995	112	76

The above figures show almost an even balance between the attendances at the day and Sunday schools in the Borough of Swansea and the parish of Llangyfelach, an industrial parish juxta-posed to Swansea. In his report on the Swansea district the Assistant Commissioner included

1 1847 *Reports*, Part 1. Parochial Summaries of the numbers attending Day and Sunday schools, pp. 43-49.

details of a statistical inquiry printed in the *Fifth Annual Report of the Council of the Royal Institution of South Wales for* 1841 on the population of the municipal borough of Swansea.[1] The territorial limits of this district extended beyond St. Mary's parish into the parishes of St. John's near Swansea (which contained the Hafod copperworks schools), Llangyfelach, and Llansamlet. Reference is made to fourteen Sunday schools then existing, with their attendances in the following denominational order: Independent, four; Baptist, three; Established Church, three; Calvinistic Methodist, two; Wesleyan, one, and Lady Huntingdon's chapel, one. Comparing them with the results of his own inquiry in 1846 he found that there had been an actual decrease in attendance of 11.1 per cent on the numbers of 1841. The reasons for this apparent lack of interest in the Sunday school may again be attributed to the type of working-class population in this region.

In the first place, adults did not attend so well because 'there was want of proper accommodation to separate them from the young, who could generally read better, and smiled at the mistakes of their seniors: this pained and drove them away'. Secondly, there was lack of equipment such as maps and books and the teachers were generally incompetent in point of information 'yet they were good persons and able to teach moral and religious truths, but were ignorant of geography and facts'. Thirdly, the more constant employment on Sundays kept them away. Fourthly, Sunday schools could not retain 'grown up lads after the age of 18 or 19. They quitted the schools thinking themselves men, and that they must join in the drinking habits of their seniors'.[2] Fifthly, the retention of children at day schools for a longer period made Sunday schools less effectual as instructional institutions. All children attending the Hafod copperworks schools had to remain there until the age of twelve. Of twenty-three children in the school chosen to read from a lesson-book for the Commissioner, the age variation was from seven to fourteen years.[3] J. H. Vivian employed no boy under the age of twelve in his various works, and when 'taken out' at the works had to supply a certificate of age and attendance at school to the works office. The same procedure was followed at the other copperworks schools at Kilvey, Margam, Llanelli, and Pembrey.

The third industrial region in south Wales, the mid-Glamorgan coalfield comprising mainly the Rhondda and Aberdare valleys presents the Sunday school in yet another sociological setting. Two points should

1 1847 *Reports*, Part 1, Appendix, p. 385.
2 ibid, p. 384.
3 ibid, p. 360.

be noted at the outset. Both districts became industrialized after 1860 and the common basis of economic exploitation was one product, coal. Secondly, coalmining developed very rapidly between 1870 and the end of the nineteenth century and beyond, during the same period when, after the Education Act of 1870, day school provision on a State pattern was being evolved. It was during this period, in one respect, that the Sunday school reached its climactic, whilst in another, it was shedding its primary and basic function of instructing the working classes. Its pedagogical role had reached its zenith. Educationally, it had kept the home fires burning on the Welsh working-class hearths. Indeed, it was the torch of learning which kept burning throughout the time when its rival—the day school—often succumbed to the problems connected with denominational factions and religious controversies within the voluntary system of the nineteenth century. As a 'school' its purpose had been achieved but it grew in stature and its popularity remained unchallenged as the social, cultural, and religious academy of working-class Nonconformity in its hey-day. Moreover, it was the custodian of the vernacular, for all activities were carried on in the Welsh language. Nowhere was this more true than in the mining valleys of south Wales in the period 1870-1920. The Sunday school, in a sense, became more glamorous and certainly more colourful in its many-sided contributions to the cultural life and social milieu of the collier. It was the nursery which produced and trained men and women who gained distinction in many fields and in more than one instance achieved national reputation.

Historically and statistically there is little to report regarding the Sunday school in this region before 1860. It was more or less the 'blind' sector of the coalfield. Whilst east and west had experienced half a century of industry and population congestion the centre remained unspoiled, undeveloped, and thinly populated. In 1841, the old parish of Ystradyfodwg (Rhondda) had a population of only 1,363 as compared with 6,741 in Aberdare, but even at this early date the Sunday school was dominant. The following two specimen areas are for the Rhondda and Aberdare.[1] The parishes of Llantrisant and Ystradyfodwg are taken together since the former contained the earliest collieries of the Rhondda district.

1   1847 *Reports*, Part 1, Parochial Tables of Sunday and Day schools.

Specimen area	Population 1841	Number attending Day schools	Number attending Sunday schools	Number of Day schools	Number of Sunday schools
Llantrisant	3,222	293	627	6	10
Ystradyfodwg	1,363	45	77	2	3
Total	4,585	338	704	8	13
Aberdare	6,741	445	986	10	17

The numbers of attendances are for all denominations including the Established Church and include only children of 15 years of age and under. In each area over twice the number of children attended Sunday schools as compared with day schools. The total attendances at Sunday schools for all ages at Llantrisant and Ystradyfodwg were 1,894 or almost fifty per cent of the total population. At Aberdare almost one-third of the total population attended Sunday schools.

After 1860 the Rhondda and Aberdare valleys developed rapidly. Population figures for the period 1860-1900 demonstrate this fantastic exploitation of the coalmining valleys. Already in 1851 the Aberdare valley had a population of 14,999 which grew to 65,949 by 1901. The Rhondda (old parish of Ystradyfodwg) had only 3,857 people in 1861, but by 1901 the Rhondda Urban District (formed in 1891) had 113,735 inhabitants.[1] Between 1860 and 1870 when the Welsh immigrants were arriving in large numbers social conditions were similar to those in the iron-smelting region of Monmouthshire and north Glamorgan during the first half of the century. New communities settled around each pit and the coalowners had to hurriedly throw up wooden huts and a street or two of stone Company houses for the first arrivals.[2] The long narrow valleys created the traditional elongated settlements, but after 1878 houses were not allowed to be built in a haphazard fashion. They were planned in an orderly way which had to satisfy minimum conditions of space and width of streets.[3] The new population came from all parts of Wales—

1 *Census Returns*, 1851 *to* 1901.
2 E. D. Lewis, *The Rhondda Valleys*, London, 1959, pp. 218, ff.
3 Harold Carter, op. cit. pp. 326-7.

from the farmsteads, slate quarrying districts, and the moorlands of Cardiganshire, as well as from the contiguous counties. The Welsh character of the population preserved the Welsh language and made the mining valleys real Welsh communities.[1] The true Rhondda miner was a character on his own and worked as hard for his chapel and his Lord as he did for his colliery and its owner.

Much time and space would be required to discuss the place of Nonconformity in this new industrial region. A brief reference to the Rhondda will suffice, for the Aberdare valley showed a similar picture. The complete story is related in detail in the several volumes of the *Royal Commission on the Church of England and other Religious Bodies in Wales and Monmouthshire*.[2] The statistics in themselves are revealing but a study of the bulky evidence afforded by scores of witnesses more than repays the labour involved. In short, the Commission proclaimed the overwhelming strength of Nonconformity in terms of people and places of worship. It also showed, if statistics are any indication, that from the beginning of the century Nonconformity (including Sunday schools) and industrialization proceeded side by side. In 1860, there were 11 Nonconformist chapels; 98 in 1880; 112 in 1890, and 151 in 1905.[3] There were 114 Nonconformist chapels in the Aberdare valley for the same year.[4] The total seating capacity of the Rhondda chapels alone came to 85,105 with 34,756 actual members and an additional 58,326 adherents.[5] The 151 chapels could accommodate three-quarters of the entire population of the Rhondda Urban District. Needless to say, there was a very close relationship between pit and chapel. Indeed it could be said that the rise and decline of Nonconformity and the Sunday schools in the twentieth century conformed—in the industrial areas—with the rise and decline of the coal industry.

In the hey-day of Nonconformity, Sunday schools abounded, took on new responsibilities, and became an indispensable feature not only of chapel but also of communal activities. They were flexible enough to adapt themselves to the demands of this new mining society, for a prosperous Sunday school meant a prosperous chapel.[6] Over one-third

---

1 *Wales Through the Ages*, op. cit., Vol. II, Brinley Thomas: The growth of Industrial Towns, p. 191.
2 *Royal Commission on the Church of England and other Religious Bodies in Wales and Monmouthshire*, 1910, 1911, *H.M.S.O.*
3 ibid, Vol. VI, 1911, p. 292. This was the time of the great religious revival of 1904-5.
4 ibid, p. 293.
5 ibid.
6 ibid, Vol. VII, Appendix XX, p. 105.

(38,252) of the total population of the Rhondda in 1901 (113,735) of all ages attended Sunday schools, i.e. 19,110 under the age of fifteen, and 19,142 over that age. In fact there were more attending Sunday schools than there were of actual chapel members.[1] Why were these schools so popular during this period among the mining populations? This question is answered in part by the prominence which has to be given to Nonconformity in any discussion on education in the industrial areas in the nineteenth century. Moreover, it must be remembered that after 1870 day schools had become an established feature throughout the country and they were respected as day schools. Later on, especially after 1902 when secondary education became available, the miner made every effort to secure its advantages for at least one of his children. But all these new developments in secular education did not affect the Sunday schools. The reasons are not far to seek. Here again the Sunday school was resilient enough to emulate the day school in the religious and social context.

It was one of the requirements of the Education Act of 1870 that every parish should elect a School Board for the provision of elementary education if voluntary effort had proved ineffective. This was done for the Rhondda in 1878 and the members included Nonconformist ministers. It is significant to note that very often ministers of religion were the educational leaders in their districts during the era of School Boards up to 1902—Nonconformist ministers representing some denominations which had been hostile to government assistance before the Education Act of 1870. Between 1880 and the turn of the century an amicable relationship developed between the new undenominational day and Sunday school, the latter evolving as the religious prototype of the former not merely from the aspect of organization, but also in teaching method and content, although the curriculum was mainly religious. This gave the collier—or at least his children—the best of both worlds. Day schools, universally available were accepted as formal compulsory institutions which provided the minimal framework of education and the basic skills. The Sunday school adopted the framework, applied the basic skills to its own purpose and by so doing was able to develop activities of a many-sided character which made it the cultural and social centre of the chapel-based mining society. It was the period *par excellence* when the day and Sunday school worked harmoniously in double-harness—but with the latter institution riding postillion.

This was the characteristic feature of the Sunday school in the last quarter of the nineteenth century—day school organization was absorbed

---

1 *Royal Commission*, op. cit., Vol. VI, p. 293. There were also 3,896 voluntary teachers.

in its entirety. The larger Nonconformist chapels of every denomination had a very elaborate system with separate classrooms, appropriate literature and apparatus, and trained teachers.[1] Generally, there were four departments, Infant (and many had a Cradle Roll), Junior, Senior, and Adult including large numbers over the age of 80. One example will illustrate this system. 'Noddfa', the largest Baptist chapel in Treorci, the capital of the Rhondda Valley, had a recorded membership of 600 and a Sunday school of 650 in 1879.[2] By 1909, this chapel had built a large hall and a Sunday school unit with several classrooms—all attached to the chapel. In that year it was host to the Welsh Baptist Union Annual meetings, with the President, the Rt. Hon. D. Lloyd George, in the chair. A whole session was devoted to the work of the Sunday school which was addressed by Mr. F. F. Belsey, J.P., of London, the chairman of the council of the Sunday School Union. The syllabus included the following:[3] 'Growing importance of Sunday schools; modern improvements; the Primary Department; The Institute; Week-night opportunities; Boys' and Girls' Brigades; School and Home; The Home Department and the Cradle Roll; Training Classes; Winter Lectures by Educational Experts; Conferences on Bible Study; Preparation Classes; Benefits of Local Interdenominational Unions of Sunday school Workers. The Address will be preceded or followed by a specimen Blackboard Lesson to a class of Boys and Girls.'

The Welsh Nonconformist Sunday school had its own denominational publications which included appropriate graded textbooks for religious instruction in all departments. Bible classes were a regular feature especially for the training of voluntary teachers. After 1890, Sunday School Unions were set up by each denomination and the final 'take-over' from the day school appeared, for after 1891 the Unions conducted annual examinations for all age groups.[4] In scores of instances such examinations prepared suitable candidates—more often than not, working colliers—for the Christian ministry and supplied the minimum requirements of entry for the different denominational Theological Colleges. The Sunday school also had its other activities such as Bands of Hope, Youth Meetings and 'Penny Readings'. The musical side developed phenomenally, especially after the introduction of John Curwen's Tonic Solfa System which became an immediate 'hit' in the industrial regions. Music classes thrived in chapel and Sunday school and the great aim was to become proficient in this

1 *Royal Commission*, op. cit., Vol. VII, Appendix XX.
2 *Llawlyfr Cyfarfodydd Blynyddol Undeb Bedyddwyr Cymru*, Treorci, 1909, p. 20.
3 ibid, p. 60.
4 Sir Owen M. Edwards deplored this aspect of Sunday school activity.

System so as to be able to read music 'at sight'. Curwen transformed Wales into a land of song and this is no mere sentimental epithet. In the Rhondda and elsewhere large well-disciplined choirs, mixed and male, appeared, and some of them sang before Royalty at Windsor and in London. 'Cor Caradog' is but one famous example. Every large chapel had its choir which regularly performed the classical oratorios. This society of the mining valleys exulted in Eisteddfodau, 'Ysgolion Chwarter', Singing Festivals (Gymanfa Ganu), and the Gymanfa Bwnc.[1] These were rich fields of cultural and mental activity, embraced all sections of the population from infancy to adulthood and played a dominant role in the education of the working classes. It was a culture which was the special creation of Welsh Nonconformity at its zenith, whose remnants remain to this day. The twentieth century is all the poorer for its decline.

It would be a simple task to assemble a most impressive array of statistics to show the magnitude of Nonconformity and the popularity of the Sunday schools in their glorious high noon.[2] There is an old proverb which says that more than we use is more than we want. In the light of this wisdom we can afford to be highly selective. Statistics for the Rhondda have already shown that over one-third of the total population attended Sunday schools. If we take the Principality as a whole the same proportion holds good.[3] But there are quite a few interesting deviations. The three following examples from north Wales are significant, particularly the Rural Districts of Gwyrfai and Bethesda-Llanllechid which are the slate quarrying districts of Caernarvonshire. Here, Nonconformity give this typical Welsh community—so similar to the Rhondda valleys—its own characteristic ethos and reaped a bountiful harvest of Sunday scholars, over sixty per cent of the population.[4] Even in the cathedral city of Bangor, out of its population of 11,264 almost fifty per cent attended Nonconformist Sunday schools.[5] If we include the Wrexham Urban and Rural Districts to represent the coalfield region of north Wales the proportion is again one-third like the Rhondda valleys.[6]

---

1 'Ysgolion Chwarter' were quarterly meetings of the Sunday school which comprised a miscellaneous programme of recitations and singing, and sometimes 'Holwyddoreg' or questions on a given religious topic. 'Cymanfa Bwnc' was a gathering of Sunday schools for the purpose of public catechising in religious knowledge.
2 *Royal Commission*, op. cit., 1911, Vol. VI, County Statistics.
3 ibid, Vol. VI, 1911, County Statistics. See Appendix 2 to this chapter.
4 ibid, Vol. I, Part 1, 1910, p. 266.
5 ibid, Vol. VI, supra, p. 96.
6 ibid, Vol. 1, supra, p. 267.

District	Population 1901	Chapel Members	Adherents	Sunday scholars and voluntary teachers, all ages
Gwyrfai Rural	29,838	15,823	8,853	17,358
Bethesda and Llanllechid	6,347	2,844	1,543	3,117
City of Bangor	11,264	7,617 (includes adherents)		5,146[1]
Wrexham Urban and Rural	70,154	14,428	19,548	25,694

Let us recall to mind Bowstead's pointed remark of 1854: 'the working classes attach the highest value to the Sunday school, and the day school is wanted for another purpose'. Had he been spared to see the end of the century he would have been more impressed than surprised by the truth of his dictum. Thomas Charles himself would have opened his eyes in wonder at its outcome. That the Welsh Nonconformist Sunday school responded so easily and quickly to the different demands imposed upon it, and had sufficient flexibility to adapt itself to widely contrasting sociological backgrounds in the three industrial regions and in north Wales, considerably enhanced its popular appeal and proved its indispensability to the Welsh working classes. For over a century, and at the height of its influence between 1870 and 1920 it was the religious and intellectual power-house of Welsh Nonconformity.

---

[1] Separate figures for members not given. Note that almost seventy-five per cent of the population of this cathedral city were Nonconformist.

NONCONFORMITY AND SUNDAY SCHOOLS

APPENDIX 1

SUNDAY SCHOOLS IN WALES

A PAPER ON THE GOOD EFFECTS OF SUNDAY SCHOOLS, ETC.

WITH

A REPORT OF THE SUNDAY SCHOOL AT HARWOOD

CHESTER:

PRINTED FOR THE PROMOTERS, 1789

The above is the title page of a pamphlet of twenty pages consisting of a section on The Good Effects of Sunday Schools, etc., including Moral Effect, Political View, Plan describing Circulating Welsh Charity Schools 'under the particular patronage of Mrs. Bean (Bevan), of Laugharne, Carmarthenshire assisted by the Rev. Dr. Stonehouse of Bristol, Thomas Jones, Esq., of the Exchequer and other Reverend and respectable Gentlemen.' This Plan appears 'by a Pamphlet published in London, A.D. 1775'. It refers to the work of the Welsh Circulating Charity Schools 'that in the short space of about 39 years the almost incredible number of 297,121 poor Children received a Christian Education; and it is not a little surprising that out of this great Number, there were only 144 educated in this large County (Denbighshire). We are also informed that Circulating Charity Schools on a similar Plan have been lately established in Merionethshire by the Rev. Mr. Charles and prosper exceedingly. As the County for which these Schools are designed, is in almost, if not all respects similar to those above-mentioned, it will undoubtedly be best for us to proceed on the same successful Plan. The Children are so scattered on these Mountains and the roads so exceedingly bad and even dangerous in the Winter time, That a Sunday School only—is not likely to have the desired Effect, nor so great a number of children educated with so small an expence, and from Experiments recently made, this Idea seems to be confirmed'.

The promoters then outlined a plan for a Charity School, the committee meeting at the Eagles, in Wrexham, the second Thursday in every month, to commence on Thursday, 12th November 1789.

'The First Objects of the Society be, the Children and others belonging to the Lead, Coal, Furnace, and other Businesses residing at Rhos-llanerchrygrog, Minera, the Furnace, and Harwood, and as the Fund increases to extend these Schools in proportion to such other places, as the Governors may see necessary.'

It goes on to say that 'every boy or Girl employed in the Lead, Iron or Coal-works shall have the preference as to Admission'. Then there follows the 'calculation of expences for a Sunday school' which amounted to £15. 8s. 0d per annum to educate 100 scholars, pay three teachers (Two men and one woman), the men to receive 1/6d. per week each and the woman 1/- per week. Other items were money for 'rent if necessary, Books, Presents, Fires'.

On the last page of this pamphlet appears the following Report of the Harwood Sunday School for the children of the workers in the above industries:

IN THE INDUSTRIAL AREAS

INSTITUTED ABOUT EIGHT WEEKS SINCE, ON HARWOOD MOUNTAINS,
AND INCLUDED IN THE PRESENT PLAN

The Schoolroom is very commodious and free of Rent, by favour of Mr. D. F. Jones, Attorney, about 100 Children and young Persons generally attend, several of whom, in this short space of Time have learned their Letters and begun to read. There is also a visible change in their Language and Manners, which is witnessed not only in their behaviour at School, but also by their Parents and Neighbours, many of whom have expressed their thanks for this Charity in the most grateful and affectionate Terms.

So that these rude Hills which have long echoed the prophanest Language, now begin to wear the more pleasing Aspect of a Christian Country, and, if the fostering hand of instructive Charity will but continue its beneficence, we may hope to see this Wilderness become a fruitful Place, and many worthy members of the Christian Church and the Community at large, spring from the barren Soil.

> Rescu'd from worse than Poverty or Pain,
> The rugged Hill shall hail the smiling Plain,
> A thousand Tongues lisping their grateful Lays,
> Whilst Angels listen and extend the Praise.

Wrexham, November 22nd, 1789. J. Fernal.

ADVERTISEMENT

Subscriptions will be immediately received at the
following Places.

At the Rev. Samuel Strong's, at Marchwiel; Mr. David Parry's, Ruabon; Mr. D. F. Jones's, Attorney, Chester or Cumma; Mr. Woollam's, Mr. Jones's Ironmonger; Mr. Fernal's, Watchmaker, and at Mr. Marsh's, Printer in Wrexham.

APPENDIX 2

NONCONFORMITY AND SUNDAY SCHOLARS IN WALES, 1901
STATISTICAL SAMPLES FROM THREE INDUSTRIAL REGIONS [1]

(a) *Region I: Ironsmelting*

Town or District	Population 1901	Chapel Members	Adherents	Sunday Scholars		Total Sunday Scholars
				Under 15	Over 15	
Merthyr Tydfil	69,228	16,685	13,761	8,839	7,675	16,514
Ebbw Vale	20,994	3,709	8,910	3,092	2,312	5,404
Tredegar	18,497	5,400	8,451	5,009	1,955	6,964

(b) *Region II: Industrial Triangle*

Swansea Urban and Rural; Pontardawe Rural (Swansea Valley)	145,460	42,360	33,973	45,658	(all ages)	
Town of Neath	14,897	3,688	3,420	2,695	1,779	4,474
Llanelli Urban	25,617	10,288	6,188	4,144	5,280	9,424

(c) *Region III: Mid-Glamorgan Coalfield*

Rhondda Urban District	113,735	34,756	52,326	19,110	19,142	38,252
Aberdare	43,365	13,764	10,584	6,260	5,947	12,207

WALES: Population, 1901: 1,720,600.

Total Nonconformist Communicants: 551,679: Sunday Scholars: 671,428.

Total Church of England Communicants: 193,081: Sunday Scholars: 169,390.[2]

1 *Royal Commission*, op. cit., Vol. VI, 1911, County Statistics.
2 ibid, Vol. V, 1911.

IN THE INDUSTRIAL AREAS

APPENDIX 3

MONMOUTHSHIRE IRONWORKS SUNDAY SCHOOLS

Ironworks	Denomination	Numbers attending	Language of Instr.	Secular Instr.	No. of Teachers	Hours
Blaina[1]	1. Baptist 2. Baptist	50 150	W & E Welsh	Nil Nil	10 26	2 3
Tredegar[2]	3. Est. Church 4. Baptist	210 60	Eng. Eng.	Nil Nil	27 12	2½ 4
Sirhowy[3]	5. Cal. Meth.	400	W & E	Nil	50	3
Rhymney[4]	6. Est. Church 7. Baptist 8. Baptist 9. Baptist 10. Wesleyan 11. Indep. 12. Indep. 13. Indep. 14. Cal. Meth. 15. Wesleyan 16. Indep.	477 29 130 57 147 39 210 175 291 129 18	W & E Eng. W & E W & E W & E Welsh W & E W & E Welsh Eng. Welsh	Nil Nil Nil Nil Nil Nil Nil Nil Nil Nil Nil	46 9 20 12 20 8 34 30 76 16 16	2 2 6 3 2 4 2 3 3½ 1½ 2
Ebbw Vale[5]	17. Wesleyan 18. Indep.	169 50	W & E Eng.	Nil Nil	24 5	2 3
Victoria[6]	19. Baptist 20. Wesleyan 21. Indep.	75 85 100	W & E Eng. Welsh	Nil Nil Nil	33 9 18	2 4 3
Panteg[7]	22. Baptist	80	W & E	Nil	23	4

1   1847 *Reports, Part II*, Appendix B, p. 328.
2   ibid.
3   ibid, Appendix C, p. 246.
4   ibid, Appendix B, p. 328.
5   ibid.
6   ibid.
7   ibid, p. 332.

APPENDIX 4

Glamorgan Ironworks Sunday Schools

Ironworks	Denomination	Numbers attending	Language of Instr.	Secular Instr.	No. of Teachers	Hours
Dowlais[1]	23. Est. Church (boys)	110	Eng.	Nil	14	2
	24. Est. Church (girls)	110	Eng.	Nil	12	2
Cwmavon[2]	25. Undenom.	160	Eng.	Script. Geog.	11 (2 paid)	1¾
	26. Baptist 27. Wesleyan 28. Indep. 29. C. Meth.	no returns available.				
Oakwood[3]	30. Undenom.	48	Eng.	Script. Geog.	2 (Paid)	1½
Bryndu[4]	31. C. Meth.	no returns available.				
Blaen-gwrach[5]	32. Undenom.	45	W & E	Writing Arith. Geog. Astronomy Script. Geog.	2 (paid)	5

Breconshire Ironworks Sunday Schools

Clydach[6]	33. Wesleyan	60	Eng.	Nil	11	4

1 1847 *Reports*, Part 1, p. 164.
2 ibid, p. 178, also p. 343.
3 ibid, p. 180.
4 ibid, p. 352.
5 ibid, p. 178.
6 ibid, Part II, p. 244.

APPENDIX 5

EXAMPLE OF A NON-DENOMINATIONAL WORKS SUNDAY SCHOOL
OAKWOOD (CWMAVON) IRONWORKS SUNDAY SCHOOL[1]

Established 1844. Unconnected with any religious body.
Size of buildings: 50 x 24. Good premises, good furniture; used otherwise as a day-school.
Number of paid teachers: 1 male, and 1 female.
Attendances: under 15: 25 males; 23 females. None above 15. 40 attend a day-school.
Sexes taught separately in English.
No secular instruction, but Scriptural Geography.
Discipline and supervision by teachers of day-school.
Duration of Sunday school: 1½ hours. It is connected with no church or chapel.

1   1847 *Reports*, Part 1, p. 180.

APPENDIX 6

EXAMPLE OF A DENOMINATIONAL SUNDAY SCHOOL
RHYMNEY IRONWORKS BAPTIST SUNDAY SCHOOL[2]

Established in 1816. Number of teachers: 15 male, 5 female. All teachers unpaid.
Attendances: under 15: 35 males; 20 females. Over 15: 70 males; 25 females.
Number who usually attend: 97 males; 40 females. 9 only attend a day-school.
Sexes taught separately by laymen in Welsh and English. No secular instruction.
65 read the Scriptures and commit to memory.
Also teach religious formulary, hymns, and Scriptural geography.
Number of hours at Sunday school: 6.

2   1847 *Reports*, Part II, p. 328.

CHAPTER X

School Attendance and Further Education

APART from the Sunday schools which provided part-time schooling, secular day schools whether National, British, Undenominational, or Works, were faced with the almost insuperable problem of getting children to attend them. This was a major recurrent theme of successive reports by inspectors of schools from 1840 to 1860[1]. True on a national basis, the problem was much worse in the industrial areas. It has already been shown that the Sunday school was the most popular and best attended institution, added to the fact that the majority of the industrial population was Nonconformist. Moreover, Sunday schools gained the support of many employers because they did not interfere with work, and similarly parents were strongly in their favour because they maintained that children should earn their livelihood as soon as possible, and were set to work at an early age for six days of the week. In short, we are dealing with the twin evils which beset the day schools—early withdrawal of children from school and irregular attendance. These undesirable features produced attempts to combat lack of schooling for young children and adolescents, one of which was the evening school or further education.

This question of school attendance in the mid-nineteenth century was related to many situations. Sunday schools were overflowing and had no problems. The day schools of whatever kind had to contend with the twin evils. The typical works school's greatest rival was the works to which the school belonged. The attitude of parents created the twin evils. On the one hand they maintained that the better the school the earlier the age at which their children could leave, especially if infants schools were available. On the other hand the prevailing view was that children should work and that schools interfered with work. Further education and evening schools were mainly of a kind which provided elementary education at a later age, i.e. they were really adult elementary schools. State intervention in the form of factory legislation appeared in the colliery regions of the heavy industries after 1844, but this brought its own problems in relation to school attendance as we shall see later.

From the official angle we have the annual reports of inspectors of schools and in 1861—a crucial year for education in more than one

1 *Minutes of Committee of Council*, 1855-56; 1856-57.

respect—the appearance of the Newcastle Commission Report and the beginning of the reign of Robert Lowe with his Revised Code and the notorious *payment by results* system. The Inspectors' Reports especially between 1850 and 1860 are filled with references to children withdrawn from school at an early age, usually between nine and ten years and even earlier, and irregularity of attendance.[1]

A study of the *Newcastle Commission Report* which, incidentally, did not cover the whole of Wales but merely Welsh specimen districts in the Poor Law Unions of Corwen, Dolgellau, Bala, Ffestiniog, Neath, and Merthyr Tydfil in north and south Wales, reveals interesting statistics of early withdrawal and irregularity of attendance.[2] But this Report is only one example, for every report and inquiry dealing with the industrial areas of Wales before 1870 shows that the works were the greatest attraction for young children in spite of the fact that scores of works schools existed in those areas. The same government publications proclaim the popularity of the Sunday schools, e.g. in 1858, particular attention was called by the Assistant Commissioner to the fact that young persons availed themselves extensively of the advantages of Sunday school instruction—long after they had ceased to attend day schools. Both parents and pupils thought it a breach of duty to omit punctual and regular attendance at the school on Sunday.[3]

In the day schools however, it was quite a different story. The causes of early withdrawal could not really be attributed to the poverty of the parents or to the necessity for children to supplement the family income. Nor was it due to improvidence or other causes of inability in the population.[4] Such reasons did undoubtedly exist, but only partly accounted for the phenomenon. The main reason, common to all industrial districts, was the lack of appreciation by parents of the importance 'for the future welfare of their children, of education being carried out beyond the time at which they are at present withdrawn from school'.[5] It is worth probing deeper into this assertion, for early withdrawal was prevalent in those districts where sobriety and good conduct were characteristics of the population; where the houses were well-furnished, the children comfortably clothed, and where the people went regularly to places of worship on Sundays: 'it appears to be not so much a simple want of appreciation of the value of education, as a low estimate of what education consists in,

1 *Minutes of Committee of Council*, 1855-56, p. 508, ff. See Appendix 1.
2 *Newcastle Commission Report*, 1861, Vol. 2, pp. 437-634.
3 ibid, p. 499.
4 ibid.
5 ibid.

combined with a notion, always much strengthened by the prospect of immediate pecuniary advantages resulting from the children's labour, that as much additional learning as may be required, can be obtained hereafter, as occasion for it may arise'.[1] In addition, it seemed that so far as south Wales was concerned, early withdrawal did not originate in the parents' disregard or neglect of their children's welfare but was an indispensable— though regrettable—aspect of the prevailing ideas of the time: 'it is not a vice or moral delinquency that we have to deal with, but a state of opinion. The parents think that they are discharging a duty to themselves and families in withdrawing their children from school at an early age, when their labour becomes remunerative. Their reasoning was, in fact, that after giving them as much schooling as was required for their sphere of life, they ought to lose no time in putting them in a way of earning a livelihood'.[2] The fact that there were good works schools in the industrial areas tended to militate against a longer school life for the children. One suggestion offered was that as the schools of this type improved, the parents took the view that education could be terminated at an earlier age and the Sunday schools could take over any further instruction. The parents' estimation of the amount of education 'required for the sphere of life' amounted to very little. This idea persisted in the agricultural districts of Wales until fairly recent years, where it was the practice for farmers in remote places to send their children to a secondary school for what they called 'chwarter o ysgol', i.e. one term or year of schooling.[3]

Generally speaking, in the industrial districts most children were withdrawn from school after only a year's attendance and in some cases would be allowed to remain for eighteen months.[4] This practice was rampant at many of the works schools, e.g. at Blaenavon, in Monmouthshire, where almost every child between the ages of nine and ten were taken into the works.[5] Similar conditions obtained at the Nantyglo and Blaina works schools in the same county where 'the children of superior workmen stayed in schools until twelve or thirteen years of age; most of the rest left school between the ages of nine or ten, and colliers' children left between eight and nine'.[6] Conditions were similar in Glamorgan. In that county, the Cyfarthfa school at Merthyr Tydfil was one of the best

1 *Newcastle Commission Report*, Vol. 2, p. 499.
2 ibid
3 In Cardiganshire in particular.
4 At Dowlais, many children left after one year.
5 *Reports from the Commissioners, Mines*, 1850, p. 409, ff.
6 *Reports from the Commissioners in the Mining Districts*, 1856, Parl. Pap. XVIII, H. S. Tremenheere's Report to the Home Secretary, p. 274.

examples of wholesale early-leaving. In 1854, the following details were extracted by the head-teacher from the school registers:[1]

(a) Children in school

Number in school under 6 years old	45
,, ,, ,, under 10 years old	45
,, ,, ,, over 10 years old	17
Total	107

(b) Children who attended school

For less than one year	95 (out of 107)
For more than one year	6 (,, ,, ,,)
For more than two years	3 (,, ,, ,,)
For more than three years	3 (,, ,, ,,)
Total	107

In 1855, at the same school two hundred and two boys left, out of a total of two hundred and ninety-five, the Inspector stating that 'the returns were of such a peculiar nature that I considered them well worthy of being recorded':[2]

Number on the school books	112
Number admitted	144
Number re-admitted	39
Total school	295
Remained at school	93
Left in one year between March, 1854-55	202

At the Venallt Coal and Ironworks school 'the parents took very little interest in their children's education; they were taken away to work before they had learnt anything well'.[3] Early withdrawal was equally active at Dowlais and Cwmavon despite all attempts on the part of the proprietors to check it. The bulk of the youthful population left as soon

[1] *Minutes of Committee of Council*, 1853-54: General Report by the Rev. H. Longueville Jones, p. 592.
[2] *Minutes of Committee of Council*, 1855-56, Report by the Rev. H. L. Jones on National Schools, p. 414.
[3] 1847 *Reports*, Part 1, p. 479. Evidence by W. Jevons, Esq. of the Venallt Coal and Ironworks.

as they could in order 'to earn good money at an early age'.[1] The works manager at Cwmavon ironworks said that 'all the efforts on our part do not reach the mass of the people, but are partial in their influence. My feeling from the experience of twenty years is, that little has been done in the way of checking early withdrawal from school; legislation cannot check it, and any interference often does more harm than good.'[2]

In the copper smelting districts the position was somewhat better than in the iron and colliery areas. In his report on the copperworks in south Wales for 1862, Mr. F. D. Longe distinguished between those employed in the various processes: 'In the town of Swansea, and at Port Talbot in Glamorganshire, there are six large works in which copper is rolled into sheets and rods. These rolling mills are similar to those in the iron trade. A large portion of the hands employed are youths and boys of twelve years of age and upwards. In the same district there are copper-smelting works, some of which are connected with the rolling mills. In these works, few young hands are employed. The boys employed in the rolling mills generally begin at about the age of twelve, for very young boys are not required in copperworks. The boys employed at these works had generally been at work before they came to the trade. Many had been some years in the tinworks. I examined or questioned twenty-nine boys of ages varying from twelve to fifteen, and found that fourteen could either read or professed themselves able to do so, and that fifteen could not. The boys are hired by the employers and their wages range from six shillings per week upwards'.[3] Messrs. Williams, Foster and Co., of the Morfa Copperworks, Swansea, stated that many of their boys had been to school for only 'just over a year'[4] but most of the boys employed at Vivian's copperworks had attended school for more than three years.[5] Mr. George Nancarrow, manager of the Grenfell copperworks, stated that 'they had for many years attempted to carry out a rule that no boys should enter the works under the age of fourteen, and that they should be able to read and write when they came. But they had not been able to carry out this regulation in practice, for many boys said that they were much older than they actually were'.[6] He went on to say that few boys were employed under the age of twelve, and that most of them had been

1 At Dowlais it has been noted in Chapter IV that great stress was laid on Infants schools and evening or Adult schools.
2 *Newcastle Commission Report*, p. 499 ff.
3 *Children's Employment Commission*, 1862: Fourth Report of the Commissioners, with Appendix, 1865, p. 221.
4 ibid.
5 ibid.
6 ibid, p. 223.

given 'a good education at the Kilvey copperworks schools'. Several of the boys could spell very well and many of them 'paid three-pence per week to attend the evening schools'.[1] At the Duffryn colliery schools special care was taken that all boys who came under the Collieries Act of 1862 attended evening classes, and the younger colliers also attended the day schools during strike periods.[2] The same thing occurred at the Dowlais ironworks in 1873 when 'a number of boys from the Dowlais Company's collieries came to school, being too young to fulfil the conditions of the Colliery Act'.[3] In the same year during a long strike at the works, an extra member of staff was appointed to the ironworks school to superintend the large number of working boys who had returned to school.[4]

However, apart from the strike periods when schooling became a convenience for boys who had nothing else to do, early school leaving continued. The continual drain of young pupils from school marred any educational progress with the result that works schools seemed to exist as a short breathing space between infancy and employment.[5] In other words, between the ages of ten and twelve when a great deal could have been achieved in the schools, only a very small proportion of pupils remained. The position was aptly summed up by the Assistant Commissioner when he said: 'the foundation was laid with much cost and labour but the superstructure was not raised; the ground was prepared, and the seed sown, but the fruits were not gathered in'.[6]

Another result of early withdrawal was the high percentage of illiteracy among young men from eighteen to twenty-two years of age. Most of the education which these young persons possessed—beyond very clumsy writing and bad reading—had been obtained at Sunday schools.[7] After 1855, in areas where tinplate works had been established, early leaving reached new proportions, for child labour was much more

1 *Children's Employment Commission*. Fourth Report of the Commissioners, 1865, p. 500.
2 *Duffryn Schools, Logbooks*, Vol. 1, 5 June 1871.
3 *Dowlais schools, Logbooks*, Vol. 1, 10 January 1873.
4 ibid, 4 February 1873.
5 In 1860, early withdrawal was so rapidly on the increase in some industrial districts that it threatened to render abortive all efforts to educate the working classes. (*Newcastle Commission Report*, Vol. 2).
6 ibid
7 ibid. Vol. 1, p. 219 and Vol. II, pp. 366-7: The obvious solution to the problem of early withdrawal was compulsory schooling. This was effected at the London Lead Mining Company's schools (established in 1818) at Teesdale and Alston Moor under the agency of R. W. Bainbridge. A population of 10,000 depended on the Company, and at the two schools at Middleton and Nenthead every boy had to remain at school from 6 to 12 years of age, and every girl from 6 to 14,. Many pupils remained for much longer, but no boy was employed by the Company until the schoolmaster provided a certificate of competency. This is probably one of the

in demand than in the other industries, and children were often employed as early as eight years of age.[1]

The Assistant Commissioner had a great deal to say about the effect of early withdrawal on the teaching efficiency of schools since it produced a marked deficiency of pupil-teachers. Parents could not be persuaded to allow their children to remain in school up to the required age for pupil-teachers for their grants were not equal to the wages which they could earn in the works by manual labour. Cases occurred where pupils were taken away from school just as they became qualified by age to become pupil-teachers. As a result, masters in the schools had the assistance of mere children, usually from ten to twelve years of age, who, under the designation of monitors, served simply to perpetuate their own imperfections by transmitting them to others. In some cases, where schools did not apply for grants for pupil-teachers, monitors were remunerated by the proprietors of works schools. Here again, the monitors were generally very young and were taken away when their earnings out of school exceeded their pay as monitors.[2] In schools under inspection, the small number of pupil-teachers available were generally only in the first or second year of their apprenticeship. Many, as soon as they had gained some teaching experience left for the works.[3] Thus, early withdrawal produced a pupil-teacher system which had all the objectionable features urged against the teaching of 'children by children'. In the Boys' school at Dowlais, the Company had to appoint qualified assistant teachers in lieu of pupil-teachers—a feature which undoubtedly made this school so efficient and successful.

In the slate quarrying districts of Caernarvonshire and Merioneth the same story was true and children were taken away from school as early as nine years of age. The operations connected with the cutting and preparation of slates demanded a very high degree of manual dexterity,

rare examples of works schools which insisted on compulsory attendance. Compared with Dowlais and other large works in south Wales the results of such compulsion are worth recording. Also, in order to ensure that the attendance regulations were strictly observed, the Lead Mining Company's Schools were visited twice a year by the Company's Inspector. The educational state of the adult population of 2,535 employed by the Company was as follows:

	Men	Women
Can read	96%	91.63%
Can write also	88%	74.18%
Cannot read or write	4%	8.37%.

1 *Reports from the Commissioner, Mines*, 1856, p. 278.
2 *Newcastle Commission Report*, Vol. 2, p. 478.
3 This was experienced in the large works schools at Dowlais, Blaina, Cwmavon, and Ebbw Vale. The Inspectors' Reports between 1855-65 are full of such instances.

and children were taken to the quarries by their parents as early as possible in order to teach them the essentials of good workmanship: 'the workmen took their children to the quarries with them from nine to ten, and eleven years of age, as it was found by experience that the earlier they began, the better workmen they became. Unless a boy began to practise at quarrying the slate by the time he was twelve at furthest, there was little chance of his hereafter becoming a good workman in that department. It was a "knack", and had to be started early in order to become perfect in it. A boy left until he was fourteen had little chance of becoming a good workman'.[1]

Next to early withdrawal, irregular attendance was the greatest obstacle which the schools had to encounter and this again reflected a common view of the period, that school was an interference with work. Irregular attendance assumed two different forms in different parts of the country. In the manufacturing districts it was resorted to for the most trifling reasons, and, as in the case of early withdrawal, required the co-operation of parents. It was also more prevalent in places contiguous to, or connected with large works. Children were invariably kept at home to look after other smaller children, and very frequently were employed to take food to the works to other working members of the family. The question of attendance was a regular subject of complaint by the masters of all the works schools, and the school log-books are crammed full of instances where pupils were constantly reprimanded. The character of this irregularity is illustrated by the following extract supplied by the master of a National school in the Neath area connected with one of the most extensive works in the district: 'In addition to early withdrawal education is most injuriously affected by the irregular attendance of the children in school. They are not only frequently absent, but they come in the morning long after the hour for commencing, and I am obliged to let numbers of them out half an hour before the close of the school, to carry their fathers' dinners to the works'.[2] In the rural areas irregular attendance occurred 'at the most pressing seasons' for harvest and other agricultural operations. From an educational point of view there was a great difference between this systematic withdrawal for longer periods and the spasmodic interruptions of the industrial areas. In the farming districts a child would be withdrawn from school for a stated period of two or three months in the year, and on returning would attend regularly for a long period thus giving teachers the opportunity to plan their work

1 *Newcastle Commission Report*, Vol. 2, pp. 478-9.
2 ibid, p. 463.

accordingly. Nothing of this nature could be done in the industrial areas and the following table shows that most of the pupils were absent for the greater part of the year. Four of the Welsh Specimen Districts are shown, of which two—Merthyr Tydfil and Neath represent industrial centres in south Wales—and two from north Wales. Ffestiniog is the slate quarrying centre, and Dolgellau a rural district:[1]

Poor Law Union	No. of schools giving returns	Total scholars	Proportion per cent attending school during year 1857-1858				
			Less than 50 days	50 to 100 days	100 to 150 days	150 to 200 days	Over 200 days
Dolgellau	15	908	9.7	8.7	18.6	27.1	27.0
Ffestiniog	15	1,147	19.2	27.7	19.9	19.8	17.7
Neath	20	1,910	25.0	21.6	23.2	20.3	10.1
Merthyr Tydfil	22	4,153	35.1	15.8	15.5	23.4	16.9

It was a most distressing situation for inspectors and Commissioners alike to have to observe that although the industrial areas had their 'admirable schools' and efficient teaching staffs, early withdrawal, irregular attendance, and long periods of absence, made educational progress almost impossible and made 'the schools almost useless'.[2] Yet, that was precisely the position, and it became increasingly clear that voluntary methods of educating the labouring classes were breaking down, and that the only long-term remedy was the provision of schools by the State with compulsory attendance. Indeed it was significant that these 'evils' appeared in their most chronic form so near to the Education Act of 1870.

Various methods were tried to combat the twin evils in the industrial areas which were again voluntary and not the result of any legislation. Firstly, many maintained that a child's education might be started earlier in infants' schools as part of the drive to overcome early school-leaving. For this reason many works proprietors paid particular attention to such schools, e.g. at Dowlais, Cwmavon, Neath Abbey, and Ebbw Vale ironworks; at Llanelli, Hafod (Swansea), and Kilvey copperworks; at Duffryn collieries (Mountain Ash), and a few slate quarry schools at Ffestiniog

1 *Newcastle Commission Report*, Vol. 2, p. 464.
2 *Reports from the Commissioners, Sub-Inspectors' Reports*, 1868, p. 239.

and other places. In such schools the promoters had been careful to appoint good, trained teachers from the Home and Colonial Institution and the quality of the teaching reached a high standard. In other schools where unsuitable teachers were used, infants' schools achieved little. It had been hoped that 'much might be done by improving the character of the preparative instruction in schools of this class, towards carrying the education of children by ten years of age to a higher point than is attained at present. Speaking generally, neither as to system, still less as to subject-matter of instruction, does the infant school come up to its original conception'.[1]

Secondly, promotion to better posts in the works on condition that the pupils remained at school for a certain number of years was extensively tried in many works schools in an endeavour to check early withdrawal. Pupils who showed the best progress were offered better posts such as office clerk ships or other situations which offered a career. The only drawback to this system was that posts of this kind were extremely limited in number but the official reports of the period show that it was generally efficacious and had a very beneficial tendency. It also appealed to the self-interest of parents and proved to them in a practical way that 'longer retention at school led somewhere, with its promise of advancement in future life for their children, in situations of trust, respect, and emolument, and when they grew up would be in higher positions than the ordinary workman'.[2] Within its limitations this plan operated with some success at the larger works schools at Dowlais, Cwmavon, Swansea, and Llanelli—schools where children did remain up to eleven or twelve years of age, and where promotions were possible. At Cwmavon, Mr. Gilbertson, the works manager, introduced several of the clerks to the Assistant Commissioner, one of whom described the system of admission of children to the works: 'I was educated at the Cwmavon Works schools. I think that the system of taking boys into the office from the school prompts parents to keep them in school as long as they can; they are otherwise taken from school generally at from eight to ten years of age. The practice here in admitting children into the works is to register them. When a child comes to be registered before he starts work, I ascertain by examination if he can read and write; if not, I report him to Mr. Gilbertson who admits him or not . . . but always on the condition that the child goes to the night school'.[3] Another clerk, stated in answer to

[1] *Newcastle Commission Report*, Vol. 2, p. 580.
[2] ibid.
[3] ibid.

certain questions, 'the system adopted in the works of appointing boys to be overlookers, etc., induces parents to keep children in school longer, in order to bring them up to something besides labour'. Gilbertson, however, had to concede that these were only partial cases. He very much regretted that in general, although boys were made to promise to attend evening classes, they did not do so willingly, and had to be threatened with dismissal for this neglect.[1]

It can hardly be believed that at Dowlais of all places, with its excellent schools, some of the worst cases of early withdrawal occurred and many children left almost as soon as they passed through the infants' schools. The headmaster, Mathew Hirst, provided illuminating evidence: 'there are about 1,800 children in these schools. In the Boys' school, there are 420 boys now on the books and 340 in regular attendance. These are the children of the men employed in the Dowlais works . . . there is no other school in Dowlais. In the head class, there are about 55 boys at the present time; out of these, 50 are workmen's sons. The majority of these boys are between ten and twelve. There are several boys of twelve years of age and a few of fourteen years of age in school . . . those who stay above twelve are the children of the better class of workmen who are intended for places in the office. Not ten per cent of the whole school ever reach the first class. There are boys working in the mills who are eight years old and the majority are sent to work by their parents at nine or ten years of age . . . many go from the infant school before they come into the day school at all . . . we have a night school in the six winter months; my average number of boys was 114. The girls made up the number to 200. The boys were between ten and twenty years of age'.[2]

Thirdly, some schools apprenticed promising pupils to special trades or processes in the works, and also provided facilities for them to train as pupil-teachers. The copperworks had better openings for this type of trainee, although at Cwmavon the proprietors encouraged boys to spend part of each day in school in order to improve their mathematics and writing. Fourthly, some employers introduced an educational test as a condition of employment for children from ten to twelve years of age. This at least demanded that they were able to read and write, but the

---

1 Other junior clerks were interviewed by the Assistant Commissioner. He was very pleased with their appearance, address, and the language of their conversation. Of these, one had been in school 'past 15; a second till 16 years, and a third and fourth till 14 years'.
2 *Third Report of the Commissioners, Children's Employment*, 1862: Vol. XXII, published 1864, with Appendix. Mr. F. D. Longe's Report, No. 268, p. 394.

standard required was easily attained by the time the child was ten years old, with scarcely the slightest intellectual training 'and in a year or so after leaving school the capacity both for reading and writing was lost from want of practice'.[1] This was especially true of those industrial districts where the children of the working classes turned to their native tongue for all uses of language. It was also evident 'that employers who insisted on such certificates of merit competed unequally with those who did not require them, and in a district where labour was in such demand, and very often exceeded the supply, the general adoption of such a practice was almost beyond the limits of rational expectation'.[2]

Fifthly, H. S. Tremenheere, in his Report to the Home Secretary in 1856, estimated that 'about seventy-five per cent of the boys who had passed through the good companies' schools had forgotten all they had learnt. Why? Because they left school between eight and ten years of age and the efforts of the works proprietors and the government to provide school-houses and masters has been thrown away'.[3] He went on to extol the merits of refresher courses to make up for lack of schooling. He reported that several works schools had arranged for boys between twelve and sixteen years of age to return to school for short periods. Here again the educational rewards were meagre, merely re-learning reading and writing, and offered nothing really attractive to young boys and adolescents. Lack of enthusiasm, understandably, caused the scheme to languish, and even those who frequented them had little benefit due to lack of continuity.[4]

Sixthly, Prize Schemes or Associations were yet another incentive to keep children at school. Such schemes had been initiated in 1851 in south Staffordshire and also in the coal and iron areas in the north of the same county, Shropshire, Northumberland, and Durham.[5] In 1856, Tremenheere in conjunction with Sir Thomas Phillips of Courtybella launched the South Wales Iron and Coal Masters' Association, which consisted of three regions: The Eastern Region, from the Pontypool valley to Rhymney valley; The Central Region, from the Dowlais Ironworks to the Rhondda valleys; The Western Region, from the Llynfi Valley to Llanelli, Carmarthenshire. The list of promoters covered most of the works proprietors who contributed sums varying from five to ten pounds. The

1 *Newcastle Commission Report*, Vol. 2, p. 578.
2 ibid.
3 *Reports from the Commissioners, Mining Districts*, 1856, H. S. Tremenheere's Report to the Home Secretary.
4 ibid.
5 ibid.

object of the Association was to induce parents to keep their children at school for a longer period and to get them to attend more regularly. The funds granted prizes awarded on the results of an annual competitive examination. In order to be eligible children were required to attend some elementary school approved by any member of the Association for a period of at least two years. Pupil-teachers were not eligible. Secondly, children had to be at least ten years of age, and thirdly, each child had to produce a certificate from one of the managers to show that he had attended the day school at least 176 days during the twelve months ending the 1st of June preceding the examination. The prize money of £100 was divided into sums from £3 down to 5/-.[1]

The first of these examinations for the Eastern Region was held at the National school, Newport, in June, 1857[2] conducted by two inspectors of schools, Mr. Bowstead and Mr. Bellairs. Twenty schools participated, presenting 219 pupils. A sum of £80 was distributed on the results, prizes being awarded from £2 down to 5/-. The tenth and final distribution of prizes was made in 1866 when nineteen schools with a total of 324 pupils were represented. After that date the activities of the Association ceased, mainly because its object had been achieved by Robert Lowe's Minute of 1861 and the Revised Code of 1862.[3] According to the report of the Assistant Commissioner the work of the Associations did not seem to be very effective and the pecuniary rewards for attending school could never match what the children could earn in the works: 'the value of a prize even of £4 or £5 can have little influence when put in the balance against the child's earning at least three or four shillings per week. Nor can the other assumption be reasonably expected to have much weight with the labouring population whose notions of supposed duty to their families are so strongly backed up by the prospect of immediate gain in the shape of an increase of income amounting in the aggregate to at least from £7 to £10 a year'.[4]

Seventhly, the provision of educational facilities in the form of evening classes and similar institutions was one of the characteristic features of all schools built or promoted by works proprietors in the nineteenth century. Evening schools varied in kind and in content for whilst many of them were merely extensions of the elementary school and taught only reading, writing and arithmetic, others catered for more

1 *Reports from the Commissioners Mines*, 1856, H. S. Tremenheere's Report. Also see Appendix 1 to this Chapter.
2 *Monmouthshire Merlin*, 22 June 1857.
3 Frank Smith, op. cit., p. 255.
4 *Newcastle Commission Report*, Vol. 2, p. 480.

solid work and were real centres of further education. It was in this latter role that the works evening schools, with their opportunities for advanced work and varied curricula differed from the ordinary National and British schools. In general, the aims of evening schools were four-fold: to combat the lack of educational training due to the twin evils; to provide some kind of technical instruction for the better type of adolescent and adult workman; to provide advanced courses and tuition for the examinations of the Department of Science and Art, and to provide educational and recreational facilities for workmen's leisure hours.

In the majority of works schools evening classes had been attempted to counteract the twin evils. This question was treated in some detail in the Assistant Commissioner's Report: 'the evening school, taking up the education of the child from the time he left school, and following him until he arrived at manhood, was a more direct agency for counteracting the evil of early withdrawal. Whether its influence could be brought to bear on the unskilled labouring class universally, or even very generally, was rather doubtful'. The Commissioner had no hesitation in stating that 'evening schools might be the means of supplying much of that which was left undone through early withdrawal, and that every school in the neighbourhood of, or in connection with, large works, should have added to it, as indispensable to the completeness of its provisions for education, an evening or night school'.[1] We have already seen that the Dowlais Educational Scheme had an elaborate system of night schools —mainly extensions of the ordinary day school in terms of what were taught—for large numbers of children left school at the age of ten. Most of the evening schools in all areas never attempted anything more ambitious. In north Wales, for example, at the New British Iron Company's ironworks at Ruabon, two boys aged thirteen and twelve respectively gave the following evidence: Witness No. 265, David Griffiths, 'I am an underhand puddler, I am going thirteen; I have worked one month here. I used to work at the rolls. I work the iron. I get one and four-pence a day. I was at school for half a year before I came to work. I cannot read'.[2] Witness No. 266, Godfrey Edwards, 'I am an underhand puddler, I do not known how old I am. I am twelve or thirteen. I have worked for two and a half years. I never went to school. I cannot read'.[3]

Such similar distressing evidence could be multiplied over and over again from boys at Merthyr Tydfil, Ebbw Vale, Rhymney, Pontypool, and

1 *Newcastle Commission Report*, Vol. 2, p. 404.
2 *Third Report of the Commissioners*, 1864, *Parl. Pap.* XXIX, p. 393.
3 ibid.

other places. Out of twenty boys questioned at the Cyfarthfa ironworks at Merthyr Tydfil only six could read.[1] This was the kind of material which the elementary night school had to deal with. At Merthyr Tydfil as distinct from Dowlais nearby—adolescents and adults attended the evening classes at the Georgetown National school 'organized by the clergy for the adult population who wished to make up for deficiencies in education incurred while young and who had no other method of informing or improving themselves. The men and boys, and the young women from the works dress themselves for the evening schools in their better clothes, come with clean hands and faces, as if to a feast'.[2] At the Dos nailworks school at Newport, owned by Messrs. J. J. Cordes & Co. the evening classes were merely a repetition of the courses held in the works day school, and were chiefly conducted for the boys employed at the works during the day. There was an average attendance of 200 boys at this evening school.[3]

The evening schools at Blaenavon and Sirhowy had a precarious existence and were unpopular with the working classes. They were badly attended mainly because 'many working men and boys were discouraged because they had forgotten what they had learnt in their short school life before going to work'.[4] The master at Blaneavon works school said that he had been at the school for ten years and found 'that few boys remained at school beyond ten years and most left at nine'. Having re-opened an evening school in order to counteract the effects of early leaving he had thirty-five names on the books ranging from fourteen to twenty-three years of age. Of these, seventeen had passed previously through his school but they all said 'that they had lost so much that they should go back to the simplest reading'.[5] The master at the Sirhowy ironworks school told a similar story and his evening classes had to cease due to infrequent and low attendances.[6]

Similar evening schools for elementary instruction were held at Llanelli copperworks school; Hafod and Kilvey copperworks schools at Swansea, and the Welsh Granite Company's school at Trevor, Llanaelhaiarn, Caernarvonshire.[7] In the colliery districts of the Rhondda and

1 *Third Report of the Commissioners*, 1864, pp. 396-7.
2 *Minutes of Committee of Council*, 1850, p. 304. The Dowlais evening schools have been discussed in Chapter IV.
3 J. Warner, op. cit., p. 64.
4 *Reports from the Commissioners, Mines*, 1856, p. 419.
5 ibid
6 ibid.
7 *Minutes of Committee of Council*, 1871, p. 362.

Aberdare valleys evening schools absorbed large numbers of young boys and adolescents as a result of the requirements of the Mines Act of 1862.[1] At Aberdare, the headmaster of the Duffryn schools had constantly to remind the colliery managers of their obligation to send the boys to the Duffryn evening schools. But here again, the schools were unpopular, the numbers falling rapidly with the passage of time after each reminder, e.g. on the 6th January, 1873 (when the reminder was given) 155 attended, but subsided to 55 by 13 March of the same year.[2]

The reasons for the general unpopularity of evening schools were not far to seek. In the first place the general labouring classes were indifferent and had little enthusiasm for instruction in any night school, even 'where established in connection with iron, coal, or other works, it was to a very inconsiderable extent that the workmen availed themselves of the advantages of evening schools, although no charge was made for attendances, or more correctly speaking, they had already paid for it in the deductions from their wages towards the general education fund, which they were compelled to contribute towards'.[3]

Secondly, a fundamental cause was the exhausting character of the employments in which the great mass of the working population were engaged: 'the energies of labouring men in such works as collieries, copper, tin, or ironworks, were so exhausted by the time their daily toil was over, that they were not only indisposed for, but unequal to any continuous mental exertion in classes or evening school. Even ministers found difficulty in giving religious knowledge on week-day evenings. In fact, the men were so completely tired that they were unequal when evening came, to any great mental labour than hearing a very plain sermon, or an address on some subject which did not require much continuous attention. The main source of hope of bringing the advantages of evening schools to bear on the unskilled labour classes, lies in such an arrangement of these schools as will combine recreation with conveying general information'.[4] But again, the serious defect of evening schools as educative institutions for working people lay in the fact that the persons for whose benefit they were established were too often destitute of a general elementary education. Even attractive lectures on scientific topics demanded a background of culture and knowledge which was universally lacking, and the provision of library facilities only reached those who

1   *Logbooks, Duffryn Colliery Schools*, Vol. 1, 1863-1885, entry for 13 January 1864.
2   ibid, entries 6 January 13 March 1873.
3   *Newcastle Commission Report*, Vol. 2, p. 488.
4   ibid, Vol. 2, p. 480.

were capable of reading intelligently. With all the goodwill in the world, such agencies could not correct the initial deficiency.

Evening schools established for the provision of technical instruction and part-time education for working men and boys were fewer in number and mainly confined to the larger works schools of the metallurgical and mining industries. They were more attractive and successful than the elementary evening schools for they provided opportunities for the better class of skilled workman (who could read and write) to enhance his knowledge of his particular trade, and also gave him a ladder for promotion in the works.

Of the Monmouthshire ironworks schools, the evening classes at Cwmbran offered several courses in science and this school excelled all others in the provision it made for technical instruction which was given at both day and evening classes.[1] Mr. Robins Davis, the works manager, himself a technician, insisted on a varied curriculum for the workmen and the boys which included geology, surveying, solid geometry, mathematics and algebra. He was a keen believer in relating technical instruction to the jobs of the persons concerned and also organized regular lectures and discussion groups in mathematics, chemistry, and machine-drawing: 'young men are encouraged to discuss the subjects connected with the operations in which they are engaged as, for instance, with reference to the changes which take place in the course of the process of puddling iron, which partly arise from chemical, partly from mechanical causes, but more frequently from chemical, and therefore coming under the laws of science. Mr. Davis justly observed that if these causes were known to the workmen, they would know better how to deal with their work, and would give them a greater interest in it, and subjects to think over, and study them at first hand; teaching them in fact to think, which is the first step to moral improvement . . . facts would be selected for discussion, which had actually occurred in the course of the work, and enquiry would be made into their causes'.[2]

In the Glamorgan ironworks schools technical instruction at evening schools was successful at Cwmavon and Neath Abbey. The Cwmavon Company attracted boys to the more highly skilled jobs by providing special facilities in school for them to learn draughtsmanship, solid geometry, mathematics, and mensuration.[3] At Neath Abbey ironworks,

1 *Sub-Inspectors' Report* for 1868, p. 239.
2 *Reports from the Commissioners, Mines*, 1850, p. 248. Also Medical Officers were recruited to give talks on physiology with 'special reference' to the conditions of health and therein to the necessity and effects of cleanliness'.
3 *Newcastle Commission Report*, Vol. 2, p. 578.

private evening schools were conducted by skilled technicians. There were record attendances, for the proprietor 'considered the mechanical employment in the adjoining works to be useful in promoting and carrying out the rudiments of education acquired in the school'.[1] The evening schools gave further tuition in the mechanical field, with the result that most of the key-men in the Bristol Company's Steamers, the chief engineers of large sailing vessels, and many others had been educated at the Abbey school.[2] The proprietors of the works school attributed the success of the Neath Abbey people in the world 'to the *tout ensemble* of the influences with which they were surrounded and not to those of the schools only'.[3]

Closely linked with technical instruction were the attempts made at many places to provide part-time education. But these attempts met with only limited success. The schools concerned were those at Dowlais, Dos nailworks, the copperworks schools at Llanelli and Swansea, and the Cwmavon English Copper Company schools. At Dowlais, workmen and boys were encouraged to attend day classes, and at the Dos school, Newport, the boy-employees were required to attend school two hours for four days of each week. The day-shift went to school from six to eight p.m., and the night shift from four to six p.m.[4] At Cwmavon, the proprietors experimented with the part-time release of their technically minded boys from the usual working hours in order to learn draughtsmanship, solid geometry, and mathematics, provided they agreed to attend a similar number of hours at evening classes. In the pattern-making and fitting departments, the apprentices were released for one hour on two days per week to learn drawing. Other boys were drafted to the various works departments to serve as apprentices to the older technicians, especially in the moulding departments and drawing-offices.[5] The pupils who were bright enough were encouraged to become pupil-teachers. In such ways the first real experiments were made in vocational education during the Victorian age.

Of the copperworks schools, only one seemed to have catered for real technical education. Whilst technical instruction of a sort was provided at the Hafod schools at Swansea, it was at the Llanelli (Heolfawr) copperworks school that the greatest headway was made—both at elementary and advanced levels. The driving force was its remarkable headmaster, J. E. Jones. Evening schools for the purpose of advanced

1 1847 *Reports*, Part 1, pp. 338-9.
2 ibid.
3 ibid.
4 *Third Report of the Commissioners*, 1864,, p. 398. Evidence of Mr. T. Charles.
5 *Newcastle Commission Report*, Vol. 2, p. 579.

SCHOOL ATTENDANCE AND FURTHER EDUCATION

technical education leading up to the examinations of the Science and Art Department, Kensington, were almost rare in Wales in 1867, and so far as can be ascertained only existed at Llanelli. Intensely interested in scientific subjects, this energetic man succeeded in passing all the important examinations of the Department in addition to his work as headmaster, and his heavy commitments of teaching a whole variety of evening classes which he inaugurated at the school. These classes were attended by pupil-teachers, qualified teachers who desired to possess other technical qualifications, technicians from the copper, iron, and tinworks, mining engineers, local mariners, and various other tradesmen.[1] The variety of subjects taught by this elementary schoolmaster in 1867 makes almost incredible reading: Plane, Descriptive, and Solid Geometry; Mechanical and machine drawing; elementary and advanced mathematics; theoretical mechanics; applied mechanics; acoustics, light and heat; inorganic chemistry; general navigation; physical geography; freehand and model drawing.[2]

The Department of Science and Art examinations were held annually in May and were conducted by the local committee on behalf of the Department. Candidates were required to answer written examinations, the papers of which were set by professional examiners in each subject. The question papers were sent day by day in sealed envelopes to the secretary of the local committee, who broke open the seals each evening in the presence of the committee and the candidates at 6.55 p.m. At 10 p.m., the papers were collected, sealed up in envelopes furnished by the Department—again in the presence of the committee—and forwarded to London by the first post.[3] The Llanelli copperworks had its own dock and shipping, and at the request of the proprietors of the schools, Jones prepared local mariners for nautical examinations which included navigation and nautical astronomy.

Evening schools of the type already described did not appeal to the ordinary working classes and two suggestions were put forward in the *Newcastle Report*. The first dealt with the possibility of making such classes more attractive 'to the unskilled section of the population' by incorporating recreational activities as well as school subjects. The second suggestion was 'a combination of the private evening school type—giving special or technical instruction—and the organizations, which under various names such as Mechanics Institutes, etc., would give variety

1 *MS letter* (undated) addressed from Beaumont House, Goring Road, Llanelli, Llanelli Public Library.
2 ibid.
3 *Llanelli Guardian*, 22 August 1867.

of interest'.[1] Various attempts were made by works proprietors and the workmen's committees to get the labouring classes interested in some form of educational activity during the winter months. Many districts had their Instruction Societies, Literary Societies, Mutual Improvement Societies, Reading Rooms, Libraries, Mechanics Institutes, and other similar organizations. At the Blaina works schools in Monmouthshire, for example, in addition to evening schools, an Instruction Society was formed in 1852 with the object of attracting young workers who had left school at an early age and to get them to use the schools in the evenings. The centre of activity was the library of between four and five hundred volumes. Honorary members, made up of Company Directors, Agents and clerks subscribed 10/- per quarter and ordinary members, 1/-. A reading room was also available containing several daily papers and the best periodicals. There were over 200 members, chiefly young workers from fourteen to twenty-five years of age.[2] Similar societies were popular in the majority of works schools. But with the exception of evening technical classes leading to some kind of qualification, or improving technical skills, evening schools were generally unsuccessful. A full review of the state of evening schools was made in 1860 after the Assistant Commissioner had visited south Wales. He stated that the ordinary working man was totally indifferent and 'apart from a few well-conducted technical evening schools the majority were attended by a very small proportion of the working population, and even many of the classes connected with Mechanics and similar institutions were very generally in a state of decadence. Many classes languished for the want of good teachers, but the majority of them fell away from lack of attendance'.[3] In many instances the Mechanics Institute had shrunk into the proportions of a newspaper reading room, often with a library attached but seldom used.

The class of persons who availed themselves of 'the advantages of these cheap reading-rooms were generally small tradesmen and their apprentices'.[4] Where evening schools persisted, those who resorted to them were generally of a very special class—the skilled artisans—young men in the fitting or engine-making departments who wished to obtain some special branch of instruction connected with their everyday work. These skilled artisans kept up their attendances at evening schools—

1 *Newcastle Commission Report*, Vol. 2, p. 580.
2 *Sub-Inspector's Report*, 1868, on the working of the Factory Acts Extensions Act of 1867, p. 580.
3 *Reports from the Commissioners, Mines*, 1856, p. 248.
4 *Newcastle Commission Report*, Vol. 2, p. 504.

normally held in the works school—where no technical evening classes were available in their area. This occurred, for example, at Cwmavon, where an ordinary evening school produced good results for enthusiastic apprentices.[1]

Factory legislation in the nineteenth century referred to earlier[2] was most relevant to the problems of early withdrawal and irregular attendance. The *Children's Employment Commission* appointed in 1841 had been directed to inquire into 'the employment of children of the poorer classes in mines and collieries' as well as in the various branches of trade and manufacture.[3] The educational state of children in mining areas such as south Staffordshire, the West Riding of Yorkshire, north Lancashire, and south Durham was described as 'disgraceful to a Christian country . . . with no provision for one-fourth of the uneducated youth . . . and almost the only provision for the education of the colliery population were Sunday schools'.[4] Lord Ashley's Collieries Act was passed in 1843[5] prohibiting the employment underground of women and girls, and that of boys under ten. The Commissioner appointed to supervise the working of the Act was none other than H. S. Tremenheere who was to become so familiar with conditions in south Wales.[6] As in the iron and other metallurgical industries of south Wales many colliery owners had established schools, e.g. in Durham, the Consett Iron and Coal Company had established eight schools by 1849.[7] Mines legislation up to this point hardly affected the Welsh industrial areas, for coalmining was not a feature of the Welsh economy until well after 1860. But, reference to other parts of Britain at this time showed that conditions were very much the same in all industrial regions.

The Collieries Act of 1861 however was to affect South Wales. Under this Act children under ten years of age were to be excluded from employment as before.[8] But employment between the ages of ten and twelve, without restriction of hours, was to be limited to children who were certified before being employed as being able to read and write, and in respect of whom monthly certificates were obtained by the mine owner

1 *Newcastle Commission Report*, Appendix A, p. 578.
2 Chapter II.
3 *Children's Employment Commission, Second Report, Parl. Pap.* 1843, XIII, p. 309
  A. H. Robson, op. cit., p. 144.
4 *Second Report*, ibid, pp. 465-8. Also *Children's Employment Commission, Parl. Pap.* 1842, XVI, Appendix to First Report, p. 630.
5 5 and 6 Vict., c.99.
6 *Parl. Pap.* XVI, 1844, p. 3.
7 *Report of the Mining Commissioners, Parl. Pap.* XXII, 1849, p. 401, ff.
8 23 and 24 Vict., c.151.

showing that attendance at school had been made for three hours a day on two days a week during the month preceding.[1] The log-books of some of the colliery schools, e.g. at Duffryn collieries, Mountain Ash, showed that schoolmasters assisted materially in the administration of the Act by reminding the managers and owners of their responsibilities.

Breaches of the law—employing children under ten years of age and also evading the production of certificates—were, according to the Assistant Commissioner 'by no means infrequent, and in some of the colliery districts very general . . . but generally speaking the evidence on the operation of the law for preventing juvenile labour in collieries under ten years of age indicates that legislative interference up to this point has been effective for its proposed objects, and in its results, so far as south Wales is concerned, beneficial'.[2]

The Factory Act which affected the heavy industries of south Wales was the Factory Acts Extension Act of 1867.[3] Hitherto, legislation had prohibited juvenile employment under ten years of age in collieries. There was considerable opposition by all industrialists to the extension of the Collieries Act to embrace iron, tin, and other works because 'where the demand for labour was so great and competition so strong, there would always be a danger that any enactment which interfered with the general labour market, would operate injuriously on commercial interests by becoming a tax on the cost of production'.[4] Protestations were general among proprietors of tinworks where child labour was much more in demand than in the iron and other smelting industries, for children were commonly employed in tinworks as early as eight years of age.[5] However, in spite of opposition the Act became law. It meant half-time attendance at school which was to be compulsory for all children between the ages of eight and thirteen, and also prohibited night work. This Act did not come into full operation until 1 July 1870 (the year of the first Education Act), so that in the two major industries of the south Wales coalfield before that date, the twin evils had held the stage uninterruptedly since the beginning of the century.

1 A. H. Robson, op. cit., p. 158.
2 *Newcastle Commission Report*, Vol. 2, pp. 490, ff.
3 30 *and* 31 *Vict.*, c. 103. Note that the Coal Mines Act of 1872 contained the clause that a boy between the ages of ten and twelve had to attend school for at least twenty-four hours in every two weeks during which he was employed, and also the employer was required to obtain weekly certificates of school attendance from the principal teacher of the school.
4 *Newcastle Commission Report*, Vol. 2, p. 498.
5 *Children's Employment Commission*, 1864, *Parl. Pap.* XXII, p. 409.

SCHOOL ATTENDANCE AND FURTHER EDUCATION

But the 1867 Act hindered rather than helped education. By 1868, the south Wales industrial districts had masses of unemployed children thrown out of the works because employers of labour refused to implement the half-time system.[1] The number of new works brought under inspection in the South Wales District by the 1867 Act amounted to 236: ninety-eight iron mills and foundries, twenty-four copper mills, twenty-four tinplate works, five silver works, five spelter works, three chemical works, and other printing, railworks, docks, and shipyards.[2] The panic on the part of the employers was, for a time at least quite genuine, for it was reported in 1868 that only one factory employed half-timers.[3] Later however, whatever inconvenience and extra expense it had entailed for employers of labour, the log-books of scores of works schools testify to the provisions made to educate the 'half-timers from the works'.[4]

By 1870 educational and factory legislation met on common ground. School Boards set up by the Education Act of 1870 were gradually covering the country and by-laws for compulsory attendance with certain exemptions for children over ten years of age if they had passed a certain standard in school, were being enforced by many School Boards. In 1876, Lord Sandon's Education Act[5] declared that it was 'the duty of the parent of every child to cause such child to receive efficient elementary instruction in reading, writing, and arithmetic'.[6] The Act prescribed that no child under ten years of age was to be employed, and no child between ten and fourteen unless he had passed Standard IV, or had attended not more than two schools in each year at least 250 times for a period of five years. Universal compulsory education was achieved by Mundella's Act of 1880.[7]

---

1 'The poorer subjects of the working classes, especially the very young, will be under the obligation, between the ages of eight and thirteen, of combining a certain and very useful amount of school instruction with wages-yielding employment.' *Parl. Pap.* XXII, Children's Employment Commission, 1864, p. 409.
2 *Sub-Inspector's Report*, 1868, p. 272.
3 ibid.
4 Logbooks of tinworks, copperworks, and colliery schools after 1869 were full of references to half-timers, reminders from school-teachers to works managers, and numbers of school certificates provided for the works offices at specified times.
5 *30 and 40 Vict.*, c. 79.
6 F. Smith, op. cit., p. 296.
7 ibid, p. 299.

APPENDIX 1

Two Reports from the Commissioners, Mines and Collieries, of 1846 (Vol. XXIV) and 1847, (Vol. XVI) to inquire into the operation of the Mines Act, 5 and 6 Vict. c.99. and into the state of the population in the district from Aberdare to Pontypool comprising a population of about 140,000 refer particularly to the employment of young children in collieries. Tremenheere, in his *Report* of 1847 to the Home Secretary, Sir George Grey, Bt., stated 'Two other points of the Act also still require the vigilance of the law in this district (*a*) the payment of wages in public houses (*b*) the employment underground of boys under the legal age. In excluding of boys under 10 years of age from working below ground it was obviously the benevolent intention of the Legislature to secure for them an opportunity of obtaining before that age some portion of elementary instruction. The inquiries of the Children's Employment Commissioners which gave rise to this Act of Parliament had clearly brought out the fact that the prevalent habit of taking children into the mines and collieries from the early age of 7 and 8 years was deeply injurious to their minds and characters, and one of the chief sources of that cramped and narrow understanding, and clannish mode of life, for which the colliery population is so generally conspicuous.

It is an evil that tends to perpetuate itself, and although the efforts of individual proprietors have of late years had much effect in promoting the establishment of schools in most localities in the colliery districts, I have nevertheless generally found, on minute inquiry, that the proportion of colliers' children attending them was much less than was due to their relative numbers in the neighbourhood. In very numerous instances, the collier in order to swell the amount of his usually high earnings, will endeavour to take his child down the pit with him at the earliest possible age, in preference to sending him to school. In all but so few cases as will not affect the general question, or may be easily provided for, the earnings of a collier or miner throughout the year are ample to enable him to give some degree of education to his children. The earnings of iron-stone miners are usually about 15/- to £1 per week: those of a collier very rarely as low as 15/- and very generally averaging from 18/- to £1 throughout the year.

In general there is a school of some kind, where at least reading and writing are taught, in or near to the colliery or mining village. These schools are steadily increasing, both in number and efficiency, and after having gone through the whole of the most important mining districts of the kingdom, I venture to assert that the localities where a child of a collier or miner would have to go much more than a mile to a school are very rare. The payments at such schools are very often only 1d. and very seldom more than 2d. per week.

It appears to me that it would be attended with very little trouble to employers and no hardship to the parents of the children concerned if it were to be enacted:

1. That no boy who shall attain the age of 10 years on or after the 1st day of September, 18 ? (Two, or at most three years from the passing of the Act) shall be permitted to work in any mine or colliery until he shall produce to the owner or manager of such mine or colliery a certificate, in the form marked (A), Appendix stating that he has attended a school or schools for 48 weeks altogether (a school year) from the time of his attaining the age of 7 years until the time of his being admitted to work in such mine or colliery.

2. That such owner or manager of any mine or colliery shall keep such certificate or certificates for one year after the receipt thereof, or, until the boy whose school attendance it certifies shall attain the age of 11, and shall produce the same to any Inspector of Mines when required during such period ... Considering the usually high rate of wages of colliers and miners ... they should have no difficulty in providing instruction at day schools for their sons during a period of 48 weeks, either previously to their attaining the age at which they are allowed to work below ground, or soon afterwards.

SCHOOL ATTENDANCE AND FURTHER EDUCATION

By the 39*th* *Section of the Factory Act* (7. *Vic. c.*15) the occupier of a factory is empowered to pay the schoolmaster towards the expenses of educating each child attending school, a sum not exceeding 2d. per week, or not exceeding the rate of one-twelfth part of the weekly wages to be deducted from the wages of each child. To meet the case of the collier not being able to afford to pay for the education of his child, while the child himself is not earning something towards its own maintenance, it would be sufficient to give a power to the owner or manager of the mine or colliery to stop from the wages, and pay to the schoolmaster, any sum expressed upon the school certificate as due to the schoolmaster for the boy's school attendance, at the rate above mentioned, such sum not to exceed the total cost of schooling for 48 weeks, at the rate of 2d. per week or 8/-.

Persons of intelligence in all parts of the mining districts have expressed to me their regret that the Legislature had not thought proper when, excluding boys under 10 from working in the mines, to place their parents under some kind of compulsion to send them to school for a limited period before they should be permitted to work underground. Parents and owners of mines were shortsighted and did not care—others demanded 1 year's school as a condition of employment at all—"Let the boy of a collier or miner be forced for one year out of the narrow circle of his home where his opportunities of acquiring any new ideas are probably most limited . . . let him come under the influence of an earnest, able, schoolmaster . . . let him see around orders and obedience, gentleness of behaviour . . . let even only a year's training of this kind be brought to bear on a child . . . it is not improbable that it will lead the way to a future progress and improvement in mind and character which would otherwise never have been obtained".' (*January*, 1847)

Report from the Commissioners, 1847, Vol. XVI, pp. 403-7.

APPENDIX 2

Mr. Hugh Seymour Tremenheere's Report to the Home Secretary

Sir,

It will be in your recollection, that in my reports for several years past upon the populations in the coal and iron areas, and the means requisite for their moral and intellectual development, I have called attention to the fact that, notwithstanding the large and liberal expenditure of late years upon school buildings, and providing well-paid and efficient masters and mistresses throughout nearly every portion of those mining districts—the spread of elementary education among the rising generation was—in England and Wales, very slow and unsatisfactory, in consequence of the very early age at which nearly all the children of the labouring classes left the day-schools to go to work, and the general absence of any effort among them to retain or to improve the little they had learnt while there.

It will also be in your memory to remember that in 1851, I succeeded in inducing all the principal iron and coal masters in South Staffordshire to form themselves into an association, and to provide adequate funds for offering prizes of some value in all the schools in their respective neighbourhoods—to children of not less than 11 years of age. In order to develop that plan, Mr. Norris (an H.M.I.) was placed to supervise it. Similar Associations were formed in the other mining districts—North Staffordshire, Salop, Northumberland, and Durham. I have succeeded in doing the same in South Wales, and hope to organize three Associations.

Report of the Commissioners, Mines, 1856.

SCHOOL ATTENDANCE AND FURTHER EDUCATION

APPENDIX 3

Iron and Coalmasters Association for awarding Annual Prizes among the schools of the Mining District, from the Pontypool Valley to the Rhymney Valley, inclusive.[1]

No. 1 Area, Eastern Association
President: Capel Hanbury Leigh, Esq., Pontypool Park

Subscribers include:

C. Hanbury Leigh	£5
Messrs. Darby and Brown, Abersychan	£5
R. Johnson, for Blaenavon Co.	£5
Thomas Powell, The Gaer	£5
Sir Thomas Phillips	£5
Messrs. Banks and Co., Pontymister	£3. 3s. 0d.
W. Williams, Snatchwood House	£10
Launcelot Powell, Clydach Co.	£5
F. Levick for Blaina and Cwmcelyn	£10
Messrs. Darby and Brown, Ebbw Vale	£5.
Messrs. Darby and Brown, Sirhowy	£5.
Tredegar Ironworks	£10.
Rhymney Iron Co.	£10.
J. Frimstone, Pontypool	£5.
etc. etc. etc.	

Hon. Secretary and Treasurer: Sir Thomas Phillips, Courtybella.

1 *Reports from Commissioners, Mines*, 1856.

APPENDIX 4
No. 2 Area, Central Association[2]

District from Dowlais Ironworks to Merthyr, Taff Vale, Aberdare Valley, and the Rhondda Valleys.

Subscriptions promised include:

Trustees of Dowlais Company	£10.
R. Forman, Esq., Penydarren	£5.
R. Crawshay, Esq., Cyfarthfa Castle	£10.
Anthony Hill, Esq., Plymouth Works	£10.
etc. etc. etc. etc.	

Hon, Secretary and Treasurer, G. T. Clark, Esq., Dowlais House.

No. 3 Area: Western Association

District from Llynfi Valley to Llanelli, and Swansea area.

Subscriptions promised:

Llynfi ironworks	£3.
W. H. Buckland, Maesteg	£3.
G. S. Ford and Son, Bryndu	£3.
R. Beveridge, Cefn Coal Co.	£3.
Messrs. Brogden, Tondu	£3.
Wm. Gilbertson, Cwmavon Works	£10.
L. Llewellyn, Aberavon	£10.
Hussey Vivian, Swansea	£10.
Pascoe St. Leger Grenfell, Kilvey	£5.
Chas. Waring, Abbey Coal Co. Neath	£5.
Robert Smith, Dafen Tinworks	£5.
Messrs. Nevill, Llanelli	£10.
etc. etc. etc. etc.	

Hon Secretary and Treasurer: Pascoe St. Leger Grenfell, Maesteg House, Swansea.

2 *Reports of Commissioners, Mines*, 1856.

CHAPTER XI

Characteristic Features of Works Schools

SOME material appropriate to this chapter has, of necessity, been incorporated in detail in other parts of this work. Nevertheless, it would not be amiss to bring it together under distinct headings in order to try to achieve some unified picture. Compared with the ordinary day schools of the nineteenth century, works schools had several important and characteristic features of their own, which sharply distinguished them from, for example, the basic National or British school.[1] Three of these features have already been discussed, namely infant schools, evening schools, and comprehensive schemes of work and organization which were a special aspect of some schools, for example at Dowlais. Other equally important features were associated with the internal and external organization of such schools. In the larger and more important ones, on the internal side, the curriculum, teaching methods, organization, staffing, and scales of remuneration were superior to the ordinary day schools. On the external side, because of certain considerations not found anywhere else, attention must be given to the various types of works schools, the school buildings and the financial outlay involved.

For the majority of day schools, a more or less fixed and stereotyped curriculum was the custom.[2] Throughout the country generally the indispensable elements of knowledge to be acquired were reading, writing, and arithmetic. These subjects were considered as constituting the finished education of the children of the lower classes if they stayed at school long enough.[3] In 1836, one writer observed 'that speaking of the schools generally, we cannot hope that more is to be attained than an imperfect power of reading (not sufficient in many cases to enable a child to read with pleasure to itself), a yet more imperfect power of writing, and an

---

1 i.e. schools established by the two Voluntary Societies as distinct from those works schools affiliated to these Societies for, mainly, inspection.
2 *Report of the Royal Commission appointed to inquire into the Elementary Education Acts (England and Wales), the Cross Commission*, 1886, XXV, 1888. This Commission made suggestions for essential and optional subjects, some of which were embodied in the New Code of 1887. Welsh was recognised as an official school subject for the first time.
3 J. W. Adamson, op. cit., p. 30.

acquaintance with the first three or four rules in arithmetic'.[1] Additionally, in all schools, children were given religious instruction. Compared with certain continental countries, more especially Germany, this was a most humble diet. German schools taught the Christian religion, German, the elements of geometry, general principles of drawing, arithmetic, elements of natural science, geography, general history with particular reference to German history, singing, writing, gymnastic exercises, and simple kinds of manual labour.[2]

The content of education in many works schools in the light of the above information deserves special consideration. Whilst there was little to choose between the smaller type of works schools and the ordinary day schools so far as the orthodox three R's curriculum was concerned, something far more ambitious and attractive, on the lines of the German schools, was offered in the larger and more important works schools. These, in addition to reading, writing, and arithmetic, introduced new and advanced subjects and initiated and developed their own schemes and courses of study. As a rule this was done a few years after such schools were established, for in the initial stages works schools based their work on the pattern of the other day schools whether British or National. Hill's description of what was taught in the day schools in 1836 had altered very little, if at all, by 1847. In the *Commissioners' Reports* of that year which presented a detailed account of subjects taught in every day school in Wales and Monmouthshire, the tabulated lists of the parochial summaries show a distressing preponderance of blank spaces in the columns with the heading 'subjects taught', apart from reading, writing, and arithmetic—with, of course, religious instruction.[3] It is true that in some schools, vocal music, grammar, drawing, geography, and history were included, but the number of such schools was limited. Of the number of day schools offering a more liberal curriculum the majority were works schools in the iron and copper smelting districts of south Wales. In addition to the three R's the ironworks schools at Neath Abbey, Ebbw Vale, Tredegar, Sirhowy, and others included geography, English history, grammar, and vocal music in their schemes of work.

1 Frederic Hill, *National Education*, London, 1836, p. 72.
2 ibid, pp. 257, ff.
3 In 1861, the Newcastle Commission defined elementary education in terms of the ability to read 'a common narrative', writing 'a letter that shall be both legible and intelligible' and knowing 'enough of ciphering to make out or test the correctness of a common shop bill', together with a little geography and the ability 'to follow the allusions and the arguments of a plain Saxon Sermon'. (*Vol. I*, p. 243) In other words, a Christian version of the 'three R's' for boys and girls up to the age of 10 or 12. P. W. Musgrave (ed.), *Sociology, History and Education*, London, 1970. p.22.

Lord Penrhyn's schools at Llandegai, near Bangor also offered manual work and linear drawing which had a close bearing on some aspects of the technical side of slate quarrying. In the large schools at Cwmavon (Port Talbot), Dowlais, Hafod, and Kilvey (Swansea), and Llanelli copperworks, more advanced subjects such as land surveying, algebra, geometry, and astronomy were taught.[1] Practical and inorganic chemistry, complete with small laboratories, figured in the schemes of work for older boys at Dowlais and Llanelli.[2] Dowlais was the only example in Wales where a modern language was introduced into the curriculum of an elementary school. Unfortunately it had an air of tragedy from the outset, and it ended in complete failure. In 1869, a Mr. T. C. Gambier was appointed to teach French and Drawing to the Boys' and Girls' schools,[3] but in 1871 it was reported that 'the results of the teaching in French were as yet a failure'. By 1873 'the teaching of French was a complete failure, but for that subject the French master alone was answerable' and in 1874, Mr. Gambier was asked to leave the school.[4]

It was in connection with the apprentices' day classes and evening schools that works schools could show variety of courses and more ambitious curricula. The day and evening classes for trades' apprentices at Cwmavon, and the excellent evening technical classes at Llanelli were unexcelled in Wales. It has already been shown that many schools failed to keep their pupils beyond the ages of nine or ten. In those schools where advanced subjects were introduced for boys who wished to qualify for entry to certain trades, quite an appreciable number stayed on until they were thirteen or fourteen years of age. For the greater part of the nineteenth century works schools were almost the only institutions where such facilities existed for technical education. Again, apart from purely technical instruction, and long before Higher Elementary 'Tops' and Higher Grade schools were established, the works schools provided advanced instruction in the ordinary school subjects.[5]

Works schools had another advantage over other day schools in that they were able to maintain a variety of curricula and continued to provide advanced instruction during a period when other schools had to confine themselves to teaching the three R's. The Revised Code of 1861 initiated

1 Logbooks of the schools concerned.
2 *Minutes of Committee of Council*, Report for 1874 by Rev. S. Pryce, p. 136.
3 *Logbooks*, Dowlais Ironworks Schools, Vol. 1, 1864, p. 164, Inspector's Report for 1868-69.
4 ibid, pp. 188, 230, and 272.
5 *Minutes of Committee of Council*, 1887, p. 340: The first Higher Grade Elementary school at Hendy, Pontarddulais, was in connection with the tinplate works in that place.

the system of 'payment by results' and henceforward grants to schools were allocated on an attendance basis combined with proficiency in reading, writing, and arithmetic. In addition, grants for teachers' salaries, pupil-teachers' stipends, and various other grants were to cease. The net result was the imposition of a fixed, circumscribed curriculum, inferior teachers, and an extreme deficiency of pupil-teachers.[1] This vexatious Code did not affect the works schools to any great extent. Many of them did not accept grants, and those who did accept aid, accepted it for the purpose of promoting efficiency by annual inspection by H.M.I.s. The Assistant Commissioner for south Wales stated: 'in the case of many of the schools which accepted grants, I was informed that the proprietors had been induced to connect schools with the Committee of Council on Education not from financial considerations but with a view to securing the advantages of pupil-teachers, and to place the masters under efficient responsiblity for the discharge of their educational duties. . . In some instances which have fallen under my observation, I have grounds for stating that the public money received for the remuneration of pupil-teachers and capitation grants is not applied to supply deficiencies in the ordinary revenue of the schools; but that it, or an equivalent amount, is expended in giving increased educational efficiency to the school by the supply of apparatus, the appointment of additional masters, or other means of raising the character of its education'.[2] Such degree of financial independence in works schools was reflected both in the varied curriculum which they offered and the quality of teaching power in spite of the Revised Code. This is borne out by the evidence contained in the schools logbooks which are full of references to the subjects taught. In 1864, the curriculum at Dowlais included the three R's, scripture, music, history, geography, grammar, drawing, physical exercises, sewing, needlework, and musketry drill![3]

The 1847 *Reports* reveal how the schools were organized and also provide much information on teaching methods. On the whole, the monitorial system held sway, and, with few exceptions, all works schools enumerated therein were organized on that system. However, by 1850, all of the larger works schools were employing substantial numbers of pupil-teachers and above the average number of trained teachers. We have already seen that many proprietors placed their schools under the vigilance of one or other of the voluntary societies, and were able, by means of the extra money received from government grants, to employ additional

1 *Minutes of Committee of Council,* 1866-67, p. 214; ibid, 1867-68, p. 169.
2 *Newcastle Commission Report,* Vol. 2, pp. 490, ff.
3 *Logbooks, Dowlais Ironworks Schools,* Vol. 1, 1864.

trained teachers and also to train pupil-teachers. Other large works schools, for example, Cwmavon, did not seek government aid, were financially independent, and were able to maintain the schools—with trained teachers and pupil-teachers—from the revenue received from the poundage levy. But for the sake of efficiency the proprietors requested the National Society to send its Inspector to carry out annual inspections.[1]

The annual reports of the Committee of Council after 1850 show that all the larger works schools were organized in classes, with trained teachers in charge of each class, together with the requisite number of pupil-teachers serving their four-years' apprenticeship.[2] In this respect again, the Revised Code did not seem to affect the recruitment of pupil-teachers, for schools like Dowlais, Cwmavon, Hafod, Kilvey, Llanelli, and Dafen (Llanelli), had their full quota of pupil-teachers doing their training.

Another feature of works schools was the remuneration of their teaching staffs as compared with the ordinary day schools. In the former schools the teachers received a higher scale of salary because in addition to the augmentation grants received from the government for improving teachers' salaries the works schools were able, even under the Revised Code, to continue to pay better salaries because they could draw on the poundage levy. Also, in some works schools where difficulty was experienced in securing pupil-teachers, 'the teaching power was wholly supplied by staffs of able assistant masters at a scale of remuneration greatly exceeding that which would be incurred by the employment of pupil-teachers, but securing at the same time for the scholars incomparably superior advantages to those which it would be possible to obtain with pupil-teachers'.[3] In all districts where they had been established, it was generally acclaimed that 'the works schools were superior to the ordinary self-supporting schools of the country; the masters were, taken altogether more competent and better remunerated'.[4]

The distribution and location of works schools has provided another feature of unusual interest. It has been possible to distinguish three types of schools. Firstly, the large, individual works schools (exclusive of the smaller ones), for example, in Monmouthshire: Tredegar, Sirhowy, Rhymney, Blaina, Cwmbran, and Nantyglo. In Glamorgan: Neath Abbey, Margam, Kilvey, Hafod, Bryndu Colliery, etc. In Carmarthenshire: Amman ironworks, Llanelli and Pembrey copperworks, Dafen tinworks,

1 *Newcastle Commission Report*, op. cit., Vol. II, Appendix B, p. 611. The Cwmavon schools did not seek government aid until 1865.
2 *Minutes of Committee of Council* from 1850 onwards.
3 *Newcastle Commission Report*, Vol. 2, pp. 490, ff.
4 ibid.

etc., and in Breconshire, Yniscedwyn ironworks; in north Wales, the Welsh Granite Company's school at Trevor, Caernarvonshire. Secondly, the parent works school and its satellites. Four large Companies, in addition to establishing their respective basic schools, also provided satellite schools which might, or might not, be tributary to the parent institution. At Dowlais, the parent Boys' and Girls' schools had four infants schools connected with them—Gwernllwyn, Banwen, Gellifaelog, and Dowlais, and two additional junior schools at Tir y Colly and Pengarnddu.[1] The Cwmavon schools (the parent unit) which comprised Boys', Girls', and Infants Departments, also had other schools at Oakwood and Bryn, with an Infant school at Tymaen, all promoted by the same Company. These were all located around Cwmavon. A similar grouping existed at the Llynfi schools, Maesteg, and the Duffryn colliery schools in the Aberdare valley:[2]

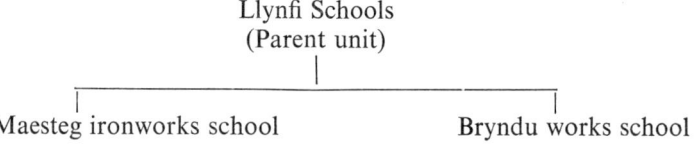

Llynfi Schools
(Parent unit)

Maesteg ironworks school   Bryndu works school

Thirdly, a group of large works schools owned or controlled by the same Company, as at Ebbw Vale, the Ocean Coal Company, Oakeley Quarries and Penrhyn Quarries. Two examples illustrate this type:

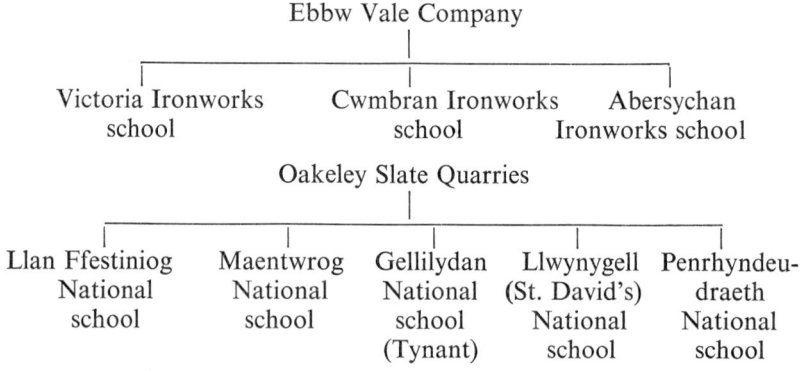

Ebbw Vale Company

Victoria Ironworks   Cwmbran Ironworks   Abersychan
school   school   Ironworks school

Oakeley Slate Quarries

Llan Ffestiniog   Maentwrog   Gellilydan   Llwynygell   Penrhyndeu-
National   National   National   (St. David's) draeth
school   school   school   National   National
                              (Tynant)   school   school

Perhaps one of the most interesting features regarding works schools was the manner in which they developed in particular districts together

1 See Chapter IV for Dowlais schools grouping. Also Dowlais schools logbooks, Vol. 1: 1869, p. 168; ibid, for 1865, p. 74 for Tir y Colly and Pengarnddu.
2 See Chapter VII for Duffryn schools grouping.

CHARACTERISTIC FEATURES OF WORKS SCHOOLS

with the actual school buildings and their cost to the proprietors. Most of the earlier and larger schools had more than one phase of development, whilst the largest, that at Dowlais went through at least three or four phases of expansion. The first phase was usually a humble one when the particular school was held in any spare room attached to the works or in disused buildings near them—or even in the lofts of stables. The Tredegar and Tremadoc schools started in rented rooms in the local Town Halls. The second phase, after about 1840, saw the provision of proper and substantial accommodation. The works proprietors usually built and paid for the school buildings but exacted a levy on workmen's wages to maintain the schools. Most proprietors also provided school-houses for the headteachers. The Reports of Inspectors and Commissioners alike after 1850 refer specifically to the works schools in their districts and employed such words as 'magnificent', 'extensive school buildings', 'good design of artistic beauty', etc. The Dowlais schools evoked superlative comments, e.g. 'the excellent buildings which were designed by Sir Charles Barry . . . and the four Gothic windows are of great interest to students of architecture'.[1] In 1850, the Mines Commissioner said 'that all the instances of liberal expenditure upon school buildings have, however, been exceeded by the magnificent structure erected by Sir John Guest and will remain a lasting tribute to the principle that, where great fortunes have been made from the labour of thousands of the working classes, a great debt is due to them, and that no reasonable efforts can conscientiously be spared which may contribute to their moral and intellectual elevation, and to their physical well-being and comfort'.[2] Details of other school buildings and amenities have already been described in connection with individual ironworks schools, and the works schools which called for special comment by the Inspectors in the other industries were those at Hafod, Kilvey, Llanelli, Pembrey, Dafen, and the Duffryn Colliery schools.[3] The financial outlay incurred by proprietors in the building of schools was quite considerable. e.g. Sir John Guest and his Trustees spent £20,000 on one phase of the Dowlais schools[4] but this was an exceptional case. In Monmouthshire, the Ebbw Vale Company 'expended upwards of £3,000 in the erection of new buildings';[5] the proprietors of the Abersychan ironworks, £3,500;[6] Rhymney, £2,200,[7]

1 *Notes on the Dowlais Schools*, op. cit.
2 *Reports from the Commissioners, Mines*, 1850, p. 244.
3 *Minutes of Committee of Council*, 1852, and 1858-59.
4 *Notes on the Dowlais schools.*
5 *Reports from the Commissioners, Mines*, 1850, pp. 248, ff.
6 ibid.
7 ibid.

and at Sirhowy, Messrs. Darby & Co., 'had, with great liberality, laid out upwards of £2,000 in very spacious school buildings close to the works'.[1] Similarly, in the western region the Hafod schools at Swansea 'cost between £2,000 and £3,000',[2] the Pembrey copperworks school 'with school houses', £1,700,[3] and the Dafen tinworks National school, £500.[4]

The most distinctive feature peculiar to works schools was the educational tax levied on workmen for the support of schools. This charge was not uniform but varied from school to school, and was levied on all persons employed in the works. It also applied to the young and unmarried men and boys, but very often persons in these categories paid at a lower rate. In many cases the unmarried employees had free access to evening schools. For these payments, books, but not stationery, were generally supplied. The 'stoppage' was compulsory, was imposed irrespective of the number of children sent to school, and 'there was a kind of tacit understanding that, in consideration of the stoppage, the proprietors would keep the schools open as long as they kept on the works'.[5] In some of the smaller works, there was not a sufficient number of workmen employed to warrant the establishment of a school, and in such cases the amount derived from poundage was transferred to a neighbouring school which the workmen's children attended. Also, in some instances, contributions from the school fund were made by proprietors to certain schools, British or National, for the convenience of workmen who resided at too great a distance for their children to attend the school connected with the works.[6]

Schools were maintained in several ways: (a) Some proprietors merely built schools for their employees, and all subsequent maintenance fell on the shoulders of the workmen through poundage payments. Some of the larger works schools were in this category: Llynfi, Maesteg, Tredegar, Rhymney (British), Blaenavon, and Cwmavon ironworks schools. Matthew Arnold, who had been impressed by this system of poundage at the Llynfi schools, expressed the hope that many other proprietors would adopt the same method to promote similar schools: 'This school is not maintained by the Company, nor by the payments of the children who frequent it, but a weekly deduction is made from the wages of every

---

1 *Reports from the Commissioners, Mines*, 1850, pp. 248, ff.
2 ibid.
3 *Reports from Commissioners, Inspectors of Factories*, 1868-69, p. 232.
4 ibid.
5 ibid. *Newcastle Commission Report*, Vol. 2, p. 568.
6 ibid

person employed in the works'.[1] This type of school, maintained entirely by the working population 'demonstrated very clearly their desire for education. Where proprietors were enlightened enough to show the way and provide the buildings, the workmen were prepared to maintain such establishments. At least, they did not resent paying their weekly pence. It is also important to note that this increased interest in education, is however due to the stimulus applied by the formation of good schools by the owners, and does not to any great extent originate with the men. The workmen do not establish day schools for themselves or support such voluntarily, but they submit to a small deduction from their wages for the school, and when to this their employers add convenient schoolrooms, and enough to support trained teachers, there is no indisposition to profit by the means afforded. Where the means are at hand, the people are very far indeed from being indifferent to education'.[2] This statement was an important part of the evidence given by G. T. Clark, one of the Trustees of the Dowlais schools, to the Assistant Commissioner in 1859. It is not wholly acceptable without some reservations, after reading carefully the Inspectors' Reports of that period. In the first place, works schools in some localities were in a very special position. Very often they were the only schools available for the working classes, and, furthermore, whether the workmen liked it or not, they were compelled to pay poundage as a condition of their employment. Secondly, the assertion that workmen did not desire to establish their own day schools was a moot point. In fact, there were several instances where workmen did establish their own schools, but in almost every case were unable to maintain them unless they were helped by the Voluntary Societies. Thirdly, as we shall see in the Merthyr district, smaller schools could not compete with works schools and had to close down. Fourthly, workmen in some areas were far from happy in 'submitting to a small deduction from their wages' to support a works National school, for out of this discontent the undenominational or neutral works school appeared. Tribute should certainly be paid to the benevolent proprietors who established such schools, but greater compliments should be showered upon the ordinary workman whose contributions, however small, in the aggregate more than covered the cost of maintaining them.

(*b*) There were some examples of schools where the proprietors provided the buildings and also maintained them. This occurred at Capel

1 Matthew Arnold: *Reports on Elementary schools*, 1852-1882. New ed., Board of Education, 1910, p. 9.
2 *Newcastle Commission Report*, Appendix B, evidence by G. T. Clark, Esq., Dowlais House, 22nd August, 1859.

Waun y Pound, Lord Penrhyn's schools at Llandegai, and Mrs. Oakeley's National School (St. David's), at Llan Ffestiniog.

(c) Some proprietors made no stoppages from workmen's wages, but the children were required to pay school pence. This happened at Rhymney (National) ironworks school, Sirhowy, and most of the slate quarry schools of north Wales.

(d) The large schools at Dowlais, Hafod, Llanelli and Pembrey copperworks, Kilvey, Margam, Dafen tinworks, Aberavon, Tondu, and others, including all the colliery schools, combined both systems of payment, i.e. school pence and poundage. At Dowlais, for example, 'for over half a century, every workman employed by the Company contributed one half-penny in the pound from his wages towards a school fund. Each child of a Dowlais workman actually attending at the schools paid a fee of two-pence per week in the Boys' or Girls' schools, and one penny per week in the infant schools. A few, children of tradespeople, who did not contribute to the school fund, were charged four-pence per week'.[1]

(e) In some places the workmen built and maintained their own schools. Religious differences caused discontent at some of the works schools in the Swansea valley, and rather than send their children to the works National schools, the workmen at Ystradgynlais, Ystalyfera, and Abercrave established British schools.[2]

The majority of works schools, when the time arrived for building new extensions, renovations, or even new schools, sought assistance from parliamentary grants. As we have already seen, many did so in order to avail themselves of inspection and for the promotion of greater teaching efficiency. In such areas less efficient schools were compelled to close down. For example, in the Merthyr district, all schools in Penywaun languished because of the Company's school; at Dowlais, all other schools, mainly of the private adventure type 'were decaying on account of the Dowlais Company's schools'.[3] Even some National Schools had to close due to the existence or enlargement of British Works schools, e.g. at Llanelli, the National school closed 'because of the Nevill's British Works schools'.[4]

It is possible to analyse the financial returns of some schools supported by stoppages. Many proprietors were unwilling to divulge the

1 *Minutes of Committee of Council*, 1880-81: Report for 1880, by W. Edwards, H.M.I., p. 311. Also, Notes on the Dowlais schools.
2 Mr. J. Bowstead, H.M.I. was one of the few who gave credit to 'the liberality and self-sacrifice of the humble workman'. *Minutes of Committee of Council*, 1868, p. 281.
3 *Newcastle Commission Report*, Vol. 2, p. 548.
4 *Report of Pakington Select Committee*, Minutes 4493-98.

details of their educational balance-sheets and very often the school fund account was mixed up with the works' sick and medical funds and other contributions. It would appear however that in most cases the amounts obtained by stoppages were more than enough to cover the cost of maintenance of the schools, although there were examples where such a fund was insufficient. The Assistant Commissioner cited three examples of schools 'returning an income arising from this taxation of the workmen'. The first produced an income of £157 per annum against an expenditure of £147 over the same period; the second, an income of £56 against £43 expenditure, and the third, of £172 against £137.[1] Full details of the income and expenditure of the copperworks schools at Hafod and Llanelli were produced, and the following anonymous ironworks school, in which there were 96 boys, 117 girls, and 143 infants:[2]

Full returns of the finances for one year of an ironworks school in South Wales employing from 2,000 to 2,100 men, boys and girls:—

Receipts	£	s.	d.	Expenditure	£	s.	d.
School pence for one year	3	2	8	Teachers' Salaries ..	112	4	8
				Teachers' Assistants	27	4	6
				Books & apparatus..	10	15	9
				Fuel & Lights ..	10	0	0
Income from stoppages	297	7	6	Rent	29	5	0
				*Other expenses .. (no details)	30	4	0
				Balance of receipt ..	80	16	3
	£300	10	2		£300	10	2

*'The works proprietors contributed to two other schools in the neighbourhood, but the amount of their contributions could not be ascertained, nor indeed, whether they were not included in the item "other expenses".'

Again, one large ironworks school, Tredegar, was in a particularly sound financial position as early as 1846. The income derived from stoppages amounted to £500 whilst the expenses of school maintenance

1 *Newcastle Commission Report*, p. 550.
2 ibid, Appendix E, p. 634.

were only £280. 4s. 0d.[1] All these examples showed that works schools were financially self-supporting. It was for this reason that many mediocre works schools who did not aspire to any additional expense of appointing fully-trained teaching staffs with a full quota of pupil-teachers carried on independent of parliamentary grants for a long time. The larger works schools however, who could well afford to remain independent of government aid, became affiliated to one or other of the Voluntary Societies, in order, among other things, to use the additional parliamentary grants to improve the efficiency of the school. Herein lay the great difference between the ordinary British or National school, and the works British, National, or Neutral school. The Assistant Commissioner made an interesting observation on the stoppage system when he stated that 'if this method of obtaining a revenue for the support of schools was equal to the cost of their maintenance, i.e. promoting educational facilities by the distribution over large numbers of small payments, then, from a financial point of view, it seemed to indicate a conclusion favourable *to general taxation for educational purposes.* Considering the condition of the population among which these schools were established and the many unfavourable obstacles to its educational progress from continuous immigration and other causes, it had to be admitted that the schools effected much for the education of the masses'.[2]

That works schools were the education authorities of their day is appreciated when consideration is given to the large populations which they served in their immediate vicinity. Taking the ironsmelting districts as examples and examining them on an area basis, the Pontypool valley had a population of 20,000 and the works schools in that valley were able to offer accommodation for 2,500 pupils.[3] On the basis of individual

1 1847 *Reports*, Part 2, p. 278.
   On the question of the ability of works schools to pay their own way, the Assistant Commissioner made out the following case: 'As, in no single instance that fell under my notice, did I find that any objection to the principle of receiving government aid influenced the proprietors of works, I think it is a fair presumption that the revenue raised by assessment on the wages of the workmen was sufficient to defray the costs of the schools: and this view is confirmed by the simple calculation that if in a works, 600 persons subscribed a 1d. per week each, it would amount in the year to £130. Deducting the young men and boys employed, we can assume 120 children at school. The master's salary would be about £70 p.a. and the payment of monitors or assistants about £30. This would, exclusive of rent of premises leave about £30 p.a. for the provision of school furniture, books, and other expenses. This estimate will, I think, fairly apply to the works schools in country districts, in which education is of a medium quality. At all events, I feel some confidence, from my knowledge of these schools, that I have not under-estimated any element in the calculation.' *Newcastle Commission Report*, Vol. 2, p. 550.
2 ibid.
3 *Reports from the Commissioners, Mines*, 1850, p. 340.

schools there were plenty of instances where large populations in smelting towns were served by a large works school—populations ranging from 8,000 to 12,000. There were populations of 12,000, 10,000 and 8,000 at Dowlais, Rhymney, and Cwmavon respectively.[1] It could be said that wherever there was a works school there was a works education authority and the poundage system was the education rate for the district. One other point was made with reference to the poundage system: 'valuable as government aid may be as an additional element to this method of supporting education, it would not have been possible to produce equal results by the existing system of voluntary agency supplemented by government assistance, which this mode of raising a school revenue had effected. I may here incidentally remark that it is to be borne in mind, in looking at the educational capacity of the two South Wales Unions, Neath and Merthyr Tydfil, that the works schools remove a vast burden of educational claims which would otherwise press on the voluntary agencies, aided or unaided by the government, of the population of these manufacturing districts'.[2] Another interesting feature of the finance of works schools was the 'guarantee grant' paid by the larger companies, mainly in the iron and copperworks schools. Where the income from poundage, school pence, and government grant proved deficient to maintain the schools, the companies concerned made up the difference. This was often implemented at Dowlais, and the Llanelli, Pembrey, Kilvey, and Hafod copperworks schools.[3]

In colliery schools stoppages on wages were carefully graded to suit different types of colliers. The school fund of a typical colliery was made up in the following manner: every adult workman paid 4d. per month; all boys working underground and earning from 6/- to 8/- per week paid 2d. per month; all boys working above ground and earning 1/6 per day paid 4d. per month; other boys engaged in sundry occupations, door-keepers, etc., paid nothing.[4] These schools were of two kinds, those which belonged to an individual colliery, e.g. Clydach Vale, Llwynypia, Dinas, Court Herbert (Skewen), Gilfach Goch, etc., which were maintained by the colliery concerned. Other colliery schools might be supported by a number of collieries, sometimes as many as five or six, e.g. at Duffryn, Ocean collieries, and the Garw collieries. Examples of the support of such schools have already been given from the wages books of the Ocean Coal

1   *Minutes of Committee of Council*, 1844, p. 226.
2   *Newcastle Commission Report*, Vol. 2, Appendix E, p. 632.
3   *Papers and Accounts of Llanelli Copperworks schools*; also excerpts of accounts from the school logbooks.
4   *Newcastle Commission Report*, Vol. 2, Appendix E, p. 633.

Company. The following is an example of the financial returns of a small individual colliery school:[1]

Estimate of annual receipts and expenditure of a colliery school assuming that 300 men and 100 boys are employed.

Receipts	£	s.	d.	Expenditure	£	s.	d.
300 men, etc., at 4d. per month	75	16	8	Salary: master	46	16	0
				Salary: Sewing Mistress	6	0	0
				Books £5			
				Repairs £2.10.0			
100 boys at 2d. per month	6	10	0	Rent £5	12	10	0
				Extras and cost of collection	5	0	0
					70	6	0
				Balance receipts	12	0	8
	£82	6	8		£82	6	8

Regarding the management or administration of works schools, ordinary National and British schools which were supported by voluntary subscriptions and parliamentary grants were managed by local committees elected from the body of subscribers, and in the case of National schools the parochial clergy were involved. But the works schools were almost exclusively under the sole control of the companies or the proprietors of the works to which the schools were attached. In such schools the management presented the somewhat exceptional feature that those who contributed a large proportion of the revenue had no part in the control of the schools. The proprietors decided whether the schools should be conducted on the National or British system, appointed the teaching staffs and prescribed the subjects of instruction.[2] In fact it was to them that every question relating to the conduct of the schools was referred and their decision had to be accepted. One example has already been given of the Tredegar ironworks school which had an annual income of £500 from workmen's contributions and only just over one-half of that amount was expended on the school. The Commissioners of 1847 were highly critical of this state of affairs and maintained that this system of sole

1 *Newcastle Commission Report*, Appendix E, p. 635.
2 *Report of Pakington Select Committee*, Minutes 3017-5871.

CHARACTERISTIC FEATURES OF WORKS SCHOOLS

control by the proprietors was far from peculiar to the Tredegar Company: 'the obvious evil of it is, that those who pay do not govern, and inasmuch as the employer causes the school to be conducted after his own views, a portion of the contributors to it are sure to feel aggrieved. No account is rendered to the men, and the surplus money may go to the payment of a church minister, or it may be pocketed by the firm and became a source of clandestine profit to the employer, without any possibility of detection ... I feel it my duty, however, to state my conviction, that the workmen do not derive an equivalent for the fund usually raised from their wages and to which they are compelled to pay. The system of a compulsory payment "under proper regulations" is one which I should be averse to condemn too hastily. It may, in many cases, prove the only efficient means of procuring a maintenance for a good school; the workmen would scarcely maintain it adequately if left to themselves, and the owners are unquestionably as likely to do it for them. The only desideratum seems to be that the money should be properly applied and accounted for, and that the men themselves should have the benefit of the surplus, if there were any. The time may come when it will be compulsory on the employers to have the children educated before they employ them and, if so, it may be expedient that the means of doing so should exist. At present, more money than enough is paid in these establishments by the people, and the end is not answered'.[1]

There is no doubt whatsoever that there was ample justification for this forthright criticism by the Commissioners, for similar examples, though on a much smaller scale have been noted where income exceeded expenditure on schools. But in the case of the larger schools, when they were rebuilt or extended, especially after 1850, and more particularly the colliery schools after 1865—when such schools maintained high standards of teaching power—the income was expended wholly on the schools. The school accounts and registers were always available for inspection by H.M.I.s. For example, when Mr. W. Edwards, H.M.I., reported on the Dowlais schools in 1880—schools where both systems of payment were combined, i.e. poundage and school pence—he mentioned that 'the payment of the weekly fees by the children which are 1d. and 2d. is easily secured, and the amount of arrears for 2,280 scholars for two years was only £18. 13s. 0d. a part of which sum is said to be recoverable. The accounts and registers at these schools are kept with admirable accuracy'.[2]

1 1847 *Reports*, Part II, p. 279.
2 *Minutes of Committee of Council*, 1880-81, p. 311, Report by W. Edwards, H.M.I. Also, *school accounts from logbooks of Llanelli and Hafod copperworks schools, Dafen Tinworks school*, etc.

Furthermore, the very existence of the guarantee fund in many schools was proof enough that money matters had to be kept under stringent surveillance.

Again, for the majority of works schools after 1870 ample evidence is obtained from the school log-books that management committees included workmen's representatives.[1] It was true that some schools considered management to be the province of the works proprietor, company, or works manager. In 1866, Bowstead claimed that one-third of the schools in south Wales were works schools which 'were generally managed by the chief person of the works, but if the proprietor does not reside there, they are managed by the principal resident whoever he may be, and perhaps he associates with himself two or three other managers and they sign the papers and are responsible for the conduct of the schools'.[2]

Reverting to the question of workmen's representatives on school management committees it is strange that Mr. John Jenkins,[3] the Assistant Commissioner in 1860 could doubt the wisdom of allowing members of the 'unskilled labour class'[4] to serve on such bodies and wondered 'what would be the operation of their participation in the management, on the character, and efficiency of the schools themselves'. Nevertheless he suggested 'that it should be a matter of experiment'—which he admitted might be quite successful—'from the examples he had in mind of the management of Mechanics and other analogous institutions by committees which are at least largely composed of working men. To these I may add the numerous sick and provident societies in which there are always found a sufficient number of persons of the same order and average of intelligence with those employed in the works to superintend (and altogether they do so very judiciously) the affairs of such societies. I do not see why the same discretion and capacity should not equally fit them for sharing in the control of a school. . . A judicious share of

1 *Logbooks Llanelli and Hafod schools.*
2 *Report of Pakington Select Committee*, p. 159, Minutes 3156-7.
3 John Jenkins (1808-84), born in Swansea: M.A. (Glasgow), 1831; Unitarian Minister-cum-Schoolmaster at Yeovil (1832-37) and Bath (1837-39), Returned to Swansea and opened a school; salaried lecturer for the Anti-Corn Law League in West Wales; appointed an Assistant Commissioner for the celebrated Blue Books Report of 1847, but his appointment withdrawn because he was a Unitarian—yet was appointed Assistant Commissioner, Welsh Districts, for the Newcastle Commission in 1858. Started a newspaper in 1847—*The Swansea and Glamorgan Herald*, which he edited for ten years. Called to the Bar (Gray's Inn), 1865, and moved to London to follow his calling. (*Y Bywgraffiadur Cymreig*, op. cit., t. 409-10).
4 *Newcastle Commission Report*, Vol. 2, p. 459. He refers to 'the right of the taxed, i.e. the workers, to have control in the expenditure of their money, and the present state of the intelligence of the unskilled labour class'.

control in the government of the schools to which they contribute is at least an experiment worthy of being tried'.[1]

Was the Assistant Commissioner so completely out of touch with Welsh working-class life and culture? Did he have reason to doubt the intelligence of the 'gwerin'? As Assistant Commissioner, Jenkins's argument that such 'unskilled people of the labour class' with their experience of other organizations might well be able to serve on school committees was quite sound. But as John Jenkins the Welshman, had he overlooked or forgotten the excellent tribute which he paid to the Welsh Sunday schools in *Volume 1* of the *Commission's Report*?[2] The simple fact escaped his attention that one of the main reasons for the phenomenal success of the Welsh Sunday schools which made them more popular than day schools was that they were *completely controlled and organized* by the working-classes![3]

It was in connection with religious instruction that the greatest difficulty arose and much bitterness displayed with reference to management and again we have the situation of Nonconformity versus the Anglican church.[4] A large part of the evidence given before the Pakington Select Committee was taken up with the question of religious instruction in British, National, and Neutral works schools. Certain schools were mentioned which were conducted on the National principle and which gave rise to much discontent between the Anglican management committee and the Dissenting workmen—namely at Cwmavon and Ebbw Vale. Bowstead, again in his evidence, stated that 'in Monmouthshire in connection with the Ebbw Vale Company's school, a clergyman manages it. There is no representative interdenominational committee, but usually

1 *Newcastle Commission Report*, Vol. 2, p. 458.
2 ibid. Vol. 1, pp. 52-3; Also Vol. 2, p. 460: Jenkins here speaks of Welsh Sunday Schools. 'As a preparatory influence, the agency of the Sunday school in this work (of raising educational standards) has been second to no other in importance and value . . . it has instilled into this portion of the community a taste for reading and other intellectual habits most favourable as preparations to the diffusion of education'!
3 Some schools in the Swansea valley, for example, at Ystalyfera, the workmen were very resentful of individual control by the proprietor of the works school. One witness stated that 'it is too bad that we should pay to the school and have no voice in what is taught to our children, nor in the choice of teachers'. (*Newcastle Commission Report*, Vol. 2, Appendix C). Another said 'the workmen do not object to the payment towards the school, but to their having no management of their own money. I think that if in a works school a mixed committee of proprietors and workmen had the management, it would be more satisfactory. It would, no doubt, create more interest in the cause of education. From what I know of the workmen, I think they would be competent to aid on such a school committee.' ibid, Evidence of the Rev. Rees Evans, Baptist Minister, Ystalyfera.
4 *Report of Pakington Select Committee*. pp. 131-295.

the officers of the Company, clergyman, surgeon, and one or two agents'.[1] The only workable solution to the religious problem was the Neutral or unsectarian school, by definition 'a school which included all Protestant denominations, including the Church of England, having no special connection with the British and Foreign School Society nor called by that name, but conducted on the same principle as nearly as possible'.[2] One example is sufficient, i.e. the Dowlais schools were Anglican until about 1855, when Lady Charlotte Guest 'thought it expedient to make them Neutral schools, at the instance of some representation from the workmen'.[3] This question of discontent between workmen and management committees of schools on the religious issue, and Neutral schools is discussed in the next chapter.

1 *Report of Pakington Select Committee,* Minutes 3090-91.
2 ibid, Minutes 3028-29 and 3233-38.
3 ibid, Minute 3238.

CHAPTER XII

Works Schools in Relation to the Voluntary Societies and School Boards

THE EXTENT to which works schools supplied the deficiencies of educational provision in the industrial areas is best appreciated and assessed by relating them to the work of the Voluntary Societies and the phase of Voluntaryism roughly between 1844 and 1854 associated with certain Nonconformist denominations notably the Baptists and Independents. Up to 1870 and to some extent afterwards, the government had encouraged the provision of elementary education through the Voluntary societies by means of its annual grants. In the *Minutes of the Committee of Council on Education* for August and December 1846 appeared statements on the 'School in its relations to the State, Church, and the Congregation'.[1] It stated that the first act of the government was a sign of confidence in the two societies organized on a religious basis. By this act the government declared that it accepted the antecedent history of elementary instruction as determining that the constitution of its schools should have a religious foundation in harmony with the institutions of the country. The two Societies however differed in one important feature. The National Society made no effort at comprehension. Its schools were founded on the doctrines of the Church, their religious constitution was in conformity with its discipline, and their management was confided to the laity of the Church who co-operated with the parochial clergyman. The British and Foreign School Society desired to comprehend in the support and management of its schools all, whether Churchmen or Dissenters, who could co-operate in communicating religious instruction from the authorised version of the Holy Scriptures without any sectarian interpretation. Voluntaryism was a protest against any form of government aid.[2]

The theme of voluntary education in the industrial areas is complex and it is within the religious framework of the voluntary system that this complexity becomes evident. It is therefore important to bear in mind that after 1833 the religious issue had an extraordinary influence on the internal organization of works schools and also in their relations with the two Voluntary Societies for two reasons: (*a*) Most of the works

---

1 The School in its relations to the State, the Church, and the Congregation, being an explanation of the *Minutes of the Committee of Council on Education in August and December*, 1846. London, 1847, pp. 7, ff.
2 ibid

schools were established after 1833 and whilst the majority of works proprietors were Churchmen, their employees were mainly Dissenters; (b) after 1850, the majority of works schools sought government aid and had, therefore, to be affiliated either to the National or the British and Foreign School Societies. Voluntary education had expressed itself not on a secular, but on a religious basis. With the creation of the Committee of Privy Council on Education in 1839, and the alteration in the grant regulations in 1846, works schools which accepted government grants became involved in the question of attachment to one or other of the Societies. This, in turn, demanded a classification of such schools on a religious basis, and moreover, created a special type—the Neutral, Undenominational, or Unsectarian school.[1]

Since workmen were required to subsidize the maintenance of schools out of their wages, embarrassing situations often arose which in some places caused considerable controversy and discontent. Although education in these schools was voluntary, i.e., the workmen pleased themselves whether their children attended or not, the payment was compulsory and was usually a condition of employment. A more serious aspect of this weekly poundage was that it again involved the question of religion. In some places works schools were conducted according to the principles of the Established Church and were inspected by the National Society, but Dissenting workmen were still obliged to support such schools which were not in accord with their religious tenets. Instances occurred in the Swansea valley where proprietors adopted an intolerant attitude and refused to accede to the workmen's demands for an unsectarian school, with the result that the workmen built their own schools conducted on British lines, but the majority of employers respected the views of their employees by allowing schools to be conducted on an undenominational or neutral basis as we shall see later.[2]

In 1843, Sir James Graham's controversial Factory Bill (which contained concrete proposals for the establishment of schools in the industrial areas and which foundered on the rocks of religious controversy) stirred the Voluntary Societies into greater activity and more especially brought Voluntaryism to the forefront. Voluntaryism appeared after 1833 as a movement against any form of government aid, which gathered momentum with varying degrees of success during the next twenty years.

1 These could only be found in the British system within the British and Foreign School Society.
2 *Report of the Pakington Committee.* Most of the minutes of evidence are packed with references to, and arguments concerning Neutral or Undenominational schools in the industrial areas.

Its most militant phase, inspired and guided by one of the leading Nonconformist ministers in South Wales was the decade 1844-1854. The bulk of its supporters were drawn from the rapidly expanding Nonconformist congregations, in particular the Independents. North Wales, as we have seen, was different. There, within the stronghold of Calvinistic Methodism, the religious leaders were prepared to accept as much State aid as possible in order to establish British schools.[1]

In south Wales, however, the Voluntaryists were extremely active and voluble. Two events added fuel to their fire. One of them, Graham's Factory Bill of 1843, has already been noted. The other, which caused a national awakening, was the appearance of the notorious Blue Books of 1847. Both events generated mounting suspicion and antagonism against the Established Church. Graham's proposals, which favoured Church schools, angered the Dissenters, and large meetings were held all over south Wales protesting against the 'oppressive and insidious Bill'.[2] For example, in April 1843, 'about eighty petitions were sent from Swansea and the neighbouring parishes against the educational clauses of the Bill . . . the petition from Zoar Chapel, Neath, and its branches received 1,426 male signatures . . . which were sent to J. H. Vivian, Esq., M.P. (of the Hafod copperworks, Swansea) while others were sent to County Members'.[3] The suspicions of the Independents were confirmed by the preponderance of Anglican witnesses in the 1847 *Reports*, and in the following years a spate of pamphlets poured forth from the Welsh press in protest. Welsh periodicals and newspapers, the voice of the Welsh Nonconformist pulpit, and some leading denominational ministers, including the Rev. Evan Jones (Ieuan Gwynedd) and the Rev. David Rees, of Capel Als, Llanelli, denounced the *Reports*.[4]

Rees was the main protagonist of the Voluntaryists and the shining star of his denomination—the Independents. Furthermore, he was the giant of the movement both in the pulpit and in the columns of the Welsh periodical '*Y Diwygiwr*' (The Revivalist) which he edited for his denomination. His influence upon, and contribution to Welsh elementary education in the mid-nineteenth century has still to be written. He used his periodical ruthlessly to express his implacable animosity against all forms of interference by the State and employers of labour in education, except on one point. Writing in 1846, he stated his utilitarian view of

1 *British and Foreign School Society, Annual Report for* 1849, p. 4.
2 *The Merlin*, 21 July, 1843.
3 *The Cambrian*, 28 April, 1843.
4 The controversy over the Blue Books (*Brâd y Llyfrau Gleision*) extended over many years, and the moral and other issues, the attacks on the Anglican Church, and the replies of the Bishop of St. David's and others, are not relevant here.

education: 'At yr addysgiaeth wladol a chelfyddol ni fuasai gennym un wrthwynebiad i dderbyn cymorth llywodraethol mewn rhyw amgylchiadau, oblegid y mae rhoi gwybodaeth yn ddyledswydd cymdeithasol . . . oblegid fod gwybodaeth fasnachol . . . yn angenrhaid er cyrraedd anrhydedd gwladol'.[1] Here he states clearly that he favoured State aid in certain circumstances for purely secular instruction. On all other matters he was uncompromising. His writings were characterized by bitter attacks on works proprietors and works schools because of the truck and shop systems, and the Anglican sympathies of the industrialists who organized education without consulting the parents. He also proclaimed that no employer of labour had the right to make a compulsory deduction from workmen's wages for educational purposes: 'Ac i ni ddweyd ein syniad yn llawn, nid oes gennym ddim golwg ar siop y cwmni, meddyg y gwaith, nac ysgol y gwaith . . . gadwer i'r dyn ddewis ei siop, ei feddyg, ei ysgolfeistr, a'i bregethwr, a rhoddi iddo ei ennillion bob ddimai goch. . . Yr ydym yn dra sicr nad ydynt wedi deall hyd yn hyn beth yw rhyddid cydwybod, amgen ni ryfygent ymgymeryd ag arolygiaeth ysgolion plant eu gweithwyr, a'u dysgu yng nghredo Eglwys y Wlad'.[2] Having described in detail the rights of the ordinary working man, he ended his diatribe in a typical Voluntaryist manner: 'Rhieni ddylai ddewis addysg eu plant . . . y mae y boneddigion hyn wedi myned dan gyfrifoldeb ofnadwy! Yn gyfrifol am addysg plant eu gweithwyr'.[3]

By 1853 it became apparent that Rees was beginning to change his attitude towards State aid and was more sympathetic to the British school system. He recanted on this issue in 1854 but his opposition to works schools persisted until his death. The reasons for his submission are not far to seek. In the first place, he realized that the working classes needed a basic education on the British or Neutral system. Secondly, the poverty of the people made Voluntaryism, however consistent, impracticable, and thirdly, an Agent had been appointed to organize schools for the British

1 *Y Diwygiwr*, 1846, Rhif. 134, p. 289.
2 ibid, 1861, pp. 221-2: 'To be frank, we have nothing to say to the Company's shop, the works' doctor, nor the works school. Let a man choose for himself his shop, doctor, schoolmaster, and minister, and let him keep every half-penny of his wages.' ibid, 1853, p. 223: 'The owners know no freedom of conscience . . . or they would not take upon themselves the education of workmen's children in the creed of the Church.'
3 ibid, 1853, p. 224: 'Parents should decide their children's education—the owners have assumed an awful responsibility—of educating their workmen's children.' See also Appendix 1.

Society in south Wales.[1] Also, in 1855, Bowstead, H.M.I. of the British and Foreign School Society, in a comprehensive report on education in south Wales, had shown the great numerical strength of Nonconformity over the Established Church in the industrial areas, and had defended the Dissenters in their attitude against the Church and the teaching of the catechism in schools.[2] Voluntaryism still persisted in some areas, and in 1868, a year before Rees died, Bowstead reported that 'Education on the principles of the Established Church has been freely and extensively offered to the Welsh people both in week-day and Sunday schools. But nine-tenths of them are Nonconformist, and instead of accepting these offers they have everywhere struggled, or are still struggling at whatever cost, to establish unsectarian schools of their own, and to free themselves from what they regard as the trammels of Church catechism, Church formularies, and Church influence. The exertions that are put forth, and the sacrifices that are made, with this view by persons, from whom such exertions and such sacrifices are least to be expected, are really remarkable'.[3]

The relation of works schools to Voluntaryism was straightforward and simple. Where Anglican employers of labour refused to meet the workmen's wishes to conduct schools on unsectarian lines, the workmen took the law into their own hands and built their own schools or sent their children as fee-payers to the nearest British school. This of course meant paying twice over for the workmen, who had in any case to submit to the usual poundage. This occurred in more than one place—at Ystalyfera, Abercrave, and Ystradgynlais—where workmen built schools and received the annual parliamentary grants. Such places however 'were in the ludicrous position of having two schools side by side, the one upheld in handsome style by the master of the works out of the workmen's poundage,

---

1 Rev. W. Roberts (Nefydd). But the Independents were more interested in the appointment of his successor, David Williams, in 1863, and it was during that period that they eventually 'came over' to the principle of State aid. '*Y Diwygiwr*', 1863, p. 247, and 1864, p. 218.
2 *Minutes of Committee of Council*, 1855, pp. 625-642.
3 ibid, 1868, p. 280. Note that the difficulty of obtaining sites (which also had to be freehold to fulfil the regulations of the British and Foreign School Society) often incensed the pure Voluntaryists, and sites were not available in some districts for the building of British schools because 'the land was the property of gentlemen belonging to the Church of England and those generally of the Tories and High Church party'. *Nefydd MSS*, Journal for 18th December, 1856. Idwal Jones, op. cit., p. 121.

and the other supported with great difficulty by the impoverished workmen themselves'.[1]

The relation of works schools to the two Voluntary Societies was intimate and of mutual concern. It was intimate in the sense that the majority of works schools built after 1850 (including the older ones which had been renovated and enlarged) received government grants through the Voluntary Societies. This involved two important changes in their organization—affiliation to either one of these Societies on a religious basis and an annual inspection by the inspectors of the particular Society on behalf of the Committee of Privy Council.

The chief reason which prompted proprietors of works schools to seek government aid and inspection was the change in the grant regulations in 1846. The new system of grants devised by Kay-Shuttleworth[2] assisted the schools with their annual expenses, replaced the discredited monitorial for the pupil-teacher system, and promoted the efficiency of the new Training Colleges. The proposals also included a suggestion that better safeguards should be included in the management of schools in receipt of grants so that the laity who supported them should have a share in their control.[3] Henceforth grants were given to apprenticed pupils and to the teachers who instructed them; retirement pensions were available for teachers, and building grants were available to schools.[4] The advantages of this scheme for works schools, in their relation to the Voluntary Societies was far-reaching. Normally such schools had no building grants, for the sites and buildings were supplied by the proprietors, but the grants they received in respect of pupil-teachers and teaching staff meant that in addition to the money they obtained from poundage (and in many instances from school pence as well) they were able to offer a higher remuneration to their staffs. In addition, annual inspection kept these schools in a high state of efficiency. At the Dowlais schools the resident manager admitted 'Inspection, such as I have found it in the government

1 *Minutes of Committee of Council*, 1869, p. 281: 'There is a class of works in which the employers use the fund got from a deduction from the men's wages to establish Church schools and to bring up in Church principles a set of children whose parents are generally Dissenters in the proportion of at least nine to one. It is at least doubtful whether the masters are legally entitled to devote wages to support schools disapproved by the workmen. A cause involving this question was recently tried in a Glamorgan County Court, and its decision, so far as it went was in favour of the right of the workmen . . . to have a voice in the choice of schools which their children attended.'
2 Dr. James Phillips Kay (1804-77), first secretary of the Committee of Privy Council for Education; known as Sir James Kay-Shuttleworth, from February 1842.
3 Frank Smith, op. cit., p. 199.
4 *Minutes of Committee of Council*, 1846, Vol. 1, pp. 1-2.

Inspectors is absolutely essential to the success of our schools. Government inspection adds wonderfully to the efficiency of schools and gives the teachers an appeal from a prejudiced manager or committee. . . I only work the Privy Council scheme of secular inspection and I feel no check on my independence'.[1]

Some of the works schools maintained their independence for a long time before accepting State aid but almost all opted for annual inspection by the inspectors of the Committee of Council. A few Anglican works schools invited diocesan inspectors to do this work, for example, at Cwmavon: 'Our day schools connected with the works do not receive government aid nor are they under government inspection.[2] We do not wish to be interfered with in the arrangements made for these schools, and there are some points which, if we accepted aid would be insisted upon, that would be unnecessary here. But the schools are visited at our request by the diocesan inspector and are noticed in his report. The Church catechism is taught in the schools but it is not compulsory on children whose parents object to their learning it. There is no compulsory attendance of the scholars at church on sundays. There are five Sunday schools held in the rooms of the day schools'.[3]

The affiliation of works schools to the Voluntary Societies relieved the pressure on the work of those societies in the industrial areas and more important still, when School Boards were set up after the Education Act of 1870 there was no need to build and equip new Board Schools. Relationships on a religious basis with the Voluntary Societies resulted in religious types of works schools, since they were classified as National or British according to the religion of the proprietor, if he insisted. Where proprietors were considerate or indifferent the schools became Neutral, Undenominational, Unsectarian, Combined, or Comprehensive. The Neutral type, outside the context of works schools, was the subject of a good deal of discussion among those who were favourable to State control during the nineteenth century.[4] It has been mentioned earlier, that the definition of Neutral in connection with works schools meant the admission

---

1 *Newcastle Commission Report*, Appendix E, pp. 634, ff., evidence of G. T. Clark, Esq., Dowlais Works.
2 The Cwmavon schools accepted government aid as from 1865.
3 *Newcastle Commission Report*, Vol. 2, evidence of William Gilbertson, Manager.
4 Frank Smith, op. cit., p. 205. Dr. Hook, Vicar of Leeds, in a published letter (1846) 'On the Means of rendering more Efficient the Education of the People', proposed 'combined' schools, that the State should take over full responsibility for secular education, giving facilities to the religious denominations to enter the schools on two afternoons a week. This met with little success.

of children without reference to religious creed. There were no religious tests for teachers and such schools were usually inspected by the British and Foreign School Society.[1] A similar kind of school, the Comprehensive, referred to a denominational school which, while teaching the distinctive creed of a church, did not exclude children of other faiths.[2] It has been noted that Neutral schools came into being as the result of requests from Nonconformist workmen, and the usual procedure was for a 'memorial' to be presented to the proprietors asking them to conduct their schools on unsectarian or neutral principles. With very few exceptions such requests were granted and the inspector was able to state in 1868 'It is much to the credit of a great majority of employers that they consulted the wishes of the workers in the class of schools which they established, and wherever that was the case, the system produced admirable results. This was the case at Dowlais, Mountain Ash (the Duffryn schools), Ebbw Vale, Sirhowy, Maesteg, Tondu, Nantyglo, and the Hafod, Kilvey, Llanelli, and Pembrey copperworks, and many others. At all these places, large and well-organized schools, in which the religious teaching is based solely on the Bible, and is strictly neutral as between the different sects, have been established by means of a poundage on wages. All the schools give entire satisfaction to the workmen, whilst most of them are in admirable condition, and if a general system of compulsory education were introduced forthwith, these works schools would be prepared to meet the demand'.[3]

Neutral works schools were exclusive to South Wales and the following lists have been extracted from sources which showed them as *inspected schools* receiving government aid[4]:

Out of a total of 109 inspected works schools, 20 were Neutral:

Monmouthshire	*Glamorgan*	*Carmarthenshire*
Ebbw Vale (Ironworks)	Dowlais (Ironworks)	Llanelli (Copperworks)
Sirhowy (Ironworks)	(after 1855)	Pembrey
Abersychan	Cyfarthfa (Ironworks)	(Copperworks)
(Ironworks)	Maesteg (Ironworks)	

1 *Report of the Pakington Committee*, Minutes 3028-40.
2 Frank Smith, op. cit.
3 *Minutes of Committee of Council*, 1868-69, p. 280. *Report of the Pakington Committee*, 1866, Minutes 3034-9 and 3040. Two schools are mentioned showing the numbers of Church of England children who attended the Neutral schools at Maesteg and Hafod copperworks schools, Swansea. These figures are extremely revealing: At Maesteg, out of 914 children, 93 were C of E; at Vivian's schools at Hafod, out of 779 children only 14 were C of E.
4 *Minutes of Committee of Council*, 1850 to 1895; *Report of the Pakington Committee*, complete Minutes of evidence.

Monmouthshire	Glamorgan	Carmarthenshire
Nantyglo (Ironworks)	Llynfi (Ironworks)	
Cwmbran (Ironworks)	Penydarren	Breconshire
Varteg Hill	(Ironworks)	Nil
(Ironworks)	Plymouth (Ironworks)	
Varteg Hill (Colliery)	Neath Abbey (Ironworks)	
	Kilvey (Copperworks)	
	Hafod (Copperworks)	
	Aberdulais (Tinworks)	
	Duffryn (Colliery)	

On a purely religious basis, works schools were either National or British. Again referring to the statistical evidence for *inspected schools*, of the 109 works schools, 40 were affiliated to the National Society and 49 to the British and Foreign School Society. Including the 20 Neutral schools, the total of unsectarian works schools was 69.[1]

The magnitude of the Works Schools System demands detailed treatment. If the classification of works schools on a religious basis is viewed from the statistical angle and related to the achievements of the two Voluntary Societies, i.e. the number of day schools which they promoted, it at once becomes evident that the Works Schools System was not only on an extensive scale, but was, moreover, an integral and indispensable element in the organization and provision of popular education in the industrial areas of Wales during the nineteenth century. This was the gap which was filled in the pattern of voluntary education by the works schools. These schools not only relieved the Voluntary Societies of their responsibilities in the industrial areas but were numerically distinctive enough to be considered an essential part of the voluntary system.

Statistically, the extent and achievements of the Works Schools System itself is most impressive. It has not always been possible to extract relevant figures, for although statistics abound, they are often, on checking, unreliable and sometimes contradictory. Anyone who attempts perfection or even correctness of figures by comparing independent sources of information or statistics for the nineteenth century cannot escape frustration and often has to admit defeat! The returns of the Voluntary Societies are a case in point. For the purposes of this analysis, *only inspected schools* as listed in the official reports of *Government Inquiries, Commissions*, and the *Minutes of the Committee of Council* form the main basis of this

1 See Appendices 2 and 3 to this chapter.

investigation. The operative word here is *inspected*, for many schools are not included if they do not come within this category although other works schools were included in the grand total of 134 in Chapter II.

A Statistical Investigation of the Extent of the Works Schools System in Relation to the Achievements of the Two Voluntary Societies up to 1865-1870:

This investigation is based on four separate groups of statistics in the following manner:

1. Abstracts from the *Reports of the British and Foreign School Society* between 1833 and 1870. Figures for the National Society are not available in complete form, for many Church schools were not in union with the National Society and, moreover, the Society did not always distinguish between scholars who attended on Sundays only, and those who attended throughout the week. The Secretary stated 'in the Church schools we do not talk of day schools. The object of the Society is to promote Sunday and day schools, or Sunday schools'.[1] Again, very often the British and Foreign School Society had no official knowledge of the provincial schools, for there was frequently no direct relationship between a British school and the parent Society.[2] However, there is far more evidence available of the work of the British Society and the first analysis is based on those returns only:

In the decade 1833-1843 . . . 28 British schools in Wales.[3]

In 1833, of the 15 British schools in Wales—13 in south Wales and 2 in north Wales—7 were British works schools. *Nearly 50 per cent were works schools.*

In 1851, 80 British schools in Wales: 36 were works schools. *Nearly 50 per cent works schools.*[4]

In 1853, 14 British Schools in south Wales, but there were 37 British works schools out of a total of 67 works schools.[5]

In 1860, in the four south Wales counties of Monmouth, Glamorgan, Brecon, and Carmarthen, there were 85 British schools (this total included all departments, i.e. boys, girls, and infants and not individual schools) of which 47, or *over 50 per cent were works schools.*[6]

1 *Report of the Committee on the State of Education*, 1834.
2 Frank Smith, op. cit., p. 133.
3 *Annual Reports of the British and Foreign School Society*, 1834-44.
4 ibid, 1852.
5 *Nefydd MSS*, xv, 276, May 5th, 1860.
6 ibid

In 1870, of the 180 British schools in the six south Wales counties, 96 were works schools, of which 66 were British works schools—*over one-third*.[1]

Bowstead, in his report on British schools in south Wales for 1860 stated: 'In 1853, the number of schools in south Wales and Monmouthshire referred to me as claimants of public aid towards their maintenance was 18. In 1860 it was 95. The 18 schools of 1853 were not all established and supported by Nonconformists, neither are the 95 schools of 1860. In each case it is probably about fair to say that two-thirds of the number owe their existence, more or less, many of them to Dissenters. In 1854, Dissenters, although in great number, had done little for education. *The remaining one-third consists mainly of large and important schools connected with works of which the owners are generally, but by no means invariably, Churchmen.* The two classes of schools (i.e. British and Works schools) have increased in nearly equal proportions. In seven years there has been an increase which has more than multiplied the number of efficient schools by five'.[2]

2. Abstracts from the *Commissioners of Inquiry into the State of Education in Wales*, for the four south Wales counties of Monmouth, Glamorgan, Brecon, and Carmarthen:

In 1846 .. .. 199 National schools: 11,724 pupils.
 .. .. 20 British schools: 2,809 pupils.
 .. .. 37 Works schools: 5,532 pupils.

Note that only 22 schools are listed in these *Reports* as works schools, but a study of the Parochial Lists of schools shows 37. This discrepancy is explained by their inclusion under the designation of National or British schools in those lists. Personal investigation of the number of works schools established up to 1846 produces a total of 58. Of these, 52 show an approximate total attendance of 7,050, i.e. 50 per cent *of the combined total attendance for the ordinary National and British schools in 1846*.[3]

3. According to Sir Thomas Phillips, the total day scholars attending National schools in the four south Wales counties in 1846 was 12,100 which is near enough to the figure given in the 1847 *Reports* above.[4]

---

1 *Minutes of Committee of Council*, 1870-71, list of grant-aided schools, Welsh counties. This confirms Bowstead's evidence to the Pakington Committee, Minute 3156.
2 *Minutes of Committee of Council*, 1860, Report on South Wales.
3 1847 *Reports*, Part I, Parochial Returns of Schools.
4 Sir Thomas Phillips, *Wales, etc.*, p. 593 ff.

4. The returns of Mr. R. R. W. Lingen, H.M.I., in the *Report of the Pakington Select Committee* for 1866 show the following:[1]

Returns of inspected schools for six south Wales counties in 1865:
National schools: 166   Number of scholars: 17,705
British schools: 122   Number of scholars: 17,230

Works schools in south Wales in the period 1865-1870 total 88. Returns from 77 show approximate total attendances of 16,081. *This is nearly 50 per cent of the above combined totals for ordinary National and British schools.*

In 1870 there were 109 works schools in Wales classified in the following manner on a religious basis:

	North Wales	South Wales
	9 National	31 National
	3 British	46 British
		20 Neutral
Total	12	Total 97

STATISTICAL SUMMARY:

The following figures show the extent of the Works Schools System compared with the two main Voluntary Societies in the industrial areas of south Wales, 1865-1870:—

INSPECTED SCHOOLS ONLY

National Schools	British Schools	Works Schools
1854: 54	1853: 14	1853: 67
1864: 154	1860: 103	1860: 79
1865: 166	1865: 122	1870: 88 (with returns only from 77)

Pupils in attendance, 1865:   National schools 17,705
                              British schools 17,230
                              Works schools 16,081
                              (1865-1870)

These statistics are approximate and have been compiled from official returns as and when they appeared, for in many cases they do not fall conveniently into annual groupings. But the general picture emerges clearly. On a numerical basis alone, works schools were so numerous and

---

1 *Report of the Pakington Committee*, Appendix 2, pp. 310-11.

the numbers attending them so large that it can be claimed that these schools constituted a system equal in importance to the Voluntary Societies:

  i. Fifty per cent of the schools within the voluntary pattern in south Wales in 1847 were works schools.

  ii. Up to 1853—when the first full-time Agent for the British and Foreign School Society was appointed in south Wales—works schools completely eclipsed British schools in that region and were the main sources for elementary and further education in the industrial districts.

  iii. In 1860, fifty per cent of the south Wales British schools were works schools.

  iv. By 1870, as the above abstracts show, the number of pupils in attendance at works schools almost equalled those of the Voluntary Societies.

For several years before 1870 it became apparent that 'the Voluntary System, however impressive might be some of its fruits, could not perform the task of instructing a nation'.[1] Arguments in favour of a State system of education had gained valuable ground partly through the influence of many eminent men of the period—of whom T. H. Huxley was one of the foremost—but mainly due to other important factors which once more brought popular education to the fore, with clear indications, which culminated in the Education Act of 1870, that the problem could only be solved at national level.[2] Sir John Pakington, when introducing his Education (No. 2) Bill, in March 1855 asserted that 'the people could not be educated by voluntary effort, and the financial demands of public education could not be satisfied by freewill offerings. The only legitimate way in which education could be provided was by calling on the people to contribute a rate for it'.[3]

Among the contributing factors to the creation of a State system were those which had worried social reformers and educationists alike during the first half of the nineteenth century and which threatened to recur. Child labour was still rampant in most factories not covered by previous legislation and although the Mines Act of 1860 had prohibited the employment of boys underground between the ages of ten and twelve

---

1 Frank Smith, op. cit. p. 285.
2 Thomas Henry Huxley (1825-1895): medical doctor, geologist, naturalist, and anatomist. Famous teacher of science and fervid exponent of a liberal curriculum. He justified a system of compulsory education and advocated infant schools, continuation schools, and technical schools.
3 J. W. Adamson, op. cit., p. 152.

unless they could produce a certificate from a competent schoolmaster that they could read and write, or, failing this, that they were attending school for not less than three hours a day during two days in each week —evasion was practised on a large scale, and at least three inspectors of schools had described the Act as a failure in 1863. Moreover, the Revised Code of 1862 had provided an effective and serious check to the building of new schools by its sharp cut in the grants for such purposes during a time when the population was growing rapidly in industrial areas and large towns.[1] Educational destitution was again a serious threat and the Voluntary System was becoming inert. Even the Voluntaryists finally capitulated in 1867.[2] In the same year, with the passing of the Reform Act which gave the franchise to nearly all householders and added a million voters to the Parliamentary Register, 'the provision of schooling became a matter of urgency in anticipation of the assumption of full citizenship by an unknown number of illiterates'.[3]

Forster's Education Act of 1870 sought to deal with the two persistent problems of the period—educational destitution and irregular school attendance. It proposed to survey the school needs of the country and to provide schools where they were needed, i.e. to 'fill up the gaps'. The Act allowed and indeed encouraged further voluntary activity and this was proved by a spectacular rush of applications which reached Whitehall from the two Societies to establish new schools. Where voluntary effort failed or was non-existent, School Boards were to be formed. Fees were to be charged and schools were to be helped partly by government grants and by rate aid. School Boards were also empowered to frame by-laws for the compulsory attendance of children between the ages of five and twelve.[4]

The existence of the Works Schools System in relation to the new administrative developments arising out of the 1870 Act was of special interest and importance in the evolution of a State system of education between 1870 and 1902. It has already been shown how they worked with the Voluntary Societies and, after 1870, although the history of works schools is that of gradual take-over by School Boards due to changing circumstances and the crystallization of a State system of education

---

1 In South Wales after 1860 there was an unprecedented rise in population, especially in the mid-Glamorgan coalfield and the new tinplate and steel manufacturing districts. See all the *Minutes of Committee of Council Inspector's Reports on South Wales*, between 1866 and 1880.
2 The Leeds group under Baines, the centre of the movement in England, could no longer maintain their position and the movement collapsed.
3 J. W. Adamson, op. cit., p. 347.
4 Compulsory attendance came in 1880, by A. J. Mundella's Act.

VOLUNTARY SOCIETIES AND SCHOOL BOARDS

their work and influence even during this period proved indispensable to the new School Boards in whose areas they happened to be located. After 1870, the elimination of these schools did not necessarily mean closure, but transference to a newly elected School Board. This procedure, in view of the attitude of the 1870 Act to the Voluntary System was an uneven and sometimes prolonged process, i.e. as stated earlier, the Act did not abolish voluntary effort but supplemented it. Indeed, instances occurred where certain large and important works schools persistently refused to surrender their independence and continued to exist under the old regime until the very end of the century. This arrangement was practicable so long as school fees continued to be paid in all schools. The Education Act of 1891, however, abolished school pence, and after that year the final crop of works schools capitulated to the central administration and became submerged in the local educational pattern. After the Education Act of 1902 which created Part 3 Education Authorities, works schools lost their identity, but in several districts even at the present time their memory is perpetuated in the original name of the school, e.g. Llanelli Copperworks school.

The transference of works schools to local School Boards raised several points of considerable importance:

1. Where such schools were taken over by School Boards, heavy expenditure on the provision of school buildings was eliminated. A complete survey of all works schools transferred to School Boards has not been practicable but fortuitously full records are available of all the larger schools, only a few of which surrendered their individuality and independence before 1890. Among those which were transferred at an earlier period, i.e. around 1880, were the Llynfi and Maesteg ironworks schools which were in excellent order and highly efficient. Some schools, because of certain local conditions—usually innumerable intermittent strikes—had been temporarily closed. In such cases schools were re-opened by the School Board, e.g. the Merthyr Colliery school at Maesteg and the Yniscedwyn Ironworks school at Ystradgynlais.[1] On the other hand, examples were found where newly elected School Boards realized that school buildings and accommodation were too poor for further use and usually new schools were built and re-organized. Two examples are given from north and south Wales—the one, a rural slate quarrying region, and the other a densely populated area where copper-smelting was important. In 1871, 'the first meeting of the Ffestiniog School Board was

---

1 *Minutes of Committee of Council,* 1877: General Report by the Rev. B. J. Binns, H.M.I., on schools in Glamorgan.

held on the 13th April . . . and the census of schoolchildren showed that 1,859 required accommodation. To meet this, there was at the time accommodation for 969 children in the existing schools.'[1] Several of the schools were those erected earlier in the century by the quarry owners, 'but most of the schools in the area were totally unfit for school purposes, and with the consent of the Department, the Board proceeded with as little delay as possible to the erection of new school-buildings in every part of the neighbourhood'. By 1875, four new Board schools had been erected at a cost of £6,434. 11s. 8d.[2] The second example comes well towards the end of the century. In 1896, 'after considerable delay, the School Board of Swansea has settled down in earnest, not only to meet the demands of a growing population, but also to substitute new and improved buildings for old ones unsuitable and condemned. New schools will be built, especially at St. Thomas, to contain 1,200 scholars, and to supply the place of the old Kilvey copperworks schools, which, when opened at the beginning of the century were thought to be equal to anything of the kind in the country'.[3]

2. Many works schools continued to remain independent—and those were the largest and most important ones—some of them remained aloof until the closing years of the century. School Boards merely took over the administration of such schools. The last to succumb were the Hafod copperworks schools at Trevivian, Swansea.

The Dowlais schools were transferred in 1892, and the Inspector noted in 1880 'the children of Dowlais are educated in the fine schools of the Dowlais Iron Company, and the Merthyr School Board have so far been saved from any expenditure on behalf of this portion of their district'.[4] The Act of 1891 which gave parents the right to demand free education for their children produced the final *coup de grâce* for these famous schools. The act of transference is given in the Trustee's own words: 'By a recent Act of Legislature, proposed at the instance of Her Majesty's Government, education, so far as it is compulsory, is in future to be provided at the expense of the country. The new Act puts an end to the school pence, but its provisions, if well worked, will rather more than cover that deficiency. It was, however, found that the Dowlais workmen were not, on the whole, disposed to continue the poundage, and as this involved

1. *Minutes of Committee of Council*, 1877: Report of the Rev. E. T. Watts, H.M.I., on Merioneth, p. 636, ff.
2. ibid.
3. ibid, 1897: General Report for 1896, Swansea District, by Mr. Munro, p. 289.
4. ibid, for 1881: General Report for 1880 by W. Edwards, H.M.I., p. 305.

a very considerable shortcoming, it became necessary to place the schools under the School Board, which has accordingly been done. In closing a school managership of nearly 36 years[1] the Trustee may be allowed to express a hope that the schools' teachers under the new management, may retain the complete respect and confidence of the parents, and that the schools may continue to deserve the high character which the Reports of Her Majesty's Inspectors shew them to possess. Dowlais, 1st March, 1892'.[2] In 1893, the Llanelli copperworks schools were transferred to the Llanelli School Board, were re-modelled and greatly enlarged.[3] The large Cwmavon schools including the satellite ones at Oakwood, Bryn, and Tymaen Infants, which had 1,500 children attending them in 1880,[4] remained independent as late as 1896 for they are mentioned with other schools in the Inspector's report of 1897: 'Indeed, of all the British and works schools once existing in the Swansea Inspection District, only Hafod, together with the Cwmavon works schools, the Bryndu (Pyle) colliery school, and the Tondu ironworks school now remain as such'.[5]

3. The Inspectors' Reports in the *Minutes of the Committee of Council* after 1870 record that works schools were 'the best and most efficient' in the manufacturing and mining districts. In Monmouthshire, the Rhymney and Abersychan ironworks schools received annual commendation and special mention.[6] In Glamorgan, the Dowlais, Maesteg, Llynfi (ironworks schools), the Duffryn colliery, and the Hafod and Kilvey copperworks schools especially pleased the Inspectors.[7] In Carmarthenshire, excellent reports were the rule for Dafen (Llanelli) tinworks, and the Llanelli and Pembrey copperworks schools.[8]

4. In addition to praising the efficiency of works schools the reports also made special comment on the 'large and fine buildings', e.g. at Dowlais, Abersychan, Duffryn, Llanelli, Dafen, Pembrey, Hafod, and Cwmavon. Another significant feature of the position of works schools in relation to the formation of School Boards was their numerical strength in terms of attendances. Taking Glamorgan as a specimen area for the

1 G. T. Clark, Works Manager and Schools Trustee, 1856-1892.
2 *Dowlais Schools Memorandum*, 1892.
3 *Minutes of Committee of Council*, 1897, Report for 1896 on the Llanelli District by Mr. Jones, p. 298.
4 *Minutes of Committee of Council*, 1881, p. 644.
5 *Minutes of Committee of Council*, 1897, p. 289, but the Minutes of 1894 state that the Cwmavon and Tondu schools had been transferred by this date.
6 ibid, 1879, Report by Mr. Waddington, H.M.I., p. 436.
7 ibid, 1873, p. 188.
8 ibid, 1874, pp. 69 and 133.

1880 survey and extracting the relevant details for the large School Boards with brief descriptions of each parish, the following information is most significant:—

    i. Merthyr Tydfil School Board: This parish is seven miles long and from three to five miles broad. Its population is about 52,000 and has not increased since 1871. Dowlais, at the north-east of the parish, is a dense mass of houses spread over a hill which rises to a height of over 1,000 feet above sea-level. Its population of 16,000 is maintained entirely by the extensive steel and ironworks, and the collieries attached to them. The Dowlais Iron Company is responsible for the education of the children of the whole of this population.[1] The town of Merthyr proper is contiguous to Dowlais, and extends from the lower part of the same hill along the Taff valley almost un-interruptedly for one and a half miles at the lower elevation of 500-600 feet. The working classes are supported by the Cyfarthfa Ironworks, which were re-started in 1879, and by the collieries. The population, including one or two suburbs is about 30,000. The remainder of the population of the parish is divided between Troedyrhiw, Merthyr Vale, and Treharris, all of which are some miles from Merthyr.

There are nine Board Schools in nineteen Departments. 'The average attendance at all is 2,942, showing an increase of only 486 since 1877. Last Spring there were 3,824 children in average attendance at the other public elementary schools of the parish. They were:

    3 "Company" or works schools with 2,081 children

    4 National (two of which were works schools) with 1,130 children.

    2 Roman Catholic—Dowlais Works schools—with 613 children.'[2]

The works schools educated practically the whole child population of the parish of Merthyr Tydfil, since the other two National schools one of which was Georgetown, were mainly supported by the Cyfarthfa ironworks.[3]

    ii. Aberdare Parish: Nearly the same area as Merthyr Tydfil with a population of 38,000, eleven Board Schools in twenty-one Departments, with a total average attendance of 2,888 children. 'There are 3,133 children in other schools:

    4 "Company" or works schools with 1,967 children.

1 *Minutes of Committee of Council*, 1881, p. 305.
2 ibid, p. 306.
3 *Report of the Pakington Committee*, Minutes 3233-38.

3 National schools with 1,087 children.
1 Roman Catholic school with 79 children.'[1]

iii. Llanwonno Parish: The population of this parish was 11,400 in 1871 but has since grown. The town of Pontypridd is inconveniently divided between three parishes of which this is one. 'There are:
8 Board schools with 1,850 children.
2 "Company" or works schools with 352 children.
1 National school with 89 children.'[2]

iv. Llantrisant Parish: This is also a large parish the boundaries of which were determined when the population was centralised at the town of the same name, but now includes several large mining villages in remote parts. 'There are:
9 Board Schools with 835 children.
2 National Schools with 411 children.
1 Colliery School with 346 children.'[3]

Summary of 1880 Survey: Mr. William Edwards, H.M.I., reported that 'the total average attendance at all the public elementary schools in his district which comprised Merthyr Tydfil, Pontypridd, and Crickhowell, Breconshire was 26,334:

Board Schools	14,915 children
Company or Colliery schools ..	6,781 children
National Schools	3,844 children
Roman Catholic	794 children

The Company or Colliery Schools were classed as British schools.[4]

v. School Boards sometimes acquired works schools by purchase. This was particularly evident after 1880 when, faced with an increase in the numbers of children attending due to Mundella's Act, School Boards took over the existing ones by purchase agreement, i.e. those schools who wished to cease functioning as works schools. Thereafter the School Boards enlarged or renovated them with the aid of government grants and also continued to extort poundage and school pence.[5] In Monmouthshire, for example, the Bedwellty School Board committed itself to a very extensive school-building programme: 'Since 31 August 1876, the Board

---

1 *Minutes of Committee of Council*, 1881, p. 306 ff.
2 ibid.
3 ibid, p. 309.
4 ibid, p. 310.
5 *Parliamentary Papers*, Vol. lix, *Education*, 1873, p. 236, ff.

has built and completed 7 separate blocks of schools, accommodating 4,484 children, and purchased, improved, and enlarged 5 existing blocks, accommodating 1,962 children more; the building, purchase, etc., of these 12 blocks has required a loan of £42,456. Since August, 1879, the Board has also arranged to purchase and enlarge the Rhymney Ironworks Schools, needing a further £4,500'.[1] The Aberystruth School Board in the same county had also erected new schools and also 'purchased and enlarged the Blaina Ironworks schools'.[2] In 1882, the Trevethin (Pontypool) Board purchased the Abersychan and Pontnewynydd works schools 'enlarging and renovating them'.[3] In Glamorgan, the Swansea School Board purchased the Hafod copperworks schools in 1898—the last of the works schools to fall.[4]

vi. The majority of works schools were British, received their grants through the British and Foreign School Society, and soon after 1880 most of them had been absorbed by School Boards. The National Society, however, redoubled its efforts to promote schools on a voluntary basis within the time limit, one year, imposed by the Education Act of 1870. Where works schools already existed in industrial areas—and most of them were either British or Neutral—National schools had to struggle for existence. Their position was particularly desperate and vulnerable when they had to compete with the Works Board Schools as the following report showed: 'for the right of educating a population in which Nonconformists so largely predominated, the parish of Gelligaer furnished several examples of the inevitable death of Church of England schools in these circumstances . . . only one exists out of the five which I inspected two years ago. The clergyman of the parish carried on these schools by exertions which might have borne valuable fruits amidst a more sympathetic community. In the older industrial centres where the Established Church has a richer flock, a National school may not only flourish financially, but may also be extremely efficient and popular. The Aberdare town National school deserves mention again for its remarkable success'.[5]

vii. Some School Boards, having taken over certain works schools, continued to use the poundage system as a basis of maintenance thus obviating the necessity of levying a local education rate, i.e. the poundage was retained in order to produce a sum sufficient, with government grants

1 *Minutes of Committee of Council*, 1879, Monmouthshire, p. 440.
2 ibid, 1883, p. 430.
3 ibid.
4 *Vivian Collection, MSS*, 1840-1923, *D/DGV*, 36, Glamorgan County Record Office
5 *Minutes of Committee of Council*, 1881, p. 310.

to balance expenditure. This method of maintaining schools operated at Merthyr Tydfil and at the Ferndale colliery schools.[1]

viii. School Boards came to the rescue of certain schools who unsuccessfully tried to exist on the poundage system—'such schools who were in difficulties took refuge under the wings of a school Board'. These schools were in the colliery districts, and one group, the Duffryn schools which were in the highest state of educational efficiency, were transferred to the School Board on account of a debt which had accumulated during a strike, and which could not be covered by any reasonable sacrifices on the part of either the managers or the colliers. In the Rhondda Valleys also, several schools 'have lately undergone a similar change of management for the same reason'.[2]

One final point should be mentioned concerning school fees. The managers of 'struggling' National schools ascribed their lack of success to the fact that School Boards charged low fees and some of them did not even press parents for school pence. Where School Boards had taken over Works schools, school pence were lower than for other children. Again, in some transferred Works schools the children of workmen paid no fees at all, whilst others, e.g. at Rhymney, had to pay—176 boys, 181 girls, and

---

1 *Minutes of Committee of Council*, 1881, p. 311. The Inspector, Mr. W. Edwards, made a further comment: 'I cannot omit to illustrate my remark by quoting the Ferndale schools, under the Llanwonno School Board, where the sum of £343. 7s. 11d. was raised by the poundage tax and £36. 11s. 0d. was paid by the children of tradesmen: the rates were not called into requisition at all. Compare the sum thus raised on behalf of 630 children with the total amount received by the Merthyr School Board for 2,942 children, viz.: £681. 17s. 11d. I draw the contrast not so much for the sake of discrediting the good management of the Merthyr School Board as of showing the immense advantage of the poundage system when it is feasible, and it is feasible to some extent wherever there are collieries giving constant employment. The school fees in Merthyr and Gelligaer are only 1d. and 2d. In the neighbouring parish of Aberdare, of which the circumstances are and have been throughout very similar, the fees range from 1d. to 4d. and have produced for 2,888 children the sum of £1,600 which, however, includes £182 drawn from poundage on behalf of 700 children.'

2 ibid, p. 310: 'These questions lead naturally to the matter of school fees. The managers of struggling National schools ascribe their want of success to the fact that School Boards charge a low fee and do not press parents for that. Some Boards certainly are lukewarm in the matter or they excuse their indulgent course of action by reference to the hard times and the difficulty of combining compulsory attendance with a severe exaction of school fees. The difficulty of making parents pay some share of the expense of school maintenance is solved with great ease in the case of schools maintained by poundage. Here the young unmarried men who compose more than half of the whole body of colliers, are made to contribute almost unconsciously to the expense of educating their little brothers and sisters. The tax may be hardly sensible, while it produces a sum sufficient, with the grant, to balance the expenditure. In some cases it has been possible to apply this system even to Board Schools.'

226 infants paid 3d. each per week.¹ At the Abersychan ironworks school controlled by the School Board, 124 boys, 164 girls, and 231 infants paid at the rate of 1½d. per week each. Workers' children at the Sirhowy ironworks schools received free education, and at the Cyfarthfa schools taken over by the Merthyr Tydfil School Board workmen's children paid a penny per week and others varying sums of 2d. and 3d.²

Tinworks schools and the Spelter works school at Maesteg were absorbed by School Boards at various dates after 1870, were enlarged and renovated, and were reckoned among the best schools in their respective districts, e.g. Dafen (Llanelli), Aberdulais, Aberavon, and Margam.³

Up to 1878, the whole responsibility of supplying education in the parish of Ystradyfodwg (Rhondda) had been thrown on Voluntary agency supported enthusiastically by the local colliery owners and colliers who worked through local committees to build, manage, and maintain the schools.⁴ The committee members were composed of ministers of religion, tradespeople, working colliers, and proprietors of collieries. The schools were all dependent on the poundage contributed at the collieries in addition to certain grants from the Voluntary Societies (mainly British) for their maintenance. A 3d. poundage was considered hardly sufficient for the medical fund but the school fund had to be satisfied with a 1d. The larger collieries were able to maintain their schools without financial worries but others had more difficulties especially when strikes and short stoppages interfered with the regular poundage payments. In addition, the long strike of the 1870s was the means of closing more than one of the National schools in the parish, e.g. the Pentre National school was closed in 1875.⁵

It became obvious that the time had arrived to tackle the problem of education on a sounder footing in an area where coal exploitation was expanding phenomenally and the child population swelling rapidly every year, and in any case the schools were, from the standpoint of accommodation inadequate. Accordingly, on 28 October 1878, a School

---

1 *Parliamentary Paper*, Vol. lix, Return of all Public Elementary Schools under Inspection within School Districts in which School Boards have been formed. pp. 236-240.
2 ibid.
3 Appendix 5 to this Chapter.
4 *Minutes of Committee of Council*, 1881, p. 305.
5 *N.L.W. MS.* 4383*D*, p. 127.

VOLUNTARY SOCIETIES AND SCHOOL BOARDS

Board was formed.[1] One of the first things demanding the attention of the Board was the compilation of a census of the whole parish which was divided into eighteen districts and the following details were required: number of families visited; number of children under 5 and 13; number of children over 13, and the number of children attending and not attending school.[2]

The results showed that there were 13,997 children under 13, and 5,637 above that age. Only 7,189 attended school, whilst 7,010, or fifty per cent, under 13 did not attend any kind of school.[3] Within a few months after its formation the Board took over the following colliery schools: Treorchy United, Bodringallt, Pentre, Dunraven, and Ystrad Rhondda, and then set about supplying the deficiency of school accommodation in the parish.[4] By 1882, other colliery schools went over to the Board, including Clydach Vale, Ferndale, Ton, Park, and Blaenycwm. More were to follow, and by 1894, Llwynypia, Penygraig, and Cwmparc joined the School Board.[5] The new schools opened by the School Board together with the colliery schools already absorbed were taken over by the Rhondda Education Authority after the Education Act of 1902.[6]

---

1. The members were: D. Evans, Bodringallt (Chairman); William Jenkins, Ystradfechan (Vice-chairman); D. Richards, Bute Merthyr Colliery, Treherbert; Wm. Walker Hood, Glamorgan Collieries, Llwynypia; Rev. William Morris, Baptist Minister, Noddfa, Treorchy; D. Davis Joseph, Tydraw, Treherbert; Rowland Rowlands, Penygraig; Thomas Owen, Collier, Treherbert; William Abraham (Mabon), Miners' Agent (who disqualified himself by being absent for over six months); Rev. William Jones, C.M. Minister, Ton Pentre; Edmund Thomas, Maindy Hall, Ton Pentre; David Rosser, Solicitor, Pontypridd, Clerk to the Board.
2. *N.L.W. M.S.* 4383*D*.
3. *Ystradyfodwg School Board Census*, 1878, D. Davies, Printer, Treorchy.
4. *N.L.W. M.S.* 4383*D*.
5. *Education Committee Minutes*, extracted by W. Morris Jones, Esq., late Director of Education, Council Offices, Pentre, Rhondda.
6. ibid.

APPENDIX 1

The Rev. David Rees wrote the following contribution to *Y Diwygiwr*, stating the case against Works Schools:[1]

Ysgolion y Gweithwyr: Ie, 'Ysgolion y Gweithwyr'! O'r goreu! Y mae y gweithiwr yn ddyn, bellach, ynte? Bu yn cael ei ystyried am gyfnodau hirfaethion yn ryw fath o anifail deu-droed wedi eu greu yn bwrpasol a'i anfon i'r ddaear yn uniongyrchol i fod yn gaethwas tragwyddol i ewyllys uchelgeisiol ei Arglwyddi gormaelus a chalon—galed. Druan ohonno! Ymladdodd ryfeloedd ei dywysogion hunanol; cochodd foroedd a'i waed, a thryfrithir meusydd y brwydrau heddiw a'i esgyrn gwynion ef. Ac yn dâl am ei drafferth, cafodd olwg mwy gwrthwynebus nag eiddo angau ei hunan, geiriau caletach a phoenusach i'w deimliad na llafnau bidogau awchlymaf maes y gwaed, a'i yrru a flangell gormes nes y syrthiodd o'i gafael i waelod bedd.

Ond y mae'r olwyn wedi troi erbyn hyn. Y mae'r gweithiwr wedi profi fod holl gynneddfau y natur ddynol yn cyd-gyfarfod ynddo. Cydnabyddir ei fod yn ddyn. Teimlir fod ei bresenoldeb mor bwysig ar y ddaear, ei enaid mor werthfawr, ei gyfrifoldeb mor fawr . . .

Gan fod y gweithiwr yn ddyn, ac yn ddyn mor bwysig, perthyna iddo hawliau, y rhai os gomeddir hwynt iddo, a fyddant yn gyfrifon duon yn erbyn y rhai a'u gomeddant neu a'u cam-gyfranant; ym mysg yr hawliau hyn saif addysg yn uchel ac amlwg.

Bu adeg yn y byd pan ystyrid rhoi addysg i'r bobl yn berygl i heddwch y wladwriaeth, diogelwch yr orsedd, a chysur y dyn ei hun. Ond y mae'r farn ysgymun hon wedi ei thaflu at y pethau a fu, a dorau teml gwybodaeth wedi ei hagor led y pen i'r gweithiwr . .

Ym mysg y dospeirth sy'n awyddus am addysg y gweithiwr gellir rhesu llawer o gwmniau a pherchenogion gweithfeydd. Y mae gan lawer ohonnynt 'Ysgol y Gwaith'. Codant dreth wythnosol neu fisol neu bunol oddiar gyflog y gweithiwr, i'w chynnal. Rhaid i bob gweithiwr, mawr a bach, hen ac ieuanc dalu y dreth, boddlon neu anfoddlon.

Y mae y cwmni neu y perchennog, neu y 'resident manager' yn dewis yr athraw, ac yn nodi allan ansawdd y ddysg i'w chyfrannu, heb ymholi dim a rhieni y plant. Ac mewn llawer o engrheifftiau y mae'r addysg yn hollol wrthdarawiadol i'r egwyddorion a broffesa y rhieni.

Mynnir eglwyswr yn athraw, dysgir catechism yr eglwys i'r plant, a denir hwynt i'r eglwys ar y Sabboth-tra yr a y rhan liosocaf o'u rhieni i addoldai ymneillduedig. Gallem nodi bagad o ysgolion sydd yn cael eu dwyn ymlaen fel hyn, ond ymataliwn y tro hwn gyda nodi ysgolion J. H. Vivian, Ysw., A.S., ac ysgolion Foxhole dan ofal P. St. L. Grenfell, Ysw., Maesteg House . . . [1]

Note: The above extract describes the workman as a person with a conscience and liberty to decide for himself as to what kind of education his children should have. Rees maintained that works schools were established to promote Church education, and quotes the Hafod and Kilvey schools as examples. But this was not strictly true for soon after they were opened, they became unsectarian (Neutral) schools.

1 *Y Diwygiwr*, Rhif. 216, Gorffennaf, 1853, Cyf. XVIII, pp. 222-224.

APPENDIX 2
INSPECTED NATIONAL WORKS SCHOOLS[2]

Monmouthsnire	*Glamorgan*	*Carmarthenshire*
Rhymney National (Iron)	Dowlais (Iron) (until 1855)	Trimsaran (Iron)
Tredegar (Iron)	Cyfarthfa (Iron) (later Neutral)	Dafen, Llanelli (Tinworks)
Machen (Iron)	Cwmavon, Bryn & Oakwood (Iron)	Carmarthen (Tinworks)
Pontypool (Iron)	Pentyrch (Iron)	
Pontnewynydd (Iron)	Ystalyfera (Iron)	
Blaenavon (Iron)	Ystalyfera (Tinworks)	
Courtybella Colliery	Hirwaun (Iron)	*Breconshire*
Trevethin (Iron)	Melincrythan (Copper)	Clydach (Iron)
	Llangyfelach Colliery	

2 *Minutes of Committee of Council*, from 1850 to 1895.

VOLUNTARY SOCIETIES AND SCHOOL BOARDS

Monmouthshire	Glamorgan	Caernarvonshire
	Penlle'rgaer Colliery	
	Margam (Tinworks)	Llandegai (Slate)
	Pontardawe (Tinworks)	Llanllechid (Slate)
	Margam (Copper)	Gerlan (Slate)
	Rhigos Colliery	
	Llansamlet (Colliery)	*Merioneth*
	Bryndu (Colliery)	Maentwrog (Slate)
	Gorseinon (Colliery)	Llwynygell (Slate)
	Cilybebyll (Colliery)	Llan Festiniog, Gellilydan (Slate)
	Court Herbert Colliery, Skewen	Tanygrisiau (Slate)
		Penrhyndeudraeth (Slate)

Total National Works Schools: 40

APPENDIX 3
INSPECTED BRITISH WORKS SCHOOLS[1]

Note: All colliery schools without exception were British schools after 1860.

Monmouthshire	Glamorgan	Carmarthenshire
Ironworks	*Ironworks*	*Ironworks*
Rhymney British	Venallt	Gwendraeth
Victoria (Ebbw Vale)	Tondu	Amman
Blaina	Tonmawr	Brynamman (Tinworks)
Cwmcelyn	Maesteg (Spelter Works)	Pontamman (Chemical)
Dos Nailworks (Newport)		Hendy (Tinworks)
	Collieries	
Tydee (Tinworks)	Bryndu	
Pits, Ebbw Vale (Colliery)	Hirwaun	
	Llanfabon	*Breconshire*
	Dinas	Yniscedwyn (Iron)
	Treherbert	
	Bodringallt	
	Llwynypia	
	Treorchy	
	Dunraven	
	Blaenycwm	*Caernarvonshire*
	Pentre	Trevor Welsh Granite Co.,
	Ystrad	Penrhyndeudraeth (Slate)
	Penygraig	Tremadoc
	Ferndale	
	Cwmparc	
	Clydach Vale	
	Blaengarw	
	Ynysybwl	
	Cwmaman	
	Garth (Maesteg)	
	Coegnant (Maesteg)	
	Merthyr (Maesteg)	
	Tynewydd	
	Gilfach Goch	
	Resolven	
	Dyhewid (Llantwit Faerdre)	
	Merthyr Vale	

Total British Works Schools: 47

1 *Minutes of Committee of Council* from 1850 to 1895.

APPENDIX 4
Works Schools listed as having been transferred to School Boards by 1894[1]

MONMOUTHSHIRE IRONWORKS SCHOOLS

School	Grants for enlarging	Scholars	Av. Attend	Annual Grants
Abersychan	£1,825	570	—	—
Blaina	—	440	—	£15 7 0
Ebbw Vale	—	870	592	£468 19 0
Lower Rhymney	—	253	244	£213 10 0
Middle Rhymney	—	695	495	£425 10 0
Sirhowy	—	435	298	£224 19 0
Upper Rhymney	—	360	264	£211 6 0
Blaenavon	£155	349	—	—
Cwmbran	£538	119	79	£51 9 0
Dos Nailworks Newport (half-time school)	—	347	41	£30 3 0
Pontnewynydd	£365 7 8	363	304	£321 19 10
Trevethin (Pontypool)	—	332	316	£340 4 7

CARMARTHENSHIRE AND BRECONSHIRE IRONWORKS SCHOOLS

School	Grants for enlarging	Scholars	Av. Attend	Annual Grants
Amman (Carms.)	£100	412	351	£294 5 0[2]
Yniscedwyn (Breconshire)	£370	280	231	—[3]

Works schools listed as having been transferred to School Boards by 1894[4]

GLAMORGAN IRONWORKS SCHOOLS

School	Scholars	Av. Attendance	Annual grants
Maesteg	543	328	£280 0 0
Llynfi	614	259	£226 12 0
Neath Abbey	231	128	£108 16 0
Tondu	826	548	£542 2 0
Ystalyfera (Wern)	564	386	£331 3 3
Cwmafon	974	667	£597 8 0
Cwmafon (Tymaen) Infants	250	129	£103 15 0
Cwmafon (Bryn)	86	42	—
Cwmafon (Oakwood)	349	219	£206 9 0
Dowlais	2,239	1,449	£1,452 18 6
Penydarren	854	551	£546 2 0
Georgetown (Merthyr)	754	577	£556 4 0
Pentyrch	332	164	£147 4 0

1 *Minutes of Committee of Council*, 1894, p. 1075.
2 ibid.
3 ibid.
4 ibid, p. 1084.

VOLUNTARY SOCIETIES AND SCHOOL BOARDS

APPENDIX 5
Schools of the Non-Ferrous Metal Industries
transferred to School Boards by 1894.

Tinworks Schools	Scholars	Av. Attendance	Annual grants		
Dafen (Llanelli)	283	234	£250	2	5[1]
Aberdulais	153	83	—[2]		
Margam	253	141	£130	5	0[3]
Copperworks Schools					
Llanelli	741	743	£611	1	5[4]
Pembrey	509	475	£549	19	1[5]
Hafod (transferred in 1898 by purchase)	1,114	889	£860	4	0[6]
Margam	704	552	£474	10	0[7]
Kilvey	842	634	£536	10	6[8]
Melincrythan (Neath)	773	724	—[9]		
Spelter Works School					
Maesteg	312	261	£228	7	6[10]

APPENDIX 6
Colliery Schools
transferred to School Boards by 1894

Ystradyfodwg School Board formed in 1878, included the following schools in 1882:[11]

School	No. of Scholars	Av. Attendance	Annual grants		
Blaenycwm	103	46	£33	7	0
Bodringallt	472	544	£487	0	0
Clydach Vale	487	213	£161	8	2
Dunraven	242	391	£300	7	10
Ferndale	660	683	£601	0	10
Park	410	284	£284	5	4
Pentre	654	550	£470	14	10
Ton	800	436	£449	3	4
Treorchy	793	607	£535	9	1
Ystrad	415	158	£116	11	0

Other Colliery Schools
transferred to School Boards:

School	No. of Scholars	Av. attendance	Annual grants		
Duffryn	1,121	669	£630	14	0
Navigation	322	280	£259	10	0
Merthyr (Maesteg)	304	259	£205	7	0
Court Herbert (Skewen)	524	558	£488	5	0
Bryndu	476	296	£285	12	0[12]

1 *Minutes of Committee of Council*, 1894, p. 1076.
2 ibid, p. 1084.
3 ibid.
4 ibid., pp. 1076-77.
5 ibid.
6 *Vivian Collection, MSS.*, 1840-1923 D/DGV 36.
7 *Minutes of Committee of Council*, 1894, p. 1084.
8 ibid.
9 ibid.
10 ibid.
11 *Minutes of Committee of Council*, 1883, p. 753.
12 ibid, 1894, p. 1084.

Epilogue

THE INDUSTRIAL REVOLUTION created many social problems, not the least of which was the lack of educational provision for the children of the new working class population in rapidly developing industrial areas. Indeed, 'our system of universal compulsory education was the outcome of the discovery in the second half of the eighteenth century, of the evil conditions to which the children of the poor of this country were exposed in increasing measure ... To the educationist nothing is more striking than the increasing recognition that the ignorance, neglect and degradation of the child population constituted a national menace'.[1] This was just another way of describing educational destitution at national level, a condition which was more acute in industrial regions than anywhere else. But the Industrial Revolution had travelled a long way, and had ruthlessly exploited its vast hordes of uneducated children, before the State took legislative action through the Education Act of 1870. This measure merely supplemented the effective, though limited achievements of the Voluntary Societies and brought them, together with the Works Schools System, into the new national framework which evolved in the period 1870-1902. Educational destitution created the Works Schools System which 'filled the gaps' of voluntary effort in the industrial areas. The State did likewise for those parts of the country not covered by the combined efforts of the Voluntary and Works Schools Systems. The final step was taken when the Board of Education Act of 1899 and the Education Act of 1902 produced the necessary machinery for the administration of education at national and local levels.

During the first half of the nineteenth century, religion, in one way, hindered, rather than helped, the establishment of schools through the agency of the Voluntary Societies. Welsh Nonconformity was sufficiently potent to maintain the principle that education was the help-mate of religion. In such an association the State could have no place. This attitude explained the tardiness and hesitancy of the Welsh people to accept government grants in aid of education. This was more true of south Wales than north Wales. Sir Hugh Owen succeeded in converting the strongest religious denomination in north Wales, the Calvinistic Methodists, to adopt undenominational schools on the British system.

1 Frank Smith, op. cit., p. 1.

EPILOGUE

In south Wales, however, the land of older Dissent—the Independents and Baptists, whose religious leaders resented both State aid and Anglican proprietors of works schools—produced for almost two decades, a Voluntaryist vacuum which considerably hampered the progress of British schools. The most militant of the pure Voluntaryists in the industrial areas, the Rev. David Rees, held out almost to his death in 1869, just a year before the 1870 Education Act.

In another way, religion considerably enhanced educational opportunities throughout the Principality. Welsh Nonconformists had a first-class native institution at hand, the Sunday school, which exhibited 'a mixture of worship, discussion and elementary education, which the congregation performed for itself, and without other agency than its own'[1] conducted wholly in the Welsh language. This institution out-shone all other competitors in the educational field, and was far more popular than day schools in the industrial areas. In addition to the religious circumstances of the time—the suspicious attitude towards State subvention obstructing the establishment of day schools, and the phenomenal success and universality of Sunday schools—the economic factor was all-important, for day schools of *any kind* were regarded as a hindrance to work, and an interference with the earning capacity of children of working class families.

It is in the light of this distinctive Welsh background that the provision of educational facilities in Wales during the Industrial Revolution has been viewed and assessed. In the industrial areas, as in other parts of Wales, Sunday schools flourished and had no difficulties to encounter. The Voluntary Societies made their valuable contribution where they were acceptable.[2] But, shunning the religious factors, and ignoring State aid in the initial stages, Companies and works proprietors set about building schools because 'an essentially economic organization

1 *Special Reports on Educational Subjects*, vol. II, p. 4, Education Department, Committee of Council.
2 Up to 1839, the State had merely been a subscriber to the two Voluntary Societies on an equal basis, and the principle was to make grants where one-half of the sum required was raised by local efforts. The British and Foreign School Society had exhausted its local funds in the first year and was unable to make a proportionate advance. The result was that gradually two-thirds, three-fifths, or three-fourths of the grant went to the National Society which had superior local resources. It also became evident that the system was defective in a most essential feature, as no provision was made in those localities where it was most required, and where education was at the lowest ebb, e.g. the industrial areas. These defects and inequalities were gradually turning the public mind to a rate-supported system, which, however, was yet far in the distance. This was the very period, 1839-1846, when many works schools were established, taking over the role of voluntary effort in the evolving national pattern.

like the works which created the industrial community became *inevitably* involved in a social function like education'.[1] It was after such schools were built and organized, that the employers confronted and *solved* the religious difficulties by conducting their schools on 'neutral' or unsectarian principles, and eventually sought government grants and inspection in order to guarantee their efficiency. In short, employers of labour had overcome—*in the sixties of the nineteenth century*—the religious problems which were perpetuated by the Education Act of 1902, and caused so much acrimony and friction between Welsh Nonconformity led by Lloyd George, and the central government, from 1902 to 1906, and long afterwards.

This assumption of responsibility for education by employers in the industrial areas deserved far greater support from those for whom the schools were intended, for the response did not always match the good intentions of employers and the outlay involved in their ventures. The reasons for working class indifference have been discussed. But, in many ways, the Works Schools System made a solid and valuable contribution to the evolution of a State system of elementary schools between 1870 and the turn of the century. The educational aspirations of employers of labour became embossed on the State pattern in many ways, as it gradually emerged.

Firstly, works schools, drawing revenue from an educational tax on the working class community and from government sources, had (apart from periods of strikes) financial stability, and were in a highly favourable position as compared with voluntary schools which had to operate according to fixed budgets and slender incomes. Secondly, ample funds and financial security meant, for the works schools, far better conditions for all concerned. Her Majesty's Inspectors had repeatedly stressed the benefits resulting from a combination of compulsory tax on workmen and grants from the central government, which became a strong argument for rate-aided education after 1870. Thirdly, regarding better conditions for all, works schools had more flexible methods of teaching and organization, could pay better salaries to teachers, and could attract and keep a full quota of pupil-teachers. The larger works schools had discarded the mechanical monitorial method at an early stage by substituting trained teachers which they could well afford. This, in turn, ensured a high degree of teaching efficiency and a good type of pupil-teacher, i.e. who remained for the full period of apprenticeship. Scales of salaries were more favourable than in voluntary schools. The

1   M. Sanderson, op. cit., p. 279.

effects of these beneficial improvements in works schools, warmly applauded by such people as Matthew Arnold and Her Majesty's Inspectors, profoundly influenced the new Board Schools after 1870, i.e. works schools, their organization, teaching staff, curricula, remuneration, etc., became the model for such schools.[1]

Fourthly, due to their financial structure, works schools had superior infants departments, and evening schools which pioneered successful experiments in further and technical education (though of a somewhat narrow vocational nature) making them the best schools in their respective areas, many of them becoming the first Higher Grade schools within the State system. Furthermore, in addition to all the advantages which works schools enjoyed due to their financial resources, had there been compulsory education in their hey-day, they would have, long before 1870, become a superior type of elementary school. Fifthly, apart from Sunday schools, irregular attendance and early school-leaving were characteristic features of all day schools throughout the country before 1880, but works schools where such conditions were most rampant, threw the problem into greater relief and again paved the way for attendance by-laws in the 1870 Act. There is no doubt that the successful compulsory attendances exercised by some employers of labour, e.g. the high standard of literacy among the working classes of the London Lead Mining Company's schools in the north of England, showed the government that compulsory education was the only effective remedy.

Two final points are worthy of inclusion in the list of contributions made by the Works Schools System to the State elementary school structure. After the Revised Code of 1862 which produced a check on school building, fresh evidence of educational destitution was accumulating, especially in large towns, cities, and some industrial areas. But in those places where works schools existed, and after 1880 when school attendances grew rapidly after Mundella's Act, proprietors of works were always able to enlarge their schools to the great satisfaction of Her Majesty's Inspectors. After the Education Act of 1870, wherever they were found, works schools—just as they had done once before, in localities where voluntary effort was weakest—took over a heavy burden of accommodation and finance from the newly constituted School Boards. In 1891, the Works Schools System came to an end with the abolition of school pence. It had served its purpose and had made no mean efforts

---

1 After 1880, some works schools had been absorbed by School Boards earlier than others. But the higher salaries paid in works schools had to be honoured, and eventually the staffs of other schools in the School Board District benefited.

for the diffusion of knowledge in a new, unstable industrial society which paid more attention to the earning power of young children than to developing their intellectual capacities. Its many-sided contributions to the State system of education is an important chapter in the history of elementary, and, to some extent, higher education, in England and Wales.

Bibliography

A. MANUSCRIPT COLLECTIONS

1. *IN LIBRARIES, MUSEUMS, RECORD OFFICES, COUNTY EDUCATION OFFICES, AND SCHOOLS*

NATIONAL LIBRARY OF WALES, ABERYSTWYTH

Nevill Documents:
I. Personal Account Book, 1770-1784, (Savill)
IV. Letter book of Charles and R. J. Nevill, 1804-7
V. Letter book of R. J. Nevill, 1823-1830
VII. Letter books of R. J. Nevill, 1830-36; 1836-1853
VIII. Letter book of R. J. Nevill, 1842
X. Journal of Carmarthenshire Collieries, 1803-1812
XXI. Resolutions of Messrs. Daniell, Savill, Guest, and Nevill, 1804-1834.
XXIII. Ledgers of the Llanelli Copperworks, 1823-1857
XLVII. Trade and Domestic Accounts of R. J. Nevill, 1808-15
XLVIII. Minutes of Annual Meetings of Sims, Willyams, Nevill, etc., 1837-1850
2705: Letter from John Jones, Llangennech to R. J. Nevill re proposed school extension, 1848.
2743: Letter from Rev. Ebenezer Morris, Vicar of Llanelli, to R. J. Nevill, 1849.
516: Llanelli Copperworks British School: Memorandum of Agreement between the Managers and a pupil-teacher, 1868.

Cyfarthfa Papers:
4378 D. Letter books and correspondence of W. Crawshay.
10364 D. Account Books of Cyfarthfa and Hirwaun ironworks.

Fonmon Documents:
39. Survey of Plymouth ironworks, Merthyr Tydfil, 1862.
2276-8, 83: Papers relating to Plymouth ironworks, 1863-1869.

Various Documents and Deeds:
25, 702-6, Williams and Williams, Haverfordwest: Documents relating to Panteg ironworks in Pontypool, 1876-81.
7, 9, Berry Deeds, relating to Aberdulais Forges, 1777-1793.

Abergavenny Deeds:
1407 Machen ironworks 1819
408 Blaenavon ironworks, 1823
406, and 409-13 Varteg ironworks, 1823

7454-7 A: 7458-60 B: Diaries of W. S. Clark, references to Dowlais ironworks and Penydarren, 1845-1858.
6093 E: Letters and Papers relating to South Wales ironworks, 1771-1841.
12628 A: Treherbert British School Account Book, 1868-1872.
7096, 7106, 7132 E: Nefydd MSS, The Journals of the Rev. William Roberts (Nefydd), of Blaina.
4383 D: The History of Ystradyfodwg, M. O. Jones.
4983 D: The Autobiography of Samuel Holland, 1803-1892.

BIBLIOGRAPHY

UNIVERSITY COLLEGE OF NORTH WALES, BANGOR
MSS. 27494, 27496, 27499: Cilgwyn Papers, Porth yr Aur Collection.

BRITISH MUSEUM
522m12(2): The Case of Sir Humphrey Mackworth and of the Mine Adventure, with respect to the irregular proceedings of several Justices of the Peace in the County of Glamorgan.
522m12(6): The Mine Adventure or an Expedient for Composing all differences between the partners of Mines late of Sir Carberry Price.
522m12(15): A General Account of the Mine Adventure, Folio 2, 1709.
522m12(44): Tracts relating to Mines, 'A representation containing a vindication of Sir Humphrey Mackworth from the many false and scandalous reflections cast upon him in the House of Commons in the year 1709.'
444a50: The Mine Adventure laid open, Folio 8, W. Waller.
816m13(76): The Case of the Mine Adventurers in relation to a Bill before Parliament for settling their affairs, London, 1711.

CARDIFF CENTRAL LIBRARY
Bute Documents:
VI. 29: Dowlais iron and steelworks and collieries by J. Thomas Lewis.
VI. 4.1034, Papers, Reports, Memoranda, and Letters re Dowlais coal and iron works.
VII. 4.1035, Reports, Letters, Memoranda.
IX. 40. (1846): Memorandum re subscriptions to the Cowbridge and Llanblethian National Schools.
X. 2 (3): Abstract of payments and receipts for the late Marquis of Bute's Executors and Trustees, 18th March, 1850-18th March, 1851.
Whitchurch School, Melingriffith: MS 4.999, Subscriptions Lists and admission tickets.

SWANSEA CENTRAL LIBRARY
Admission Registers of Hafod Copperworks Schools, 1852.
Miscellaneous Papers dealing with Hafod Copperworks schools.
Logbooks, Hafod Copperworks schools, 1863-1900.

LLANELLI PUBLIC LIBRARY
Returns of the Llanelli Free School, March and April, 1818.
Names of Subscribers to the Llanelli Charity School, 1823.
Contributions to Llanelli British School, 1864-5.
Llanelli Copperworks Schools, Statements of income and expenditure for 1864-66 and 1878.
Llanelli School Report for year ending February, 1870.
Measurements of Copperworks (Heolfawr) School, 1871.
Llanelli Copperworks Schools, scales of salaries, 1893.

CARNEGIE FREE LIBRARY, PORT TALBOT
Miscellaneous Papers dealing with details of admission to the Cwmavon works schools; references to school administration, evening schools, etc.

MERTHYR TYDFIL EDUCATION OFFICE
Memorandum issued by the Trustee of the Dowlais Schools.
Notes re Dowlais Schools.

ABERYSTWYTH COUNTY EDUCATION OFFICE
Deeds of the Goginan, Ysbyty Ystwyth, and Esgair Hir Schools.

COUNCIL OFFICES, BLAENAVON
Documents and Deeds relating to Church schools, Blaenavon.

BIBLIOGRAPHY

COUNCIL OFFICES, PENTRE, RHONDDA
Education Records and Papers relating to elementary education in the Rhondda.

CAERNARVONSHIRE COUNTY RECORD OFFICE
County Deeds and Leases:
E259: Welsh Granite Company's School at Trevor, Llanaelhaiarn.
EA/5/18. f.66: Gerlan National School.
EA/5/18. f.25: Llandinorwig National School.
ES/1/Llandegai 2: Llandegai National school logbook.
Logbooks of the Welsh Granite Company's School, Trevor.
B.J.C. Index No. 603, Records of Messrs. Breese, Jones, and Casson, Penrhyndeudraeth National School.

GLAMORGAN COUNTY RECORD OFFICE
D/DGV. 36. Vivian Collection, MSS. 1840-1923.
D/DGV. 1A. Business Note book kept by A. P. Vivian, 1840-1898.

School Boards:
E/SB. 1/1. Aberavon: Minute Book, 1893-1899.
E/SB. 2/1. Aberdare: Minute Book, 1871-1877.
E/SB. 2/11. Aberdare: Committee Minute Book, 1873-1881.
E/SB. 2/15. Aberdare: Report and Letter Book, 1876-1885.
E/SB. 7/1. Cilybebyll: Minute Book, 1871-1875.
E/SB. 30/1. Llansamlet Higher: Minute Book, 1877-1883.
E/SB. 31/1. Llantrisant: Minute Book, 1871-1880.
E/SB. 40/1. Llanwonno: Minute Book, 1871-1879.
E/SB. 37/1. Margam: Minute Book, 1881-1896.
E/SB. 58/1. Ystradyfodwg: Minute Book, 1878-1885.

School Logbooks:
E/MA Duffryn Colliery Schools, 4 Volumes, 1863-1930.
E/M Merthyr Colliery Infants School, Maesteg, 1887-1904.
E/M Merthyr Colliery Mixed School, Maesteg, 1882-1900.
E/M Tondu Ironworks school, 1863-1888.
E/W Ystalyfera (Wern) Ironworks schools.
E/W Abercerdin (formerly called Dinas Main Colliery Board School) 1874-1902.
E/W Margam Tinworks school: 1874-1899.
E/W Margam Copperworks school: 1868-1907.
E/W Kilybebyll Infants School: 1874-1897.
E/W Cwmavon Works Schools, 6 Volumes.
E/W Neath Abbey Ironworks school.
E/W Bryndu Colliery school.
E/W Maesteg Spelter Works school.

School Logbooks consulted elsewhere:
Dowlais Ironworks schools, at Dowlais Schools: 6 Volumes, Boys and Girls, Vol. 1, 1862-1883; Vol. 2, 1883-1894; other volumes after 1894.
Llanelli Copperworks Schools, at Llanelli Copperworks School.
Penydarren Ironworks School, Merthyr Tydfil, Penydarren School.
Amman Ironworks and Brynaman Tinworks Schools: loaned from these schools.

2. *PRIVATELY OWNED*

Ocean Coal Company, Ltd., Treorchy (before 1949):
Private Account Ledgers; Private Letter Books; Miscellaneous Files; Wages Books for the following collieries showing miners' contributions to colliery schools:

Maindy Wages Book No. 1; Park Wages Books, Nos. 1 and 6; Dare Wages Books, Nos. 1, 5, and 6; Eastern Wages Books, Nos. 1, 2, and 3; Garw Wages Books, Nos. 1, 2, 3, 4, and 6; Lady Windsor Wages Books, Nos. 1, 2, 3, 5, 6, and 7.

B. OFFICIAL PAPERS

Reports from the Select Committee on the State of Education among the lower orders: 1816, IV; 1817, III; 1818, IV.
Parochial Returns made to the Select Committee on the Education of the Poor, 1819, IX.
General Table showing the State of Education in England and Wales, 1820, XII.
Education Inquiry: Abstract of Answers and Returns made pursuant to an Address of the House of Commons, 24th May, 1833. Vol. 2, Monmouth; Vol. 3, Surrey-Radnor (containing Glamorgan).
First Report from the Commissioners appointed to collect information in the Manufacturing Districts relative to the employment of children in Factories with Minutes of evidence and Reports of District Commissioners, 1833, XX.
Second Report of the Commissioners, of 1833, XXI.
Supplementary Reports of same, 1834, XIX, XX.
28th Report of the Commissioners of Inquiry into Charities, 1834.
Report from the Select Committee on the Education of the Poorer classes in England and Wales. 1834, IX; 1835, VII; 1837-38, VI.
Abstract of Answers and Returns relative to the State of Education in England and Wales, 1835, XLI; XLII; XLIII.
Reports from each of the Four Factory Inspectors on the educational provisions of the Factory Act, together with a joint Report, 1839, XLII.
Parliamentary Papers: Accounts and Papers, Education, 1839, Vol. XLI.
Minutes of Her Majesty's Committee of Privy Council on Education, 1839-1899.
Reports from the Select Committee on the Act for the regulation of Factories, together with Minutes of Evidence, 1840, X; 1841, IX.
First Report of the Commissioners for Inquiring into the employment of children in Mines and Manufactories, 1842, XV.
Reports and Evidence of Sub-Commissioners on same, 1842, XVI, XVII.
Second Report of Commissioners on same, 1843, XIII.
Report of R. J. Saunders upon the establishment of schools in the Factory Districts in February, 1842; 1843, XXVII.
Bill for Regulating the employment of children and young persons in Factories and for the better education of children in Factory Districts, 1843, II.
First Report of the Committee for Inquiring into the employment of children in agriculture, 1843, XLI.
Bill for Regulating the employment of children, young persons, and women in Factory Districts, 1844, II.
Six Reports of the Commissioner on the operation of the Mines Act, 1844-49.
Reports of the Commissioner appointed under the provisions of the Act 5 and 6 Vict. c.99 to Inquire into the working of that Act and into the State of the Population in the Mining Districts, 1844-1859.
Reports of the Commissioners of Inquiry into the State of Education in Wales, appointed by the Committee of Council on Education. In three Parts, 1847.
The School in its Relations to the State, the Church, and the Congregation, being an explanation of the Minutes of the Committee of Council on Education, 1847.
Hansard's Parliamentary Debates from 1846.
Report of the Commissioners on Popular Education in England; Reports of Assistant Commissioners, Minutes of Evidence, 1861, XXI, Parts 1-6.
Return to an Address of the House of Commons dated 25th July, 1861, Printed 28th April, 1862, Llanelli, etc. Schools.
Third Report of the Commissioners, Children's Employment Commission, 1862, Parliamentary Paper, 1864, XXIX.

BIBLIOGRAPHY

Fourth Report of the Commissioners, ibid, with Appendix, 1865.
Report from the Select Committee on Education, together with the proceedings, Minutes of Evidence, Appendix, and Index, 1866.
Reports from the Commissioners, 1868-9, Parliamentary Paper XIV; Report of Sub-Inspectors for 1868 on the working of the Factory Acts Extensions Act of 1867.
Reports from the Commissioners, 1870, Vol. XV. Reports of Inspectors of Factories for the half-year ending 31st October, 1869, Half-yearly Report by Robert Baker.
Parliamentary Papers, Accounts and Papers, Vol. LII, 1873. Returns from all School Boards up to 30th September, 1872.
ibid., Vol. LVIII, 1875. Nominal Return of all schools in England and Wales transferred to School Boards under Section 23 of the Elementary Education Act of 1870.
School Attendance and Child Labour. Report of Departmental Committee, 1893-4, LXVIII.
Royal Commission on the Church of England and other Religious Bodies in Wales and Monmouthshire, 1910, 1911. HMSO.
Censuses of England and Wales, 1801-1901.

C. REPORTS, PERIODICALS, NEWSPAPERS

1. *REPORTS*

Reports of Inspectors of Mines from 1854.
Reports of Inspectors of Factories from 1834.
Reports of the Society for Bettering the Condition and Improving the Comforts of the Poor, 1797-1808. Digest of same, 1801.
Reports of the Central Society of Education.
Reports of the South Wales Prize Association.
Diocesan Reports of the Monmouthshire Education Board from 1840.
Reports of the British and Foreign School Society from 1815.
Reports of the National Society from 1812.
Results of the Returns to the General Inquiry made by the National Society into the State and Progress of schools, 1846-47, published 1849.

2. *PERIODICALS AND JOURNALS*

Quarterly Journal of Education, 1831-1835.
Chambers' Edinburgh Journal, 1852.
Wales: ed. J. Hugh Edwards, Vol. IV, 1913.
Geographical Journal, 1919.
Archaeologia Cambrensis, 6th Series, Vol. XIX, Parts 1 and 2, 1919.
Transactions of the National Association for the Promotion of Social Science, 1859.
Transactions of the Honourable Society of Cymmrodorion, 1897-8; 1904; 1931-32; 1969-70, Part 1.
West Wales Historical Records, Transactions of the Historical Society of West Wales.
Journal of the National Library of Wales, iii, V, 1953-54, xiv, 4, 1966; xv, i, 1967.
Sociological Review: Journal of the Institute of Sociology, xliii, 1951.
The Advancement of Science, Vol. VI, No. 23, 1949.
Economic History Review, 2nd Series, Vol. XX, 1967.
Past and Present, No. 38, December, 1967.
Economica, 10, 1930.
Economic History, February, 1939.
Economic Journal Supplement, February, 1935.
Population Studies, 19, 1966.

BIBLIOGRAPHY

Welsh Periodicals

Y Dysgedydd
Seren Gomer
Y Drysorfa
Y Cymmrodor
Y Cyfarwyddwr
Welsh Outlook

Y Diwygiwr
Y Bedyddiwr
Y Geninen
Yr Adolygydd
Y Traethodydd
Yr Athro

Newspapers

The Swansea Cambrian
Aberdare Times
Monmouthshire Merlin

Merthyr Express
Llanelli Guardian
Yr Herald Cymraeg

D. BIOGRAPHIES, DIARIES, AND LETTERS

1. *BIOGRAPHIES*

Y Bywgraffiadur Cymreig Hyd 1940, Llundain 1953.
The Dictionary of Welsh Biography, London, 1959.
Y Bywgraffiadur Cymreig, 1941-1950, Llundain 1970.
Dictionary of National Biography, Supplement, Vol. II, 1901.
Davies, Owen (Rev.): Cofiant y Parch. Dr. Pritchard, Llangollen, 1880.
Davies, T.: Bywyd ac ysgrifeniadau D. Rees, Llanelli, 1871.
Davies, W. E.: Sir Hugh Owen, his Life and Work, London, 1885.
Evans, E. Wyn: William Abraham (Mabon), Cardiff, 1959.
Evans, Daniel: Life and Work of William Williams, M.P., Llandysul, 1940.
Evans, J. J.: Morgan John Rhys a'i Amserau. Liverpool, 1935.
Hammond, J. L. & B.: Lord Shaftesbury. London, 1923.
Jenkins, D. E.: The Life of the Rev. Thomas Charles of Bala, 3 Vols., Denbigh, 1908.
Jones, D.: Life and Times of Griffith Jones of Llanddowror. London and Bangor, 1902.
Jones, Henry: Old Memories. London, 1923.
Jones, Thomas: Rhymney Memories. Welsh Outlook Presss, 1938. Reprinted, Gwasg Gomer, 1970.
Morgan, E.: The Life and Labours of the Rev. Thomas Charles, 1828.
Morgan, J. V. (ed.): Welsh Political and Educational Leaders, London, 1908.
Palmer, A. N.: John Wilkinson and the old Bersham Ironworks, Trans. Cymm. Soc., 1897-8.
Podmore, F.: Robert Owen, 2 Volumes, London, 1906.
Reid, T. W.: Life of W. E. Forster. London, 1889.
Roberts, T. R.: Eminent Welshmen. Cardiff, 1908.
Smith, Frank: Life and Works of Sir James Kay-Shuttleworth. London, 1923.
Southey, R. & C. C.: The Life of the Rev. Andrew Bell. London, 1844.
Williams, R.: A Biographical Dictionary of Eminent Welshmen, Llandovery, 1853.

2. *DIARIES AND LETTERS*

Bessborough, Earl of: The Diaries of Lady Charlotte Guest. London, 1950.
Bessborough, Earl of: Lady Charlotte Schreiber, 1853-1891, London, 1952.
Bowstead, J.: Letters Concerning Education in South Wales, Stroud, 1861.
Letters of the Rt. Hon. H. A. Bruce, G.C.B., Lord Aberdare of Duffryn, Private Edition, Vol. 1, Oxford, 1902.
Baines, E. (Jnr.): Letters to Lord John Russell on State Education, London, 1846.
Lloyd, D.: Letter to J. Bowstead. Carmarthen, 1861.
Williams, W.: Letter to Lord John Russell on the present defective State of Education in Wales. London, 1848.
Williams, W A Second Letter to Lord John Russell on the Report. London, 1848.

BIBLIOGRAPHY

E. OTHER WORKS

(*Selected List*)

Adams, Francis: History of the Elementary School Contest in England, London, 1882.
Adamson, J. W.: English Education, 1789-1902. Cambridge, 1930.
Addis, J. P.: The Crawshay Dynasty. Cardiff, 1957.
Aeron Afan: Cyfansoddiadau Buddugol Eisteddfod Iforiaid Aberafan, Mehefin 23ain, 1853. Caerfyrddin, 1855.
Anon: Adroddiad Ysgolion Sabbothol y Methodistiaid Calfinaidd yng Ngogledd Cymru, Llanrwst, 1827 a 1829, Caerlleon, 1829.
Anon: Crybwylliad am ffurfiad a sefydliad Ysgolion Sabbothol. London, 1821.
Anon: The Welsh Education Question and the Bishop of St. David's. Bristol, 1861.
Anon: Yr Ysgolfeistr fel y bu: Yr Ysgolfeistr fel y mae. Yr Adolygydd, 1850.
Anon: A brief history of the Hafod Copperworks School from its foundation. Swansea, 1905.
Anon: Sunday Schools in Wales. A paper on the good effects of Sunday Schools and a Report on the Sunday school at Harwood. Chester, 1789.
Armytage, W. H. G.: Four Hundred years of English Education. Cambridge University Press, 1964.
Arnold, Matthew: Reports on Elementary Schools, 1852-1882. London, 1889; New ed., 1908.
Ashton, T. S.: The Industrial Revolution, 1948.
Aspinall, A.: Lord Brougham and the Whig Party. London, 1927.
Astle, J. G. E.: The Progress of Merthyr Tydfil. Merthyr Tydfil, n.d.
Aquilonius, K.: Det svenska folkundervisningsvasendet, 1809-1860 (The Swedish Popular Educational System), Stockholm, 1942.
Baines, E. (Jnr.): The Social, Educational, and Religious State of the Manufacturing Districts. Leeds, 1843.
Balfour G.: The Educational Systems of Great Britain and Ireland, Oxford, 1903, 2nd ed.
Barber, J. T.: A Tour through South Wales and Monmouthshire. London, 1803.
Barnard, H. C.: A Short History of English Education, 1760-1944. London, 1947.
Bartley, G. C. T.: The Schools for the People. London, 1871.
Bernard, T.: Of the Education of the Poor, 1809.
Binns, H. B.: A Century of Education. London, 1908.
Bowen, Lane: Rise of the Tinplate Industry. Llanelli, 1892.
Bowden, W.: Industrial Society in England towards the end of the Eighteenth Century. London, 1925.
Bowles, N. L.: Thoughts on the Education of the Poor. London, 1820.
Birchenough, C.: History of Elementary Education in England and Wales from 1800 to the present day. London, 1938, 3rd ed.
Boyd, R.: History of the Coal Trade. London, 1892.
Boyd, R. W.: Coal Mines inspection: its History and Results. London, 1879.
Briggs, Asa (ed.): Chartist Studies. Macmillan, 1959.
Brooke, E. H.: Monograph on the Tinplate works of Great Britain. 1932.
Browing, L.: History of Blaenavon. 1906.
Bruce, Henry Austin (Lord Aberdare): On Amusements, as the Means of Continuing and Extending the Education of the Working Classes. Cardiff, 1850.
ibid. The Present Condition and Future Prospects of the Working Classes . . . in South Wales, 1851. Reprinted in Lectures and Addresses, London, 1896.
Buer, M.: Health, Wealth, and Population, 1760-1815. London, 1926.
Carter, Harold: The Towns of Wales. Cardiff, University of Wales Press, 1965.
Chappell, E. L.: Historic Melingriffith. Cardiff, 1940.
Clapham, J. H.: An Economic History of Modern Britain, Vol. 1, Cambridge, 1930.
Clarke, T. E.: A Guide to Merthyr Tydfil. Merthyr Tydfil, 1848.
Clarke, W. K. L.: A Short History of the S.P.C.K. London, 1919.

BIBLIOGRAPHY

Clement, Mary: The S.P.C.K. and Wales, 1699-1740: the history of the S.P.C.K. in Wales from its foundation to the early years of the Welsh Methodist movement. London, 1954.
ibid. Correspondence and Minutes of the S.P.C.K. relating to Wales, 1699-1740 (ed). Board of Celtic Studies, University of Wales, History and Law Series, No. 10, Cardiff, 1952.
Cliffe, C. F.: The Book of South Wales, 1848.
Cole, G. D. H.: Life of Robert Owen. London, 1925.
Couling, S.: Our Labouring Classes: their Intellectual, Moral, and Social Condition Considered. London, 1851.
Coxe, William: A Historical Tour of Monmouthshire, London, 1801.
Craik, H.: The State and Education. London, 1884.
Davies, D. J.: Economic History of South Wales prior to 1800. Cardiff, 1933.
Davies, E.: Hanes Porthmadog. Caernarfon, 1913.
Davies, E. T.: Religion in the Industrial Revolution in South Wales, University of Wales Press, Cardiff, 1965.
Davies, W.: Agriculture and Domestic Economy of South Wales, Vols. 1 and 2. London, 1815.
Dawes, R.: Observations on the Working of the Government Scheme of Education. London, 1849.
Dobbs, A. E.: Education and Social Movements, 1700-1850. London, 1919.
Dodd, A. H.: The Industrial Revolution in North Wales, 2nd ed, Cardiff, 1951.
Dufton, J.: National Education, London, 1847.
Dunlop, O. J. and Deman, R. D.: English Apprenticeship and Child Labour. London, 1912.
Edmunds, W.: Traethawd ar Hanes Plwyf Merthyr. Merthyr, 1864.
Edwards, H.: Elementary Education: the Importance of its Extension in our own Country. London, 1844.
Elsas, M. (ed.): Iron in the Making. Dowlais Iron Co., Letters, 1782-1800. Cardiff, 1960.
Engles, Friedrich: Condition of the Working Class in England, translated and edited by W. O. Henderson and W. H. Chaloner, Oxford, 1958.
Evans, Benjamin: Bywgraffiad y diweddar Barch. T. Price, Aberdar. Aberdare, 1891.
Evans, D.: The Sunday Schools of Wales. London, 1883.
Evans, J.: Some Account of the Welsh Charity Schools and the rise and progress of Methodism in Wales through the means of them, under the sole management of Griffith Jones, Clerk, Rector of Llanddowror in Carmarthenshire, etc., London, 1752.
Evans, J.: History, Antiquities, and Customs of South Wales. 1803.
Evans, John and Britton, John: A Topographical and Historical Description of the County of Monmouth. London, 1809.
Evans, Leslie Wynne: Ironworks Schools in South Wales, 1784-1860. Sociological Review, xliii.
ibid. Schools established by Industrial Undertakings in Caernarvonshire and Merionethshire during the nineteenth century. Trans. Caerns. Hist. Soc. 1954.
ibid. Bron y Foel School, Caernarvonshire, ibid, 1955.
ibid, Voluntary Education in the Industrial Areas of Wales before 1870. N.L.W. Journal, xiv, 4, 1966.
ibid. School Boards and the Works Schools System after 1870, ibid, xv, 1, 1967.
Evans, T.: Cambrian Itinerary. 1801.
Evans, Thomas: The Background of Modern Welsh Politics, 1789-1846. Cardiff, 1936.
Fay, C. R.: Life and Labour in the Nineteenth Century. Cambridge, 1920.
ibid. Great Britain from Adam Smith to the Present Day. London, 1928.
Fenton, R.: Tours in Wales, 1804-13. 1917 ed.
Flower, P. W.: A History of the Trade in Tin. London, 1880.
Floud, J. E.: Social Class and Educational Opportunity. London, 1956.
Freidlander, D. and Roshier, R. J.: A study of internal migration in England and Wales: Part 1, *Population Studies*, 19, 1966.
Francis, A.: History of the Cardiganshire mines. 1874.

BIBLIOGRAPHY

Francis, G. Grant: The Smelting of Copper in the Swansea District. 2nd ed. London, 1881.
Fraser, W.: The State of our Educational Enterprises. 1858.
Fredriksson, V. (ed.): Svenska folkskolans historia, under redaktion av. (History of the Elementary School in Sweden), Albert Bonniers forlag, Stockholm, 1940.
Gaskell, P.: Artizans and Machinery: the Moral and Physical Condition of the Manufacturing Population. London, 1836.
Gibbins, H. de B.: English Social Reformers, 2nd ed., 1902.
ibid. Industrial History of England, Revised ed., 1926.
Giffen, R.: Progress of the Working Class in the Last Half-Century. London, 1884.
Grant, P.: History of Factory Legislation. London, 1866.
Gray, K.: History of English Philanthropy. 1905.
Gregory, R.: Elementary Education: Some Account of its Rise and Progress in England. 1895.
Griffith, D. M.: Nationality in the Sunday School Movement. Bangor, 1925.
Griffith, Parch D.: Yr Ysgol Sabbathol a'r Oes. Wrecsam, 1858.
Hamilton, H.: The English Brass and Copper Industries to 1800. London, 1926.
Hammond, J. L. and B.: The Rise of Modern Industry. London, 1926.
ibid. The Age of the Chartists. London, 1930.
Heckscher, F.: Svenskt arbete och liv (Swedish work and life). Stockholm, 1941.
Hicks, W. R. C.: The Education of the Half-Timer, Econ. Hist., February, 1939.
Hill, F.: National Education. London, 1836.
Holman, H.: English National Education. London, 1898.
Horner, L.: On the Employment of Children in Factories. London, 1840.
Hughes, H. D.: Hynafiaethau Llandegai a Llanllechid. Bethesda, 1866.
Hutchins, B. L. and Harrison, A.: A History of Factory Legislation. 3rd ed., London, 1926.
Inglis, K. S.: Churches and the Working Classes in Victorian England. London, 1963.
James, J. Spinther: Hanes y Bedyddwyr yng Nghymru. 4 cyfrol, Caerfyrddin, 1893-1907.
James, L.: A Short History of Elementary Education in South Wales. Llanelli, 1904.
Jenkins, R. T.: Hanes Cymru yn y Ddeunawfed Ganrif. Caerdydd, 1931. ibid: Hanes Cymru yn y Bedwaredd Ganrif ar Bymtheg. Cyf. I, 1789-1843. Caerdydd, 1933.
Johansson, H.: Den svensksa socknen under 1700—talet (The Swedish Parish in the Eighteenth Century). Tome 7, Svenska folket genom tiderna. Malmo, 1938.
John, A. H.: The Industrial Development of South Wales, 1750-1850. Cardiff, 1950.
Jones, David: Hanes y Bedyddwyr yn Neheubarth Cymru. Caerfyrddin, 1839.
Jones, Edmund: A Geographical, Historical, and Religious Account of the Parish of Aberystruth. Trevecka, 1779.
Jones, E. (Ieuan Gwynedd): The Dissent and Morality of Wales. London, 1847.
ibid. A Vindication of the Educational and Moral Conditions of Wales. London, 1848.
ibid. Facts and Figures in Support. London, 1849.
Jones, E. D.: Mackworth and the S.P.C.K. N.L.W. Journal, V.iii. 1953-54. ibid: The Journal of William Roberts (Nefydd), (ed.), viii, 1953-54; ix, 1955-56; x, 1957-8.
Jones, G. J.: Winning poem on Hafod schools, Morriston Eisteddfod, 26th September, 1854.
Jones, Idwal: The Voluntary System at Work. Trans. Cymm. Soc., 1931-32.
Jones, J. Clifford: A History of the Schools and Education in Buckley. Flintshire Hist. Soc. Pubns. xv, 1954-55.
Jones, J. S.: A History of Rhymney and Pontlottyn. Denbigh, 1904.
Jones, M. G.: The Charity School Movement in the Eighteenth Century. Cambridge, 1938.
Jones, R. W.: Bywyd Cymdeithasol Cymru yn y Ddeunawfed Ganrif. 1931.
Jones, Theophilus: A History of the County of Brecknock, Vols. I and II, 1805-9. 2nd ed., Brecon, 1898.
Jones, R. J. (Alltud Eifion): Y Gestiana, sef Hanes Tre'r Gest. Tremadoc, 1892.
Jones, W. H.: A History of the Port of Swansea. Carmarthen, 1922.

BIBLIOGRAPHY

Jones, J.: Traethawd ar Ddysgeidiaeth . . . London, 1837.
Jones-Roberts, K. W.: Education in the parish of Ffestiniog. Jnl. Mer. Hist. and Rec. Soc., ii, 1956.
Kay-Shuttleworth, J.: Four Periods of Public Education. London, 1862.
ibid. Public Education as affected by the Minutes of the Committee. London, 1853.
Keeling, F.: Child Labour in the United Kingdom. London, 1914.
Kenrick, G. S.: The Population of Pontypool and the Parish of Trevethin. London, 1840.
Knowles, L.: Industrial and Commercial Revolutions in Great Britain in the Nineteenth Century. London, 1921.
Lancaster, Joseph: Improvements in Education as it Respects the Industrious Classes of the Community, etc., London, 1803.
ibid: Outline of a Plan for Educating Ten Thousand Poor Children. London, 1806.
ibid: The British System of Education, London, 1810.
Levi, T.: Canmlwyddiant Ysgol Sabbothol Cymru. London, 1885.
Lewis, E. D.: The Rhondda Valleys. London, 1959.
Lewis, Henry: Ysgolion Brutanaidd Arfon. 'Cymru', 1912.
Lewis, J.: The Swansea Guide . . . Swansea, 1851.
Llewellin, William: Iron and Wire Works of Tintern. Arch. Camb. III, ix, 291.
Lloyd, J.: The Early History of the South Wales Ironworks. London, 1906.
Lloyd, J. E. (ed.): A History of Carmarthenshire, Vol. II, Cardiff, 1939.
Low, S. and Sanders, L. C.: The History of England During the Reign of Victoria. London, 1907.
Ludlow, J. M. and Lloyd Jones: Progress of the Working-classes, 1832-1867, London, 1867.
Mackworth, H.: A Familiar Discourse concerning the Mine Adventure. 1700.
Maclure, J. S.: Educational Documents, England and Wales, 1816-1963, First ed., 1965.
Malkin, B. H.: The Scenery, Antiquities, and Biography of South Wales. 2 Vols., London, 1807. Reprinted, S. & R. Publishers, Wakefield, Yorkshire, 1970.
Mann, H.: Educational Census, 1851. London, 1852.
Mantoux, P.: The Industrial Revolution in the Eighteenth Century. London, 1961.
Meade, R.: The Coal and Iron Industries of the United Kingdom. London, 1882.
Morgan, K. O.: Wales in British Politics, 1868-1922. Cardiff, 1963.
Morris, D.: Hanes Tredegar o Ddechreuad y Gwaith Haiarn hyd yn Bresenol. 1868.
Morris, J. H. and Williams, L. J.: The South Wales Coal Industry, 1841-1875. Cardiff, 1958.
Musgrave, P. W. (ed): Sociology, History and Education, London, 1970.
Newcombe, R.: National Schools in North Wales: A Sermon preached in the Cathedral Church of Bangor on September 11th, 1821, on behalf of the Bangor Diocesan Schools by Richard Newcome, M.A., Warden of Ruthin, Canon of Bangor, etc., Denbigh, 1821.
Norberg, P.: Avesta Skola, Stockholm, 1924.
North, F. J.: The Slates of Wales. 3rd ed., Cardiff, 1946.
O'Brien, J.: Old Afan and Margam. Port Talbot, 1926.
Owen, Evan: Workmen's Libraries in Glamorgan and Monmouthshire. Cardiff, 1895.
Owen, Robert: A New View of Society and Other Writings. Everyman Library, 1927 ed.
Parry, Edward: Llawlyfr ar Hanes y Diwygiadau Crefyddol yng Nghymru. Corwen, 1898.
Parry, G. T.: Llanberis, ei Hanes, ei Phobl, a'i Phethau. Caernarfon, 1908.
Parry, O.: Y Dosbarth Gweithiol yng Nghymru. Caerfyrddin, 1865.
Parry, W. J.: Chwareli a Chwarelwyr Caernarfon. Caernarfon, 1897.
Pennant, T.: Parishes of Whiteford and Holywell. London, 1796.
Phillips, E.: A History of the Pioneers of the Welsh Coalfield. Cardiff, 1925.
Phillips, D. R.: The History of the Vale of Neath. Swansea, 1925.
Phillips, Thomas: Wales: the Language, Social Condition, Moral Character, and religious opinions of the people considered in relation to education. London, 1849.
Pollard, Sidney: The Genesis of Modern Management: A Study of the Industrial Revolution in Great Britain, London, 1965.
Powell, D. and E.: The History of Tredegar. Newport, 1902.

BIBLIOGRAPHY

Pritchard, D. Dylan: The Slate Industry of North Wales: a study of changes in economic organisation from 1780 to the present day. Unpublished M.A. thesis, University of Wales, 1935.
Rees, E.: Hanes Brynaman. Ystalyfera, 1883.
Rees, T.: History of Protestant Nonconformity in Wales. London, 1861; enlarged ed., 1883.
Rees, Thomas and Thomas, John: Hanes Eglwysi Annibynol Cymru. 4 cyfrol, Lerpwl, 1871-5; Cyfrol V gan J. Thomas, Dolgellau, 1891.
Rees, William: Industry before the Industrial Revolution, Two Volumes, Cardiff, 1968.
Richard, Henry: Letters on the Social and Political Conditions of the Principality of Wales. London, n.d.
Richards, D. M.: Aberdare in 1837. Aberdare, 1897.
Richards, Thomas: The Puritan Movement in Wales, 1639-53. London, 1920.
ibid. Religious Developments in Wales, 1654-62. London, 1923.
Roberts, O. O.: Addysg yng Nghogledd Cymru. Caernarfon, 1847.
Roberts, R. Owen: Ysgol weithfaol yr Hafod gan mlynedd yn ol. 'Yr Athro', Mehefin-Gorffennaf, 1952.
Robson, A. H.: The Education of Children Engaged in Industry in England, 1833-1876. London, 1931.
Roderick, A. J. (ed.): Wales through the Ages, Vol. II. Llandybie, 1960.
Scott, W. R. The Constitution and Finance of Joint-Stock Companies to 1720. Vols. 1 and 2, London, 1912.
Senior, N. W.: Suggestions on Popular Education. London, 1861.
Shankland, Thomas: John Myles. Trafodion Cymdeithas Hanes Bedyddwyr Cymru, 1910-22.
Silver, Harold: The Concept of Popular Education: a Study of Ideas and Social Movements in the Early Nineteenth Century. London, 1965.
Simon, Brian: Studies in the History of Education 1780-1870. London, Reprint, 1964.
ibid. Education and the Labour Movement. London, 1965.
Skeats, H. S.: Popular Education in England: being an Abstract of the Report of the Royal Commissioners on Education. London, 1861.
Smelser, N. J.: Social change in the Industrial Revolution, London, 1959.
Smith, Frank: A History of English Elementary Education, 1760-1902. London, 1931.
Spurrell, W.: Carmarthen and its Neighbourhood. 2nd ed., Carmarthen, 1879.
Taylor, W. C.: Factories and the Factory System. London, 1844.
Thomas, Brinley: The migration of labour into the Glamorgan Coalfield, *Economica*, 10, 1930.
Thompson, E. P.: The Making of the English Working Class. London, 1963.
Trevelyan, G. M.: British History in the Nineteenth Century. London, 1922.
University College, Swansea, Faculty of Education: Pioneers of Welsh Education. Four Lectures, Session 1961-62.
Waller, W.: The Answer of Mr. Waller to Mr. Hawkins' Report Given in at the General Court of the Governour and Company of the Mine Adventure of England, December 15th, 1709. London, 1710.
Ward, Gertrude: The Education of Factory Child Workers 1833-1850. (Econ. Journal Supplement, February, 1935).
Warne, A.: Den svenska folkundervisningen fran reformationen till 1809 (Swedish Popular Education from the Reformation to 1809). Stockholm, 1940.
Warner, J.: Local Government in Newport, 1835-1935. Newport, 1935.
Wilkins, C.: The South Wales Coal Trade and its Allied Industries from the Earliest Days to the Present Time. Cardiff, 1888.
ibid. History of the Iron, Steel, Tinplate, and other Trades of Wales. Merthyr Tydfil, 1903.
ibid. The History of Merthyr Tydfil, new ed., Merthyr Tydfil, 1908.
Williams, David: John Frost: A Study of Chartism. Cardiff, 1939.
ibid. Modern Wales. London, 1950.
ibid: The Rebecca Riots, Cardiff, 1955.

BIBLIOGRAPHY

Williams, D.: Monmouthshire. London, 1796.
Williams, G. J.: Hanes Plwyf Ffestiniog o'r Cyfnod Boreuaf. Wrecsam, 1882.
Williams, J. R. D.: Parish of Rhymney, Mon., Centenary, 1843-1943. Cardiff, 1943.
Williams, James: Traethawd buddugol ar arferion drwg ieuenctyd y gweithfeydd, a'r moddion goreu i'w diwygio. Merthyr, 1860.
Williams, Raymond: Culture and Society, 1780-1950, Penguin Books, 1963.
Williams, W.: An Examination of the Principles on which the British and Foreign School Society is Established. London, 1823.
Wing, C.: Evils of the Factory System. London, 1837.
Wyse, T.: Education Reform: or the necessity of a National System of Education. London, 1836.

F. BIBLIOGRAPHIES

Blackwell, H.: Bibliography of Local and County Histories. Old Welsh Chips, Brecon, 1888.
Jenkins, R. T. and Rees, William (ed.): A Bibliography of the History of Wales, Cardiff, 1931.
Second Edition, Cardiff, 1962.
Supplement I, 1963, offprinted from The Bulletin of the Board of Celtic Studies, Vol. 20, Part 2, May, 1963.
Rees, J. F. and Rees, William: A Select Bibliography of the Economic History of Wales. Economic History Review, ii, No. 2, January, 1930.
Rowlands, W.: Llyfryddiaeth y Cymry. ed. Silvan Evans, Llanidloes, 1869.

Index

Aberavon, 62, 67, 159, 243, 292, 326.
Abercrave, 44, 161, 292, 309.
Abercwmboi, 185.
Aberdare, 25, 37, 41, 59, 109, 172, 179, 182, 246-249, 272, 322; Free Schools, 172, 182.
Aberdare, Lord (Henry Austin Bruce), 183, 183n.
Aberdulais, 158, 160, 326.
Abergavenny, 176.
Aberkenfig, 61.
Abersychan, 26, 46, 51, 52, 288, 289, 321.
Abertillery (Blaenau Gwent), 236.
Aberystruth, 53; school board, 324.
Act of Union, iv.
Acrefair, 208.
Adamson, J. W., 2n, 283n, 317n, 318n.
Adolescence, 257.
Adult Education (see also schools), 57, 257ff.
Allendale, v.
Alston Moor, v.
American West, 235.
Amlwch, 222.
Amman, 37, 162, 242.
Amman Ironworks, 287.
Amman Ironworks British School, 37, 68-69, 70n, 162n.
Ammanford, 121.
Anglesey, 205, 207.
Anglican, 29, 39, 60, 66, 205, 236, 299, 307, 309, 311, 334.
Annual Reports—National Society, 16n, 17n, 39n, 50n, 176n; British and Foreign School Society, 18n, 29n, 128n, 208n, 212n, 213n, 214n, 216n, 221n, 306n, 307n, 314n.
Apprentices, 213, 221, 263, 267, 276, 310, 335; education of, 221.
Arfon District, 209.
Armenschulen, v.
Armytage, W. H. G., 65n, 97n.
Arnold, Matthew, 60, 61n, 65, 290, 291n, 336.
Ashley, Lord, 277.
Assistant Teachers, 263.
Associated Miners of Cornwall, 124.
Atkinson & Barrow, 50.

Attainment, 39, 96, 132, 135-136, 171, 219, 221, 246, 262, 265, 268, 272, 273, 283.
Attendance, 21, 22, 24n, 43, 47, 48, 63, 66, 100, 101, 105, 106, 108, 127, 128, 134, 135, 159-160, 161, 162, 171, 172, 176, 205-206, 208, 217, 219, 220, 221, 222, 232, 237, 239, 240ff, 252, 257ff, 267, 293, 294, 315, 316, 322ff.
Avesta (School), iv.

Bagillt, 208, 210.
Bailey, Crawshay, 172, 182.
Bailey, Joseph, 43.
Bainbridge, R. W., v.
Bala, 208, 258.
Bangor, 205, 209, 210, 218, 219, 252; Girls' School, 210, Boys' School, 210, British School, 221, Dean of, 219; Normal College, 162, 206, 209; Sunday schools, 252.
Bank of England, 64, 65.
Banwen, 99, 292.
Baptists, 182, 210, 232, 237, 243, 244, 246, 305, 334.
Barnard, H. C., 2n.
Barry, Sir Charles, 97, 289.
Battersea Training School, 97.
Beaufort, 27, 236.
Beaufort, Duke of, 124.
Beaumont, Wentworth Blackett, M.P., v.
Bedwellty, 23, 48, 176; School Board 323.
Bellairs, Rev. W. H. 96, 269.
Belsey, F. F., 251.
Bernard, Sir Thomas, 3.
Bersham, 211.
Bessborough, Earl of: 58n, 97n, 100n, 102n, 103n.
Bethel British School, 221.
Bethesda, 217, 252; Quarry band, 220.
Bevan, Madame, 2.
Bible Society, 174, 233.
Bible Study, 251.
Biddulph, Mr. J., 65.
Biddulph, Col. Myddleton, 211.
Birchgrove, 127.
Birmingham, 133.
Blackboard lessons, 251.
Blackwood, 26.
Black Boy Colliery, (Darlington) v.
Blaenau Ffestiniog, 214.

351

INDEX

Blaenavon, 25, 26, 37, 38, 43, 235, 259 271, 290.
Blaenavon Church School, 39n.
Blaengarw School, (1833), 183.
Blaengwrach, 42, 239, 244.
Blaenau Gwent, (Abertillery, qv), 236.
Blaenycwm, 327.
Blaina, 26, 53, 54, 259, 267, 287;
Blaina school, 54; ironworks, 54; British school, 54.
Blaina & Cwmcelyn Co., 54.
Blue Books (1847) 15, 17n, 18n, 19n, 26, 38n, 39n, 40n, 41n, 43n, 45n, 47n, 48n, 49n, 53, 55n, 56, 59n, 61n, 63n, 67n, 68n, 69n, 70n, 95n, 98n, 123n, 126, 130n, 134n, 135n, 136n, 137n, 158n, 159n, 160n, 171, 172n, 173n, 177, 179n, 205n, 210, 211n, 212, 213n, 214n, 219n, 222n, 235n, 237n, 238n. 239n, 241n, 243n, 245n, 246n, 247n, 260n, 274n, 286, 294n, 296, 297n, 307.
Bodringallt (Ystrad), 180; British School, (1861), 180.
Bonsall, Sir Thomas, 136.
Booker, S. W., 43.
Booker, Thomas W., 159.
Boys' Brigade, 251.
Bowring, Dr., M.P., 60.
Bowstead, Joseph, 45n, 68, 129n, 172, 231, 232, 239, 253, 269, 292n, 298, 299, 309, 315.
Breconshire, 25, 26, 37, 46, 53, 54, 68, 131, 173, 287, 314, 315, 323.
Bridgend, 67.
Bristol, 40, 70.
Bristol Co. Steamers, 41, 274.
British and Foreign Bible Society, 233.
British and Foreign School Society (1814), 18, 20, 28, 29, 44, 48, 53, 106 108, 126, 128n, 131, 158, 161, 172, 176, 177, 178, 180, 182, 203, 204, 205, 206, 207, 208, 210, 211, 212, 213, 214, 216, 220, 221n, 231, 245, 300, 305, 306, 307n, 308-309, 312 314ff.
British Iron Co. (Abersychan), 51, 52, 78, 79.
British Ironworks School (Rhymney), 48.
Brooke, E. H., 60n, 62n, 69n, 159n, 160n, 161n.
Bron y Foel School, 220.
Broughton, 211.
Brymbo, 210, 211.
Bryn, 288, 321; Bryn School, 62, 66.
Brynamman Ironworks School, 69; Tinworks School, 69.

Bryndu, 26, 67; colliery, 287.
Brynmawr, 27.
Buckley, 212.
Budd, James Palmer, 59, 160.
Buildings (schools), 15, 26, 27, 29, 39, 44, 49, 52, 59, 104, 126, 133, 135, 209, 218.
Building Fund, 210.
Burry Port, 157.
Bute, Marquis of, 25, 172, 178, 182.

Cadoxton, 134.
Caernarvon British School, 182.
Caernarvonshire, 122, 176, 204, 205, 207, 208, 209, 212, 214, 217, 220, 252, 263, 287.
Caerwys, 212.
Caird, Edward, 162.
Calvinistic Methodists, 29, 204, 205, 208, 209, 210, 211, 222, 232, 233, 234, 237, 246, 307, 333; connexion meetings, 208.
Cambrian Education Society, 208.
Cambrian Co. (Maesteg), 60-61.
Cambrian, The 63n, 307n.
Canford Manor (Poole), 97.
Capel Als, Llanelli, 244, 307.
Capel Waun y Pound, 9, 25, 37, 50, 292.
Cardiff, 25, 43, 172.
Cardigan, 159.
Cardiganshire, 6, 8, 43, 122, 135, 249.
Carmarthen 158, 159, Tinworks, 160.
Carmarthenshire, 10, 19, 26, 121, 122, 157, 186, 242, 268, 287, 312, 314, 315.
Carmel (Flints.), 212.
Carneddi (Bethesda), 209.
Carneddi British School, 221.
Carr, J. M., 128.
Carter, H., 58n, 235n, 248n.
Casson family, 215, 216.
Catechism, 171, 211, 221, 309, 311.
Census Returns, 47n, 95n, 122n, 129n, 239n, 240, 248n.
Chambers Edinburgh Journal, 122n, 125n.
Charity School Movement, 1, 243.
Charles, Rev. Thomas, 2, 175n, 178, 233, 253.
Chappell, E. L., 158n.
Chartered Companies of the Mines Royal; Mineral and Battery Works, iv.
Chartist Movement, 18, 25, 27, 126, 173, 174, 235.
Child labour, 20ff, 263ff, 317ff.
Child savings, 216.

352

INDEX

Children's Employment Commission, 277.
Chirk, 211.
Chirk Charity School, 211.
Choirs, 252.
Chwarel y Cae, 219.
Cilgwyn Co., 220.
Cilybebyll (Crynant), 25; colliery school, 173.
Circulating Schools, 1, 9, 233.
Clark, G. T., 25n, 104, 291.
Clark, T. E., 95n.
Clydach, Breconshire, 27, 37, 68, 70, 173, 179, 185.
Clydach Vale, 295, 327; British school (1872), 181.
Colston School (Bristol), 40, 41n.
Cockett, 127.
Coegnant Infants School, 185.
Coffin, Walter, 172.
Collections, 209, 210, 222.
Collieries Act, (1843), 277, 278; (1861) 277; (1862) 262.
Colliers and Miners School (Hirwaun, 1820), 171.
Combined schools, 311.
Commissioners (Mines, 1846) 60n; (Mines, 1861) 24; (Education) 19n, 22, 47, 98, 124, 130, 136, 211, 212, 213, 221; Commissioners Reports, Mines: 19n, 25, 27, 38, 44, 50n, 52n, 57n, 60n, 61n, 62n, 63n, 64n, 65n, 69n, 95n, 99n, 108n, 123n, 127n, 176n, 179n, 243n, 259n, 268n, 273n, 276n, 277n. *See also* entries under 'Blue Books', Newcastle Commission, Pakington Select Committee.
Committee of the Privy Council on Education, 4, 15, 16n, 19n, 23n, 28n, 38n, 40n, 42n, 44n, 47n, 48n, 49n, 50n, 52, 54, 55n, 57n, 58, 61n, 63, 66, 67n, 96n, 97n, 98n, 99n, 100n, 102n, 103n, 104n, 105n, 107n, 108n, 110n, 123, 126, 127, 128n, 131n, 133n, 134, 135n, 158n, 159n, 161n, 162, 171n, 173, 175n, 176, 185, 186n, 216, 217n, 220n, 231, 232n, 240, 241n, 257n, 258n, 260n, 271n, 285n, 286, 287, 292n, 295n, 297n, 305, 306, 309n, 310, 311, 312n, 313, 315n, 318n, 319n, 320n, 321, 322n, 323n, 324n.
Comprehensive schools, 311.
Compulsory contributions, (*see also* Poundage), 8, 24, 28, 29, 41, 42, 44, 56, 123, 126, 130, 160, 180, 219.
Compulsory education, 3, 22n, 51, 265, 311, 312, 333.

Consett Iron and Coal Co., v, 277.
Co-operative stores, 174.
Coppleston, Bishop, 174.
Côr Caradog, 252.
Cordes, J. J., 54, 271.
Cornwall, 242.
Corwen, 258.
Cotton Co., Mold, 29.
Cotton manufacture, 204, 221.
Council of the Royal Institution of S. Wales, 246.
Court Herbert Colliery School, 129, 186, 295.
Courtybella, 26, 268; Colliery School, 174, 176.
Cradle Roll, 251.
Crane, George, 43, 44, 68.
Crane, Moira (Cwmtwrch Colliery) 178.
Crawshay, F., 41, 96, 171.
Crawshay, Robert, 56, 178.
Crickhowell, 323.
Crimean War, 231.
Crown Copperworks (Neath), 121.
Crown Copper and Spelter Works, (Neath), 134.
Cuba, 242.
Cumberland, v, 5.
Curriculum, 3, 8, 23, 43, 59, 63, 97, 98, 105, 132, 171, 175, 218, 219, 221, 222, 239, 244, 251, 273, 275, 276, 283ff.
Cwmavon, 16, 17, 26, 56, 62, 65, 66, 121, 157, 239, 243, 260, 261, 266, 273, 274, 277, 284, 286, 287, 290, 295, 299, 311, 321.
Cwmbran, 51, 287, 288.
Cwmcelyn British School, 54.
Cwmllynfell, 178.
Cwmparc British School, (1871) 181, 182.
Cwmpennar, 183.
Cymro, Y, 220n.
Cwmtwrch, 178.
Cwmyglo British School, 220.
Cyfarthfa, 56, 57, 95, 271, 322, 326; school, 259.

Dafen, 158, 161, 287, 326.
Dafen tinworks, 287.
Dalarna, v.
Daniel, Alfred, 132.
Daniel, Benjamin, 179.
Darby of Sirhowy, 37, 50, 290.
Darby, W. H., 211.
Darbishire, Col. W. A., 217.
Dare Collieries, 181ff.
David, Morgan, 172.

INDEX

Davies, David, Ocean Collieries, 181ff.
Davies, Rev. Owen, 137n.
Davies, W. E., 206n.
Davis, Robins, 273.
Davy, Sir Humphrey, 125.
Day release, 102.
Democracy (*see also* workers' control), 233, 234.
Denbigh, 203, 205, 208, 209, 210, 220.
Department of Science and Art, 270.
Dinas, Rhondda, 25, 172, 180, 295; Boys School, (1845), 173; Girls' School (1838), 173.
Dinorwic, 209, 220; quarries, 214, 220.
Diphwys Quarry, and Diphwys Casson, 215.
Discipline, 43, 97.
Dissenters, 39, 48, 49, 136, 171, 204, 205, 211, 213, 214, 216, 232, 236, 243, 305, 306, 307, 309, 315.
Dissenting Sunday Schools, 232, 236.
Diocesan Education Boards, 15, 18.
Diwygiwr, Y, 308n, 309n.
Dolbadarn British School, 220.
Dolgellau 258, 265; British School 216.
Dodd, A. H., 203n, 217n, 221n.
Dos Nailworks School (1848), 54, 55, 274.
Dowlais, vii, 16, 24, 25, 37, 42, 56, 57, 58, 95, 96n, 99, 169; Dowlais Iron Co., 57, 95ff, 96n, 169, 183, 235, 236; schools, 95ff, 110n, 237, 239, 260, 262, 263, 266, 267, 268, 270, 271, 274, 283, 284, 285, 286, 297, 288, 289, 291, 292, 295, 297, 300, 310, 312, 320, 321, 322; Catholics, 106.
Druce, Mr., 130.
Duffryn, 173; Colliery Schools, 109, 182, 262, 272n, 278; National school, 183-184, 262n;
Duncan & Co., (Llancaiach), 197.
Dunraven, 180; Colliery School 327;
Dunraven British School, 180, 182.
Durham, v, 268, 277.
Dutchmen, ivn.
Dyhewid (Llantwit Faerdre) Colliery School, 186.

Ebbw Vale 19, 37, 52, 53, 236, 270, 284, 289, 299, 312.
Education Acts, 1870: viii, 4, 22, 157, 170, 209, 247, 250, 265, 278, 279, 311, 319, 324, 333, 334, 336; 1878: 279; 1880: 279, 318n; 1891: 319, 320; 1899: 333; 1902: 319, 327, 333, 335.

Education Authorities (Part 3), 319.
Education Bill (1820), 4; (1855), 317.
Education census, 47.
Education Department (1856), 4, 206.
Education of Factory Children's Bill, (1843), 21.
Education fund, 176; Inquiry, (1833) 18, 38n, 39n, 42n, 63n, 64n, 123n, 125n, 158n, 159n, 171n, 244n.; part time education, 22; education tax, 290, 335; technical education, 274ff; educational testing, 267.
Edwards, William, HMI, 110, 301, 325n.
Eglwysilan, 159
Elementary education, (*see also* schools), 2, 10, 15, 17, 18, 42.
Elizabeth I, 5.
Elliot, Sir George, 185n; school, 185n.
Endowed Schools, (*see also* schools—grammar), 39.
Enlightened employers of labour, vii.
English Copper Co., 62, 63, 64, 66, 67, 157, 274.
Eryri, 204
Escomb ironworks school (Durham) v.
Esgair Hir, 6-8, 135.
Established Church, 18, 28, 205, 232, 233.
Evans, Daniel, 19n, 26n.
Evans, J. J. 175n.
Examinations, 132, 267, 275.

Factory Acts, ii, 4, 20, 21, 22, 221; 1802, 20; 1819, 20; 1833, 20, 21, 221, 222; 1844, 21; 1860, 21; Extension's Act (1867), 22, 278.
Factory Bill (1843), 25, 213, 306, 307.
Factory schools, ii, 21, 26.
Faraday, Sir Michael, 125.
Felinfoel, 244.
Ferndale, 179; British school 179; colliery school, 325, 327.
Ffestiniog, 213, 214, 215, 258; School Board, 319; Slate Quarries British School, 216.
Ffynongroew, 212.
Field Quarry, 219.
Feilding, Viscount, 212.
Finlay, Mrs., 127.
Fireman's School, (Hirwaun), 41, 171.
Fletcher, Mr. J., 216n.
Flintshire, 29, 203, 205, 210, 211, 220, 221.
Ford, H. H., 67, 179.
Francis, A., 136n.
Freeman, Charles, 57.
Freeman, John, 122.

INDEX

French, 285.
Frere, Cook & Powell, 70.
Frost, John, 16, 243.
Furnace School, (Hirwaun), 41.
Further Education, 257ff.

Gambier, T. C., 285.
Garth, 222.
Garw Collieries, 295; Garw Valley, 179, 182.
Gelli, 179.
Gellifaelog, 99, 288.
Gelligaer, 26, 179, 324.
George, David Lloyd, 251, 335.
Georgetown National School, (1843), 58, 271.
Gerlan School, 218.
Germany, iv, 124, 284; education system in, 97.
Gibea Chapel, Brynamman, 69.
Gilbertson, W., 63, 266.
Gilfach Goch, 295; Colliery school, 185.
Girls' Brigade, 251.
Glamorgan, 6, 8, 16, 25, 26, 30, 37, 67, 157, 170, 171, 172, 174, 178, 185, 231, 234, 259, 261, 287, 312, 314, 315, 321, 324.
Glamorgan Ironworks Schools, 273.
Glamorgan Coal Co., 181.
Glais School, 162.
Glanogwen, 218.
Gloddaith, 122.
Gloddaith Lead Mines, 137.
Gloucester, 53, 236.
Glyncorrwg, 42, 239, 241.
Glyn Neath, 239.
Glyn Tâf, 67.
Goat Street School (Swansea), 40.
Goginan, 122, 135, 137.
Goginan Lead and Silver Mining Co., 136.
Gorseinon, 25, 172.
Gorseinon Girls' and Boys' School, (1846), 172.
Gouge, Thomas, 1n; Gouge Trust, 1.
Government grants, 21, 27, 28, 44, 48, 49, 52, 176, 306, 308, 309, 334n.
Gower, 244.
Grading, 97.
Graham, Sir James, 21, 25, 126, 213, 306, 307.
Graigddu, 172.
Grammar School (Swansea), 243.
Gray, James Rosewarne, 110.
Great Exhibition, 231.
Great Orme Copper Mines, 137.

Grenfell Copperworks, 261.
Grenfell, Pascoe St. Leger, 27, 122, 126.
Greenwich, 215.
Guarantee Fund or Grant, 295, 298.
Guest, Lady Charlotte (and Schreiber), 42ff, 58, 95, 182, 300; Sir John (d. 1852), 37, 42, 57, 95ff, 126, 182, 289; Ironworks Schools, 95ff, 237; Education Scheme, 99, 107, 123, 182.
Guppy, T. R., 63.
Gwaunadda, 172.
Gwendraeth, 37, 58, 242.
Gwernllwyn, 99, 288.
Gwyn, Howell, 173.
Gwynne, Richard, 123n.
Gwyrfai, (Rural District), 252.

Hafod, (Swansea), 3, 123, 124ff, 169, 271, 284, 287, 289, 292, 295, 307, 312, 320, 321, Copperworks School (Swansea), 122, 124, 126n, 127n, 128n, 169, 246, 324.
Half Day Pupils, 54.
Halkin, 212.
Hamilton, H., 124n.
Hanbury, Capel (of Pontypool), 70.
Hansard, 126n.
Harford, John, 43, 50, 158, 159.
Harford, Samuel, 159.
Harford & Bailey, 37.
Harries, Rev. G., 44.
Harris, H., 173n.
Harwood, Sunday school; Charity school: 233n, 254.
Hawkins, Mr., 7.
Hayle Foundry School (Cornwall), 110.
Health, 16, 40.
Hendy Higher Grade School, 158, 162.
Heolfawr School (Copperworks, Llanelli), 122, 274ff, 131ff.
Heolyfelin (Aberdare), 182.
Hereford, 53.
Hill, Frederick, 284.
Hill, Thomas, 38, 96.
Hill & Hopkins, 37.
Hirst, Matthew, 97, 98, 108, 267.
Hirwaun, 25, 41, 171, 172, 178, 180, 235; British school, 178.
Hogg, Walter, 128.
Holland, iv.
Holland, Samuel, 214, 217.
Holywell, 210, 212, 221.
Home and Colonial Infant School Society, 44.
Home and Colonial Institution, 127, 266.

INDEX

Homfray, Samuel (of Tredegar), 37, 49.
Hood, Archibald, 181.
Hopkins, Samuel, 38.
Hopkins, Sarah, 39.
Howell, T. Jones, 222.
Hubbuck, G. P., 48.
House of Commons, 17, 19.
Housing, 16, 17, 60.
Hughes, Hugh Derfel, 219n.
Humanists, 3.
Humanitarian movement, vi.
Huntingdon, Lady, 246.
Huxley, T. H., 317.

Ilston, 243.
Immigrants, 204, 231, 235.
Independia Fawr, 244.
Independents, 232, 243ff.
Indiscipline, 236.
Inquiry into the State of Education in the Principality (*see* entries under 'Blue Books')
Inspectors of Factories (*see also* Commissioners), 22, 221.
Inspectors of Schools (*see also* Commissioners), 41, 124, 128, 310-311.
Institution for the Formation of Character, 3.
Instruction Society (Blaina), 54.
Ireland, 16.
Irish families in Wales, 235.
Iron and Coalmasters Association, 178.
Iron and Wireworks School (Tintern), 5, 6.
Islington, 207.
Itinerant Masters, 9.
Itinerant Schools, 2.

James & Aubrey, (Cwmllynfell Colliery), 178.
Jenkins, Rev. E., Dowlais, 98.
Jenkins, John, 298, 299.
Jenkins, R. T., 8n, 236n.
Jenkins, William, 28n, 182.
Jersey, Earl of, 178.
Jevons & Wood Co., 42.
John, A. H., 37n, 122n, 169n.
Johnson, H. Vaughan, 212.
Jones, A. Gray, 9n, 37n.
Jones, E. D., 6n.
Jones, Rev. Evan (Ieuan Gwynedd), 307.
Jones, Rev. Griffith, 1, 2, 9, 233.
Jones, Rev. H. Longueville, 57n, 65, 99n, 101, 104n, 106n, 260n.

Jones, Sir Henry, 162.
Jones, Rev. Hughes, Maesteg, 61.
Jones, Idwal, 206n, 208n.
Jones, J. E., 132, 133, 274.
Jones, M. G., 1n, 2n, 3n, 233n.
Jones, M. O., 180.
Jones, Rhys Williams, 19.
Jones, Thomas, 47n, 48n.
Joseph,, T., 182.
Juvenile Clubs, 216.

Kay-Shuttleworth, Dr. (formerly Dr. J. P. Kay), 3, 310, 310n.
Kenfig Hill Colliery School, 186.
Kensington, Science and Art Department, 132, 275.
Kenthouse Lead Works, 124.
Kilvey, (Swansea), 40, 123, 246, 271, 284, 287, 289, 295, 312, 320, 321; Copperworks school, 40, 123, 262.

Laboratory equipment, 98.
Lancaster, Joseph, 9, 158.
Landore, 124.
Lefel Fawr Leadmining Co., 135.
Leigh, C. Hanbury, 52.
Lettsom, S. F., 62.
Liberalism, 2.
Libraries, 42, 49, 52, 60, 64, 174, 220, 272, 276.
Licswm, 212.
Lindsay, Hon. Capt., 134.
Lingen, R. R. W., 316.
Literacy, 233.
Literary Societies, 276.
Liverpool, 214.
Llanaelhaiarn, 220, 271.
Llanberis, 214; British School 220; County Secondary School, 210.
Llancaiach, 179.
Llandaff, 172, 236.
Llanddeinolen, 214.
Llandegai, 214, 284, 292; School, 218.
Llandeilo Fawr School Board, 162.
Llandudno, 25, 122, 137.
Llandwrog, 212.
Llanellen, 176
Llanelli, 10, 25, 27, 121, 129; Free School: 10, 130; 158, 161, 169, 242, 243, 244, 245, 266, 268, 271 274, 275, 284, 285, 287, 289, 292, 295, 307, 312; Copperworks School 121, 319, 321; Higher Grade School, 132; School Board, 133, 321.
Llanelly, (Breconshire), 70, 173.

INDEX

Llanfabon Colliery School, (Gelligaer), 179.
Llan Ffestiniog, 214, 292.
Llangennech National School, 133.
Llangyfelach, 25, 127, 172; Church School, 172.
Llangwm, 215.
Llanidloes, 204, 221.
Llanllechid, 209, 218; British School 221.
Llanpumsaint, 19.
Llanrug, 209.
Llansamlet, 178.
Llantrisant, 172, 178, 247, 248, 323.
Llanwenarth, 236.
Llanwonno, 185, 323.
Llechryd Tinworks, 159.
Llewellyn, Llewellyn, 69, 172.
Llewellyn, William, 160.
Llwynypia, 179, 295, 327; British School, 181.
Llynfi, 26, 60, 61, 268, 290, 321; Iron Co., 60, 61, 185.
Locke, John, vi.
Lock, (Lloc), 212.
London, 37, 40, 173, 207, 275; Borough Road School, 128; Lead Mining Co., v, 336; School Board, 97.
Longe, F. D., 261.
Lords of the Abbey (Neath), 39.
Lowe, Robert, 258, 269.
Luther's catechism, v.

Machen, 25, 43, 176.
Machynlleth, 222.
Mackworth, Sir Humphrey, 1, 6, 7, 8, 9, 10, 121, 135, 169.
Maentwrog, 214.
Maesteg, 26, 37, 60, 67, 134, 179, Merthyr Colliery School, 185, 319 288, 290, 312; Ironworks Schools, 321, 326; Spelter Company, 121.
Maindy Colliery, 181.
Malaren, Lake, v.
Malin and Robinson, 67.
Mann, H., 239.
Mardy, 179.
Margam, 25, 121, 158, 159, 241, 244, 287, 326; Copperworks School 134; Tinworks, 159, 160n.
Marshall & Co. (Shrewsbury), 222.
Mason & Elkington Co., 133.
Mechanics Institutes ii, 52, 65, 68, 276.
Melincrythan, 158, 162.
Melindwr School Board, 137.

Melingriffith, 25, 158, 159.
Menai Straits, 207.
Mancott, 212.
Merthyr, vii, 16, 26, 37, 42, 57, 59, 235, 239, 241, 243, 258, 259, 265, 270, 271, 295, 322; School Board, 110, 320, 322, 326.
Merioneth, 204, 205, 208, 213, 263.
Methodism, 231ff.
Midlands, 37.
Miers, John, 160.
Mines Act, 26, 272, 317.
Mine Adventurers, 1, 6, 7, 8, 136.
Minera, 211.
Mines Regulations, 184.
Mineral and Battery Co., 5, 6.
Miskin Infants School, 109, 183.
Model Schools, 40.
Moeltryfan, 220.
Mold, 29, 212, 220, 221.
Mold Cotton Mill Co., 221.
Monmouthshire, 9, 16, 18, 19, 27, 37, 47, 52, 53, 54, 157, 173, 174, 177, 179, 185, 231, 232, 236, 242, 248, 259, 273, 276, 284, 287, 299, 312, 314, 315, 321, 322; School Board, 176.
Monmouthshire Merlin, 207n, 269n.
Monitorial System, 109, 263, 335.
Montgomeryshire, 204, 205, 221.
Moral standards, 18, 22.
Moravia, 124.
Morfa copperworks, 261; Tinplate works, 161.
Morgan, Robert, 160.
Morning Standard, 123n.
Morris, Rev. William, 28n., 41.
Morris, William, 41.
Mostyn, 212.
Mostyn, Hon. E. M. Lloyd, 212.
Mostyn, Lord, 212.
Motley and Winkworth, 161.
Mountain Ash, 183, 278, 312; Comprehensive School, 183n.
Mundella, A. J., 279, 318n, 323.
Mutual Improvement Societies, 276.
Myles, Rev. John, 243.
Mynyddislwyn, 176.

Nancarrow, George, 261.
Nant, 211.
Nantlle, 214.
Nantyglo, 25, 26, 37, 43, 53, 259, 287, 312.
Nantymoel Colliery School, 186.

INDEX

National Society, 3, 15, 17, 18, 28, 43, 44, 49, 58, 59, 63, 96, 106, 125, 126, 130, 160, 174, 176, 177, 182, 203, 204, 205, 206, 211, 212, 213, 217, 296, 305, 306, 313, 314ff.
National Society Reports, 17n, 39n 50n, 176n.
National Society, Welsh Education Committee, 177.
'National' System, 21, 28, 39, 43, 44, 57, 58, 96, 175, 182, 205, 217.
Neath, 6, 42, 62, 121, 160, 169, 173, 243, 258, 264, 265, 295, 307.
Neath Abbey, 25, 39, 169, 273, 288, 291.
Neath Mechanics Institute, 68.
Nefydd's *Journal*, 45n, 48n, 55n, 66n, 67, 106n, 131n, 135n, 171n, 172n, 178n, 179n, 182n, 309n, 314n.
Nevill, Charles, 129, 130.
Nevill, Richard Janion, 10, 12, 13, 27, 122, 130.
Nevill, W. H., 133.
Newborough, Lord, 216.
New British Iron Co., Abersychan, 51.
Newcastle Commission Report, 4, 25n, 45, 64, 107n, 109n, 110, 173n, 258, 261n, 263n, 264n, 265n, 267n, 268n, 269n, 270n, 272n, 273n, 274n, 276n, 278n, 286n, 287n, 290n, 291n, 294n, 295n, 296n, 298n, 299n, 311n, 314n.
New Dock School (Llanelli), 158, 161-162.
New Lanark 3.
Newmarket, (Flintshire), 212.
Newport, 37, 54, 173, 235, 271, 274.
Newport National School, 269.
Newtown, 204.
Newtown (Mountain Ash), Infants School, 183.
Nicholas, S., 182n.
Nixon Collieries, 182, 183, 185.
'Noddfa' Baptist Chapel, Treorci, 251.
Nonconformists, 305, 307, 309, 311, 312, 315, 324,.
Nonconformity, 18, 28, 48, 59, 60, 66, 106, 126, 160, 205, 206, 231, 257, 297, 333.
Normal Schools, 39, 176.
North, F. J., 215n.
North Wales Association, 209.
North Wales Gazette, 215n.
Northumberland, 268.
Norton, Upperton and Stone, 69.

Oakeley, W. G., 214, 218.
Oakeley, family, 214ff.
Oakeley, Mrs. L. J., 216.
Oakeley Quarries, 214ff, 218.
Oakwood Works School, 63, 66, 288, 321.
Ocean Coal Co., 181, 182, 295.
Ogmore Valley, 61, 179, 182.
Ollivant, Bishop, 174.
Owen, Edward, 160.
Owen, Sir Hugh, 26, 205, 206, 207, 208, 213, 333.
Owen, Rev. Owen, 136.
Owen, Robert, vi, 3.

Pakington Select Committee, 44n, 58n, 60n, 102n, 106n, 110n, 177n, 178n, 211, 292n, 299n, 306n, 312n, 316, 322n.
Pakington, Sir John, 317.
Pant, Dowlais, 106.
Parental attitudes, 21, 40, 41, 43, 99, 212-213, 257, 258, 259, 264, 266.
Park Colliery, 181; Park Colliery School, 327.
Parliament (*see also* Acts, Bills, Commissions), 3, 4, 25.
Parliamentary Register, 318.
Parochial Table of Day Schools, 134.
Parsons, W., 160.
Part-time education, 273.
'Payment by Results', 258.
Pemberton, R. S., 13, 130.
Pembrey, 133, 234, 246, 287, 289, 295, 312.
Pembrokeshire, 2, 186.
Penclawdd, 124.
Pengarnddu, 106, 288.
Penllergaer, 25; Church school 172.
Peninsular War, 125.
Penmaenmawr, 217.
Penmachno British school, 221.
Pennant, Col. (Lord Penrhyn), 214, 218, 220, 284, 292.
'Penny Readings', 251.
Penrhin Colliery and school, 180.
Penrhyn Castle, 218.
Penrhyn, Lady, 218.
Penrhyndeudraeth, 214, 216, 217.
Penry, Henry, 135.
Pensions, 310.
Pentonville, 207.
Pentre, 179; British School, 181, 327; National School 181, 326.
Pentre Bach, (Merthyr Vale), 186.
Pentremoch, 212.
Pentrechwyth, 123.
Pentyrch, 25, 37, 43, 159.
Penycae, (Cwmavon), 62, 66.

358

INDEX

Penydarren, 56, 58, 95.
Penygraig, 179, 327; British School 181.
Penygroes County Secondary School, 210.
Pen yr Allt Goch National School, 215.
Penywaun, Merthyr, 296.
Pestalozzian principles, 44, 127.
Philipps, Sir John, 2.
Phillips, D. R., 8n, 11n, 38n, 40n.
Phillips, E., 124n.
Phillips, Rev. John, 17, 208, 209, 210, 213.
Phillips, Nunes & Co., 161.
Phillips, Rev. Thomas, 174.
Phillips, Sir Thomas, 19, 173ff, 178n., 204n, 205, 206n, 268, 315.
Plas Tan y Bwlch, 214.
Plymouth Ironworks, 56, 58, 95.
Pollard, Sidney, i, 5n.
Pontamman Chemical Works, 121, 134.
Pontardawe, 158, 160.
Pontarddulais, 127, 162, 243.
Pontrhydyfen, 62.
Pont Walby, 180.
Pontypool, 26, 37, 42, 53, 173, 234, 236, 239, 268, 270, 294.
Pontypridd, 171.
Poor Law, 3.
Poor Law Commission, 207.
Poor Law Unions, 258.
'Popular' Education, 3, 4, 313.
Population: (*see also* census); 47ff, 247, 248, 250, 294, 295, 322ff; Chirk, 211; Denbighshire, 210; Dowlais, 95; Flintshire, 212; Hirwaun, 171; Llanllechid, 218; Llanelli, 129; Margam, 159; Merthyr, 95; North Wales, 205; Rhondda, 179; Swansea, 122; Ystradyfodwg, 179.
Port Talbot, 62, 121, 157, 234, 261, 284.
Porth, 179.
Portmadoc, 217, 221; British School, 221.
Port Penrhyn, 219.
Poundage (*see* levy, compulsory contributions), 28, 44, 60, 63, 67, 70, 127, 133, 159, 160, 161, 171, 176, 178, 180, 181, 182, 185, 211, 214, 287, 290, 291, 292, 294, 295, 297, 306, 308, 309, 312, 320, 324, 325, 326.
Powell Duffryn, 183.
Presbyterian College, (Carmarthen), 43.
Prestatyn, 212.
Price, Joseph Tregellis, 39 ff, 71, 72.
Prichard, Rev. Dr. John, 137, 137n.
Primrose Colliery, 173.
Prize Association and Schemes, 177, 268, 269.
Prussian System, 97.
Pryse (of Gogerddan), 136.
Pryse, Sir Carbery, 6.
Pupil Teacher System, 61, 97, 109, 123, 124, 128, 132, 217, 263, 267, 269, 275, 286, 287, 335.

Quakers, 25, 39, 211.

Radicalism, 234.
Raikes, Robert, 236.
Rebecca Riots, 243.
Rees, Rev. David, (Capel Als, Llanelli), 129, 244, 307, 308, 334.
Rees, M. John, (Llandudno), 137.
Reform Act (1867), 318.
Reform Parliament, 126.
Religious differences, iii.
Religious teachings, 15, 19, 22, 27, 49, 98, 126, 206.
Resolven Colliery School, 186.
Revised Code, (1862), 258, 269, 285, 286, 287, 318, 336.
Revivalist, (*Y Diwygiwr*), 307.
Rhandirmwyn, 122, 137.
Rhigos, 178, 179, 180.
Rhiwlas British School, (1844-1854), 220.
Rhondda, 27, 28, 172, 178, 179, 180, 182, 231, 246, 248, 249, 250, 252ff, 261, 268, 271; Urban District, (1891), 249; Education Authority, 327.
Rhosbeiro, 222.
Rhosllannerchrugog, 210, 211.
Rhostryfan British School (1844), 220.
Rhosymedre, 208, 210.
Rhymney, 48, 235, 268, 270, 287, 289, 290, 295, 321, 324, 325; Iron Co. 48; iron works National School 48, 169.
Rhys, Morgan John, 175.
Richards, Rev. P. M., 210.
Richardson, Evan, 207.
Risca, 176.
Roberts and Smith, 159.
Roberts, Ellis, 215.
Roberts, Robert, 215.
Roberts, Rev. William ('Nefydd'), 28, 39, 42, 54.
Robson, A. H., 21n, 278n.
Rolant, Evan, 215.
Roman Catholic Schools, 102, 106.

INDEX

Rowen British School, 221.
Rowlands, Moses, 173.
Royal Commission on the Church of England and other Religious Bodies in Wales and Monmouthshire, 249, 252n.
Royal Institution of South Wales, 246.
Royal Observatory, 215.
Royal Society, 125.
Ruabon, 208, 210, 270.

St. Asaph, 205.
St. David's, (Blaenau Ffestiniog), 215.
St. John's Girls School, (Swansea), (1825), 125.
St. Thomas, (Swansea), 122, 123, 320.
Samuel and Knight, 221.
Sanderson, M., ii, 335n.
Sandon, Lord, 279.
Saunders, R. J., 20, 170n.
Schools: adolescent evening: 99, 104, 105, 107; adult day: 99; adult elementary: 257; adult night: 99, 104, 105, 107; private adventure: 15, 57, 130, 241, 243; age: 40; boards: 22, 28, 44, 305ff, 336; building: 288ff; comprehensive: 312; costs: 105, 126, 133, 161, 171-172, 176, 206; day schools: 23, 42, 43, 52, 53, 54, 60, 64, 99, 110, 159, 207, 208, 210, 221, 231, 241, 250, 285, 311,; equipment: 98, 123, 219; finance: 293, 296; free schools: 25, 39, 130, 172; higher grade: 285, 336; Infant: 39, 40, 41, 44, 97, 98, 99, 106, 134, 161; Junior: 99, 101; neutral: 300, 306, 335; night: 49, 51, 53, 54, 58, 59, 64, 98, 99-101, 184, 219, 270ff; pence: 310, 326, 336; secondary: 210, 250; Sunday: ii, 1, 2, 15, 18, 19, 23, 43, 49, 50, 53, 60, 66, 159, 175, 182, 207, 221, 222, 231, 232, 233-241, 249, 250, 251, 252, 253, 257, 258, 259; Sunday school attendance: 231; Sunday school sessional time: 239; Sunday school union: 251; technical schools: 102; school trips: 219; unsectarian: 20, 106, 123, 134, 206, 207.
Scientific Institution, Rhymney, 48.
Scotland, 181.
Select Committee on Education, 18, 22, 44.
Seaton Colliery School (Durham), v.
Shankland, Rev. T., 7n, 8n, 9n, 169n.
Sheere, W., 6n.
Shropshire, 203, 268.

Sick Fund, vii, 50, 52.
Silver, Harold, i.
Simon, Brian, i, 3n.
Sirhowy, 26, 271, 284-287, 292, 326.
Sketty, 127; National school, 129.
Skultuna, v.
Smalley, Christopher, 221.
Smith, Adam, vi.
Smith, C. M., 178.
Smith, Frank, 4n, 236n, 269n, 279n, 310n. 311n, 312n, 314n, 317n, 333n, Smith, G. W. Duff Assheton, 214, 220.
Smith, Robert, 159.
Snatchwood House, 53.
Snowdonia National Park, 204.
Social conditions, 16ff, 210, 234ff.
Social welfare, 5, 16, 104, 174.
Society of Mines Royal, (1568), 5.
Solfa system, (John Curwen), 251.
South Wales Association, 209.
South Wales Iron and Coal Masters Association, 268.
S.P.C.K., 1, 2, 6, 8.
Special Reports on Educational Subjects, 334n.
Squire, Rev. E. B., 125.
Staffordshire, 39, 268, 277.
Stansty, 211.
State control, 265.
State finance, 20, 21.
State intervention, 257.
State system, 15, 233, 311, 317 318, 336, 337.
Stockholm, v.
Stow, David, 3.
Strick, Francis and Thomas, 70.
Subordination, 126.
Sunday schools (*see* Schools).
Sweden, iv.
Swansea, 25, 37, 43, 59, 121, 122, 157, 160-162, 172, 178, 241, 249, 261, 266, 271, 284, 306, 307, 320; School Board, 128, 320, 324; ticketings, 122.

Taff Vale Iron Co., 68.
Tafodog, 180.
Tai (Dinas), 173.
Taibach, (Port Talbot), 121, 134, 159.
Talacre, 212.
Talbot, C. R. M., 159.
Talsarn British School, 220.
Talybont British School, 221.
Tanygrisiau, 217.
Tawe Valley, 121, 234.
Taxation (for educational purposes) 294, 335.
Taylor, Messrs. J. & Co., 136.

INDEX

Teachers—finance of, 23, 43, 127, 135, 180, 221, 287, 335; inspection of, 123; quality of, 15, 40, 105, 109, 123, 135; number of, 19; selection of, 41, 110, 136; training of, 43, 110, 123, 127, 136, 177, 209, 240.
Technical education, 125, 336.
Temperance Movement, 244.
Testing, (*see also* examinations), 267.
Textbooks, 251.
Theological Colleges, 251.
Thompson, E. P., i.
Thomas, J. W., (Arfonwyson), 215.
Thornley Colliery School (Durham), v.
Tinworks Schools, 37ff.
Tir y Colly Junior School, 288.
Ton, 179; British School (1869), 181; Colliery School, 237.
Tondu, (Bridgend), 37, 67, 292, 312.
Tonmawr, 67; Iron and Coal Co., 67.
Tonypandy National School, (1870), 181.
Tophill Colliery, 178.
Training Colleges, 310.
Treacher and James Co., 59.
Trealaw, 179.
Tredegar, 27, 235, 236, 284, 287, 289, 290, 293, 296, 297; Ironworks Baptist School 239.
Treforest, 171.
Tregoning and Morewood, 162.
Treharris, 322.
Treherbert, 179, 180; British School (1860), 180; National School, (1862), 180.
Trelogan, 212.
Tremadoc, 214, 289.
Tremeirchion, 212.
Tremenheere, Hugh Seymour, 18, 23, 25, 26, 27, 42, 52, 65, 69n, 175, 259n, 272, 281, 285.
Treorchy, 179, 180, 181, 250; Colliery School, 327.
Trevethin, 42, 43; School Board, 324.
Trevivian, 124, 320.
Trevor, 220, 287.
Trim Saron School, 68, 69.
Trinity College, Carmarthen, 177.
Troedyrhiw, 322.
Trosnant, 173.
Trueman, A. E., 16n.
Turner, William, 214, 215.
Tydee, (Rogerstone), Tinworks School, 158, 162.
Tylorstown, 179.
Tymaen, 288; Infants School, 63, 66, 321.

Tynewydd, 180, 186.
Ty'ntwr Undenominational School, 218, 219.

Unitarians, 43, 239, 244..
United Collieries British School, Treorchy (1866), 181.
University College, Bangor, 210.
University College, Swansea, 125n.
University of Glasgow, 162.

Varteg Hill Iron Co., 42.
Varteg Hill (Trevethin), 25, 185.
Vaughan, John (of Derllys), 1.
Vernacular, 23, 204.
Venallt, 25, 42, 239.
Venallt Coal and Ironworks School, 260.
Vener, Lake, v.
Victoria Ironworks, 26, 239.
Vigurs and Smith, 62.
Vivian, John, 124.
Vivian, John Henry, 27, 122, 124, 125, 186, 246, 261, 307.
Vivian, Pendarves, 134.
Vivian, Sir Hussey (Lord Swansea), 125.
Vivian, Richard Hussey (Lord Vivian) 125.
Voluntary Societies, 3, 10, 15, 20, 21, 27, 29, 62, 89, 128, 170, 180, 203, 305, 306, 310, 311, 313, 316, 317, 318, 319, 326, 333, 334.
Voluntary Society of the Established Church, 7.
Voluntaryists, 129, 209, 232, 244, 305, 306. 307, 308, 318, 334.
Voluntary System, 317.

Wages, 25.
Waller, William, 6, 7n, 8.
Walloons, ivn.
Warde, (Llanelli), 130.
Warner, J., 46n, 54n, 271n.
Washington Chemical Works school (Durham), v.
Watney & Co., 69.
Watson, Mr., 8.
Watts, Rev. E. T., 320n.
Waunfawr, 209, 221.
Waunycoed, 173.
Weardale, v.
Wearmouth Colliery School (Durham), v.
Welsh Baptist Union, 251.
Welsh Bibles, 233.
Welsh Circulating Schools, 233.

361

INDEX

Welsh Granite Co., 220, 271, 287.
Welsh Language (*see also* vernacular), iii, 2, 23, 29, 41, 159, 231, 236, 246, 334.
Welsh Specimen Districts, 269.
Welsh Training Schools, 177.
Welsh Trust, 233.
Wesleyans, 210, 231.
Whitbread, S., 3.
Whitchurch, (Cardiff), 159; school, 158n.
White Rock (Upper and Middle Bank Co.) School, 122.
Whitford, 212.
Wilkins, C., 38n, 42n, 50n, 55n, 57n, 68n, 70n, 95n, 98n, 134n, 181n, 183n.
Williams, David, 169n, 235n, 243n.
Williams, David, (Llanelli copperworks school), 131.
Williams, D. M., 217.
Williams, Foster & Co., 261.
Williams, Joshua, 212.
Williams, Owen, 217.
Williams, William, M.P., 19, 26, 126.
Williams, W., 53.
Willoughby, Lord, 219.
Windsor Castle, 173.
Wirral, 203.
Witton Park Ironworks School, (Durham), v.
Wool manufacture, 204.
Workers control in education, 298, 299.
Workmen's schools, vi.
Working class, 3, 4, 15, 16, 17, 21, 23, 24, 28, 104, 125, 174, 204, 231, 234, 235, 246, 253, 268, 299, 333n, 334.

Works Board Schools, 324.
World War (1914-1918), 180.
Wrexham, 208, 210, 252.
Wynne, John, 220.

Y Cymro, 220n.
Y Diwygiwr, 308, 309.
Y Foel, 207.
Y Gwladgarwr, 216.
Yard School (Charles Pit Colliery), 186.
Yniscedwyn, 25, 26, 37, 43, 44, 68, 287, 319.
Ynys y Geinon Colliery, 173.
Ynysfeio, 180.
Ynysgarth, 173.
Ynyshir, 179.
Ynysybwl school, 182.
Yorkshire, West Riding, 277.
Ysbyty Ystwyth, 122.
Ysbyty Ystwyth Miners School, 135, 136n.
'Ysgolion Col. Pennant', 218.
'Ysgolion Chwarter', 252n.
Ystrad, 179, 180.
Ystalyfera, 296, 309.
Ystalyfera, Iron and Tinplate Co., 59; Wern Girls School, 59; Tinworks School, 59.
Ystradgynlais, 44, 157, 161, 234, 292, 309.
Ystradyfodwg, 28, 178, 179, 180, 248, 326.
Ystrad Rhondda, 327.

Zoar Chapel, (Neath), 307.